ASPECTS OF GREEK AND ROMAN LIFE

General Editor: H. H. Scullard

★ ★ ★

LAW AND LIFE OF ROME

John Crook

LAW
AND LIFE
OF ROME

John Crook

CORNELL UNIVERSITY PRESS
ITHACA, NEW YORK

CORNELL UNIVERSITY PRESS

1967

Library of Congress Catalog Card Number: 67-20633

PRINTED IN ENGLAND

CONTENTS

Iuris consultus abesto

CHAPTER I

INTRODUCTION

This is not quite a book about Roman law, on which there already exist any number of excellent treatises.[1] Neither is it quite a book about Roman social and economic life; that subject, too, is already illuminated by massive works of scholarship.[2] It is about Roman law in its social context, an attempt to strengthen the bridge between two spheres of discourse about ancient Rome by using the institutions of the law to enlarge understanding of the society and bringing the evidence of the social and economic facts to bear on the rules of law. Nowadays, with good reason, the nature of law is usually discussed in sociological terms; we insist on asking what role laws and lawyers and courts actually play in the life of their societies.[3] No one supposes, of course, that by looking only at the law you can get a whole picture of society, neither are the detailed legal institutions of a particular society a product of nothing but its social and economic patterns. Nevertheless, law is certainly some reflection of society (usually of its more conservative aspects, because of the law's function as a guarantor of stability), and not only a reflection, but also in some degree an influence upon it (usually a brake, providing only cautiously and tardily the mechanisms to fulfil the changing desires of society as a whole, but sometimes an accelerator, a tool in the hands of a particular section of the community such as an intelligentsia for achieving new ends that people in general do not actively want but will not positively oppose).[4]

In complex societies everyone is enmeshed in a vast network of legal rules, although people may go through their lives unconscious of most of them (even if 'ignorance' of them 'is no defence'). Roman society was quite complex enough for this to be true of it, but it is likely that more Romans knew more about their legal institutions than Englishmen do about theirs. For reasons connected with the amateurism (until quite late in its history) of Roman public life—whereby the standard education included forensic rhetoric,[5] and the law was run by members of a financially independent upper class in the interstices of pursuing political careers or just managing their estates, so that the talkers of law were also the readers and quite often the writers of literature—for such reasons, legal talk and terminology seem rather more frequent and more at home in Roman literature than in ours. Legal terms of art could be used for literary metaphor, could be the foundation of stage jokes or furnish analogy in philosophical discussion. And a corollary of this is that many a passage of Latin *belles lettres* needs a knowledge of the law for its comprehension.

Society and law are subject to change, and Roman history went on for a long time. The present book cannot possibly provide a chronological account of the relations between law and society at every stage of that long history.[6] The picture must be a 'still', and must therefore be focused on a particular stage. However, the period chosen is itself a long one—simply for convenience, in order to exclude as little as possible of the interesting evidence— and there is no need for it to have a very precise beginning or end. One way of describing it would be to say that it goes from Cicero to Ulpian; Cicero's earliest surviving oration, *pro Quinctio*, was delivered in 81 BC, and Ulpian, the most famous of all the Roman jurists, was murdered by the praetorian guard between December, AD 222 and May or June 224.[7] Another way of describing it would be to say that it goes from the legislation of 90–89 BC by which all free persons in Italy south of the River Po became entitled to possess Roman citizenship, to AD 212, the traditional date[8] of the legislation of the emperor Caracalla by which almost all free persons in the whole Roman empire became possessors of Roman citizenship. This stage of Roman law and society (which will be called 'our period' in all that follows) corresponds neither to the 'classical' period of Latin literature, which runs roughly from Cicero to Tacitus, nor to the 'classical' period of Roman law, which runs roughly from Augustus to Ulpian; the latter discrepancy calls for comment and, as some scholars would hold, for apology. To the experts in Roman law the age of Cicero, the late Republic, is 'pre-classical' in an important sense, its legal institutions being significantly different from those of the 'classical' period of law and, where uncertain, not to be casually extrapolated from what we know about the 'classical' period.[9] Consequently our picture of a period that embraces both Cicero and Ulpian cannot be a unity, and the 'still' is bound to be out of focus. In the present book this undeniable truth will nevertheless be boldly ignored, partly because for the matching up of law and society the evidence of Cicero is too valuable to sacrifice, and partly because for our purposes it is not as devastating as it might seem. The fact is that by Cicero's day the whole structure of Roman society, and enough of the fundamental structure of Roman law, were already there; the 'Roman Revolution' was a revolution of government, not of social structure; and in the age of the Principate the ground-bass of both society and law remained the same, however subtle and remote the variations played above it. There were of course important developments, not least as a result of the legislation of the emperor Augustus;[10] of course neither society nor law remained static for three hundred years. But these changes are comparatively easy to take into account, and will indeed often be our theme.

As to the appropriateness of treating Roman law as a reflection of, and using it to throw light on, Roman society, some further preliminaries are necessary in order that the reader may not be under any illusions about the difficulties and limitations of the whole enterprise. To begin with, it is simply not possible to do a proper 'sociology' of Roman law.[10a] Sociology depends on measurement, upon statistical techniques for discovering what most people mostly do, and so upon measurable evidence. Notoriously, the ancient world very seldom provides such evidence, only particular statements of individual alleged facts.[11] The sociologist will supplement his material by the use of models, and he will assume that if the community he is studying behaves in certain ways like some other known group of communities it probably does so in other ways too, unless there is specific evidence to the contrary. Dangers arise, however, if you apply this technique in comparing imperfectly known societies with other societies that are also imperfectly known.[12] A second difficulty is due to the fact that Roman society was very oligarchical. It perpetuated enormous differences in wealth and social power, and the upper class which determined its legal rules enshrined in them a code of values relevant to itself which cannot automatically be assumed to have been equally relevant to the lives and habits of the mass of people. Furthermore, the intellectual power and subtlety and thoroughness of the great Roman jurists, which made their surviving writings a justly admired paradigm of law for later ages, was achieved at the price of concentration on certain groups of rules (those most relevant to the oligarchy of which they were members) and unconcern for what might in fact be going on below or outside that sphere.[13] The nature of Roman legal training and discussion puts in our way another stumbling-block. In the schools of rhetoric and law they invented, and argued the *pro* and *contra* of, imaginary legal tangles,[14] so that a proportion—very difficult to estimate—of what looks like case law in our sources is imaginary-case law.

The problem is indeed the same as in considering the relation to society of the elaborate legal systems—the codes, particularly—of other peoples remote in time: the Babylonians, Assyrians, Egyptians, Hindus. How far do the texts reflect what actually happened?[15] How available were the remedies of the law? What were its delays and its costs? To what degree was it at the mercy of power, bribery or corruption?[16] What practical chance had the slave of getting freedom from his master, or the shopkeeper of getting his bill out of the consul, or the miner of getting damages for injury in the course of his employment? How many people just broke the laws, and which laws did they break? How much of the law was enforceable, in any case?

Even then the tale of difficulties is not fully told. One more question arises: what are we going to mean by 'Roman' law and 'Roman' society? The dominions of Rome embraced many culturally very un-Roman people: Greeks, Egyptians, Semites, Celts and so on. Rome did not (or only in a sense that will be briefly discussed at the very end of this book) impose a unitary system of legal institutions like a giant dishcover upon all these diverse sets of people. Their legal relationships inside their own communities went on in most ways as before, at least in our period, and it would be quite impossible to describe them all—not least because of some of them virtually nothing is known.[17]

Can one, then, obtain only so vague, partial and distorted a reflection of Rome in its heyday, by looking through the eyes of the law, as to make the entire undertaking worthless? One or two considerations, at least, can be set on the other side of the scale, and how far they help to tip it the reader will judge by results. In the first place, although one might suppose that in the slums of Rome or the remote countryside of Gaul the rules laid down by the jurists, the Labeos and Ulpians, had little significance, this is not entirely so. The great (perhaps the emperor) owned the land on which you were a tenant, they owned your habitation, they were the employing class; the rules of debt and damage and wages would indeed concern you. Ambition might take you up in the world, and, as you rose, more and more of the rules of Roman law would be relevant to you; above all, if, having been a foreigner, you became a Roman citizen (as during our period more and more people did) the Roman law would become your law. Secondly, to redress the balance of the evidence, there is much that we can add to the juristic treatises.[17a] On the one hand there are hundreds of references to legal affairs in Roman lay literature. Here, indeed, we are still in the upper brackets of society, but at least we are in the realm of practical, everyday law, not the meshes of technical professional theorizing (and such references also provide useful chronological indications). On the other hand, and much more important still, there survive in remarkable richness, on stone and bronze and papyrus and wooden tablets, actual documents of day-to-day legal business—*instrumenta* and *negotia*. We can read the humble man's will, the auctioneer's receipt, the sale of a horse, the miner's contract of service. Not only does this take us down into the middle-class world of Pompeii, of Trimalchio's Dinner Party, and further down still to the barmaids and common soldiers and apprentices, and out

into the countryside and the provincial towns; it also enables us
to judge, a little, how far this lower world did order its lives
according to the rules made by the great men in Rome. Many
such everyday documents survive from the even older Near
Eastern societies of Babylonia and Assyria,[18] but only in the
Roman case are we fortunate enough to have all four kinds of
evidence in abundance: the legislation, the juristic commentaries
on the law, the lay literature referring to the law, and the documents of daily legal relationships.[18a]

Of these materials, then, the present book will be made; but
before they are set out in greater detail a word must be put in
(not with apology) about what it does not contain. Nothing will
here be found about the origins of Roman substantive or
procedural law; the Twelve Tables, the *legis actiones*, even the
extensive, though tricky, evidence of Plautus for the law of his
age, will hardly be mentioned. Secondly, there will be almost
nothing about the local law of people in the provinces. We shall
see under what conditions the metropolitan law of Rome applied
to them, but for more there is not room; and this has the effect of
excluding one massive subject: the law of Roman Egypt.[19] From
Egypt we have an overwhelming mass of legal and economic
papyri; here more than anywhere else it is possible to make
contact with the legal relationships of ordinary folk. But because
of the diversity of its population and the pedantry of its bureaucracy the law, like the administration, of Egypt remains a thing
apart from all the rest. It would burst the modest bounds of this
book, and so will not appear as such, though this need not
preclude our occasionally taking into account an illuminating
papyrus. A third omission of a different kind must be signalled.
We cannot go, as a textbook of Roman law would, into the
details of the legal rules and how they were applied to innumerable complex sets of facts; we can only sketch the main institutions
and state some of the basic rules. This has an effect which the
author does much regret. It makes it impossible to view the
Roman law in one of its most characteristic and impressive lights
—as a mode of argument. The law reflects not only the social and
economic but also the intellectual life of a people, and the Roman

jurists, arguing in their pragmatic, case-to-case way, provide important evidence for the strengths and weaknesses of the intellectual equipment of the Romans; but another volume would be needed to embrace the subject, and sadly we must leave it.

Two aspects in particular of what follows may give pain to those accustomed to the usual presentation of the grand theme of the Roman law. The first is this: unlike the Roman jurists and the modern scholars who study them, who were and are accustomed to separate very rigidly the sacred law, the administrative law, the criminal law and the pure civil law of relations between one individual and another, the present book treats of all these indiscriminately as its historical purpose seems to demand. Secondly, for the same reason (but perhaps more heinously) the traditional divisions of the civil law—persons, things, obligations (contracts and then delict) and actions—will be quite ignored here, and topics will be taken up in an order designed to bring out their social relationships.

It would not be possible to set out in a page or two all the evidence for Roman law,[20] but a sketch of the principal sources actually to be used in this book is necessary, if only to introduce the reader to some further difficulties.

First there is the great mass of juristic literature. We have the benefit of a quite good 'Introduction to Roman Law' written by a learned lawyer in the second century AD—the *Institutes* of Gaius.[21] The enormous treatises of the most famous lawyers, however, survive only in excerpt. The emperor Justinian, in the sixth century AD, attempting to revive from Byzantium the physical reality of the Roman empire, set out to revive also its law as a universal code.[22] He entrusted this enormous task to his most learned academic lawyers, headed by Tribonian, and they were required to perform it in a furious hurry. The ultimately resulting 'Corpus of Civil Law', which we possess, contains *Institutes*, an elementary textbook based on Gaius; the *Codex Iustinianus*, a collection of legislation by emperors from Hadrian onwards; and the *Digest* (or *Pandects*), published in AD 533.[23] To compile the *Digest* Tribonian and his colleagues gathered

together copies of the principal juristic writings of the eminent
lawyers of former days (many were already very hard to come
by), chopped them up, and redistributed them under Titles or
headings, each Title concerning some particular rule of law—
'Concerning military wills', 'Concerning *peculium*' and so forth.
Each Title, therefore, was composed of a number of Fragments
or Excerpts, each fragment being a passage from a named work
of legal literature.[24] Thus we have at first sight a great mass of
the actual written arguments and discussions of all the eminent
jurists from Cicero's day to Ulpian and beyond. The great bulk
of the material is from Papinian, Paul and Ulpian, the giants of
the 'classical' period of Roman jurisprudence in the late second and
early third centuries AD, which creates the problem that the bulk
of our evidence for the Roman law of our period comes from
treatises composed at the very end of it. But there is a very much
more serious problem, deriving from the simple fact that the
whole of Justinian's 'Corpus of Civil Law', including the *Digest*,
was given the force of law; it was to be living law, not history,
and it alone was to govern the lives of the people and the practice
of the courts. Now since the writings of the eminent jurists of
the distant 'classical' past, though in general too valuable to lose,
contained much that was by Justinian's time obsolete and had to
be abolished, it was necessary to alter or 'interpolate' their
excerpts in the *Digest*, to bring them up to date, expunge references to dead institutions, contradictory opinions and so on (which
added to the scale and so to the extreme haste of the whole opera-
tion). Only, therefore, if we can distinguish the original from the
interpolated in these fragments can we say what the law was in the
opinion of Ulpian and the rest; and in very many cases we cannot
do this with conviction. If all the places in the *Digest* that have
been incriminated for interpolation in the last hundred years
were laid end to end and expunged there would be little left;
but many a passage has passionate defenders, too. Moreover, in
fairly recent years the problem of alterations in the *Digest* has
been shown to be even more complex. It has become apparent
that those precious texts of the old jurists on which Tribonian
and his fellow commissioners set to work as the data of their

task had already suffered change in the 'post-classical' centuries
lying between Ulpian and Tribonian, and the same is true of
other independently preserved works, like Gaius' *Institutes*. Men
had been re-editing them all the time to bring them into line
with changes in the law.[25] Views as to the extent of all these
interpolations vary like other fashions; from our present point
of view there is no need to despair, because on the whole controversy is concerned with the details of the law rather than its
broader rules, and because for the existence of those broader rules
we often have other evidence which will save us from gross
anachronism.

A difficulty already referred to is that of knowing whether legal
situations discussed in the *Digest* are real or imaginary. We very
often do not know, but the range of uncertainty can be circum-
scribed a good deal. First, there are many references to specific
enactments by the emperor or senate on named dates, and
answers to petitions by particular emperors or discussion of cases
in their presence; with these there is no problem. Secondly, we
know something of the imaginary cases that were argued in the
rhetorical schools;[26] they were fantastic *Arabian Nights* sort of
stuff, and the cases in the *Digest* have a quite different ring of
practicality—even if imaginary they are in terms of law and
society always *ben trovato*. The *Digest* often gives its litigants
stock names (Seius, Titius and so on), and cases where these
names appear may well be invented for discussion; but often it
uses specific names unlikely to have been invented or indeed
patently real, as in the discussion of the wills of Pannonius Avitus,
procurator of Cilicia, and Seius Saturninus, senior helmsman of
the fleet of Britain, or the concubine of Cocceius Cassianus.[27]
And the cases discussed under these real names are not different
in character from those discussed under stock names. Sometimes
the jurist concerned is found saying 'I remember a discussion on
the following actual circumstances' (*ex facto consultum, ex facto
tractatum*),[28] or he quotes letters to him asking for advice, or
remembers an argument he had when sitting on the panel of the
praetor,[29] or even an argument with the emperor.[30] As far, then,
as this difficulty goes the *Digest* can be used confidently enough.

Besides Gaius and the *Digest* there survive some other substantial fragments of juristic writings, particularly the 'Vatican Fragments', the 'Titles from Ulpian' and the 'Opinions of Paulus', all post-classical, but based on works by the classical jurists. But the second main category of evidence for the law consists of legislative and administrative texts found on inscriptions in stone or bronze and in papyri. (This is the point at which to say parenthetically that, apart from the *Digest*, almost every text the reader could want or this book will use is collected in the three small but marvellous volumes of *Fontes iuris Romani anteiustiniani*, compiled by the finest Italian Romanists of the last generation.)[31] There would be no point in formally listing these texts here, as we shall use them in due place; they include the municipal charters of Urso and Salpensa and Malaca in Spain, the Lex Rubria from Gaul and the Table of Heraclea from Italy, Augustus' edicts for the province of Cyrenaica, the 'Gnomon of the Idiologos' (part of the rules of the Department of Special Revenues in Egypt), and 'Apokrimata', a collection of legal rulings of the emperor Septimius Severus.[32]

In the third category of evidence come the *negotia* and *instrumenta*. Again, since they will be a constant preoccupation in all that follows, they need not be set out in detail now; most of them will be found in the third volume of *Fontes*. Amongst them are several substantial archives belonging to a single person, place or time, such as the records of loans and sales and labour contracts of Dacian miners that come from Verespatak in Hungary (the 'Transylvanian Tablets'), and the documents from the strong-box of Caecilius Iucundus, the banker-auctioneer of Pompeii, which lay buried beneath the dust of the earthquake of AD 79. One marvellous collection of eighty-seven documents has turned up quite recently from the other buried Campanian city, Herculaneum: the 'Herculaneum Tablets',[33] which include several important groups, especially the dossier of proceedings concerning the claim of a woman Petronia Iusta to a declaration of free birth. Another such homogeneous collection is the archive of documents relating to a single Greek family from Tebtunis in Egypt and running from AD 89 to 224.[33a] And some of the papyri from

Dura-Europos, the 'caravan city' on the Euphrates, offer a glimpse into the legal life of a community on the fringe of the Roman world.[34] That even wooden tablets, smeared with wax, and writing incised in the wax, should survive to be read today, is astonishing; but the reader who looks at these texts in the print of modern books should permit himself two reflections: first, that the originals are mostly very broken indeed, full of holes and cracks and smudges—often therefore very heavily filled in by editorial conjecture, and so to be assessed critically and cautiously; and secondly, that he owes the possibility of making use of them at all to the brilliant and patient detective skill and the limitless erudition of some of the giants of classical scholarship. These are the tasks of the flourishing academic disciplines of 'juristic epigraphy' and 'juristic papyrology'; there also exists 'juristic archaeology',[35] for the law of land and buildings must be compared with the actual remains (types of shops and houses, air-photographs of centuriation and so on), and the sculptured reliefs on tombs and public and private monuments sometimes refer to or represent procedures of the law.

It remains to bring in the evidence from lay literature.[36] We are fortunate in having, distributed along the path of our period, two large mines to quarry and a third quite substantial one. The largest by far is Cicero, of whom it should be remembered that he was a famous barrister, so that on the one hand he knew plenty of law but on the other hand his statements of it are advocate's statements, not necessarily to be believed because he says so. There are four surviving civil law speeches of Cicero (all defences),[37] but naturally many of his criminal law speeches contain important legal references (especially the Verrines and the defence of Archias). So also do the works on rhetoric, particularly de oratore and Topica. But, above all, the massive unexpurgated correspondence not only abounds in legal details but, through the family and property and commercial transactions of Cicero and his friends, gives a detailed picture of the nature of aristocratic society in the late Republic. Hardly less illuminating, this time for the age of Trajan, is the collection of letters of the younger Pliny—except that he only allowed in what was respectable and redounded to his credit. The famous tenth book (a separate collection of his official correspondence with the emperor) is exceedingly important for the way Roman law worked in the provinces under the Principate. Thirdly, the *Apologia de magia* of Apuleius, his defence of himself on a charge of using magic arts to secure the affections of a wealthy widow, delivered before the governor of Africa in about AD 160, is not only superb rhetoric but also an important legal source for its period. Some law can be got from his fictional work, the 'Golden Ass', and some from the *Satyricon* of Petronius. That great novel gives a picture of 'low-life' which, however much its colours may have been enriched by the author's powerful imagination, nevertheless recreates as nothing else does the actualities of small-town life—including law—in the first century AD. Of course, Tacitus and Suetonius and Dio, the historians, and Valerius Maximus and Aulus Gellius, the collectors of antiquarian information, are not without profit for our purposes. Of the Latin poets it is naturally the satirists, closest to everyday life, who abound most fruitfully in legal evidence—Horace in his *Satires* and *Epistles*, Persius, Martial, Juvenal; but wherever the element of 'social realism' is present, as sometimes in Propertius and particularly in Ovid, in comes the law. Beyond this list we come to the territory of mere legal allusions, of which no Latin author is free; but in their case it is not so much a matter of their being useful to elucidate the law as of knowledge of the law being required to elucidate them.

All in all, then, there is a huge body of information which, though scattered, complicated and difficult to assess, gives the historian some chance of escaping (at least for the purposes of such a work as the present book) from the vicious circle of 'interpolation doctrine' to which the most massive single source of our knowledge, the *Digest*, is subject.

*

One more preliminary question must be gone into: what *was* law at Rome? The question is not here intended as a jurisprudential or philosophical one, but simply signifies: of what propositions might a Roman have said 'You can't get away from that; it's the law'? This is virtually the same as asking how and by whom the law was made, or what the 'sources of law' were at Rome.[38] Cicero gives an answer for his day:[39]

> 'Partitive division of a subject is dividing it like the limbs of the body, as when one says that the civil law consists of legislation [leges], resolutions of the senate [senatus consulta], decided cases, the formal opinions of the jurisprudents, the edicts of magistrates, custom, equity.'

Some of these 'limbs' are awkward and difficult, so consideration of them may be postponed until we have looked at the more professional answer of Gaius for his day (200 years later):[40]

> 'The laws of the Roman people consist of legislation, enactments of the plebeians [plebiscita], resolutions of the senate, constitutions of the emperors, the edicts of those who have the right to issue edicts, and the answers of the jurisprudents.'

'Leges' and 'plebiscita'. These are the ancient formal legislation of the Roman Republic. In its early days the Republic's only law-making authority was the populus Romanus assembled and voting in its comitia, thereby making leges. Subsequently equal authority was accorded to the plebs Romana, assembled and voting in its concilium and thereby making plebiscita. These two kinds of enactment were equally 'legislative', and they were the only 'laws of Rome' in the full sense of the word.[41] In the earlier part of our period, the late Republic and the principate of Augustus, important legislation in this full sense was still enacted, but as a genuine organ of the people's will the assemblies inevitably declined, and after Augustus legislation was very rare; the last known 'law of the Roman people' was passed under the emperor Nerva in AD 97.[42] (These laws were based on a bill, rogatio, put to the people; they were leges rogatae. It is customary to list and treat separately the big municipal charters of Urso and Malaca and so on, and to call them leges datae, on the ground that, while they did indeed count as legislation for the community on which they were imposed, they need not necessarily have been passed as formal leges by the community of Rome which imposed them; they could be 'given' by a Roman magistrate on his executive authority. This belief has been recently and powerfully challenged;[43] the distinction is not a genuine ancient one, and the charters were based on formal legislation at Rome but written up locally and adapted to the community to which they applied.)

Constitutions of the emperors. It will be convenient to take this heading next, because as might be expected the command of the emperor, from the beginning of the Principate, to all intents and purposes replaced the vote of the people as supreme authority in the state. A bald statement such as this is constitutionally speaking shockingly incorrect, for the Principate began constitutionally as a concatenation of magistracies—executive, not legislative powers.[44] Technically speaking the emperor's command, though you had better obey it, did not at the beginning make law. At the end of our period it did, and Ulpian could say:[45]

'That which has been decided by the emperor has the force of law.'

It was being treated as such already by Hadrian's day, in the early second century AD, though Gaius, having included it amongst his sources of law, has to give a few sentences later a rather illogical reason for doing so:[46]

'because the emperor himself is given his *imperium* by a law.'

However, from a practical point of view this does not matter very much. It is more important to consider the different forms in which the emperor's will was expressed. To begin with, one must note that both the few 'laws of the Roman people' that were still passed and the many important 'resolutions of the senate' (to which we shall come presently) were enacted at the emperor's instigation, or at least as far as we know never without his approval. Imperial decisions proper can be subdivided in many ways, and more minutely than is needed here;[47] Gaius says they are 'by *decretum* or *edictum* or *epistula*'. *Decreta* are judicial decisions (and of the emperor as judge there will be more to say in a later chapter).*Edicta* are the pronouncements of an officer of the people to the people (or to some particular set of them), saying what he requires to be done—not only about the law but about anything; for example:[48]

'Imperator Caesar Augustus, pontifex maximus, in the seventeenth year of his tribunician power, says: if any persons of the province of Cyrene have been granted the privilege of [Roman] citizenship, I order that they shall nevertheless be rated for municipal charges. . . .'

Epistulae, letters, cover several phenomena. On the one hand the emperor might take the initiative and (as a result of requests, an embassy or such like) write a letter to a community; for example:[49]

'Imperator Caesar Vespasian Augustus to the magistrates and local senators of the Vanacini, greetings. . . . The privileges accorded to you by the deified emperor Augustus after his seventh consulship, which you retained down to the reign of Galba, I confirm.'

Or he might write an answer, to a petition (*libellus*) that had been sent in, on the bottom of the petition itself (*subscribere*, to write a *subscriptio*); the legal *Apokrimata* of Septimius Severus are actually a collection of such answers.[50] These two kinds of answers to people's appeals are most commonly lumped together under the name of 'rescripts', *rescripta*; Marcianus says:[51]

'If anyone, when he has one will already made, makes another, even if in the second one he has instituted heirs to specific things, the former will is rendered void, as the deified emperors Severus and Antoninus wrote in a rescript, the words of which I append. . . .'

And since appeals on points of law, before ever a case came on, were much the commonest, we hear of a great many more *rescripta* than *decreta*. Very many rescripts in the *Digest* are in fact answers to the queries of officials about the state of the law; many of Trajan's replies to Pliny are just this. There is one other category of imperial enactment which Gaius does not mention, perhaps because he thought of it (quite reasonably) as another kind of letter, namely the *mandatum*. *Mandata* were instructions to officials (again not necessarily about the law), either to an individual official or to all relevant ones, like Trajan's confirmation of the military will:[52]

'. . . moved by a sentiment of honest dealing towards my noble
and loyal fellow-soldiers I have decided to make provision
for their simple natures by allowing their intentions to be
fulfilled irrespective of the form of their wills. Let them therefore make wills in whatever way they wish and can.'

Ulpian says that this decision 'came to be inserted in the mandates',
which suggests that the mandates came to be a kind of official
code.[52a]

Resolutions of the senate (*'senatusconsulta'*). The decisions of the
senate, like those of the emperor, did not at first strictly speaking
have the force of law. The senate of the Republic, though
technically only the advisory council of the state's executive
officers, acquired a wide competence which did not conflict with
legislation because it was exercised mainly in a different field, the
day-to-day running of foreign policy and dealing with states and
peoples outside Rome. From Augustus onwards *senatusconsulta*,
named usually after the magistrate who had proposed the bill
in the senate-house, became a frequent and important engine of
development of the law. Sometimes the proposing speech was
made by the emperor himself, sometimes it was read on his
behalf:[53]

'Since a set of rules about all this was made by resolution of the
senate, it is best to give a commentary on that resolution, and I
begin by quoting it [says Ulpian]: "Quintus Julius Balbus and
Publius Juventius Celsus Titus Aufidius Hoenius Severianus,
consuls [AD 129], brought forward a bill based on a paper of
Imperator Caesar Hadrian Augustus, son of Trajan Parthicus,
grandson of the deified Nerva, greatest princeps, father of the
state, on 3rd March. On the question what action to be taken,
the senate resolved: i. Since . . . etc. etc." '

Consequently, *pari passu* with the emperor's word coming to be
treated as making law, so did the *senatusconsulta* proposed by him,
and eventually his speech in the senate-house came to be quoted

without reference to the formal resolution to which it was supposed to lead, as one more form of imperial legislation:[54]

> 'The deified Marcus [Aurelius], by an oration spoken in the senate, laid down that a pact to convert an annuity into a lump sum should be valid only if approved by the praetor.'

The 'Edicts of those who have a right to issue edicts'. Magistrates had this right—the consuls, praetors, aediles and governors of provinces (and indeed also the tribunes, who were—in the end—magistrates, and the censors and *pontifices*, none of whom had *imperium*; but they will not concern us). We possess edicts of governors laying down particular rules for the province in their charge:[55]

> 'Marcus Mettius Rufus, prefect of Egypt, says: I am informed by Claudius Areius, the controller of the Oxyrhynchite district, that both private and public property are in confusion because of long-standing failure of management of the property registry office. . . . I therefore order all owners, within six months, to register in the property registry office their personal property etc. etc.'

But for the law there is an enormously more relevant aspect of the edicts of magistrates, which can be approached by looking at a third and even later definition of the 'sources of law', that of Papinian:[56]

> 'The civil law is that which derives from laws, decisions of the plebeians, resolutions of the senate, decrees of the emperors and the formal opinions of the jurisprudents. The praetorian law is that introduced by the praetor in the public interest, to support, supplement and correct the civil law; it is also called *ius honorarium* from the office [*honos*] of the praetors.'

A full historical description of this vital and characteristic development cannot be attempted here,[57] but very roughly it is this. The urban praetor (from 367 BC) and the peregrine praetor (added in 241 BC) were in practice in charge of the courts of the Republic.

They had, to work with, a primitive system of law based on the Twelve Tables, standard and rigid forms of procedure, and ancient custom. What they did was to build up alongside that primitive system more flexible institutions, enabling the law of the Republic to keep pace with its economic and social development and its increasing contact with foreign peoples. This was the *ius honorarium*, the 'Roman Equity'. The Edict was the tool they employed; it was the right and duty of each praetor to publish an 'annual edict', *edictum perpetuum*, when he entered on his term of office, which was for a year, and the annual edict set out what actions at law he would allow—in what circumstances he would grant a legal action or other remedy (such as an injunction) if requested to do so, or in what circumstances he would refuse. The praetor could not legislate; if there was legislation he must provide actions to give it force (though he might refuse an action in an individual case). But where there was none he had it freely in his discretion to grant or refuse legal remedies, and the remedies and protection he gave were in effect legal rights as against all the world except a superior magistrate or someone claiming under legislation or the civil law.[58] The praetor's edict was his own, but as the praetors were simply career politicians, not necessarily learned in the law, their edicts tended to copy that of their predecessors, occasionally being added to or improved by a legal luminary who happened to be, or advise, the praetor. Thus a basically permanent set of rules grew up, and already Labeo, in Augustus' time, was able to write a 'Commentary on the Perpetual Edict' on a large scale.

The edict of the aediles governed the markets of Rome, and had an importance which will be seen later. Governors of provinces also had to publish an edict when they entered their province, both to provide the special rules of law applicable to their territory and to make available to Roman citizens in the province a set of legal remedies parallel to those they had at home. The provincial edict tended, for the same reason as the urban, to become standardized, though in Cicero's day it was still subject to modification by governors who had the learning or interest. We hear a lot about it from Cicero, both in what he says about the administration of his *bête noire* Verres[59] and in his description of his own edict for Cilicia. He writes, for example, to his precursor:[60]

'I worked my edict out in Rome. I've not added anything, except what the tax-companies, when they came to see me at Samos, asked me to copy straight out of yours.'

And to Atticus he says:[61]

There's nothing unusual about Bibulus's edict except the clause you told me about in your letter, when you said it was a "slap in the eye for the whole equestrian order". But I've got a counterpart to it, only less crudely put, taken from Mucius Scaevola's edict for Asia . . . and I've followed a lot of the clauses of Scaevola, including the one that gives the Greeks a great feeling of liberty bestowed—that in suits where all parties are Greeks they can use their own laws.'

The praetor's edict, which was not wholly static in the first century AD, was finally codified by Hadrian's most eminent jurist, Salvius Julianus,[62] and it was as commentaries on the codified edict that the largest works of interpretative jurisprudence were written in the latest part of our period, especially that of Ulpian.

Answers of the jurisprudents. It is well known that in no society does the law consist entirely of legislative enactments; it may rest on very few, or none—most tribal law is entirely non-legislative. We must therefore turn to the non-legislative sources of Roman law, and can begin with the last source mentioned by Gaius, the 'answers of the jurisprudents'. It will be seen in a later chapter how the learned lawyers, by advice to judges and counsel and litigants, influenced how the rules of law should be applied to particular cases, and so made law rather as the courts do today. And the published works of jurisprudence, available to practitioners, were simply an extension of oral advice. Now this was a quite informal process. Acceptance of a jurist's statement of the law would depend on his distinction, and his distinction would depend on the learning and subtlety of his replies. Was there anything more formal, any rule, for example, for deciding between the conflicting opinions of two distinguished jurists? Not until long after our period (in AD 426) was a formal rule of thumb promulgated, a 'law of citations'[63] for a generation of lawyers to whom not much in any case was left of the old un-wieldy—when not inaccessible—mass of juristic publications. Within our period there is only one phenomenon to record, and this will be done briefly, because its significance is furiously controversial and, unless new evidence turns up, likely to remain so. From Pomponius's historical excursus quoted in an early title of the Digest[64] we learn (though the passage may have undergone a whole series of interpolations) of a 'right to give answers publicly with the authorization of the emperor', established by Augustus;[65] and Gaius in the Institutes says that 'answers of the jurisprudents' are the decisions and opinions of those who 'have received permission to lay down the law', and if they are unani-mous what they so hold has the force of law, if not, a judge may (and must) think for himself.[66] Some scholars hold that from the beginning of the Principate anyone who wanted to be called a iuris consultus and give formal legal advice had to have an imperial patent. Others hold that there was an inner circle of patented jurists (perhaps connected with the emperor's advisory council) whose opinions if unanimous made law, whereas the opinions of others remained mere advice. Again, it is held by many that in spite of Gaius[66a] no opinion of any jurist or group of them had in our period the force of law—the imperial patent just improved your standing. From our point of view what matters is that it is never stated in the sources that such-and-such is a rule of law because it was so laid down by jurists X and Y and Z; beyond that the problem is not worth pursuing here. Nor can we do more than mention a much more important connected topic—the way in which the influence of the jurists on the law underwent change. Two outstanding books in recent years have shown how this happened. It was a result partly of the increasing bureaucratization of the Roman empire (law became less aristocratic and amateur, and more and more formally tied to the emperor and his council), and partly of the changing social origin of the jurisprudents (again from aristocratic amateurs to salaried officials of equestrian and provincial background).[67]

Decided cases. The modern Englishman is accustomed to the rigid principle of *stare decisis*, whereby a court's decision in a particular case is binding for the future, if such a case comes up again—makes law, in fact—unless it is either overruled by a higher court or the new case can be shown to be significantly different from the one decided. Did Rome have such a source of law? Cicero, in the passage of the *Topica* with which we began, appears to say so; but the short answer is that he cannot mean what, with our background, we are liable to assume him to mean. What he probably meant is suggested by a parallel passage in the treatise *ad Herennium*;[68] the courts in Republican times might have precedent or the 'current of decisions' quoted at them by counsel, but the decision in the case on hand did not necessarily follow such precedent. What the emperor said when he decided a case was naturally law, but even he did not, like the House of Lords until the other day, bind himself or his successors absolutely, though they would normally quote and follow him, and the existence of a final and central court of appeal put a different complexion on things.

'*Custom*' *and* '*equity*' (Cicero). The latter was not so much a 'source of law' as a principle by which cases could be judged and the law interpreted and developed—the guiding principle, above all, of the *ius honorarium*.[69] The former is the subject of long stretches of every treatise on jurisprudence; for of course in the broadest sense, if we maintain that law somehow reflects society we are implying that in some way and to some degree what people actually normally do comes to influence the law, and the notions of ancient tradition, 'time out of mind' and so on are very general characteristics of legal systems. But as soon as one asks specific questions, such as 'how does this particular system decide what *is* a custom?', or 'what does it do if alleged custom conflicts with legislation?', one begins to see that custom plays different roles in different systems. On the role of custom in the

Roman system there are many excellent discussions[70] and some important disagreements. Certainly, from quite early days the Roman jurists clearly and rather ruthlessly distinguished between legal customs and mere social observances, in which they were quite uninterested. As to 'custom of the realm', the law of the Roman Republic, according to historical tradition, began its serious career with a statute or code, the Twelve Tables, which no doubt partly enshrined contemporary custom and partly made new rules. (It was convenient later, when the original significance of those hoary but often parroted clauses was no longer understood, to attribute to them meanings which gave venerable legislative sanction to what were in fact more recent Roman customs.) The jurists in interpreting the law might be influenced by what they believed to be men's general habits—of agreement and the like; and they might look to such habits when there was no express law on a point. But no general theory was developed about the part played by custom as against, for example, legislation, or of how custom was to be determined. There is indeed a famous text in the *Digest*, attributed to Salvius Julianus:[71]

> 'Ingrained custom is not unreasonably maintained as as good as law; this is what is known as the law based on men's habits. For since actual legislation is only binding because it is accepted by the judgment of the people, those things of which the people have approved without any writing at all will justly be binding on everyone. And therefore the following principle is also quite rightly accepted, that legislation can be abrogated not only by the vote of a legislator but also by desuetude, with the tacit agreement of all men.'

It is usual, though not unanimous, to regard both the positive and the negative parts of this assertion as 'post-classical' interpolations and not, at the very least, applying to our period.[72]

Local custom is a different matter. On the one hand, precisely because local custom is local, the law of a large unified state will inevitably impose certain uniformities that override what the people of such-and-such a village or valley have always done. On the other hand one meets a number of cases in the *Digest* where local custom is specifically looked to. Thus we are told[73] that:

'if land is sold, security against eviction must be taken according to the custom of the region in which the transaction takes place;'

and that under certain circumstances a guardian may have to pay interest on his ward's property 'according to the habit of the province'.[74] And one of the letters of Pliny to Trajan, with the emperor's reply, gives a very neat case.[75] 'Several of the cities of Bithynia-Pontus,' says Pliny, 'claim that they are privileged creditors of bankrupts as against private creditors. Many governors have accepted this, and it is now taken as settled law here; but I should be happier with a general ruling.' 'It depends on the charter of each city,' replies Trajan. 'If they have such a privilege, uphold it, but I am making no general rule to the detriment of private creditors.'

This leads us on to Rome's relationship to the general legal customs of the non-Roman peoples in her dominions. *Ius civile* is opposed in one sense to *ius gentium*, 'law of the peoples'. Now *ius gentium* certainly does not mean (as it came in the seventeenth century to mean)[76] 'international law'. What it does refer to is those legal habits which were accepted by the Roman law as applying to, and being used by, all the people they met, whether Roman citizens[77] or not. (Thus, slavery was *iure gentium*—everybody had it; whereas *sponsio* as a form of verbal contract was *iure civili* and available only to Roman citizens.) Rome did not destroy the legal systems of her subjects, in respect of their dealings amongst themselves; what is more, Rome borrowed some legal institutions from the highly sophisticated standard practice of the Greek-speaking part of her dominions (though the degree of borrowing is rather variously estimated).[78] So some customs of foreign peoples did become part of the law of Rome. Nevertheless, if you, a Greek, came into a Roman court it was by Roman law your case was judged (though the provincial courts were not necessarily deaf to peregrine legal traditions);[78a] it would be no use, for example, pleading a national custom which had not been accepted by Roman law. And in numerous important spheres the Romans stoutly refused to take any notice of quite widespread eastern customs.

Having surveyed the sources of Roman law we must return to that part of it which consisted of specific enactments, to enquire what was the scope of their validity in space and in time. *Leges* proper could, according to Julianus (as we saw, but saw also the doubtfulness of the passage), be abrogated by disuse; otherwise they were perpetual unless abolished by the passing of something else. The characteristic Roman way in fact was to set up a new legal institution, such as a more flexible form of procedure, alongside the old and let the old gradually be forgotten or survive for some limited purpose to which it was best adapted. The most famous case of this is the way in which the *ius honorarium* in its long development simply got round the old *ius civile* without abrogating anything. In respect of extension, *leges* at their widest applied only to Roman citizens; but they determined the law that was applied in the Roman courts, so that it would be no use a non-citizen saying 'by my law I am allowed to inherit from a Roman citizen', since he could only make such a claim before a Roman magistrate, for whom the rule was that non-citizens could not inherit from Roman citizens. *Senatusconsulta* were valid, as far as we know, without limit of time. They were not confined in extension, in the time of the Principate, to 'senatorial' provinces;[79] and especially those numerous *senatusconsulta* that regulated the private law applied to all Roman citizens everywhere, governed the Roman courts, into which non-citizens might come, and sometimes extended the application of *leges* to non-citizens.[80]

When we come to the pronouncements of magistrates the situation is different. Edicts of magistrates were technically valid only for the term of the magistrate's office, though in the provinces it was probably normal to assume that rules made by one governor went on unless his successor enacted something different, and to quote them to his successor. We have seen that the edicts most important for the law, the annual edicts of the urban and peregrine praetors, were in effect handed down with less and less change. What of imperial constitutions? It has been much argued whether they were valid only under a given emperor, and subject therefore to ratification by the next. A recent reconsideration has led to the conclusion that 'constitutions of all sorts continued in effect long after the deaths of their authors'; even 'abolition of the memory' of a hated emperor did not necessarily cancel his *acta,* though evil ones might be individually abrogated. For 'the stability of society in all its phases demanded that the imperial pronouncements, which reached into every corner of the empire and touched its life in every aspect, should remain in force unless specifically changed'.[81] The emperor Nerva made much the same point:[82]

> 'Since the arrangements of everything, which were begun and completed in former times, need to be maintained, we must stand by even the letters of Domitian.'

Many imperial constitutions were for particular provinces or sets of people, and so only applied to them.[83] We have seen the reluctance of Trajan to be jockeyed into issuing general rules; it is exemplified again in the famous letter about the Christians:[84]

> 'It is not possible to lay down anything general that will have a kind of set formula.'

Nevertheless, imperial decisions could apply to everybody; they were not constitutionally confined to the 'provinces of the emperor',[85] nor to Roman citizens:[86]

> 'Imperator Caesar Vespasian Augustus, pontifex maximus, in the sixth year of his tribunician power, imperator for the fourteenth time, pater patriae, consul for the fifth time and designated for the sixth, censor, says: since the pursuits suitable for free persons are held in all cities to be for the public and private good and sacred to the gods, the profession of elementary and higher school-teachers who raise the minds of the young to civility and public virtue being sacred to Hermes and the Muses and the profession of doctors and physical trainers to

Apollo and Asclepius (for to the disciples of Asclepius only is given the care of physical health, since they are hailed as sacred and divine); I therefore order that these persons aforesaid shall not be liable to billeting or to taxation of any kind.'

What may surprise those accustomed to think of the Romans as an administratively efficient people is that it seems to have been quite difficult even for the authorities to discover what currently valid legislation there was on problems with which they had to deal.[87] Evidence comes from several of the official letters of Pliny—as extraordinary imperial commissioner governing the province of Bithynia-Pontus—to Trajan, with the emperor's answers. He forwards a petition and appends copies of letters of Domitian and an edict of Nerva.[88] On another occasion, requesting advice about a legal difficulty, he writes: 'Numerous imperial constitutions have been quoted to me about this—an edict, said to be of Augustus, for Andania, a letter of Vespasian to Sparta, etc. None, however, apply either specifically to this province or to all areas generally. I am not appending copies, because their authenticity and textual accuracy is dubious, and I expect you have proper copies in Rome.' Trajan replies: 'Yes, there are many enactments, but no general ordinance; here is a decision for your case.'[89] He seems to have the copies, as Pliny surmised; but when in another letter Pliny asks: 'On certain legal questions previous proconsuls of this province have given judgments, and there is a letter of Domitian; but the *senatusconsultum* on this branch of law mentions only proconsuls. May I (who am technically not a proconsul) give judgments on these questions?', Trajan sends back the astonishing answer: 'Send me a copy of the *senatusconsultum* and I'll tell you whether you may.'[90] Finally, in another letter Pliny actually encloses the text of the relevant clauses of the *lex Pompeia*, the ancient charter of the province, and of an Augustan edict.[91] It may be that the firing of the Capitol in the civil war of AD 69 had disastrous effects on the archives; certainly Vespasian set up a committee to recover documents.[92] The situation was therefore perhaps worse for *leges* and *senatusconsulta* than for imperial constitutions, copies of which were presumably kept by a bureau of the emperor's administration. But it does appear that the safest way to preserve a decision that concerned you was to take a copy of it yourself when it was promulgated; and this is in fact how our surviving documents have mostly come down to us.

★

In the Greco-Roman world litigation was a public spectacle. Rhetoric (which of course was not only forensic but also political and sometimes just 'epideictic'—for display) and rhetoricians fulfilled in ancient society the role that the stars of entertainment hold today. And these rhetorical performances, including the speeches of the great barristers in legal actions, took place in public, in the stoas and basilicas the remains of which are still to be seen. Pliny gives a vivid picture, congratulating himself on success in a *cause célèbre*:[93]

> 'There they were, one hundred and eighty jurors (for that's what the four panels come to when they are joined together), a huge collection of counsel for both plaintiff and defendant, rows and rows of seats in court, and a deep ring of auditors standing up, surrounding the whole huge court in a multiple circle. The magistrate's dais was crowded, and even from the upper stories of the basilica men and women peered down in an effort to hear, which was difficult, and see, which was easy enough. . . . I piled on every canvas—indignation, rage, distress—and sailed the seas of that tremendous action like a ship before the gale.'

Besides this, it was a part of the philosophy of the Romans that the duty of a citizen included taking his share of the burdens of the law: acting as judge, arbitrator or juror and supporting his friends in their legal affairs by coming forward as witness, surety and so on. Many a familiar passage of Latin verse testifies to this; Juvenal's recipe for the good citizen:[94]

> 'be a good soldier, good guardian, honest arbiter, unperjured witness;'

or Horace's answer to the question 'Who is a good man?':

c

'the man who keeps the resolutions of the senate, the statutes and the law, before whom many great suits are brought to judgment; when he is surety affairs are safe, when he is witness causes are upheld;'

or Horace's description of the daily legal life of Rome in his encounter with the Bore, and his complaints about all the legal business a man gets involved in.[95] Still more exacting were the claims on those who professed legal learning; Pliny says:[96]

'I've done a lot of speaking in court; I've often been a judge; I've often been on a judge's panel of advisers,'

and:

'I'm almost more often a judge than a barrister.'

It is, as was suggested at the beginning of this introduction, the constant sense of the omnipresence of legal concepts amongst the Romans that gives the stimulus to closer study of the relation between their law and their life. This could be carried out in an anecdotal way; one meets in the legal sources, not least the formidable bulk of the *Digest* itself, many human circumstances and predicaments—piquant, comic, pathetic—which help, like a first sight of Pompeii or Ostia, to bring us closer to the ancient world and to make us feel that in their attitudes and activities they were 'people rather like ourselves after all'. Since we shall not return to this anecdotal approach, the reader may care for a few samples: There is the man who runs into a shop to escape the police and is bitten by a dog (D. 9. 1. 2. 1); the quarrel over removal of a street-lamp, which might as easily come out of Petronius or James Joyce (D. 9. 2. 52. 1); the question whether robbers can have an action for division of profits (D. 10. 3. 7. 4), reminiscent of the English 'Highwaymen's Case' of 1725;[97] the argument for holding that no fare need be paid in respect of a baby born on board a ship (D. 19. 2. 19. 7); the problem of the slave who spends too much time in picture-galleries (D. 21. 1. 65 pr.); and the disgraceful story of the knight who took to burglary (D. 47. 18. 1. 2). There are rules for punishing wreckers (D. 47. 9. 10)

and for the better ordering of snake-charmers (D. 47. 11. 11).
Both sides of the law are represented: the lawyer's sigh of
despair at the unbusinesslike habits of laymen (D. 19. 1. 38. 2):

> 'What happens if neither buyer nor seller has forseen this
> eventuality, as is usually the situation in such cases?';

and the layman's contempt for the niceties of law (D. 31. 88. 17):

> 'I, Lucius Titius, have written this my testament without any
> lawyer, following my own natural reason rather than excessive
> and miserable diligence.'

Valerius Maximus has a splendid cautionary legal tale (VIII,
2, 2) about a man who, being mortally ill and wishing to leave
money to his mistress, adopted the legal 'dodge' of letting her
put him down in her account-book as owing her a large sum
(which his heir would have to pay); but he recovered, and was
sued on the account by the rapacious object of his affections. And
anyone who cares to look up the facts stated in a case judged by
the emperor Augustus in 6 BC (they can be read in *Fontes* III, no.
185) will find them piquant indeed.

There is an endless variety of matters of this sort, but we shall
not pursue our subject by way of them, because such an approach
is both trivial and misleading. Of course men of all ages have the
same quirks and tend to get into the same scrapes, but it is the
differences, not the similarities, between one society and another
that call for comment and investigation, and for an attempt to
fathom some of their reasons; and it is to this task that the
chapters which follow will be addressed.

CHAPTER II

THE LAW OF STATUS

The first difficulty for the modern reader wishing to understand the legal lives of people in Rome and her dominions is to think himself back into a world where men's rights and duties depended on fundamental differences of formal legal status; and a clear conception of these principles is an unavoidable prerequisite to everything else, even what might otherwise have seemed the natural subject to begin with, the machinery of justice and the courts.

It is simple enough to draw up (as Gaius does in the *Institutes*) a table of the statuses that implied more or less completely different sets of rights and duties in the eyes of Roman law, thus:

1 People (male and female) are either slaves, or they are free.

2 Free people are either free by birth, *ingenui*, or free by grant of freedom from slavery, 'freedmen', *libertini*.

3 Free people are also either Roman citizens, or 'Latins' (and if Latins either coloniary Latins or, under the Principate, Junian Latins), or peregrines (and if peregrines either citizens of some particular peregrine community or of none).

4 Roman citizens are either independent—'in their own power', *sui iuris, suae potestatis*—or in the power of someone else, *alieni iuris*.

5 Persons *sui iuris* are either under guardianship, *tutela*, or caretakership, *cura, curatio*, or under neither of these.

This dull catalogue, however, does not, in the first place, exhaust the complexities, for there were numerous other status categories which involved partial differences of rights and duties which could nevertheless be quite important, such as age and sex (the special position of infants and of women), being married with a stated number of children, married without children, or unmarried, being a soldier, being a senator or member of the equestrian order or neither, and in the provinces being a magistrate or councillor of your city or neither (or in Egypt being a citizen of Alexandria, a citizen of another Greek city or just a plain Egyptian). Also there arose the question where a man lived—whether he was domiciled in the place of which he was a citizen or in some place of which he was not a citizen but only a permanent resident, *incola*. And in the second place the catalogue gives in itself no notion of the profound effect which his particular status had on a man's life.

The origins of the complexities of citizenship and non-citizenship lie in the history of archaic Greece, when the Greeks (for reasons, indeed, only dimly understood even today) organized themselves politically not into a nation but into a large number of tiny nations, city-states, whose members had rights and duties within their own state but were without duties or rights—were foreigners—in the state the other side of the mountain. This pattern of life the Greeks themselves exported, both before and after Alexander; Rome, beginning herself simply as one city-state, inherited it, in spite of becoming a world power, and the notion of citizenship of small municipalities and strangership outside remained, notwithstanding some modifications, basic to the structure of Rome's dominions. 'Roman citizen', therefore, is not just a vague term meaning an inhabitant of the Roman empire, but a precise expression of one particular set of rights and duties.

Thus, if you had visited the market-place of, say, Tarsus in the time of the apostle Paul you would have found there Roman citizens, citizens of Tarsus (some of whom would be Roman citizens as well, like Paul, others not), citizens of other places domiciled but only having the rights of *incolae* there, and free persons who were not citizens of anywhere.[1] Of all these some would be free-born, others freedmen, some independent, others under the power of fathers or guardians. And the rest of the population would be slaves. Each kind of person would be carrying round with him a different bundle of rights and duties in the eyes of Roman law, though it might take little cognizance of some of them. An easy way to perceive why it took Gaius a whole book out of the four of his *Institutes* to describe the law of status is to ask oneself how one would determine the status of children born of mixed marriages across any of these status boundaries.

Citizenship in the ancient world, we are accustomed to say, was based on a principle of personality, not of territoriality; your status depended on birth—the status of your parents—or on grant of one kind or another. However, territoriality was not altogether unimportant.[2] For one thing, there were many people domiciled in places of which they were not, by the 'personal' principle, citizens, and unless the state of their domicile granted them its citizenship they remained *incolae* (what the classical Athenians called 'metics'). The Spanish charters, that of Urso (which goes back to Julius Caesar) and that of Malaca (Flavian in date), refer to them. The Urso charter gives places at its city festivals separately to citizens of Urso, *incolae*, and guests and temporary visitors.[3] That of Malaca has a piece of historical tit-for-tat; in the Roman Republican age, Latins domiciled in Rome were allowed to vote in Roman citizen assemblies, in one voting-group picked by lot on the day, and now Malaca repeats the arrangement in reverse, allowing *incolae* who are Roman citizens or Latins to vote in *her* elections in a group picked by lot.[4] In the *Digest* there is a title 'On the municipal law and on *incolae*', which makes rules about how far *incolae* must be bound by the laws and pay the taxes of the community they live in, such as:[5]

'An *incola* must obey the magistrates both of the community of his domicile and of that of which he is a citizen.'

It discusses what constitutes domicile as opposed to mere transience, how the domicile of wives is determined, and so on.

The notion of territoriality received a further importance from the extension of Roman citizenship, which came to represent not an exclusive 'belongingness' such as would preclude a man from belonging any more to his own original citizen community but a privileged extra status that a man could have, like Paul, over and above his existing rights. (This topic has been the subject of passionate debate in recent years, under the label of 'double citizenship';[6] the reader must note that what is said here about it is not an 'agreed view', for there is at present none.) By the time Cicero died the free inhabitants of Rome and all Italy were Roman citizens, and Rome had begun to plant émigré communities of Roman citizens, *coloniae*, overseas. The ancient city-states of Italy that had received citizenship were called *municipia*. Julius Caesar and Augustus proceeded fast with the creation overseas of new *coloniae* (by settlement) and *municipia* (by grant). Also there had already begun, sporadically, the practice of granting Roman citizenship to individual foreigners, for services rendered, and this naturally raised the problem, for such an individual, whether he must abandon all his former legal rights, and could escape all his former legal duties, in the peregrine community in which he no doubt continued to live. Now the idea that a man could be a citizen of more than one city at once was not unknown to classical Greece, and in Hellenistic times citizenship was sometimes treated just as an honorary status ('freedom of the city of X') and one man could have several. Rome had begun as a state with an exclusive principle, at least to the extent that if a Roman took another citizenship he lost his own. This somehow, by some stages, was modified, though Cicero could still boom impressively on the subject when it suited his case.[7] Certainly from Augustus' time the regular principle, when granting Roman citizenship to foreigners, was to require them to continue their civic duties in their original community, or specifically to exempt them from some or all of them.[8] Whether this is correctly described as having two citizenships or not perhaps does not much matter; it is certainly possession simultaneously of two sets of legal relationships,[9] and Roman citizenship is henceforward an extra status, leaving its possessor the right to sue and be sued in his native courts[10] and hold office in his native city, but also not depriving that city of him as a taxable head for local taxation so long as he lived in it. A recently discovered inscription from the remote Moroccan town of Banasa (reported but not yet published, so one can only speak of it at second hand)[11] records the grant of Roman citizenship to a chieftainly Berber family in the second century AD 'without prejudice to the law of their tribe', *salvo iure gentis*. (Another recent discovery—to show how knowledge of Roman society grows all the time, piecemeal, by tiny additions—is a Milesian lady of the first century AD, Claudia Paula, a Roman citizen, whose husband is a senior local official as well as a Roman citizen, and who is described in an inscription as 'of Italic right'. Hitherto the 'Italic right' has only been known as an immunity of certain lands from Roman tribute, but here it seems to signify some kind of personal immunity from local obligations.)[12] The Banasa inscription contains another remarkable novelty. It refers to a schedule in the imperial archives of all new citizens (which must mean new individual grants) from Augustus onwards. Certain family details had to be entered in the schedule; and this links up with Trajan's demand for 'age and property rating' when granting individual citizenship to certain protégés of Pliny.[13]

*

The conditions for acquiring Roman citizenship can be set out as follows:

Birth. To be a Roman citizen by birth you had to be a child of a true Roman law marriage, *iustae nuptiae* or *iustum matrimonium*, the condition of which was that both parties must possess *conubium* —which meant simply the right to contract a true marriage, and was possessed by all Roman citizens but also by some others, as will be seen. Theory held that in *iustae nuptiae* (which were *iure civili*) the child followed the status of the father, whereas in any other sort of marriage (which was *iure gentium*) it followed the status of the mother; but as a result of certain modifications by legislation the effect of the rules in practice, during the whole of our period, was that you could only be a Roman citizen by birth if your father was, and even then only if your mother was either a Roman citizen or otherwise possessed *conubium*—except that the theoretical rule stayed unmodified in one case (very remarkably): children of a Roman citizen woman and a slave or an unknown father took her status and were therefore Roman citizens.[14] It must not be forgotten, therefore, that children of

Roman citizen fathers might well not themselves be Roman citizens, and might even be slaves.

Manumission. One of the most extraordinary facts of Roman law is that a slave manumitted (that is, given his freedom) in proper form before a magistrate[15] or by will, and not in contravention of certain Augustan legislation, by a Roman citizen master, became himself a Roman citizen. We shall see presently that he was in many ways a 'second-class' citizen; he was *civis Romanus libertinus* instead of *ingenuus*. But he had the precious *conubium*, so that his children, if he married right, could be *ingenui*.

Government grant. The cases are numerous,[16] and it would be tedious to go through them all. The most important were:

1 To whole peregrine communities *en bloc*. This is the main process whereby Roman citizenship spread during our period, sometimes via the 'Latin right' as a half-way stage. Many inscriptions record such grants;[17] some emperors were more lavish with them than others, especially Claudius, who was criticized for overdoing it:[18]

> 'He had decided to put all the Greeks, Gauls, Spaniards and Britons into togas.'

2 To the soldiers of the auxiliary regiments and other non-citizen branches of Rome's forces, including the navy, on completion of their years of engagement or honourable discharge when they left the service. (To be a regular legionary you had to be a Roman citizen, though many men of non-citizen origin were simply given citizenship on enlistment to qualify them if they wished to enter the legions, but the auxiliaries were mostly peregrines during our period.)[19] Of these grants evidence survives in many *diplomata*, copies on bronze tablets of the official record which were issued to the individuals concerned. They certify[20] that the emperor:

> 'has given citizenship to them, their children and descendants, and *conubium* with such wives as they already had at the date of the grant, or if otherwise with such wives as they should subsequently marry, but only to one wife for each individual'.

The interesting feature is retrospective citizenship for children born during service (when marriage was forbidden). Surprisingly, it seems that the legionaries, who were citizens, were worse off; they did not get such retrospective citizenship for children born 'in the camp'.[21] But the questions of succession to them that arose were partly settled in other ways, as will be seen in Chapter IV. Also since, if a man wanted to enter a regular legion, he could be given citizenship on recruitment, children born during their father's service could get citizenship by thus following in his footsteps.

3 To the magistrates (and in some cases, from the second century AD, the town councillors) of 'Latin' communities. The right of 'Latin' magistrates to get Roman citizenship goes back to Republican times,[22] and the charters of Salpensa and Malaca in the Flavian period contain this right—and no more. But by the second century this had become the 'lesser Latin right', *minus Latium*, and there was a *maius Latium* which gave Roman citizenship to all members of the town council. It appears first under Hadrian, and may well have been an innovation of his.[23]

4 To Junian Latins (who will be explained presently) marrying a Roman citizen or Latin wife and having a child, by application to the courts when the child reached the age of one. Citizenship was granted to all.

5 In certain cases where the parties to a marriage were under a mistake as to the status of one of them, if there was a child, they could by a *senatusconsultum* of unknown date apply to the courts, prove mistake, and receive citizenship for all. The complex rules are summed up by Gaius:[24]

> 'From what we have said it is apparent that if a male Roman citizen marries a peregrine woman, or vice versa, their child is a peregrine; but if the marriage was entered into in error [*i.e.* error of status] its defect is cured by the *senatusconsultum*'.

6 Grants by the emperor to individuals, either for services rendered or expected, or simply as a favour to themselves or powerful patrons requesting it on their behalf. This was a potential door to traffic in Roman citizenship. The tribune who told the

apostle Paul that he had 'paid a lot of money for his citizenship' must be referring to bribery to obtain a grant through someone with power at court.[25] (He cannot be a freedman who has paid for his manumission and hence citizenship, because a freedman would not be a tribune; and there was no legitimate citizenship by purchase.) He is very *insouciant* about admitting this, which might imply that it was common, but on the other hand there is astonishingly little reference elsewhere to it as an abuse—except precisely for the principate of Claudius, when Paul's tribune received his citizenship.[26]

Of free persons who were not Roman citizens the only category that needs special discussion at this point is the 'Latins'. This status had two separate historical origins:

Coloniary Latins. There is no place here to enter into the early history of the status. During the whole of our period the Latin municipalities were communities with a 'half-way' position, not Roman citizens but possessed of some of the citizen rights. The status, which ceased to exist in Italy after 49 BC, continued to be granted in the first century AD to hitherto peregrine communities[27] (not to individuals).

Junian Latins. It seems to have been the emperor Tiberius under whom a law was passed which greatly complicated the Roman law of status. The story begins with the laws inspired by Augustus, *lex Fufia Caninia*, 2 BC and *lex Aelia Sentia*, AD 4, designed to limit the numbers of slaves who could be manumitted, by will or by lifetime acts respectively. Now people had in the Republican era sometimes just intimated informally to slaves that they regarded them as free instead of performing a formal manumission—by letter or by announcement 'among friends'; the praetor would protect the personal freedom of the man concerned,[28] but he had no status, and in the law's eyes he was still a slave. The effect of the Augustan laws was to put all those manumitted in contravention of them (if the slave was under thirty, or the master under twenty, or the total number freed by will in excess of the permitted maximum, and so on) in this precarious limbo of the 'informally free'. By a *lex Iunia Norbana*

of AD 19[29] a new status was invented for these people; they were
to be not citizens but a kind of Latin. They gained a recognized
and no longer precarious position at law, though a severely
restricted one, as will be seen. Informal manumission 'among
friends' went on, making Junian Latins, for a long time. Pliny
refers to it (showing that they could rise to full citizenship either
by a subsequent formal manumission or by a grant of 'citizen
right' from the emperor),[30] and a lady called Helen kept her
certificate of such an informal manumission in the year AD 221:[31]

> 'Marcus Aurelius Ammonion, son of Lupercus, grandson of
> Sarapion, mother Terheuta, of the ancient and famous borough
> Hermoupolis Maior, manumitted among friends his slave
> Helen, born in the household, aged circa thirty-four years, and
> ordered her to be free, and received for her liberty from
> Aurelius Ales son of Inarous . . . two thousand two hundred
> drachmas.'

The rights of the Latins, both coloniary and Junian, can to some
extent be spoken of together. *Conubium* they did not have, except
by special concession (such as to the wife of a discharged soldier);[32]
but the odd consequence of this, that the offspring of a Latin
father and a Roman citizen mother (taking *her* status because there
was no *iustum matrimonium*) would be a Roman citizen, was
upheld for coloniary Latins and allowed to Junian Latins by a
senatusconsultum of Hadrian's time,[33] whereas the similar odd
consequence for children of a peregrine father and a Roman
citizen mother had been rejected by legislation many generations
earlier.[34] What the Latins did possess was *commercium*, another
part of Roman citizen rights;[35] but exactly what that included
is by no means clear. Most scholars have tended to assert that it
covered practically all the rights of a citizen except *conubium*:
the right to participate in formal conveyance by 'mancipation'
and so to own property by full 'citizen right', to contract, to have
access to the urban praetor's court, to adopt, and to make and
inherit under civil law wills—with the agreed exception that
will-making rights were not allowed to Junians.[36] Ulpian,
however, speaks only of 'mancipation', and some modern authori-

ties would give *commercium* a more limited scope, excluding, for example, full 'citizenship right' ownership of property.[37] In any case, it may be doubted whether in our period this separate and complex status of Latins was of much real social importance. For Latin males absence of *conubium* was, as we have seen, unimportant; as we have also seen, the magistrates—and sometimes councillors—of coloniary Latin cities acquired Roman citizenship *ex officio*. Moreover, the state needed many services and was prepared to pay for them by granting its citizenship, and to judge by the long list of ways given by Ulpian in which Latins could rise to Roman citizenship,[38] they were the prime beneficiaries; 'any enterprising Latin must have been able to raise himself to the citizenship'.[39] As for *commercium*, whatever its content may have been in archaic times, by our period the old formal rights and actions of the *ius civile* were so small a proportion of the law compared with the new branches of *ius honorarium* which peregrines (and *a fortiori* Latins) enjoyed as much as Romans that their 'peregrinity' in these matters can have been small obstacle. The lack of right to benefit under a Roman will was the most significant private law disability that remained to peregrines, and that right the coloniary Latins probably had.[40] The special disabilities of Junians derived not so much from the fact that they were Latins as from the fact that they were freedmen (of a specially restricted sort).

All the rest of the free inhabitants of Rome's dominions (and of course those outside as well) were simply peregrines, *peregrini*. The great majority were citizens of some municipal community, with their own local laws with which Roman law concerned itself hardly at all. A slave freed by a peregrine owner was just a peregrine;[41] what particular rights he had would depend on the law of his owner's community. But criminous slaves freed by Romans fell, by the *lex Aelia Sentia*, into that sub-class of peregrines called *dediticii*. The main point about them is that they could never be promoted to Roman citizenship; even the constitution of Caracalla that gave all other free persons citizenship continued expressly to exclude them.[42] But whom the category contained besides these criminous freedmen we do not really know. They had no citizenship of any community; this was the situation of most of the population of Egypt, but the Egyptians were not excluded from Caracalla's grant. By AD 212 there were still a great many peregrines for Caracalla to promote, especially in the Greek-speaking lands; the 'upward' movement to Roman citizenship had been going on steadily all the time, but much more massively in the west than in the east, and it was of course the upper classes who had been getting it.[42a]

Everybody not so far mentioned was a slave.

*

In a society where status determines all your rights and duties it may be very important to prove your status. Proof that you were a Roman citizen and not a peregrine; that you were free-born and not a freed slave; most fundamental of all, that you were a free man and not someone's slave. How difficult or easy was it to establish status? Leaving aside for the moment the last and most crucial case let us consider first the proof of citizenship.

The situation in the Republic was that proof of citizenship depended on your name appearing on the census-list, which was normally brought up to date at five-year intervals. Just at the beginning of our period, when the bulk of Italy was being enfranchised after the 'Social War', those with a new right to citizenship either had to make a personal appearance in Rome before the praetor or were supposed to be enrolled by the censors under their whole community, now raised *en bloc*. This was neglected, for numerous political reasons, and people claiming to be new citizens by grant were not on the roll. In 65 BC, therefore, when a *lex Papia* was passed expelling peregrines and requiring prosecution of people falsely claiming to be citizens, many were put in peril. Cicero defended one of them, the poet Archias, which is how we learn about the matter.[43]

For citizens by birth the *lex Aelia Sentia* of AD 4 established a system of birth registration.[44] Why was it established by this particular statute? Perhaps to check age in determining whether masters freeing slaves were aged twenty or under; we know that these registers were used for proof of age.[45] The *lex Papia Poppaea* also relied on the registers; to encourage the increase of family size amongst the upper classes it gave certain privileges to those with not less than three children; presumably proof of family size depended on the registers. The parent (it could be the mother)[46] made a formal statement before the authorities, a *professio*, and they put the child in the register as stated, without enquiry,[47] so that the *professio* was essentially evidence rather than proof. Individuals could obtain a copy of the entry; here is one dated AD 62:[48]

'In the consulship of Publius Marius and Lucius Afinius Gallus, 23 July ... at Alexandria beside Egypt. Certified copy from the list of birth attestations open to public inspection in the Atrium Magnum, in which occurs the following item: Lucius Julius Vestinus, prefect of Egypt, published the names of those who had declared the birth of children in their households in accordance with the *lex Papia Poppaea* and *Aelia Sentia* in the consulship of P. Marius and L. Afinius Gallus. 18 July: Lucius Valerius Crispus, son of Lucius, tribe Pollia, property three hundred and seventy-five thousand sesterces, reported the birth of a son, Lucius Valerius Crispus, son of Lucius, tribe Pollia, to his wife Domitia Paulla, daughter of Lucius, on 29 June prox.; c. r. e. ad k.' (unintelligible).

From another document we learn the rule that illegitimate children were not allowed on the register; instead of a formal *professio* parents just made a private declaration of such children under seal:[49]

'. . . because the *lex Aelia Sentia* and *Papia Poppaea* forbids illegitimates to be reported on the register'.

A tablet from Herculaneum also records one of these private declarations, dated AD 60 (though one cannot see why the child was illegitimate):[50]

'In the consulship of Gaius Velleius Paterculus and Marcus Manlius Vopiscus, 24 July, L. Vennidius Ennychus testified that a child was born to him of Livia Acte his wife.'

Apuleius in his defence of himself has a spirited passage that mentions the birth registers:[51]

'As to the age of my wife Pudentilla, about which you have confidently (and falsely) asserted that I married her at 60, I shall make a brief reply; a long one is not needed when the facts are so plain. Her father made a declaration of the birth of a daughter, as everyone does. The entries are preserved both in the public archives and at their home: here they are now, under your nose. Hand Aemilianus the tablets; let him examine the binding, identify the seals, read the year, work out the age . . .'

As to citizenship by grant, we now have the evidence of the Banasa tablet that there was a register of all new citizens by individual grants and that copies of the entries could be obtained; and there was a register of all grants to discharged veterans, of which the auxiliary *diplomata* were copies for the individual to keep. The main 'everyday' sign of being a Roman citizen was possession of the 'three names', *praenomen*, *nomen* and *cognomen*, and it was a criminal offence to usurp these, a kind of forgery, sometimes very severely punished.[52]

An exceedingly interesting new dossier from Herculaneum concerns the efforts of a young woman called Petronia Iusta to establish that she was free-born and not a freedwoman.[53] It was not, it seems, contested that her mother had been a slave in the household of a couple, Petronius Stephanus and Calatoria Themis, and had been freed by them; the problem for Iusta turned on whether her own birth had been subsequent to her mother's manumission (in which case she was free-born, though admittedly illegitimate—very likely a bastard of Petronius, who seems to have been fond of her) or previous to it, and she herself manumitted by Calatoria Themis after Petronius' death. Iusta apparently could produce no birth declaration (and, incidentally, a *lex Visellia*, probably of AD 24, made it a crime for a freed person to pretend to be free-born),[54] but neither could Calatoria Themis produce any formal record of manumission. The only important *Digest* text on such cases is 22. 3. 14, which concerns who is to be plaintiff and who defendant; in the present action

we do not know, nor what the outcome was. The documents are
of two categories: first, a set of records of mutual promises,
vadimonia (bails) by the parties for appearance before the urban
praetor in the Augustan Forum at Rome on a given date at the
usual unconscionably early hour, on pain of agreed fines, which
will be looked at later in a different context; and second, a category
of documents consists of a number of *testimonia*, sworn statements
of witnesses on both sides (themselves formally sealed and
witnessed):[55]

'I, Gaius Petronius Telesphorus, have written and sworn by the
spirit of the emperor Augustus [*i.e.* Vespasian] and his sons that
I know the girl Iusta, object of suit, to have been born free, the
child of my fellow-freedwoman Petronia Vitalis; and that it
was I who arranged with Petronius Stephanus and Calatoria
Themis that he should accept reimbursement for the child's
upbringing and restore her to her mother; from which facts
I know that the woman Iusta, object of suit, was born in freedom as daughter of Petronia Vitalis—which is the question at
issue.

'I, Quintus Tamudius Optatus, have written and sworn by
the spirit of the emperor Vespasian Caesar Augustus and his
sons that I was present when Petronia Vitalis discussed the girl
her daughter with Calatoria Themis; and that I heard Stephanus
the husband of Themis there and then say to Petronia Vitalis
"Why are you upset with us about the child, considering that
we are treating her as our own daughter?" From which I know
that the woman, object of suit, is the daughter of Petronia
Vitalis and is free by birth—which is the question at issue.

'I, [name illegible], have written at the request of Marcus
Calatorius Marullus and in his presence, because he said he was
illiterate, that he has sworn by the spirit of the emperor
Vespasian and his sons that: "I know that Calatoria Themis
manumitted both the girl and myself; from which I know that
the girl is the freedwoman of Calatoria Themis—which is the
question at issue." '

★

D

If 'the woman who calls herself Petronia Iusta' was a freed-woman, the widow Calatoria had over her the rights of a patron. We must look more in detail now at the legal position of persons whose freedom and Roman citizenship were based on manumission, for although the Roman law stated with exemplary firmness that 'all men are either free or slaves'—that is that it recognized no helots, serfs or villeins—the legal, let alone the economic, reality was a good deal more *nuancé*. Another reason for taking the class of freed men and women very seriously is that it supplied the nearest thing Rome ever had to a middle class. To say that they 'were probably the most intelligent class of the community'[56] underestimates the range the class covered, for many humble, illiterate menials were manumitted; nevertheless, the freedman class certainly did include many people of high intelligence, literacy, energy and ambition, and what is more, already by the time of Cicero's death they probably comprised a high proportion of all Roman citizens, in the urban communities at least, so that, psychologically and culturally speaking, the status-line of demarcation, free as against slave, was blurred and ultimately annihilated by the fact that so many of the free had once been slaves, and replaced by the simple distinction between 'haves' and 'have-nots'.[57] The most famous of all Roman freedmen is an imaginary one: Trimalchio. Petronius paints him in detail, mocking, *en grand seigneur*, the characteristics of his class; but behind the satirical picture can be seen many of the traits of a bourgeoisie —emphasis on material values, connection with commerce, urbanism, aping of the 'gentry'. The scorn and dislike of freed-men amongst the senatorial class springs from the complex attitudes towards slavery which will be spoken of presently. The hatred of imperial freedmen in politics is well known; more general social dislike is trenchantly expressed by Persius, on a slave just freed by formal ceremony:[57a]

'One twist, and Dama is Marcus Dama now. What, Marcus is surety and you refuse to lend? Marcus is judge and you have no confidence? Marcus has spoken it; it must be true. Come, Marcus, be a signatory to my will!'

Even the formally manumitted *civis Romanus libertinus* had once, says Cicero, been treated almost as a slave.[58] All through our period he was under a series of legal disabilities compared with the free-born.[59] Some were disabilities of public law; freedmen could not serve in the regular legions; they could not aspire to the senatorial or equestrian orders (except by extraordinary grant of the emperor); and in most citizen towns they were not eligible for local magistracy. By Augustan legislation a senator could not contract a *iustum matrimonium* with a freedwoman. These bans affected the whole class; those whose patron or patron's children were alive were under numerous further limitations, based on the ancient notion that they owed 'dutifulness' to the family who had conferred on them the benefit of citizenship. This notion may originally have been part of social *mores* rather than law; but in our period 'patron's rights' were certainly no mere vague general clientship. There are several *Digest* titles about them, and they were actionable in the courts.

First, the freedman must not act to the harm of his patron. He might bring civil suits against him only by permission of the authorities, and 'infaming actions'[60] not at all; and the only criminal proceedings he might initiate against a patron were for treason. And the patron could apply reasonable chastisement to him:[61]

> 'for the praetor is not obliged to put up with a man who was yesterday a slave and today is free, complaining that his master has been rude to him or mildly struck or corrected him.'

Officium involved the freedman in undertaking general services on behalf of his patron, such as accepting the guardianship of his children or supporting him if he fell into poverty. Under this heading a word may also be said about manumission 'for the purpose of matrimony'. By Augustan legislation it was ruled that a slave woman freed by her patron so that he could marry her (though she was not in terms forced into the marriage)[62] could not divorce him and go into marriage or concubinage with another without his consent.[63] Matrimonial reasons were treated as a valid cause for relaxation of the age minima for formal manumission laid down by the *lex Aelia Sentia*,[64] and in this case the woman must actually marry if her manumission was to be good (and her status as a citizen valid). The reverse case is interesting (though the relevant text is often suspected of interpolation):[65] a woman might free a male slave 'for the purpose of matrimony', but only if she herself was a freed slave and he her fellow-slave. This is a hint of what must have been a common case, of the slave of either sex, given freedom, buying or begging from the master the partner with whom they had been in sexual relationship (marriage of slaves being impossible) and freeing him or her so that a proper marriage might at last begin.

Again, a slave could be required, as a condition of obtaining freedom, to swear an oath that he would perform so many *operae*, man-days of work, for his patron, and was then obliged to repeat this oath when free because the law treated the *operae* as actionable. (It has been pointed out that when a free bread ration was established for the city plebs in the late Republic numerous masters saw their chance to free slaves, put them on the national bread line, and continue to use their *operae* without having to pay their keep.)[66] There were some limits:[67]

'Only those *operae* are taken to have been imposed, which can be performed without indignity or danger to life. Thus if a slave who has worked as a prostitute is manumitted she does not have to provide the same *operae* to her patron.'

Operae could be either domestic and personal services or skilled craftsman's work. They were units of value convertible into cash, and sometimes a freedman could offer money in lieu; in any case, the praetor gave an action for them just as if they were a money debt.[68] Freedmen with two free children, and freedwomen over 50, were exempt. The *operae* of slaves could be hired out by the master; the *lex Aelia Sentia* ruled that a patron could not hire out his freedman's *operae* for reward, but so many modifications were made to this principle that in the end it did not amount to much.[69]

What, then, of the freedman who failed in general 'dutifulness'? There was no legal mechanism of the praetor for reducing him to slavery again. Nevertheless, the famous debate staged in Tacitus' *Annals* under the year AD 56 shows that many wealthy patrons hankered after such a mechanism,[70] and that, though they did not get it, Nero (like his predecessor)[71] was quite prepared to re-enslave 'undutiful' freedmen in individual cases. By the end of our period, to judge from the *Digest*, there had come to exist a criminal punishment for freedmen who failed in 'dutifulness'.[72]

Another category of rights of patron over freedman was automatic; it gave him a hold over his freedman's property, especially on death. Augustus' legislation resulted in very complicated rules which are not interesting enough to be worth stating in detail. Very roughly put, the basic principle was that if a freedman had legitimate children they could inherit from him, but if he had any heirs (whether by will or not) outside this narrow range the patron could claim a half share against them. The Augustan rules modified this in numerous details—particularly, that where a freedman's estate was large the patron would henceforth get a share even as against the freedman's legitimate children.

Here we must bring in parenthetically the special disability of Junian Latin freedmen. Upon their death everything they had reverted entirely to their patron just as if they had remained slaves, and this reversion could be bequeathed or sold to third parties.[73] Justinian's *Institutes* get rhetorical and emotional about this:[74]

'In life they were free, but with their last breath they lost both life and liberty.'

However, the fair point has been made that since, if a Junian Latin had children, he could be promoted to citizenship, only the childless necessarily breathed their last as Latins.[75]

The rights of succession of patron to freedman sound even more crushing in the light of a *Digest* title 'On actions in fraud of patron' (D. 38. 5), from which it appears that any alienation of property by a freedman before he died, or any legacy, which could be regarded as defrauding the patron of his due share of the estate, was subject to a legal action against the freedman's heirs:[76]

'In life a freedman can make gifts to friends who have deserved well of him; but he cannot make legacies even to deserving friends if by so doing he diminishes the patron's share.'

Another title in the *Digest* reveals a sinister practice by which masters would impose on slaves as a condition of freedom some enormous sum of money or total of *operae* 'for the sake of burdening the liberty';[77]

'so that if the freedman offends his patron it can be exacted, and consequently the freedman will be forever under his patron's thumb through fear of the exaction, and he will agree to do anything if it is demanded by the patron.'

The praetor gave an action to repress this.

The patron's right to succeed was supplemented by his right to guardianship of all freedmen who were minors and all freedwomen of any age (except that Augustan legislation released all women from perpetual guardianship if they had a requisite number of children). Those under guardianship could only alienate property with their guardian's consent, so this was another element in the control by patrons of their freedmen's property.

All this sounds very harsh. The Romans liked to think of a freedman's relationship to his patron as having something filial about it, and this was not wholly 'doublethink'. It need not be doubted that often there was a 'faithful retainer' relationship like that of Tiro to the Cicero family.[78] And the law was not entirely one-sided. Even the rules about succession must be looked at in the light that the foundation of a freedman's property was the slave-*peculium*, legally belonging to the master, which he had been allowed to keep on manumission; if, as often, the slave had 'paid' for his freedom by, in effect, renouncing some or all of his *peculium*, the patron could not then defeat his will and claim part-succession.[79] Other limits to the patron's power were similarly secured by making his right to succession or *operae* depend on them. Thus he could not, on pain of this, initiate criminal actions against his freedman involving the death penalty (except treason), and he had to support his freedman if impoverished; in fact a common kind of legacy was an annuity, *alimenta*, to freedmen. And finally, the sense of freedmen as part of the family and a continuance of the family name (which they took upon manumission) comes out strongly in the tradition of sepulchral monuments, as will be seen.

We hear a certain amount—not only in the *Digest*—about ways in which a freedman could come to count as free-born. First, by the 'grant of the gold rings' by the emperor, which was naturally only for freedmen with special favour at court. They were released from the disabilities of public law and from their patron's rights to services during their lifetimes, but counted still as freedmen on their death so that their patrons (doubtless usually the emperor himself) preserved rights of succession.[80] Secondly, just as a man held as a slave might prove in the courts that he was in truth free-born, so might a freedman. This was sometimes abused in collusive actions in which patrons put up no proper defence against the claim (which is no doubt what Encolpius means in the *Satyricon* when he describes Ascyltus as 'freed by lust and free-born by lust'),[81] and the law tried to stop such collusions.[82] The emperors sometimes granted 'restitution of free birth' as a fiction.[83]

★

About slaves there is much literature,[84] and this is not surprising. The slave is regarded by many historians as the determining factor in the economic, social and intellectual life of antiquity. There can be scarcely a title of the *Digest* in which he does not figure. Precisely for that reason he will not be treated in a single place in the present book, but will appear where he belongs, which is everywhere. For the moment all that concerns us is his (and, it cannot be too much emphasized, her) place in the law of status.

In many ancient societies everybody was more or less unfree. Greco-Roman society, by polarizing freedom and unfreedom with a sharpness rare in human history,[85] provided itself with a sharper version than most societies of the puzzle: what is a slave? Is it a thing or is he a person? In Roman society and law this ambivalence is everywhere. The slave is a *res*, a *mancipium*, thing, chattel; *res mortales*, 'mortal objects', slaves are called at one place in the *Digest*.[86] The slave is an object of buying and selling; damage to a slave is damage to property; you can own part of a slave—that is, the slave can be owned by several people at once, like a field. Few things could read more callously than *Digest* 21. 1, on what constitutes 'sickness or unsuitability' of a slave in the market; for instance:[87]

> 'The slave who does anything to remove himself from mankind is regarded as vicious; as, for example, if he makes a noose or drinks medicine as a poison or throws himself from a height, hoping to achieve death. For one who will do this to himself will have no scruple about what he does to others.'

The slave has no rights or duties. If he commits offences his master can choose between paying damages and handing him over. He cannot sue in the courts (except for one thing) or enter public life or join the army.[88] There is no such thing as slave marriage. 'What, you fool! A slave a man?'[89]

Yes, also a man. In the agricultural society of early Roman times the farmer worked the land with his whole family, sons and slaves. And between sons and slaves in the old man's power there was not all that much difference—except in ultimate expectations. To the end of Roman law the rules about *filius familias* and *servus* are curiously alike; the 'power of life and death' applies over both, neither can own anything—they can have only *peculium*—and so on. The very word for 'slave' in old civil law formulas is *homo*. The law of the Twelve Tables on assault treated slaves just as less privileged adults; the penalty was smaller, that was all. With the great influx of slaves after the Punic Wars, when Roman society and economy were transformed, there began Rome's great heyday of 'slave economy', and the chattel status of slaves grew more severe; and then under the Principate (as indeed slaves became rarer and dearer again, but not wholly for that reason) the status was subjected to a long, slow, tentative process of amelioration by legislation on humanitarian grounds:[90]

'The power of masters over their slaves must indeed be unimpaired, and no man must be deprived of his rights; but it is in the interest of masters that assistance against cruelty or starvation or intolerable injury should not be denied to those who have just complaints.'

The labour of the slave was needed at all levels of intelligence and subtlety, and thus he will be found managing estates and businesses and shops and ships, contracting as agent for his master, joining in partnerships with his master or others on the basis of his *peculium*, nursing, healing, teaching his master's children. There was one matter on which the slave might (through an intermediary) come into court—namely his liberty.[91] Deliberate killing of him was not only damage to property; it was also murder.[92] He could on manumission become a Roman citizen, and a Roman citizen could for crime be reduced to slavery; and the children of a Roman citizen might be, and probably often were, slaves. The offices of the public administration were staffed by 'slaves of Caesar' and 'freedmen of Augustus'.

Every sort of treatment by masters, therefore, and every sort of relationship between master and slave can be found in the sources, depending on what part of the labour force the slave belonged to, just as every condition of slave life can be met with from the treadmill to the boudoir—and to the office. And none is more typical than another. Nevertheless, through the pattern there does run a thread of those 'spiritual stresses and unremitting social tensions' which make it analogous to the old American South.[93] Cases of masters killed by their slaves haunt the literature and the law.[94] The most celebrated literary reference is Tacitus' account of the debate that followed the murder of Pedanius Secundus, with a fierce and powerful speech by a famous jurist, Cassius Longinus;[95] even more significant is the gentle and *bien pensant* Pliny, writing about the murder of Larcius Macedo:[96]

'and no one can think himself secure merely because he is easy-going and mild; it is not cold calculation that leads to masters being murdered, but simply criminality.'

★

The most important question that could arise about a man or woman was: slave or free? And proof of status could be difficult, for many reasons including the fact that:[97]

'it is difficult to distinguish a free man from a slave.'

In spite of the Roman law's insistence on sharply distinguishing between slave and free, the evidence suggests that in social, cultural and economic terms there was something much more like a 'continuum' of statuses, quite apart from labour conditions in which the free worker might be worse off than the slave.

To confine ourselves here to formal legal process: *causae liberales*, suits concerning liberty, might occur both ways round—either the man held as a slave claiming to be free or the man living as a free man claimed by another as his slave. And this question of status might be a necessary preliminary to actions of other sorts. We hear in the *Digest* of two frauds: one is the suppression of clauses in wills granting freedom to slaves;[98] the other is a nasty blackmail, the extortion of money under the threat of suppressing evidence of a man's free status when he is claimed (perhaps by yourself) as a slave.[99] To plead liberty, if you were held as a slave, you had to have an *adsertor libertatis* to approach the court for you. There was an action 'for production', *ad exhibendum*, so as to ensure that you were produced in court. One important case of the suit for liberty resulted from the common practice of exposure of unwanted infants, who might be picked up by people and brought up as their slaves. Roman law insisted that their free status was unimpaired, so that if they could find an *adsertor* they could recover their freedom. In the Greek-speaking parts of Rome's dominion[100] it was a condition of such recovery that someone should pay 'ransom' representing the costs of the child's upbringing, but successive emperors refused to allow that any such payment was obligatory.[101] However, the practical problem remained: had you any proof, and could you get an *adsertor*? Many must have failed.

A curious figure appears frequently in the pages of the *Digest*: the *liber homo bona fide serviens*, 'free man in a state of slavery in good faith'. The good faith, is, in our period, that of the person who holds him as a slave—he believes him to be so.[102] How could a free man find himself in this unfortunate situation? We have seen one case, exposure in infancy.[103] Another was kidnapping, *suppressio*, which the Augustan Peace never succeeded in stamping out—perhaps just because as other sources of slaves dried up the dealers turned to it as a channel of supply; Pliny has some curious tales of disappearances.[104] Again it was a matter of how you were to prove, against someone who had bought you in the market in good faith, that you had ever been free. Yet another case was that of the slave made free by the provisions of a will of the contents of which he was unaware; such a situation is made the starting point for a discussion about a quite different matter in the *Digest*:[105]

> 'A man had a slave Stichus in charge of a loan-bank on his estate in the provinces. In his will, which was opened in Rome, Stichus was down as free and part-heir. Stichus, in ignorance of his status, went on lending and calling in moneys on behalf of the deceased. . . .'

What the *Digest* is mostly taken up with are complex puzzles about acquisition by the *bona fide serviens* as agent of his supposed master, when it turns out that, having been really a free man all along, he was not capable of acquiring for a third party; but these are only of technical interest. More important for us is to hear Dio of Prusa in the second of his speeches 'On Slavery':[106]

> 'Enormous numbers of free people sell themselves so as to serve as slaves according to contract, sometimes on terms not light but the most severe imaginable';
> 'Are not many people held as slaves actually free men serving unjustly? Some get to a court and prove themselves free, but many for ever fail to do so, being unable to supply clear proof of their free status, or simply because their so-called master is not harsh.'

The last phrase is perhaps the most significant of all. There might be reasons why a man would wish to sell himself into slavery or stay in slavery, and not least because slavery might be less hard than freedom. We hear of other motives; one of Trimalchio's guests boasts:[107]

> 'Actually, my father was a king. Why am I only a freedman now? Because I handed myself into slavery of my own free will. I wanted to end up a Roman citizen, not a tribute-paying peregrine.'

We hear in the *Digest* of self-enslavement in order to secure the post of *servus actor*, the chief accountant of a big private household (and with normal luck to become later their freedman procurator in the same post and finish up a rich citizen with free-born children). And all this is quite apart from the case of which most is heard, which was a plain fraud: you got someone to go through the farce of selling you as a slave to an unsuspecting customer, you and your accomplice divided the price, and then at once you proclaimed your freedom and got an *adsertor libertatis*.

What, then, was the legal position about self-sale into slavery? Did it make a man irrevocably a slave in the eyes of the law? Dio is of course addressing peregrines, probably about peregrines; Roman law might be otherwise. The truth is that we cannot say what it was, so problematic are the sources; and the reason for this may well be that the law was not altogether in line with the facts of life at this humble level.

Possession in bad faith of a free Roman citizen (that is, knowingly detaining him) was *plagium*:[108]

> 'Anyone is liable under the *lex Fabia* (*de plagiariis*) who has concealed, sold, imprisoned or acquired a Roman citizen, whether free-born or freed, or another man's slave.'

It is important to note that the *lex Fabia* dealt also with detaining slaves. It made the offence, perhaps to the very end of our period, only a civil wrong, actionable for a money penalty:[109] and this rather suggests that it was originally and primarily intended to cover slaves. The praetor gave an interdict for the actual recovery of the free man out of his detention, a kind of *habeas corpus*,[110] which could be had as well as the suit under the Fabian law.

But we still ask: could he legitimately sell himself so as to make himself irrevocably a slave? First one might consider whether the contract as such was a valid sale; there seem to have been differences of opinion, settled in favour of the view that if the buyer knew the object offered was a free man there was no valid contract, but if he did not, and was buying in good faith, the sale was good.[111] Ulpian tells us that there was an action given to the purchaser for damages, against 'the cunning of those who, knowing, have allowed themselves to be sold' and against their vendor[112]—except, he says, in those cases in which the man who has sold himself is not allowed to assert his liberty. The cases to which Ulpian refers are the frauds already described; the penalty is that you can't escape from your own trap, and the implication is that apart from fraud you always can escape from slavery. The difficulty remains, that there are texts that seem to imply other cases besides fraud from which you could not escape. Selling yourself to become a *servus actor*, for example, is not necessarily fraud, nor is being given as gift or dowry or pledge, which Paulus mentions in one text as making a man a slave.[113] One cannot be sure of the answer.[114] What one can be sure of is that there were people who did sell themselves into the practical situation of slavery; and if they were content to remain in it no one was ever the wiser. If they did repent there were some circumstances in which the law would not let them escape. But of course a prospective buyer who knew their free status might hesitate.

So there were other possibilities. One was self-hire. In the eastern part of the Roman realm there were sometimes transactions looking like contracts for services, which in effect bound the servant even for life, or at least for terms of years; you could hire out yourself or your children on this basis. It might be a way of working off by service an actual debt, or the debt might be a fiction spoken of to ground the contract. Self-hire had a very long Near Eastern history;[115] Roman law ignored it, though the *auctoramentum*, or oath of free men hiring themselves as gladiators, is like it,[116] and we shall meet later the judgment debtor who has suffered 'seizure by hand' to work off his debt.

★

The law talks about formal ways of going down in the status scale, *capitis deminutio*, with its three degrees, *minima, media* and *maxima*.[117] The first of these concerns such things as a person *sui iuris* becoming *alieni iuris* by adoption, and will occupy us later; the other two are almost entirely penalties of the criminal law, and them too we postpone, except for two cases. One is the famous Roman rule that a man captured by the enemy suffers *maxima capitis deminutio* in the eyes of the law, losing both citizenship and freedom, but if he returns 'from beyond the frontier' he recovers by this *postliminium* his full status just as it was before; it is a survival of the old 'city-state' principle—citizen inside, stranger outside. The second case of an important *capitis deminutio* not resulting from a criminal conviction concerns the status of free citizen women cohabiting with someone else's slave, and of the resulting offspring. A *senatusconsultum Claudianum* of AD 52 laid down (to state a controversial position in outline) that if such a cohabitation was with the consent of the slave's owner the free-born citizen woman was reduced to the status of a *liberta*; if it was without such consent the citizen woman, whether free-born or freed, suffered *capitis deminutio maxima* and became the slave of the slave's owner (except if—and for so long as—she was in *patria potestas*). The *senatusconsultum* also, perhaps by inadvertence of wording, permitted private agreements whereby, although the woman remained free (even though a *liberta*) her children became slaves—which might well be the only terms on which her partner's master would give his consent; but this anomaly was abolished by Hadrian. The purpose of these rules cannot have been to prevent the contamination of free with slave genes. For one thing, they applied to freed as well as free women; and for another, there was nothing to prevent a free citizen woman cohabiting with her own slave and producing free children thereby, so if her partner's master was willing to sell him, and she to pay the price (or to pay the master the price of his manumission), no penalty at all resulted. What else may the purpose have been?[118]

There was one field of society in which free women often married slaves and freedmen—namely, when the latter were *servi*

Caesaris and *liberti Augusti*, imperial slaves and freedmen. This class has been the object of important recent studies, which show how seriously we must take it.[119] These were the real 'civil servants' of the Empire, the men who ran the administration from the executive side. They were a 'white-collar' class, proud of their nomenclature and conscious of their hierarchy, and they could attract wives 'above them'. The emperor was their master or patron respectively, and he wanted a hereditary service—sons born as slaves of the imperial household, *vernae Caesaris*. Now the inventor of the rules of the *senatusconsultum Claudianum* was the most famous of all imperial freedmen, Pallas, the powerful financial secretary of Claudius, and he was 'decorated' for his invention.[120] Part of its purpose, at least, may therefore have been to give the emperor control over the children of his civil servants without wholly withdrawing the chance of *servi Caesaris* to marry free women. However, it must not be forgotten that many freed slave women left a beloved partner behind in slavery. If they continued to cohabit with the slave partner any subsequent children were free; but this was a financial loss to masters. The Claudian legislation produced the effect that a master could not lose the offspring of his male slaves without a pecuniary *quid pro quo*.

The imperial slave, if of ability to rise high in the service, would normally expect manumission at about the minimum statutory age of thirty, and it appears that he would normally pay for his freedom. The one special status rule of which we hear refers to 'public slaves', but it probably applied to the *servi Caesaris*: they had the right to make a will on the basis of half their *peculium*.[121] Whether they retained this half on manumission is not known. The *libertus Augusti*, as our ambitious civil servant has now become, has the emperor as his patron, with those rights over his property at death which we have seen, and which are worth remembering in reading of the great fortunes accumulated by Pallas and Narcissus. He may have remained single hitherto; otherwise he may divorce the wife he now has and make a yet grander marriage. It is for such as him, when he reaches the senior posts, that the 'gold rings' or fictitious 'restitution of free birth', and thus even the equestrian order, are not beyond the bounds of dreaming. He is the most socially mobile figure in the picture, a 'symptom of the interpenetration of classes in Roman Imperial society',[122] a projection of the 'spectrum of statuses' upwards as well as downwards.

*

At the highest end of the 'spectrum' were the two formal 'orders', the senate and the *equites*. They are so frequently described in books on Roman history that little need be said about them here.

Entry to the senate depended on being free-born and possessing property worth not less than a million sesterces (a modest barrier, really; many were many times wealthier than that—Seneca was worth three hundred million, the younger Pliny perhaps about sixteen million).[123] It was also necessary in the ordinary way to begin with certain military posts and then, as in Republican times, be elected to the first post that actually qualified a man to sit in the senate, the quaestorship. The senate was to this extent a hereditary body, that sons of senators were entitled to the 'broad stripe' of purple on their tunic which enabled them automatically to set foot on the ladder; but others could be granted the 'broad stripe',[124] and the emperors, as censors, increasingly made use of the right to 'adlect' comparatively senior men of proved ability to an appropriate standing within the senate. As is well known, many posts in the government of the empire were throughout our period open only to senators.

Entry to the equestrian order depended on being free-born and possessing property worth not less than four hundred thousand sesterces. Beyond this there is something of a puzzle. There was a 'grant of the public horse', and those with the 'public horse' took part in an annual parade and 'choosing of the *equites*' in Rome. But it is inconceivable that all the people who call themselves *equites* in the inscriptions of the empire had the 'public horse' and indeed clear that the 'public horse' was an additional distinction. On the other hand, in that case, what is the definition of an *eques Romanus*?[125] The impression, at least, is that many people all over the Roman world, conscious of possessing the necessary

birth and wealth, called themselves *equites Romani*. To take a
post in the administrative part of the civil service, which began
originally, like the senatorial career, with military tribuneships,
you would have to have imperial permission, and that would
confirm your status. What seems certain is that the class of
equites in economic terms was enormously wider than the quite
small number of men who took up salaried careers in government
service, and was not much less landowning and *rentier* than the
senators.

In the municipalities of Rome's dominions, both citizen towns
and others, entry to the *ordo*, the local senate or town council, was
subject to severe rules. Roman policy in this matter was consistent,
and only weakened in the latter part of our period when it began
to be difficult to find men to offer themselves; it was the one
thing that Rome minded about the internal arrangements of even
the peregrine cities, that they should be governed by the best
people—that is, the wealthy. One of Cicero's attacks on Verres
shows the principle as expressed in the late Republic:[126]

'For three years no one in any town in all Sicily has been made
a senator without payment, no one by suffrage, which is what
their laws require—all by Verres' instructions or letters. And
in the cooptation of all these senators not only was there no
suffrage, but neither were the categories respected from which
senators are supposed to be picked—no property qualification,
no age qualification, none of the rules for Sicily . . . nor the
rules laid down by the senate and people of Rome.

'Halaesus had rules laid down by C. Claudius in accordance
with a *senatusconsultum*; there were many provisions: no one
under 30, professions the exercise of which disbarred, property
rating and so on; . . . from Verres even an auctioneer bought a
place on the *ordo*.'

Nearly two hundred years later rules of the same kind were in
force in Bithynia:[127]

'My lord, the *lex Pompeia*, the charter of Bithynia, has a rule that no one may be a magistrate or sit in a senate if under 30 years of age . . .'

For towns of *cives Romani* the famous and formidable list of disqualifications is given in the 'Table of Heraclea'—arrangements probably made standard by Julius Caesar. The following are not allowed to sit in the senate:[128]

'he who has been convicted of theft committed by himself or has settled out of court for theft; he who has been convicted in actions of pledge, partnership, guardianship, mandate, assault or fraud; he who has been convicted of offences under the *lex Laetoria* [protecting minors against confidence tricks]; he who has taken an oath as a gladiator; he who has [?] taken an oath of insolvency in court or an oath of solvency, or has informed his sureties or creditors that he is insolvent or settled out of court on a basis of insolvency, or whose sureties have paid out on his behalf; he whose property has been sold up by edict of the magistrate [with certain exceptions]; he who has been condemned in a criminal trial at Rome so as to be exiled from Italy, and has not been restored; he who has been condemned in a criminal trial in the city of his origin; he who has been convicted of bringing suit or otherwise acting either calumniously or collusively; he who has been reduced to the ranks in the army for ignominy or dismissed from the army ignominiously; he who has taken money or other reward for accusing a Roman citizen on a capital charge; he who has been a professional prostitute; he who has been a master of gladiators or a brothel-keeper.'

And we have already been told a little earlier in the same document that persons actually engaged in the occupation of auctioneer and undertaker cannot enter. The charter of Urso adds a domicile qualification, and also a clause providing for proceedings against councillors alleged to be 'unworthy of their place'—which at Urso did not include being a freedman; the implication is that elsewhere being a freedman did disqualify.[129]

This matter of 'unworthiness' is given additional piquancy by the discovery that at Herculaneum L. Vennidius Ennychus (whom we have met already making a birth attestation) had been judged unworthy, and probably refused permission to stand, and made an attempt to get this stigma removed.[130] The documents are very fragmentary; it is a marvel that the editors could wring anything out of them. The first begins:

'Lucius Vennidius Ennychus announces to Lucius Annius Rufus, by way of testification, that he is eligible for the right of office; and if Rufus is willing [? to name] as arbiter one of the ten members of the senate and Augustales nominated by him, Vennidius . . .'

Of the second the editors could only read:

'. . . whom you have named above'. '. . . I am ready to go to Festinius Proculus as arbiter, otherwise I shall be necessarily obliged to proceed with you by judicial wager.'

We do not know on what grounds the unhappy Ennychus had been blackballed, nor the outcome of his suit; but the tablets waft a faint scent from the past of passions and indignities arising out of small-town status that adds a little to the famous election posters of Pompeii:

'Gaius Iulius Polybius for magistrate: called for by the Mule-drivers' Union.'

CHAPTER III

THE MACHINERY OF THE LAW

The most formal aspect of this subject, with which it will be best to begin, is the structure of the civil and criminal courts. After this initial exposition everything else relating to criminal justice will be left aside for a later chapter. The establishment of the Principate by Augustus resulted in important changes in the organization of Roman jurisdiction, so we must deal with the courts in two stages, first those of the late Republic and then those of the Principate.

In the time of Cicero the main civil jurisdiction for all Italy reposed in the two courts, in the city of Rome, of the urban praetor (the 'praetor who gives justice between citizens') and the peregrine praetor (the 'praetor who gives justice between peregrines'). There is controversy about how their functions were divided as to the middle ground: who gave justice between a citizen and a peregrine?[1] Whatever the original division may have been, it has been shown to be probable that by Cicero's time the court of the peregrine praetor was not confined to suits between peregrines;[2] and in the time of Gaius (and very likely long before) you could even have that most solemnly 'civil' of all suits, the *legis actio*, before either praetor,[3] although particular statutes might lay down that suits based on them must be brought in the court of a specific praetor. Constitutionally speaking the consuls, who had the highest *imperium*, were always entitled to exercise jurisdiction or to quash that of the praetors, but they had a great deal else to do, and so seldom appear in this role in the late Republic.[4] Magistrates with equal *imperium* could quash one another's acts; a famous case is that of the colleague of Verres, when Verres was urban praetor, to whom (according to Cicero) litigants flocked to rectify the arbitrary rulings of Verres.[5] In addition the tribunes of the plebs were available to aid citizens in trouble who appealed to them, and this aid was sometimes exercised against the proceedings in the praetor's court.[6] But all this fell short of being a regular system of appeal against civil judgments, for reasons which will appear.

In the municipalities of Italy, all of whose citizens, south of the River Po, were also Roman citizens after the Social War of 91–90 BC (and the 'Transpadanes' north of the Po were enfranchised in 49) there was a civil jurisdiction of the local magistrates; but it was limited, probably uniformly, to suits where not more than the small sum of fifteen thousand sesterces was in issue—or even ten thousand in the case of suits involving 'infamy' on conviction;[7] and even then it seems to have been possible for litigants to demand transfer of the action to Rome.[8]

The ancient criminal jurisdiction of the assembly of the Roman people was certainly not defunct in the late Republic, but it was not often called into play.[9] Essentially the criminal courts of Cicero's day were the 'standing jury courts', *quaestiones perpetuae*. Their scope will be treated less summarily in a later chapter; here, it is enough to say that each court dealt with a particular statutory offence and had a large jury and a majority verdict from which there was no appeal. The penalties were also standard and not at the discretion of the jury or the president of the court. The juries were drawn from an annual list; they were upper-class, and the offences dealt with by the *quaestiones* were mostly of the kind committed by the upper-class. As to how the great bulk of ordinary crime amongst the humble folk and slaves in the cosmopolitan alleyways of the city of Rome was dealt with we are exceedingly ill informed. There was probably little real jurisdiction, only summary punishment. There existed a very junior magistracy, that of the *tresviri capitales*, who certainly had the job of imprisoning malefactors and seeing to the carrying out of executions. The scholiast on Cicero says they punished 'thieves and evil slaves',[10] and from this and other references it has recently been deduced that they had a wide criminal jurisdiction amongst the lower orders;[11] it is doubtful, however, whether they could have sentenced anyone to death.

In the provinces the governor was the sole independent jurisdictional authority, and although he could delegate his power it is
clear that one of his principal duties was to tour the province
holding assizes. From Cicero's self-congratulation it sounds as if
he was unusual in following Scaevola's edict and leaving civil
suits between peregrines in the hands of their local and traditional
courts; certainly the governor was not obliged to do so unless
(as in Sicily) the charter of the province imposed this rule on him,
and, contrariwise, he might be urged by the provincials themselves to hear their suits. All suits involving a Roman citizen in
principle came to him, though some inscriptions recording grants
of citizenship to individual provincials (a rare thing in Republican
times) give them choice of jurisdictions.[12] It was apparently possible for a citizen to request transfer of his suit to Rome, but pretty
uncertain whether he would get it unless he had powerful patrons.[13]
In criminal jurisdiction the governor had sole authority, and over
peregrines it was exercised without limit. In the case of Roman citizens there was a limit, set by their famous right of appeal to the
people, *provocatio ad populum*. In Cicero's day all Roman citizens
everywhere possessed it, and it meant that they could not be executed, flogged, tortured or put in chains by a governor if they appealed—in effect, that for capital crimes he must remit them to
Rome for trial by the appropriate jury court. Apart from this he
had a very free hand, for he was not bound by the list of statutory
offences or penalties but could try and punish in any form anything he thought contrary to the good order of his province.[14]

The Principate brought substantial changes, initiated by
Augustus (by what constitutional authority we shall not here
discuss)[15] and brought to completion by a long development over
the whole of our period. Julius Caesar had thought of codifying
the civil law;[16] it would have been a huge task already. But in
two big statutes, the loss of all but a few references to which is
one of the most serious gaps in our knowledge, the *leges Iuliae
iudiciorum publicorum et privatorum*,[17] Augustus seems to have
produced at least a code of procedure for the existing structure of
courts, civil and criminal, settling such matters as the qualifications

of jurors and witnesses, judicial vacations, bail, and the form of criminal indictments, and (incidentally) reaffirming the right of *provocatio*. In fact, the great praetorian civil courts and the standing jury courts went on as before; the novelty was the growth alongside them (in a wholly characteristic Roman way) of more and more jurisdiction by the emperor himself and his delegates and by the senate (that is, technically, the consuls reviving their dormant powers with the senate as their *consilium*). The emperors probably never did much civil jurisdiction at first instance; they were mostly busied with settling points of law by rescript and with civil appeal, which now became freely available. The only other new civil jurisdictions were certain specialized tribunals introduced at one time or another: that of the 'fiscal praetor' and the 'praetor for trusts'; except that in the latter part of our period steps were taken to provide more accessible justice in Italy by the appointment of four *iuridici*.[17a]

In the criminal law the obvious differences were much greater. The senate became the regular court for the two principal 'upper-class' crimes, treason and extortion by provincial magistrates, and we find it sometimes trying other cases that would normally have gone to the standing jury courts, which the senate had always hated when non-senators were included on the panel of jurors, since it took the view that senators had a right to be tried by their peers. From Augustus onwards the panel for the jury courts consisted largely of non-senators,[17b] so as a *quid pro quo* the senate got the privilege of this concurrent jurisdiction (which, in the case of treason, it came to regret). We hear a lot in the pages of Tacitus and Suetonius about criminal jurisdiction by the emperors themselves 'within the bedchamber', and where opposition to the regime was involved or suspected this sinister procedure was used without scruple; but in the broader context of crime generally appeal was again probably the main field for the emperor's intervention, for 'appeal to the people' became 'appeal to Caesar' as a kind of universal Ombudsman.[18]

'Ordinary' crime in the city of Rome badly needed new measures, and this became the principal sphere of the urban prefect, *praefectus urbi* (who, though appointed by the emperor, was a magistrate in his own right). The first reference to his criminal jurisdiction, of the time of Nero, shows the way in which the new concurrent tribunals gradually overwhelmed the old:[19]

> 'Valerius Ponticus was also disgraced, for laying indictments against people before the praetor [*i.e.* so as to take them before a standing jury court] in order to prevent them being tried in the prefect's court, and so secure their acquittal first by apparent legal scrupulousness and secondly by collusion.'

It was, then, still technically correct in AD 61 to be given a jury, but it was already normal to be hailed before the prefect, whose methods were quicker and less at the mercy of gerrymandering. By the end of our period the principal authorities for criminal jurisdiction had come to be the urban prefect for Rome and a hundred miles radius and the praetorian prefect for the rest. This latter, who was not a magistrate at all but the commander of the guards, began with no more in the legal field than the custody of people sent to Rome for trial. The steps by which, by the end of our period, he had become—besides much else—a kind of 'principal law officer of the crown' are strangely untraceable; the earliest evidence for his having a jurisdiction is Hadrianic.[20] The prefect of the night watch, *praefectus vigilum*, is found executing a slave burglar;[21] he probably came to have powers concurrent with those of the old *tresviri*,[22] and ultimately supplanting them.

From Augustus onwards the provinces fall into two categories: 'provinces of the Roman people', governed as hitherto by men each with his own individual *imperium*, subject only to the overriding *maius imperium* of the emperor, and 'provinces of Caesar', really just parts of the 'province of Caesar' and so governed by men who were technically *legati*, delegates of the emperor. Civil appeal was automatically possible from the latter to their delegator; it was allowed also to citizens in the 'provinces of the Roman people', by some constitutional formula the nature of which remains uncertain. As for criminal appeal from capital sentences, *provocatio ad populum* turned into 'appeal to Caesar', and a strong case has been made for thinking that in spite of its reaffirmation in the *leges Iuliae* it was subjected to new restrictions and that at least for the statutory crimes (which in Rome fell to the inappellable jury courts) governors of the 'provinces of the Roman people', where the bulk of Roman citizens were, could now inflict the death penalty without appeal.[23] In other respects provincial jurisdiction remained as it had been in Republican times, except that in Treasury matters the fiscal procurators came to possess an authority; Ulpian gives a warning hint:[24]

> 'Note, however, that if the case is pecuniary and concerns the Treasury, which is the business of the emperor's procurator, he (the governor) will do best to keep out.'

Governors had always been entitled to delegate non-capital jurisdiction to their *legati* and others if there was more than they could manage themselves; but governors of 'provinces of Caesar' were already delegates, could not delegate further, and had no *legati*. Under the Principate inscriptions record a number of men with the formal title *legatus iuridicus* (or just *iuridicus*), who seem to have been appointed specifically to take the legal burden of a 'province of Caesar' or part of one off the shoulders of the governor.[25] Apart, however, from the regular *iuridicus* of Egypt they are only found in one or two provinces, and in the rest there must have been a huge burden of litigation for the governor to get through—or fail to get through.[25a]

Much the most important innovation in the machinery of justice made by the Principate was appeal.[25b] The volume of civil appeals was very great, and from Augustus onwards the emperors took various means to delegate them, but during the whole of our period the emperor himself remained the final instance.[25c] Besides contributing to the correction of justice, appeal must have worked as a unifying and integrating force upon the law, providing a source of ultimate legal decision which the Republic had lacked.

★

Civil suits at Rome, then, began in the court of the praetor. They did not normally end in it; an important fact about Roman civil procedure is that the praetor did not try anybody. His business was not to try cases but to settle between the parties, in a way analogous to the 'pleadings' of the old English common law, the exact nature of the dispute between them and of their claims and counter-claims, to appoint someone to try the action, and to issue to him a 'formula' containing a precise and unequivocal statement of the question he had to try.[26] These proceedings might involve counsel for the parties, and argument as to law and fact,[27] but they were not the trial of the action; they were the proceedings *in iure*, 'in presence of the law officer', and when they were completed the praetor's function was over. He was not a professional lawyer, and his praetorship was part of a political career; he was one of eight men (in Cicero's day; later twelve and then sixteen) elected annually to praetorships, who drew lots for their respective spheres of action, two of whom would draw the two great jurisdictions. He was a magistrate, and his job was seeing that the law was carried out. He also had, as a magistrate, many functions that were relevant to the law but not jurisdictional at all, as can be seen by looking at the rubrics of the praetor's edict in its codified form:[28] slaves were manumitted before him; he was the recipient of legal declarations such as *professiones* of birth; he issued orders putting people into possession of property and heirs into inheritances; he gave injunctions requiring actions such as production of documents or persons or restraining actions such as building; he appointed guardians and caretakers.

Who was entitled to bring someone into court? In the civil (as opposed to the criminal) law it must be some specific person or group of people claiming under an interest such as ownership or possession or contract or damage. If there were several valid claimants to be plaintiff the praetor would choose. Certain people could legitimately sue on behalf of others: guardians for their wards, *adsertores libertatis* for persons in slavery, agents for their principals; and in such cases the praetor would usually require security that judgment would be accepted by the person on whose behalf the action was brought. There were, however, a few 'popular actions', *actiones populares*, civil actions which any member of the public might bring—and receive the damages if he secured a conviction. They were based, it has been suggested, on the idea that though these things were not crimes it was in the general interest to secure their repression; characteristic examples were the 'action for misuse of a tomb' and the 'action for things poured or dropped' (*i.e.* from upper stories).[29]

Where must suit be brought? The *Digest* titles on this are interesting.[30] Though there were complications, in general the Roman principle was that suit must be brought in the *forum* of the defendant, that is to say his domicile (the place absence from which would lead people to say 'he is abroad'), or where his shop was, if he was a travelling merchant.[31] Cicero mentions this as a privilege the peregrine Sicilians were given by Republican Rome:[32]

'that no man can be obliged to give bail for appearance elsewhere than in his own *forum*.'

However, agreement between parties to litigation as to a jurisdiction is allowed by Ulpian to be good,[33] and if a clause in a contract stated where it was to be fulfilled, that was also where it would have to be sued upon.[34] A letter of Cicero refers to a man who owed money to a friend of his 'in Gaul', the praetor at Rome would not accept the suit:[35]

'the case has been handed on to Gaul by Volcatius who has jurisdiction in Rome.'

Cicero therefore writes to the governor of Gaul asking him to 'expedite' the collection of the debt by the freedman whom his friend has sent to Gaul for the purpose.

How did a plaintiff get his man into court? Originally by 'calling to law', *in ius vocatio*. In early Roman law you could seize a recalcitrant defendant (if you had the power), and this was never repealed; but the normal process in our period is well illustrated by documents from Herculaneum: the parties took bail, *vadimonium*, that is to say mutual promises on pain of a money penalty for appearance in court on a due day:[36]

'Bail taken with Calatoria Themis for 3 December next at Rome in the Forum of Augustus before the tribunal of the urban praetor at the second hour: promise of one thousand sesterces called for by Petronia Iusta of unknown father (as she styles herself), promise duly given by Calatoria Themis with authorization of her guardian C. Petronius Telesphorus.'

Cicero in his speech *pro Quinctio* also deals at length with an (alleged) bail of this kind.[37] Alternatively, the parties might offer persons instead of money promises as security for appearance, a procedure referred to by Horace, especially in his encounter with the Bore.[38] If your opponent simply could not be got into court and would not appoint a representative, no action and hence no judgment against him was possible; but he counted as *indefensus*, and the praetor would grant you entry into his property, which it would then be up to him to contest.

Let us, however, suppose that both parties are before the praetor. At this point the whole action may come to an end—not merely by the possible veto of another magistrate or of a tribune. First, the praetor might simply refuse the plaintiff an action if he thought the claim misconceived; *denegatio actionis* was a most important praetorian right.[39] The plaintiff naturally need not despair; he could go to the other praetor, or wait till next year when there would be two fresh ones, or appeal to the tribunes or (under the Principate) to the emperor. Secondly, the defendant might confess the plaintiff's right, and this counted as judgment against him.[40] Thirdly, one of the parties might invite the other to swear an oath as to the justice of his case; if the oath was sworn the swearer won the case without more ado, and it was over. The *Digest* has a title on these judicial oaths (12. 2) which unfortunately conflates certain complex differences; but the broad pattern is important—the oath offered and sworn to had sanctity, and is throughout our period a factor to be reckoned with in the judicial process. Even the cynical Juvenal thought that perjurers met the fate at least of a nagging conscience.[41]

Supposing that none of these things has happened and the suit is to continue, it is now the praetor's business to get the parties to accept a *formula* or statement of the issue to be tried. The subtle structure of these *formulae* is a fascinating study, and Gaius tells us a lot about them,[42] but there is not space to develop it here; the simplest possible one is given as an example:

'Let Titius be judge. If it appears that the defendant ought to give ten thousand sesterces to the plaintiff, let the judge condemn the defendant to the plaintiff in that sum; if it does not so appear, let him acquit.'

The basic types of *formula*, it is commonly held, were set out as an appendix to the praetor's edict,[42a] but flexibility was the whole purpose; probably the plaintiff, with expert advice, chose the one most appropriate and if necessary asked for modifications to it that would more precisely meet his contentions, and the defendant could make objections and ask for other modifications. For the defendant there were *exceptiones*, clauses that could be added to the *formula* to permit account to be taken of reasons (other than simply denying the charge) why the action should not succeed, such as fraud or coercion or agreement not to sue or case already tried before, thus:

'If it appears that the defendant ought to give ten thousand sesterces to the plaintiff, *unless it was agreed between them that suit should not be brought for this sum within a year*, let the judge condemn the defendant to the plaintiff in that sum . . .'

To the *exceptiones* the plaintiff could append *replicationes*, and so on.

The final business *in iure* was for the parties to accept from the praetor a person or persons to try the action (of whom more in a moment). Though the parties might be allowed much latitude to argue about what issue should be tried and who should try it, the praetor was not a mere referee; he was a magistrate, and could in the long run coerce a recalcitrant litigant into accepting *formula* or judge, on pain of being treated as *indefensus*. This is made sufficiently clear by what Cicero says about Verres (though the context is actually provincial governorship);[43] no one can get his rights if

'a bad praetor, with no one to veto him, appoints anyone he likes as judge.'

With the appointment of one or more persons to judge the action the stage of *litis contestatio* is reached, proceedings *in iure* are over, and the case must go on to judgment, *iudicium*.

Who are these persons who judge? The figure most commonly spoken of in the law-books is *iudex unus*, the 'single judge'. He is not necessarily a professional lawyer, any more than the praetor. If the parties were agreed, he could be anyone at all, even a peregrine (there were some exceptions, particularly women).[44] Eminent jurists, or eminent orators like Pliny,[45] were naturally often asked to perform this service, but we hear sometimes of humble *iudices*, chosen no doubt by humble litigants.[46] If the parties did not have anyone in particular in mind, or could not agree, the praetor would propose names from the annual list of 'select jurors' who were also used to man the criminal jury courts, with certain rights of rejection by the parties.[47] An alternative system of drawing by lot names from the annual list (with rights of rejection) is widely attested, especially for *recuperatores*—to whom we shall come—and in the provinces.[47a] Sometimes the single judge is called *arbiter*; it has recently been argued that he originally dealt with different categories of case from the *iudex*,[48] but in our period no significant difference is apparent. One characteristic sphere of the *arbiter*, however, was actions for division of land or inheritances, where all parties were equally anxious for an answer, and where he might be (or bring in) an expert such as a surveyor.

Here in parenthesis must be mentioned the practically not much different figure of the 'arbiter by agreement', *arbiter ex compromisso*. Technically he differs because he is extra-judicial, a good neighbour or an expert called upon without resort to the courts, particularly to settle boundary disputes.[49] The law made some rules, however, particularly that the arbiter who accepted such a commission must carry it through. A decision by an arbiter between a private citizen and a municipality survives on a stone inscription,[50] but better still, the Herculaneum Tablets have recently given us (rather fragmentarily) the whole process of such an arbitration in AD 69:[51]

'Concerning the dispute between L. Cominius Primus and L. Appuleius Proculus over the bounds of the estate called "Numidianus", property of L. Cominius Primus, and that

called "Stratanicianus", property of L. Appuleius Proculus, . . .
Ti. Crassius Firmus is to be arbiter by agreement between
L. Cominius Primus or his heir and L. Appuleius Proculus or
his heir; and is to give a decision, formal or informal, or order
a decision to be given, openly in the presence of both parties;
and provided that he gives the decision or orders it to be given
before 1 Feb. next or postpones the day of agreement or orders
it to be postponed, then if anything is done or not done
contrary to the agreement one thousand sesterces are to be
paid. It is agreed that no fraud exists or shall exist with respect
to this matter and arbitration.'

Then we have the acceptance by the arbiter, pieces of notes of the
proceedings 'in the house of M. Nonius P . . . ', and pieces of the
arbiter's decision, 'having brought in the surveyor L. Opsius
Herma'.[52]

Civil suits by no means always went to a single *iudex* or
arbiter; there were juries, of two sorts. First, instead of a single
iudex the praetor might appoint 'recoverers', *recuperatores*, a small
jury of three or five *iudices*. The institution had an old history,
connected with the early legal relations of Rome with foreign
states, as a kind of international civil jury; but by Cicero's day it
appears as a standard alternative to the single judge—whether
the parties had a choice we do not know.[52a] Two of Cicero's
private law speeches were delivered before *recuperatores*, *pro
Caecina* and *pro Tullio*, and those two cases concerned forcible
ejection from property; but a speech of the emperor Claudius in
the senate implies that in his day the main sphere of *recuperatores*
was suits for freedom:[53]

'Do at least lay this down, that no one of only 24 years of age
be appointed to recoverers. For it is not unreasonable, I think,
that only those persons should judge issues of slavery and
freedom who cannot plead the privileges of the Laetorian law
in their own affairs.'

Many civil actions went before a much bigger jury, the Court
of One Hundred, *centumviri*. This was the home of *causes célèbres*;

Cicero furnishes a resounding list of suits that could come before it,[54] but its main business was with the inheritances and fortunes of the noble and rich—petitions of heirs, suits against unreasonable wills and so on. The famous *causa Curiana* which Cicero remembered as a 'classic' was heard before it,[55] and it was the stamping-ground (*harena*) of Pliny, who gives most information about it. It did not actually consist of one hundred; the full court, for very big suits, on an occasion when Pliny pleaded before it, was one hundred and eighty,[56] but it usually sat in four divisions. The *centumviri* had no exclusive competence in any particular field; inheritances, for example, could equally well go before a single *iudex*. The intention of the parties was decisive here, for if they wanted to go to the *centumviri* they had to open their suit with the archaic ceremony of the *legis actio*.

The judge (for we shall speak of *unus iudex* in what follows, for simplicity's sake) had to try the action and acquit or condemn (on the basis of the *formula*)—not the praetor:[57]

> 'What if the defendant denies? What if he is not liable at all? Is it the praetor's business to pronounce on his liability?'

To serve as judge if called upon was not only a social duty but a public office, from which you must be officially excused. It could be an extremely arduous and complex task, and the judge who performed it with prejudice or partiality was liable to legal action against him.[58] 'When I was first put on the panel', says Gellius, 'I read all the manuals, but it didn't help. I had an allegation of debt—no evidence at all, but the plaintiff a known man of honour and the defendant a known twister.' He consulted his friend Favorinus the philosopher but in the end had to pronounce a *non liquet* and retire.[59] The judge appointed time and place; before him counsel for the parties orated ('I give them all the time in the world; truth must come before convenience', said Pliny),[60] and testimonies, oral and otherwise, were produced. There were singularly few rules, either to bind or to assist him; such as there were appear mostly in a few titles of Book 22 of the *Digest*. The plaintiff was required to produce *in iure* documents on which he was going to rely before the judge—a wholly one-way arrangement in the interest of the defendant, who could not be made to produce anything in advance.[61] The jurists developed some rules of interpretation of documents, which could help a judge—for example, on legacies:[62]

> 'the significance of words must not be departed from unless it is manifest that the testator meant something different.'

There was a principle similar to our own, that ignorance of the law was no defence though ignorance of facts might be, and Labeo at the end of the Republic was already giving thought to the question what degree of knowledge or ignorance was appropriate to the 'man in the street'.[63] One title concerns 'burden of proof' and one concerns witnesses.[64] On the latter it looks as though Augustan legislation laid down some rules; a great deal was made to depend on the status and reputation of those who gave testimony, at least as time went on and the distinction between *honestiores* and *humiliores* grew more and more marked.[65] Written testimonies could be put in; we have seen the sworn statements in Petronia Iusta's dossier. A rule is given, based on a *senatusconsultum*, that the census and public documents must prevail against oral testimony.[66] As for private documents— receipts, contracts and so on—their force was purely evidentiary, not necessarily clinching as against other evidence (though they might, of course, be the best or only evidence of a transaction). The only exception, apart from the 'contract *litteris*' which will be explained later, was that the tablets of a will *were* the will; and Suetonius records that under Nero a formal requirement was made that the tablets must be secured with thread through holes at their edges in a special way, and then sealed.[67] A *senatus-consultum* of unknown date (but perhaps itself Neronian) generalized this formality for all documents on tablets; documents which fail to conform to these specifications were of no effect.[68]

To reach a decision on his *formula* the judge might well have to decide matters of law as well as fact, though it was recognized that the latter were peculiarly his province:[69]

> 'When judges enquire about the law governors usually give a

F

reply, but about matters of fact they ought not to offer guidance, but tell the judge to decide according to his conscience; for this is something that sometimes mars reputations and opens the way for graft and unscrupulousness.'

One has only to read a Ciceronian speech to see how difficult it must have been, with limited rules of procedure and opposing counsel using every rhetorical trick known to man—especially irrelevance—for a judge to reach a true verdict (though it is fair to say that the very rigid modern English rules of admissibility which we tend to use as a criterion are under critical fire, and would be regarded in some other modern systems as deleteriously limiting). Moreover, he might have to do far more than just condemn or acquit. Many suits were *bonae fidei iudicia*, 'actions of good faith', in which the judge must decide 'what in all fairness the defendant ought to pay or do'; all contracts, partnerships and guardianships were of this kind.[70] And there were the divisory actions for the *arbiter*, involving elaborate financial calculations, valuations, set-offs and collations. All this done, judgment must be delivered in the presence of the parties. Judgment (*condemnatio*) was always in a sum of money; that is, even if what the plaintiff wanted was his slave or his land back, the judge could not directly order this 'specific performance' to be done. The common law of England had the same rule when the Chancellor stepped in with Equity; it 'aimed, not at making a party carry out his contract, but at making him pay for not doing so'.[71] In practice, however, Roman law also got out of this, though by a different route, the *formula arbitraria*, a clause instructing a judge to convict 'unless the thing be restored'; if it was not restored the plaintiff might make his own assessment, under oath, of the value of his thing.[72] This was sufficient; the *Digest* title on suing for one's property as owner (6. 1) seems to assume all through that one can in fact get it back.

Judgment given, the duty of the judge was over. If the convicted party did not obey the judgment it was up to the plaintiff to take further steps. He was not given physical help by the authorities, but the legal consequences for the recalcitrant

JUDGMENTS AND THEIR EXECUTION

defendant were severe. First, after thirty days the plaintiff could bring an 'action on the judgment'.[72a] This apparently time-wasting formality may have been primarily to ensure that he did not take the next steps he was entitled to without the backing of an unquestionable judgment. For the next steps were first 'personal execution', that is, the plaintiff could seize the judgment debtor and keep him in private imprisonment until the debt was discharged,[73] and secondly authorized entry into the whole of the debtor's property to sell it up. The 'action on the judgment' was not a procedure of appeal; and it is usually said that while there were various methods of contesting proceedings *in iure*, against a *iudicium* there was in Republican times no appeal. It has recently been argued on the basis of a distinction made by Gaius[74] that appeal was possible from all except *iudicia legitima* (judgments given in Rome or within the first milestone by a single *iudex*, he and the parties all being Roman citizens) in the Republican period as well as under the empire.[75] In the absence of clear evidence either way one cannot be sure of this. At any rate, the defendant could contest the 'action on the judgment' on the ground that there had been no proper judgment because of coercion or fraud,[76] or he could have an action against the *iudex* for corrupt judgment.

One consequence of conviction in certain civil suits and (probably) all criminal trials was 'infamy', *infamia* or *ignominia*. Infamy could indeed arise in other ways, and it could have other consequences besides legal ones; the subject is complicated and much has been written about it.[77] The concept enshrines very characteristic Roman attitudes. The small aristocratic society of early Rome, valuing above all overt esteem (*existimatio, dignitas*), dreaded its loss exceedingly. The disapproval of a man's peers was channelled through the censors, the customary guardians of public morality, who provided a sharp extra-legal sanction against behaviour that offended accepted canons by their 'censorial mark', the *nota censoria* entered against a man's name in the census-lists,[78] which was both an expression and at the same time a cause of his being held 'infamous'.[79] The censors, part of whose function was to revise and control the lists of members of the senate and equestrian order, could also deprive a man of his place,[80] and this deprivation and the *nota censoria* would naturally (though not inevitably) be connected. Independently, the praetor in his edict deprived persons judged guilty of certain civil law offences of the right of appointing representatives in litigation or acting as representatives of others. Gaius tells us this,[81] and gives a list— perhaps not meant to be exhaustive—of actions condemnation in which resulted in this 'ignominy', carefully pointing out that the praetor did not use the word but that 'ignominy' was a consequence of the deprivation. Theft, violent seizure of goods and *iniuria* (principally defamation) appear in the list, and actions on partnership, pledge by *fiducia*, guardianship, mandate and safekeeping. Another list is given in the *Digest*;[82] they fail in curious ways to coincide, and neither mentions loan or the actions for intimidation or the corruption of slaves. It is in fact very difficult to get a general theory out of them; on the one hand not all the *bonae fidei iudicia* were infaming (*e.g.* not sale or hire); on the other not every condemnation even in a *bonae fidei iudicium* such as partnership could have justified 'infamy' on the ground which otherwise one might have seized on as its essential basis, namely fraud. It has recently been argued that this infamy resulting from condemnation in private law actions ceased to be a reality in the late Republic because it only arose if you yourself were condemned 'in your own name'—but you could appoint a representative to defend the suit, and if he was condemned *he* would be condemned in your name.[83] The logic is unassailable, but does not allow for the difficulty that a man might have in finding a representative; and while the fact that the lawyers went on talking about civil *infamia* might be put down to obsession with dead theory it is harder to explain why imperial constitutions went on dealing with it (surely as a practical issue) with reference to the praetor's edict.[84] (They dealt, it is true, with the cases of theft and rapine and *iniuria*, where a man might indeed find it hardest to get a representative.) This sort of *infamia* was also a practical issue in the municipalities, as will be seen in a moment. Conviction in the standing criminal courts also produced effects of infamy (not necessarily the same effects as the edict), and so did being sold up as a bankrupt. The consequences of all these patterns of disesteem put together can be seen in that long list of persons in the *Table of Heraclea*, quoted in Chapter II, who are not allowed to present themselves for municipal office.[85] It includes persons criminally convicted, bankrupts, persons convicted in the civil actions, including theft, persons discharged from the army with ignominy and persons exercising certain despised professions. This is a very mixed bag, and it is now usual to hold that there was no general 'law of infamy'. Nevertheless there can be no doubt that 'stigma' remained an element of legal and social sanction all through our period, and in the criminal law it was extended from the *quaestiones publicae* into the penalties of the *cognitio extra ordinem*.[86]

Jurisdiction other than that before the praetors at Rome was on an entirely different footing. The governor of a province, as fount of all procedural law, was entitled simply to *cognoscere*, try a case, which (as opposed to the *ius dicere* of the praetors) meant to try it completely before himself with any procedure he thought fit—summon the parties, determine the issue, hear the evidence, pronounce the judgment, and see to its execution. This right he had with respect to the Roman citizens in his sphere no less than the peregrines, and sometimes he exercised it:[87]

'Verres put in the plaintiff, Verres ordered appearance, Verres heard the case, Verres gave the judgment.'

But if there was more work than he wished to cope with directly he was equally entitled to 'give a judge'.[88] In theory this was very different from the formulary system; there was no question of choice of judge by the parties nor of *formula*—the instructions to the judge could be in any form.[89] But if we escape from excessive fixation on the technical mysteries and theoretically voluntary nature of the formulary system we must admit that the practical effects were probably much the same. Normally, as between peregrines in the Republican age, in so far as the local courts were not left to their own procedures, the 'charter of the province' might lay down rules (as, for example, about choice of juries in Sicily),[90] and the ordinary formulary system would prevail; we hear from Cicero of recuperatorial actions between peregrines in the provinces of Asia and Sicily,[91] of *formulae* and choice of *iudices*;[91a] and, *a fortiori*, Roman citizens will have had no less privilege. The distinction between the two procedures open to a governor is well brought out in a Verrine passage:[92]

> 'Having got a rich source of profit from the cases which he had decided to try himself with his advisers, which simply meant the personnel of his suite, Verres then discovered another endless vein to tap. You must all realise well enough the extent to which everybody's goods depend on the power of those who grant *iudices* and those who deliver judgment . . .'

There is no reason to suppose that things were different under the Principate. In Cyrene, a 'province of the Roman people', under Augustus, *iudices* were normal for all civil suits and even in criminal trials except capital cases.[93] The only evidence we have for 'provinces of Caesar' comes from Egypt, but there too *iudices* were given,[94] and some of their judgments survive. Here is one of the Julio-Claudian period:[95]

> 'Suit between discharged trooper Dionysius son of Manlius (defended in absence by M. Trebius Heraclides son of aforesaid Dionysius, trooper of the Aprian squadron, troop of Acamas) and M. Apronius and M. Manlius, troopers of the Vocontian squadron, troop of Domesticus, concerning degree of relationship, which of them was the nearer relative, so as to be granted the estate, of Dionysius son of Manlius, trooper of the Aprian squadron, alleged deceased intestate: L. Silius Laetus camp prefect having given as judge P. Matius, centurion of legion III Cyrenaica, and ordered him to pronounce:
>
> P. Matius, centurion of legion III Cyrenaica, with an advisory panel, namely M. Marcius Optatus son of Publius, tribe Falerna, corporal of the Choitan squadron; L. Herennius Valens, corporal of the Aprian squadron; and Octavius

Domesticus, corporal of the Vocontian squadron: each party having pleaded its case and the affidavits having been read out, announced his verdict as follows:

That he held that Dionysius son of Manlius was the brother of his brother Dionysius alleged deceased, and Apronius and Manlius sons of the said Dionysius, according to their own affidavits of relationship; that therefore the property of Dionysius, object of suit, belongs to the said Dionysius son of Manlius, discharged trooper, and should be adjudged to him.' (Place and date follow.)

No formalities bound the emperor; his decisions were pure *cognitiones* arrived at in any way he chose. So were those of the new courts under his officials, the urban and praetorian prefects, and of the specialized tribunals of the *fiscus*,[95a] the praetor for trusts and so on. Thus the formulary system and its element, however slight, of voluntary arbitration by the parties gradually slipped into the background and civil jurisdiction became a part of the administrative machine.

★

The praetor was not necessarily a legal expert, neither were the judges. There was therefore in Rome no Bench. As to barristers, their training was in the schools of rhetoric—simply, indeed, a more protracted and purposeful immersion in the secondary education that everybody had.[96] There was plenty of law in it, and in so far as the rhetoric was forensic, which it came to be more exclusively under the Principate when political oratory ceased to be a reality, it dealt with legal situations, however fantastic. But the barrister's job was to make a case; he was not *amicus curiae*, as Cicero did not scruple to confess:[97]

'Anyone who supposes that in my forensic speeches he has got my personal views under seal is making a great mistake . . . We orators are brought in to say not what we personally think but what is required by the situation and the case in hand.'

Cicero's friend Aquilius Gallus, who was a jurist, used to say, if consulted about matters of fact (Cicero records the remark himself):[98]

'Nothing to do with the law; go to Cicero.'

And Horace, to flatter a friend, says there are three (not two) fields in which he could easily make himself a master:[99]

> 'whether you sharpen your tongue for litigation or prepare to give opinions on Roman law or write charming poetry . . .'

In this situation one might wonder how the law ever got done, or at least how it became so precise, detailed and technical. Who could tell the praetor, the governor, the judge and the advocate what the law was?

The people who did so were the 'learned in the law', *iuris prudentes* or *iuris consulti*. First, the praetor or other jurisdictional magistrate sat with an advisory panel, a *consilium* of *assessores*; though the decisions were his responsibility he might well take them on a vote.[100] Pliny refers to an occasion when he was assessor to the urban prefect,[101] and Ulpian records a case when he was assessor to a praetor.[102] Most illuminating is Aulus Gellius:[103]

> 'I remember being an assessor on the tribunal of a praetor [a learned man]; and a barrister, quite well known, was pleading altogether off the point, not coming to the matter in hand at all. The praetor told the defendant that he was not being represented by counsel, and when the barrister exclaimed "but I am over the defendant, m'lud", the praetor replied (quite amusingly) "You're over him all right; and you're over the rest of us too".'

Provincial governors also sat with a *consilium*. Cicero is always going on about how Verres packed his with his minions,[104] but Verres was quite entitled to choose whom he wished, though normally some eminent men of the province would be brought in. And a *iudex* would have his panel also. Gellius tells us how once, being a delegated *iudex*, told by the consuls to hold a *cognitio* and pronounce judgment 'within the Kalends', he asked an erudite philologist whether this empowered him to pronounce *on* the Kalends. His friend replied:[105]

> 'Why do you ask me rather than one of the learned practi-
> tioners of the law whom you fellows usually get on to your
> *consilium* when you have to act as judges?'

(to which Gellius' answer was that his question was about Latin,
not law. 'Very well,' said his friend, 'I'll tell you about Latin;
but for what terms mean in law you must look to the usages of the
law'). Furthermore, all these people (unless they happened to be
jurisprudents themselves), and also private people thinking of
litigation, went to the jurisprudents for legal opinions, *responsa*.
Publice respondere, to give opinions on the law to all comers, was
their ancient and honourable function—Labeo's for example,[106]
and we hear of specialists in particular branches:[107]

> 'Quintus Scaevola, the most celebrated and reliable prophet of
> the laws, used to refer those who consulted him to Furius
> and Cascellius when the matter concerned land law, because
> they had devoted themselves to that particular subject.'

In Republican times even the eminent jurisprudents helped with
'cautelary' jurisprudence, *i.e.* the drawing up of proper processes
and documents,[108] but later this was mostly left to lesser fry.

It would be wrong to think of jurisprudence in the Republican
age as a profession. Its practitioners were members of the Roman
upper class, for whom even public and political office were only
incidents in lives of leisure, and it was therefore an amateur
activity just as much as being a historian or an agricultural expert.
In the late Republic, however, we find Aquilius Gallus giving up
the ladder of public office after the praetorship to devote himself
to the law, and Labeo likewise; and men begin to come into
jurisprudence from less exalted backgrounds.[109] Under the
Principate it takes on more of the character of a profession. The
career of an expert in the law might now often lead him to one
of the offices under the emperor that had big jurisdictional
functions, and the emperor himself needed jurisprudents to call
on to his *consilium*, as he himself became the main source of legal

advice through his rescripts.[110] We hear, in Gaius mostly, of two 'schools' of jurists, the Proculians and the Sabinians, who took opposite sides about numerous legal problems. Every book on Roman law discusses them—but inconclusively, owing to paucity of evidence. The tendency nowadays is to hold that they were actual colleges,[111] but the case is not convincing. There is no doubt that eminent jurists taught law, but another passage from Gellius suggests rather that it remained an informal activity:[112]

'When I first came out of the retired corner of books and schoolmasters into the world of life and the light of the forum, I remember that a question was going round several of the haunts in Rome of those who gave public lessons in the law or jurists' opinions (*stationes ius publice docentium aut respondentium*), whether a quaestor of the Roman people could be summoned to court by a praetor. . . .'

At any rate, by the end of our period the science of the law, like much else in Roman society, had become very much more bureaucratized and linked to the imperial administration than at the beginning.

The bar, in our period, was not organized in the elaborate and rigid way that characterizes the later empire.[113] It covered an enormous range of talents and standards, from the star performers in Rome to the humble *causidici* who pleaded in the provincial assizes.[113a] The main rule, going back to a law of 204 BC, was that barristers were not allowed to take fees. Of course, the great advocates of the Republic had no need to do so directly; if Cicero did a client proud the client's purse, friends and influence would be available to Cicero later at call. Nevertheless, the rule was constantly being infringed and as constantly reiterated. Augustus re-enacted it;[114] there was a terrible fuss about its evasion in Claudius' time, when a maximum fee was set at ten thousand sesterces;[115] and another terrible fuss raised by a conscientious urban praetor in Pliny's day, from which it appears that even the allowed sum of up to ten thousand sesterces must be a present, and nothing could be bargained for in advance.[116] One might bear in mind that the English barrister today cannot bargain or sue for fees, but 'it is believed that the services of barristers are not in fact wholly gratuitous'.[117] Ten thousand sesterces was not a very large sum in the upper brackets of Roman society, and Juvenal thought the bar a poorly rewarded profession:[118]

> 'There's no money in it. Argue yourself hoarse before some bumpkin of a judge—what do you get? A couple of bottles of *vin rouge*; and you've got your clerks to pay. The only way to get a name is to live like a lord; that's how clients pick their counsel. And Rome soon eats up your capital that way. If you're thinking of making a living by speeches you'd better get off to Gaul or Africa.'

This is more impressive than the complaints, common to every age, of the wealth and avarice of advocates.[119] At any rate, it does not look as if at any level the litigant often pleaded his suit in person unaided.

The voice of the provincial barrister is sometimes audible through the documents, such as the testamentary probate action of AD 184 from Egypt, in which four counsel argue:[120]

> 'Action brought by Cassius, also called Hegoumenos, of Antinoopolis, present also Isidore son of Tiberinus, a minor, assisted by Longinus Chaeremonianus his half-brother and advocate:
>
> Philotas, counsel for Cassius, said: "My client's relative, being a Roman citizen, on point of death, wrote his will and sent for my client and begged him to accept its custody, . . . etc.";
>
> Longus, counsel, said in reply: "Our opponent, fearing the penalty for opening the will, comes and says he received this will from his relative and wishes to produce it. That the testator is no relative of his I herewith assert, . . . etc.".'

A considerable bulk of the surviving prose literature of Rome consists of treatises on the art of oratory, and some of the technique seeped down to the humble bar, as is exemplified by a delicious epigram of Martial:[121]

'My suit is not about assault or murder or poison but about three she-goats that I say my neighbour has stolen; and that's what the *iudex* expects you to prove to him. But you go on about Cannae and the Mithridatic War and the treacherous behaviour of the wicked Carthaginians and your Sullas and Mariuses and Muciuses—all in a voice of doom and waving your arms about. I say, Postumus, get on to my three she-goats!'

Traces also survive of the 'cautelary' activities of the town and village notaries and scribes who wrote legal documents for people,[122] and not merely in those numerous cases in which it is said 'I, so-and-so, have written this on behalf of so-and-so, who declares that he is illiterate'. There is, for example, a papyrus containing specimen forms for testamentary clauses,[123] and a bronze tablet (evidently hung on the wall of some notary's office in Spain) with similar specimens for 'fiduciary mancipation'.[124] The scribes clung fast to the magic words of their formulas, even when they understood them little or not at all, and even when the institutions to which the phrases referred had been modified or abolished.[125]

★

A celebrated nineteenth-century essay set out the reasons for believing that in the antique age of Roman law, the age of the *legis actiones*, legal procedure weighted the scales of litigation heavily in favour of the rich against the poor.[126] Both parties must begin a suit by putting cash down; defendant in a suit for debt must find a representative (liable for double if the case was lost). How could the humble litigate at all under these conditions? The money element was a disincentive, a penalty for litigation. The powerful man could seize the humble man and drag him into court; what chance did the humble have of seizing the powerful? Judgment meant that you were haled off in chains and could be sold into slavery abroad. And so on. The argument went on to show that already in the *legis actio* period some democratic reforms were made, and that the formulary system marked a great revolution—the notion of free litigation as opposed to penalized litigation. We here meet the fundamental question, how the machinery of law worked in practice, how far men could really obtain their rights through the law; and we must ask it for our period, the classical age of Roman law.

'One law for all, whether rich or poor' sounds splendid, but in all ages it has put the poor at a disadvantage against the rich, if only because they cannot keep litigation up for so long against the rich man (or corporation). Only by having one law for the rich and another (more favourable) law for the poor can this be remedied, and the recentness of the English introduction of 'legal aid', designed to achieve this deliberate unbalance, should be a warning against exaggerated criticism of the Romans. Medicine is a parallel; but then medicine was often given free in the ancient world, and there was one immensely important side to Roman law and society to which, even for archaic Rome, the essay described above gave insufficient weight. The wheels of Roman society were oiled—even driven, perhaps—by two notions: mutual services of status-equals (I help you in your affairs; I then have a moral claim on your help in mine) and patronage of higher status to lower. In the early Republic each noble family had many 'clients', and the relation of client to patron was akin to serfdom (akin, indeed, to the freedman's relation to *his* patron); and it could be entered into voluntarily.[127] The fact that the word *patronus* came also regularly to mean an advocate helps to stress that the relationship was not one-sided. It was the patron who came to the legal rescue of his client, paid his money down for litigation, paid his debt to prevent him being haled off, stood as his representative; you might hesitate to 'lay the hand' on a humble plebeian with his patron standing by. In the old scale of 'duties' clients came below none but parents and wards.[128] Clientship of this ancient formal pattern did not survive into our period (except for the relation of patron and freedman), but its philosophy did, in public law as well as private. Nor must the informal clientship of the late Republic be thought of merely in terms of the humble 'hanger-on' waiting for his meal or present, with whom we are familiar from the satirists. Wealthy families were clients of wealthier families—that is how they got their sons into politics. Clientship was what might enable a provincial (Roman citizen or not) to get help and protection against a governor; Verres picked on one wealthy victim because:[129]

> 'he had no patrons except the Marcelli whom he could appeal to personally.'

Fides, 'faith', it has recently been argued, was originally an aspect of clientship.[130] As to the complementary concept, *officium* or mutual serviceableness between status-equals, the origins at least of many legal institutions which will be studied later are unintelligible unless it is borne in mind—such things as 'personal security':[131]

> 'If our friends hold to their duty (*officium*) there'll be plenty of funds;'

or *negotiorum gestio*, looking after your friend's legal position in his absence:[132]

> 'I'll make sure you're not down as absent on the census; I'll see placards are posted about everywhere.'

And then, finally, there was the patron *par excellence*, the emperor, the universal Ombudsman. This was not just an amiable fiction. Evidence can be found of the freedom of speech of the humble before the emperor:[133]

> 'He was a cobbler, and of course people who are no bodies can say things with more freedom before emperors than the great ever could,'

and the humble did find their way to him at times, as the *sententiae Hadriani* show,[134] and felt that there would be justice there if only they could get his ear:[135]

> '. . . which has compelled us humble men once more to petition your divine forethought, and so we ask you to come to our aid, most sacred emperor.'

The imperial *responsa* have a significant feature; the highest legal department in the empire is often found patiently explaining elementary legal points to unsophisticated petitioners, for example:[136]

> 'To (name missing) daughter of Ambrelus, petitioning by the hand of Abdomanchus, her son; women are not forbidden to borrow money or to pay on behalf of others.'

Nevertheless, many of the criticisms made of the law of the later Roman empire[137] can be made of our period with equal justification, so long as one remembers that not only Roman law is open to social criticism, and that law is in all ages a focus of social argument because it is a social regulator and an expression, at any moment, of the *status quo*. After all, only since Tolpuddle has it ceased to be the case in Britain that 'freedom of contract is the freedom of the powerful to impose terms', and until yet more recently justified pursuit of legal claims was impossible to those who could not afford it.[138] The costs of the law at Rome were not confined to what you might have to pay a barrister (as to which it may be worth noting that ten thousand sesterces was made the maximum honorarium at a time when a private soldier's pay was nine hundred sesterces a year, a centurion's perhaps fourteen thousand, and that of an equestrian procurator of the lowest grade sixty thousand). For many processes legal security had to be given in the form of promise of a fine or introduction of a substantial friend as surety: bail for appearance in court, for example, where we have seen the Herculaneum figure of one thousand sesterces, or security of an agent for ratification by his principal. And not only for litigation; there was security for right use of a usufruct, security of guardians for the property of their wards and of heirs for due payment to legatees. Legal appeals also cost money; in order to stem frivolous appeals a sum had to be paid down, to be forfeit if the appeal was lost.[139] Characteristically, however, 'maintenance' (financially supporting someone else's litigation) was not an offence in Roman law, unless it was done for profit.[140]

It has been pointed out that when we say things like 'the praetor gave an action to repress this abuse' we are assuming the standards of regularity and impartiality of justice that Western European states have attained to in modern times.[141] There was, to begin with, no professional control of the standards of Bench and Bar in Rome, because there were no Bench and Bar of a kind that would have made such standards possible. And secondly, *clientela, amicitia* and *officium* worked for ill as well as for good, since the praetor and the provincial governor and the *iudex* were enmeshed in their network as much as the litigants—under pressure to give weight to the pleas of personal friends, the letters of the great and so on. (These facts in any case ruin our chance of estimating how good or bad the system was in practice, because where improper influence is known to be a possible factor every disappointed litigant will tend to allege it.)

Then there were—what people in all ages have grumbled about—the law's delays:[142]

'a thousand vexations, a thousand hold-ups';

even worse, perhaps, its hastes—thirty days to pay up or be sold up and haled off (for private imprisonment for debt was a reality, quite calmly referred to by Ulpian, who includes in a list of those who can get a conviction in absence annulled 'a man put into public or private chains';[143] the great, as will be seen, had a different procedure applied to them, and the great could get lawsuits delayed, for themselves and others).[144] Or consider distances: the principle of *'forum* of the defendant' was all very well if the plaintiff was well-off, but even apart from that, litigation meant getting to Rome or to the provincial assize and waiting about in hired rooms; a man must be given time to 'find a hotel, lay out his luggage, and contact a barrister', says Ulpian.[145] The extreme centralization of jurisdiction upon Rome and a few provincial assize towns must have been a very real disincentive. Also, except in the cities, the aid of the law might be too remote to prevent violent self-help by the powerful; Apuleius has a horrid tale (pure fiction, but significant none the less) of the local magnate who set savage dogs on a neighbour's sons when they disputed his boundaries.[146] More or less at the beginning of our period two remedies were invented, the 'action for intimidation', *actio metus causa*, and the 'action for cunning', *actio doli*—and there were *exceptiones* for a defendant on the same grounds.[147] But it seems that already in Labeo's time the praetor would refuse an *actio doli* of a humble man against a noble:[148]

> 'it must not be given to a humble person against one prominent in dignity, to a plebeian, for example, against a consular of accepted stature.'

In a rather late text of the *Digest* we are told that the *bona fides* of humble witnesses will be scrutinized[149] (though only in a very late one is it said that the poor may not bring criminal actions except on their own behalf);[150] and this leads to one last point. By the time that virtually all free men in the empire were finally given Roman citizenship (by the *constitutio Antoniniana*) the Gilbertian situation had been reached, that 'when ev'rybody's somebody, nobody's anybody'. The 'humble' in the *Digest* texts quoted above are a status category, not the poor as against the rich—the *humiliores* as opposed to the *honestiores* or 'distinguished'. Even in Labeo's time the dichotomy was recognized and the *humiliores* were under some disadvantages; there was one law for the distinguished and another (but worse) law for the humble. But in the second century AD it appears much more rigidly and explicitly, and in the criminal law there arose a double scale of penalties for the same offence, less severe for the *honestiores* and more severe for the *humiliores*.[151] Nowhere in the legal sources is there an exhaustive official definition of who belonged in each of the two status groups. The upper group included the decurions —the town councillors of the municipalities, whom (presumably with all above them) Hadrian had already exempted from the death penalty.[152] All below, however wealthy, were *humiliores*. The consequences of this sharpened distinction, along with the decline of *provocatio*, as more governors besides the proconsuls came to be empowered to exercise death sentences on Roman citizens without appeal, were that '*honestiores* retained the privileges which had once belonged to all Roman citizens, and *humiliores* were degraded to a status slightly if at all superior to that which *peregrini* had held'.[153]

CHAPTER IV

FAMILY AND SUCCESSION

In modern English the word 'family', when we are not just using it as a general term for all our relatives (ascendants on mother's or father's side, descendants and collaterals), means a household—a man and wife and their unmarried children, a single conjugal group. This 'nuclear family' is only one of several types of family organization, both in the past and still today, classified by anthropologists;[1] the most familiar alternative is the 'joint' or 'extended' family of several conjugal groups under a common head. During our period the normal Roman family seems to have been a 'nuclear family' like our own, but to this bald assertion certain qualifications need to be made. First, the Roman word *familia*, besides meaning one's relatives and also a household, had another very common significance, namely a body of slaves. It was so used quite outside the domestic context; the slave personnel of a tax-farming company, for example, was *familia publicanorum*. Nevertheless it did also (and no doubt originally) mean the slaves of the household, all your servants as a group; the Roman household had its own individual cult of tutelary spirits, and for cult purposes it included the slaves as well as the free members. In the second place, when the Romans talked about *familia* in connexion with descent (a noble family, a wealthy family, the family of the Marcelli, and so on) they usually meant the line of people with the same name. Names, and with them 'family', were inherited like our surnames, through males, and this 'agnatic' principle of descent (as opposed to 'cognatic', in which descent is counted by blood from both father's and mother's side) had certain important consequences in property and succession which will be seen presently. Thirdly—and this is the most important qualification—one feature of the Roman family is anomalous in relation to what we think of as the standard 'nuclear family'; the authority of the head of family over his descendants lasted not merely until they grew up and married and formed their own conjugal groups but (unless deliberately broken by certain legal procedures) until the day he died. This very odd lifelong familial authority is usually supposed to be a survival from a time when the Romans lived in 'extended' families.[2] However that may be, its continued existence in an age when people certainly did not live in 'extended' families was responsible for some curious features of Roman family law.

With the one further proviso that Roman law did not interfere with the internal structure of the peregrine family, and that what follows is about the families of Roman citizens, we can examine Roman family law more closely.

The family begins with marriage,[3] to understand which it is important (but not easy) for the reader to make a clean break with all the Christian notions of marriage. To the Romans marriage was an honourable estate, for the purpose of concordant life together and the begetting of children;[4] many a tomb inscription testifies to a *bene concordans matrimonium*. But it was not sacramental, not 'holy' matrimony; it was not thought to be maintained or sanctioned by anything beyond the will of those who were parties to it—or their heads of families. The opposite of *iustae nuptiae* was not 'living in sin'.

The status requirement of *iustae nuptiae*, *conubium*, has been explained in Chapter II. There were certain other requirements. First, there existed certain statutory bars to marriage between people who would not otherwise have lacked *conubium*. (*a*) By an Augustan statute, senators and their sons could not have *iustae nuptiae* with freedwomen or other women of undignified condition; Paulus quotes a section of the statute,[5] mentioning specifically freedwomen and actresses (which included prostitutes) and showing that the law applied vice versa to women of senatorial rank and men of low condition. (*b*) Ordinary soldiers could not, until the time of Septimius Severus, marry during their service, and even children of marriages contracted before entry, if born during service, did not count as born of *iustae nuptiae*; the prefect of Egypt is found affirming this principle in AD 115 and 117:[6]

> 'Martialis could not have a legitimate son during his military service; though he quite legitimately made him his heir. . . . It is not possible for a soldier to marry.'

(*c*) Officials in the provinces could not marry women of their province, nor (by a constitution of Marcus and Commodus) could guardians marry their wards. Secondly, there were, as in all societies, certain 'taboo' or 'prohibited' degrees—ascendants and descendants, and in our period anything nearer than first cousins. Marriage of an uncle with his brother's daughter was allowed on the precedent of Claudius and Agrippina.[7] Thirdly, there was a minimum marriageable age, based on the general notion of puberty but fixed at twelve for females and fourteen for males (although in the case of males some held that it must depend on physical inspection). If either of the parties was younger the union simply counted as an engagement until the legal age was reached;[8] it was in no way an offence to enter upon such a union. The striking thing is the extremely low minimum age of marriage for girls. It has been shown by statistical study of inscriptions that females in Roman society did in fact marry extremely early; the latest survey gives a modal marriage-age for women of twelve to fifteen, and argues forcibly the unlikelihood that the age of puberty of Roman girls was as low as twelve.[9] This is an important set of facts for the understanding of Roman society. It made the likelihood of early widowhood great, and second marriages of women common (Antonia the wife of Drusus was regarded as exceptional in remaining a widow);[10] and whether or not it was possible in law for a father to force his daughter to marry, little girls of twelve or less cannot have had much practical freedom of choice.[11]

Consummation was not a necessary requirement of a valid marriage.[12] What is more, although marriage was normally begun to the accompaniment of many forms and ceremonies, none of these was of the essence. Marriage was a matter of intention; if you lived together 'as' man and wife, man and wife you were. What, then, about more than one? The Romans were monogamous, and Gaius says:[13]

'The same woman cannot be married to two men, nor the same man have two wives.'

But bigamy was not an offence; the situation is similar to 'marriage below the legal age'. The law simply assumed that people could not have the necessary intention to live as man and wife with more than one partner, so only one would count as a *iustum matrimonium*. Cicero records the problem raised by a man who left his wife in Spain and married another in Rome; it turned, in the Republic, on whether there was an automatic divorce even though nothing had been said, and, if there was not, the second 'wife' was just a concubine.[14] Gellius says that *paelex* was the ancient name (implying disesteem) of a woman who cohabited with a man who had a wife *in manu*.[15] Under the Augustan marriage legislation, though bigamy as such was still not an offence, a married woman who cohabited with someone other than her husband would be committing the grave criminal offence of adultery (and so would the man who cohabited with her) and a man who had non-marital sexual relations with an unmarried woman of high class would be committing criminal fornication, *stuprum*.

If you did not intend (or the rules did not allow you) to live together as man and wife you could live together as something else. Concubinage was regular and accepted in the life of Rome, and was in no sense thought sinful. It did not carry the respect attendant upon marriage, but this was because one of the partners was usually socially inferior; as Ulpian said, 'the difference is only in dignity'.[16] Emperors sometimes had concubines. Vespasian, after his wife's death, lived faithfully with a freedwoman, but never counted her as a wife;[17] and Marcus Aurelius, when his wife died, refused to marry the woman (almost certainly freeborn) with whom he subsequently lived, 'so as not to

introduce a stepmother over all his children'.[18] We hear of
persons who, having lived in concubinage, subsequently enter
into *iustae nuptiae*,[19] and there is plenty in the *Digest* about legacy
to concubines. A large body of evidence is available on this
institution from tombstones, and it has been the object of more
than one study.[20] One striking feature is the predominance of
concubinage between women of high status and men of a humbler
sort. Perhaps unhappy first marital experience and early widowhood are relevant here. To marry a man of low class for whom she
had a true affection might be impossible by the rules, or just
socially declassing, for a woman of high family; but the alternative was there. It has often been held that the frequency of
concubinage was forced upon Rome by Augustus' legislation
making it impossible for the senatorial order to contract a full
marriage with *humiliores*. But numerous cases have been shown
of concubinage between couples whom the Augustan rules
would not have debarred from full marriage.[21] There are certainly
difficult problems of source-criticism in considering how far the
status was legally regulated. Thus, the 'Opinions of Paulus' give
a rule that a man cannot have a wife and a concubine simultaneously,[22] but this must be post-classical. Not only do we hear
of a wife making her husband promise on pain of a money
penalty that he would not associate with a concubine during the
marriage,[23] but there are tombstones erected by men to wife and
concubine in situations where it is pretty certain that the women
exercised their respective functions concurrently.[24] Again, at
some stage it seems to have been held that concubines, or some
concubines, could be prosecuted for adultery.[25] And finally
there lurks the difficult question whether only such women
could be concubines who were sufficiently humble for relations
with them not to constitute *stuprum*. Some legal texts suggest
this, but the better view is that the lawyers were themselves
uncertain.[26]

Marriage, then, was a condition of fact dependent on the
intention of the parties. How did you prove that you were
married? Normally there would be the evidence of all those
ceremonies that are described in the books on 'Daily Life in

Rome'. There would be betrothal,[27] with its family pacts and property bargainings:[28]

'Taking a wife, eh, Postumus? There you are, in this generation, preparing pacts and agreements and betrothal ceremonies and getting a master-barber's haircut.'

There would be the actual marriage ceremony itself, of great elaboration. Above all there would be the evidence of dowry, to which we shall come.

But first it must be explained that in the time of the Republic there were two kinds of marriage (or rather two sets of effects of marriage), according to what the parties decided. In one (doubtless the earlier and original) form the woman passed into the *manus*, the hand, of her husband; which is to say that she left the agnatic family of her birth entirely and became part of that of her husband just as if she had been adopted. Whatever property she took with her (for she might own property if she was already *sui iuris*, not in the power of a *paterfamilias*) belonged henceforth to her husband or his *paterfamilias*. In the second form of marriage the woman did not pass into her husband's *manus* or his agnatic family. She stayed entirely in her own (though of course she and her husband formed a new matrimonial home), was not agnatically related to her husband or children, and continued to be in the power of her own *paterfamilias*, or, if none existed, remained legally independent, *sui iuris*, and in ownership of her own property. This second, non-*manus* form of marriage gradually prevailed over the former kind. We do not know how completely it had prevailed by Cicero's day; there were certainly still *manus*-marriages, referred to casually and not as freaks.[29] But within our period it became to all intents and purposes the only form of marriage; for simplicity's sake, therefore, in all that follows marriage will mean marriage without *manus*.

It is not possible to evaluate satisfactorily in general terms the much-asserted (or implied) independence of Roman women in the late Republic. The pieces of evidence that can be adduced point in different directions, or not unequivocally in any direction, and one must beware of generalizing from the notorious political women and the antics of Roman 'night-club' society. *Manus-* and non-*manus* marriage are really neutral here, for the choice in first marriages must normally have been made by the woman's family, not by herself with an eye to ultimate independence. It has been argued that non-*manus* marriage was actually unfavourable to the wife, since she would acquire no share in her husband's acquisitions during the marriage;[30] so the fact that it prevailed would suggest that it was the families of the males who, on average, determined the marriage pattern. In any case, non-*manus* marriage is attested in Rome for quite early times, long before there can be any question of feminine 'emancipation'. Divorce is equally neutral; again, it must normally have been at the decision not of the man and wife but of their families, and in upper-class circles, where divorce seems frequent, the decisions were often political ones, while in humbler circles we do not know whether it was frequent. The family limitation of the upper classes, deplored by Augustus, is likely to have been at least as much for reasons of property and succession as because women were able to make their distaste for childbirth prevail. The early age of marriage tells, if anything, against 'emancipation'. So, at first sight, does the Roman dowry system, in which only the woman's side made a contribution to the marriage (not until after our period do legal rules appear about 'gift in contemplation of marriage' by the bridegroom); it suggests that it was the women who had to compete for husbands. But here too there are complicating considerations.

Dowry, *dos*, was a transfer (or promise to transfer) of things having a money value from the bride's side—her family or friends—to the husband. In so far as it consisted of land or such other things as were susceptible of full ownership, the husband became owner during the marriage, though there was an Augustan rule that he could not alienate land in Italy that was dotal.[31] The scale of dowry would naturally depend on the wealth and rank of the parties, but it was not trivial—not just a sort of wedding-present. There was no rule that it had to be the bride's 'intestate portion', *i.e.* what she could expect from her father's estate in any event, but that this was at least the socially expected order of magnitude is suggested by the rules of *collatio dotis*,[32] whereby a woman claiming a share of a paternal inheritance might have to bring her dowry into account. A clear figure is given by Apuleius; his bride, the widow Pudentilla, had a fortune of four million sesterces, and he says he was content with a very modest dowry of three hundred thousand (and only promised at that).[33] A good deal of negotiation prior to a marriage would be about dowry agreements, *pacta dotalia*.[34] Almost any sort of agreements could be made, depending on the relative bargaining position of the parties. Some might secure that the wife would maintain herself out of her own, or her father's, property;[35] others might involve acceptance of the dotal property at a cash valuation—a weak position for the husband.[36] It is these variations that make it difficult to deduce an overall dominance by the male side. Most important of the dotal arrangements were those settling what was to happen to the dowry on dissolution of the marriage;[37] this was the crucial question. In default of any specific arrangement there was a rule of law, roughly as follows: if the wife died, her family would recover what they had given as dowry, except for a fraction for children, but the husband could keep any dowry that came from outside the wife's family; if the marriage came to an end for any other reason, including divorce, everything went back, except again a fraction for children and certain other fractions, mostly penalties for misconduct by the wife.[38] Return of dowry was, of course, vitally important when women married young and were liable to be widowed young, to secure them a second marriage.

If the Romans were matter-of-fact about marriage, they were equally so about divorce. It could take place at any time, either by mutual consent or by the unilateral decision of either party (or their *paterfamilias*). In the Republican age marriages were often an aspect of politics amongst the upper class; marriages cemented political alliances and divorces uncemented them. Valerius Maximus quotes cases of divorce for causes so petty that one suspects that politics may have lain behind them,[39] and although there is a tendency to believe that the rules about return of dowry may have imposed some curb on frivolous divorce, readers of

Cicero's correspondence who remember his long financial embarrassments over returning Terentia's dowry and getting back Tullia's will be conscious that he proceeded in his courses undeterred by them. It may be that the frequency of upper-class divorce in the late Republic testifies to the political rather than the moral weakness of Roman society, but Augustus at any rate thought that their family life left something to be desired. How much social effect the *leges Iuliae de maritandis ordinibus* and *de adulteriis* and the *lex Papia Poppaea* had is hard to decide, but they certainly complicated the law of family and inheritance.[40] What concerns us here is that Augustus for the first time made adultery by a woman, and condonation of it by her husband, a crime; he must divorce her, and he or someone else must prosecute her. And extra-marital intercourse with any free woman of high status, 'living honourably', also became a crime. It consequently became vital to be able to prove that you were *not* married—for a man to show that he was not condoning adultery, and for a woman, when she married, to show that she was not married already. Hence a new formal procedure for divorce:[41]

> 'No divorce is valid unless made in the presence of seven adult Roman citizens . . .'

One gets the impression that marriages were 'steadier' amongst the upper class during the Principate. Augustus' settling of the rights of retention of dowry may have helped, but it was perhaps more due to the dying out of political faction. Antoninus Pius, for example, prohibited fathers from breaking up a *bene concordans matrimonium*.[42]

Of legal relations between husband and wife one other rule needs mention: gifts between them were forbidden. A long title in the *Digest* deals with the boring details of this subject;[43] the only one worth mentioning is that a wife was allowed to bestow on her husband such property as would enable him to rise in rank where a fixed *census* was required.[44] The purpose of the prohibition was for the sake of family property, to prevent either party from parting with it to the other.

*

Children born of *iustae nuptiae* had the status of their fathers and were subject to *patria potestas*. This *potestas*-relationship expresses completely the agnatic principle of the Roman family; every member, male and female, was in the *potestas* of the oldest surviving male ascendant, the *paterfamilias* (*i.e.* if your grandfather was alive you and your father were in his *potestas*). Wives not *in manu*, it must be remembered, were not part of their husband's agnatic family; your wife was in the *potestas* of *her* oldest male ascendant. We have seen that a man might well have children born otherwise than of *iustae nuptiae*, 'natural' or illegitimate sons and daughters. No disgrace attached to them, though it will be recalled that they might well be slaves, and if he was a freedman with children born of a slave mother during his slavery they would still be slaves until he could obtain their manumission.[45] Quite a lot is said about natural children in the *Digest*.[46] Twice, for example, we are told that if a man's whole property is sold up or pledged this does not include his concubine and her children (all obviously slaves);[47] and one case is discussed of a man instituting as heirs his legitimate and his natural son.[48] Surprisingly, we never hear of quarrels over great estates between bastards and legitimate sons. Bastards, not being *in potestate*, would have a very low claim on a man's succession unless he made a will and instituted them as heirs. One imagines that if a man had left his property to a bastard to the exclusion of legitimate children they would have had an 'action of undutiful will', but no such case is discussed, and the Romans, whose society was non-feudal and who had no primo-geniture, tended to institute all their children.

Patria potestas was lifelong. Those subject to it could have no property of their own, and their lives were almost wholly controlled by their *paterfamilias*. His *potestas* included the well-known 'power of life and death', which was undoubtedly a reality in Republican times. His household jurisdiction, with a family council, dealt with offences of its members (such as sexual offences) that threatened the reputation of the family, and he could inflict chastisements and even death. This extreme is rarely heard of in the period of the Principate—only as a concession by the government to avoid odium (which had happened also in the

Republic—you handed over criminous women to their families for punishment), as in the case of Aulus Plautius' domestic trial of his wife recorded by Tacitus:[49]

> 'She was accused of foreign superstition, and her husband was allowed to try her; and so in the old style, before a family council, he held trial over his wife's life and reputation—and declared her not guilty.'

In one sense, though not what the Romans meant by *ius vitae et necis*, a 'power of life and death' was regularly exercised: it was the right of the *paterfamilias* to decide whether new-born children should be reared or exposed (their mother had no voice in the matter), and exposure was common and not a crime. The *paterfamilias* could force his married children to divorce,[50] and they could not marry in the first place without his consent. Whether he could force them to marry particular persons is a slightly more complex question. He could not do so in the case of sons; not only is *Digest* 23. 2. 21 formal on the point,[51] but it is implied by Gellius, discussing the moral (*n.b.* not the legal) duty of a son:[52]

> '. . . he ought to obey; but if his father orders him to take a shameful or criminal wife . . . he should not obey, for if turpitude enters into the question these things are no longer "indifferent".'

Of course, fathers might be jolly angry and make things difficult:[53]

> 'Father blazes with wrath when his son, mad on some tart, refuses to wed a wife with a huge dowry;'

all the more might they make things difficult for daughters. The law is less clear about this; *Digest* 23. 1. 11–12 says a daughter's consent is necessary for betrothal, but adds that anything short of positive resistance is taken for consent, and consent can only be refused if the proposed bridegroom is morally unfit. Little girls of twelve can have had small practical chance to refuse; but it must be remembered that your children *in potestate* might not be little girls or boys.

This lifelong power over children, however extraordinary it may seem (and did to the Romans),[54] was a reality, and we must not water it down. It did not apply in the sphere of public affairs:[55]

'A *filius familias* counts as a *paterfamilias* in public affairs, *e.g.* for holding magistracies or guardianships.'

We hear in the *Digest* of sons *in potestate* as consuls and provincial governors, as senators, and as local magistrates;[56] and a famous disquisition of Gellius arose out of a courtesy visit paid by a provincial governor and his father to a private house and the question who should sit on the one chair provided—which led to the telling of a story about how Quintus Fabius Maximus the proconsul dismounted from his horse on the orders of his son who was consul.[57] But in private life it mattered nothing that you might be forty years old or married or consul of the Roman people; if you were *in potestate* you owned nothing, whatever you acquired accrued automatically to your *paterfamilias*, you could make no gifts,[58] and if you borrowed money to give a dowry to your daughter it was a charge on your *paterfamilias*.[59] Loans of money to sons *in potestate* produced various frauds, as can be imagined, and so in Vespasian's principate a *senatusconsultum Macedonianum* made it impossible for a lender to sue on most loans so made—and therefore unlikely that anyone would make them; and Ulpian in the *Digest* title on the rule expressly says:[60]

'even if the son is consul, or has any other position of standing, the *senatusconsultum* applies.'

One might well wonder how such a society can possibly have worked. How did the *filius familias* with a wife and family and separate conjugal home and so on run his life and his household, if he could own nothing? An answer might be sought in two directions, but it is an irritating fact that we cannot back it with positive evidence. First one might look at 'emancipation', *emancipatio*, which, as will be seen below, took you out of *potestas*. Were adult sons, then, normally emancipated? On the whole the

evidence suggests that this was not so in the Republican age—
that emancipation was usually a penalty for misbehaviour;[61] and
that the same was true in the rest of our period is suggested by a
letter of Pliny in which he tells how his *bête noire* Regulus
emancipated his son in order that the son might take an inheritance from his mother. This was clearly a special case, the mother
having imposed it as a condition of making her son her heir, since
otherwise the property would simply accrue to Regulus.[62]

The other institution to look at, with greater hope, is *peculium*.
The son *in potestate*, like the slave, could have a fund which,
though ultimately belonging to the head of the family, was in
practice his to manage, and on the basis of which he could contract. As an economic device the slave's *peculium* was of very
great importance; we hear much less of the *peculium* of sons
and daughters, the rules governing which were the same, so
that it is not discussed separately in the *Digest*. It is, however,
overwhelmingly probable that married sons living independently
had such a fund; but the limitations must be borne in mind:
it belonged to the *paterfamilias*, there was nothing to stop him
withdrawing it, and it was part of his estate when he died.
It seems, once again, to have been Augustan legislation that
made a substantial modification to this position, by inventing a
new extra *peculium*, *peculium castrense*, the 'military fund'.[63] Over
this fund, which consisted of what he acquired by or for the
purpose of military service, the son *in potestate* had a right much
nearer to ownership; above all, he could leave it by will (which
became one of the facts of Roman law which 'everybody knew').[64]
If he did not do so it reverted to his *paterfamilias* as ordinary
peculium. He could also alienate it at any time, and his *paterfamilias*
could not touch it. It was, however, strictly limited to what was
acquired by or in connection with military service. And this is
curious; one might have expected this institution to be for the
benefit of the sons of the upper classes; but the big salaries were
for governorships and procuratorships, whereas it is likely that
military service meant here what it meant for the 'military will'—
that is, up to the junior officers, tribunes and prefects, but not
beyond. Not until after our period did sons get control over

official salaries in general. One must conclude that *castrense peculium* was invented as a privilege to encourage volunteer recruitment into Augustus' new professional army.

The *potestas*-relationship (or agnatic kinship) could be created otherwise than by birth. First, a man could be given *potestas* over his children by government grant. Gaius tells us that a peregrine who acquired citizenship for himself and his children by petition did not automatically get *potestas* over them, but only if it was specifically part of the grant.[65] He says that Hadrian laid down some rules about this, but we can see the principle working in a petition from Pliny to Trajan:[66]

'Please will you give citizenship to Chrysippus the son of Mithridates and to his wife Stratonice the daughter of Epigonus and to his children Epigonus and Mithridates, so that they may be in the *potestas* of their father.'

We must confine this to cases of petition. It cannot apply to the great block grants of citizenship to communities, to auxiliary soldiers and so on. Their grants never mention a specific privilege of *potestas* over their children, but it is inconceivable that they can all have been left without it.[66a]

An immensely more important case was adoption. A well-known feature of the social history of Rome is the infertility of the governing class, its failure to rear enough children to maintain its numbers. There were many factors involved: disease and high death-rate, the desire of society women to avoid childbearing, the danger of splitting up estates, and so on; but the point to observe here is that the characteristic remedy for a family in danger of dying out was adoption, and that that was the primary purpose of the institution. It had nothing to do with the welfare of children, and those adopted were often adults. Anyone with a spare son was in a strong position to link his family with some other noble house by giving him in adoption. With the forms we need not be concerned; they are described by Gaius and Gellius.[67] There were, however, really two institutions of very different

origin: 'adrogation' of a person *sui iuris*, which always required
public sanction, since such a person was in principle head of a
family (whether he actually had one or not) which, along with
its cult, would suffer extinction by being merged in yours; and
'adoption' in a technical sense, the transfer of someone *alieni
iuris* from the *potestas* of his or her *paterfamilias* into yours. A man
adrogated brought all his property and descendants across with
him automatically; a man or woman 'adopted' came by themselves, leaving their children (if any) under their original *paterfamilias*—and of course they would own no property to bring.
Since the purpose of the institution was to create *patria potestas*,
women could not adrogate or 'adopt'; they could be 'adopted'
but not adrogated. Another purpose, or, at least, another result
that could be achieved in this way, was the legitimization of
natural children. If the child was a *civis Romanus* you could
adrogate it, and if it was a slave you could manumit it and then
adrogate it[68]—unless it was a girl, for whom, adrogation being
impossible, you could do nothing. If the child was a peregrine
you could do nothing either, for this whole institution was
confined to *cives*; but the rules about error and Latinity (described
in Chapter II) might sometimes relieve this difficulty. Ulpian
seems to have thought it undesirable for people to adopt if they
already had legitimate children alive or were still capable of
having them,[69] but Cicero's furious fuss about the illegality of the
adoption of his enemy Clodius[70] must not be taken too seriously,
and the rules about the effect on a will of the arrival of a new son
in the family by adoption[71] imply that it was perfectly possible.
One thing which the law texts tell us nothing about, but which
certainly happened and was accepted in high society, is adoption
by will; that is how Augustus' relationship of son to Julius
Caesar came about.[72] It may have counted technically not as
adoption but as 'inheritance on condition of taking testator's
name', but the silence of Gaius and the *Digest* is still strange.
The unmarried and the childless were saddled by Augustus'
laws with various penalties, and Tacitus records a fraud which
had to be repressed in the time of Nero, whereby, in order to
qualify for public office, they hastily carried out adoptions and

then, when the offices were in the bag, equally hastily emancipated the adopted persons.[73]

Having examined the creation of *patria potestas* we must look for a moment at its dissolution. When your *paterfamilias* died, if you had no other ascendant in the male line into whose *potestas* you could fall you became independent, *sui iuris*, irrespective of your age or sex (for example, when grandfather died, if your father was alive you would now be in his *potestas*, but if not you would be *sui iuris*). Besides this natural dissolution of *potestas* there were artificial ones. If the *paterfamilias* underwent *capitis deminutio* (either minor, like adoption, or major, like criminal conviction) the tie broke, and equally so if it was the person *in potestate* who underwent the *capitis deminutio* (by adoption, for example, or in the case of a woman passing into someone's *manus*). And secondly there was a way by which a *paterfamilias* could actually release his son or daughter into independence: 'emancipation'. Gaius describes the ancient ceremony which it involved;[74] it may in early times have helped sons to escape from cruel fathers, but in our period it mostly seems to have been a penalty—cutting your child out of the agnatic family as it were with a shilling (though not necessarily so, since you could always leave him his portion as a legacy or make over property to him on emancipation, and the fact that there was a rule that a son could not force his father to emancipate him implies that it was sometimes desired).[75] If you performed the rigmarole correctly you could emerge as *parens manumissor* of your emancipated child, that is, in the same position as a *patronus* who had manumitted his slave, with patronal rights against his will; the *Digest* title 37. 12 'concerning those manumitted by a parent' is illuminating about this.

*

The fact that infants might often, by the death of their *paterfamilias*, be *sui iuris* threw considerable weight on the Roman institution of guardianship, *tutela*. Like adoption, this had originally nothing to do with the welfare of orphans, as is sufficiently shown by its application also to women, who had to have a guardian all their lives if they were *sui iuris*. It originated as a right of agnate relatives to keep a hold over property which, if the

H

infant did not grow up and have heirs, was due to come to them—
to see that the infant was not cozened into squandering it; and
similarly with the woman *sui iuris*, to prevent her from disposing
of family property. As early as the Twelve Tables a man making
a will had the right to appoint a 'testamentary' guardian to his
children (to the exclusion, if he wished, of the agnate relatives);
if he did not do this, or if the will failed, 'agnatic' guardianship came
into effect automatically. Already in the middle Republic the
concept of the welfare of infants began to enter into guardianship,
and a third kind, 'statutory' guardianship, arose: if no other
guardian existed the authorities would appoint one.[76]

Males were released from guardianship when they reached
puberty, since they were then capable of having children of their
own who would legitimately exclude the agnates; there was
dispute as to whether this depended on physical inspection or just
meant the standard age of fourteen.[77] Women were never
released (for even if married—except with *manus*—they were
sui iuris, and their husband was not their guardian). Astonishment
at this fact would be misplaced; subjection of women's legal acts
to some male authority was virtually universal in antiquity.
What does need comment is that this lifelong guardianship was
whittled away by legal devices, though as a formality it hung
grimly on. In the Herculaneum Tablets, for example, when
Calatoria Themis went bail to Petronia Iusta for appearance in
court she promised 'with authorization of her guardian' (who was
a freedman of her deceased husband). Pudentilla, the wealthy wife
of Apuleius, bought a farm; even as a married woman she did
so with her guardian's authorization, and he was brought into
court to testify that she had bought it for herself and not for
Apuleius.[78] And a document of AD 198 records the granting of a
guardian by the prefect of Egypt:[79]

'Q. Aemilius Saturninus, prefect of Egypt, at the request of
C. Terentius Sarapammon, granted a guardian to Maevia
Dionysarion in accordance with the *lex Iulia et Titia* and the
senatusconsultum, to wit M. Iulius Alexander—this grant not
being to the prejudice of any legitimate guardian'. . . . 'I,

Maevia Dionysarion, have requested the above-named guardian, Iulius Alexander, as stated. I, Gaius Iulius Heracla, have written this on her behalf, she being illiterate.'

This is illuminating; for certain legal acts a woman must have authorization, but if she said she had no guardian the authorities would appoint one for the purpose, without enquiry but with a saving clause. The acts needing authorization were alienation of *res mancipi* (mainly land and slaves, as will be seen), making a will, and any contract that put the woman under an obligation. If a guardian refused she could apply to the authorities to force him to assent; if he was absent she could get a temporary guardian of her choice. (Calatoria Themis' guardian was however a witness for Petronia Iusta.) Moreover, the automatic guardianship of agnates over women was abolished by the emperor Claudius; and already under Augustus' legislation to encourage family size, three children (four for a freedwoman) released a woman altogether from the requirement of guardian's authorization. So women *sui iuris* did in practice, in our period, manage their own property and affairs; it has been pointed out that we hear a good deal about the business transactions of Cicero's wife Terentia, but never who her guardian was.

Guardianship of infant males was a different matter. It was a necessary institution, involving administration of property as well as mere authorization, and though for agnates there might be advantages it was on the whole regarded as a great burden. Dealing with the fortunes of infants of wealthy families could be an immense task. There might be several guardians, and we hear more than once in the *Digest*[80] of division of the ward's estate, one set of guardians dealing with property in Italy and another with that abroad. It was the business of the guardian to get in debts to the ward's estate, to buy landed property if at all possible, and to put any liquid funds out on loan at proper rates of interest.[81] He must also see that the ward received out of the fund of the estate education or training appropriate to his station in society.[82] At the end of this stewardship there must be an accounting, and the now adult ward had an action (*actio tutelae*) against his guardian if the administration had been fraudulent or negligent; it was one of the actions conviction in which resulted in 'infamy'. Guardians, like stepmothers, were proverbially wicked, and people were for ever complaining and demanding their removal.[83] They must have thought themselves fortunate when they secured a clear pact not to sue, like that of 14 BC recorded on a papyrus:[84]

> '16th year of Caesar, month Tybi, ?6th day. To Protarchus, from Lucius Pomponius Rufus, son of Lucius, tribe Pollia, and Marcus Cottius Atticus. Since the father of Lucius Pomponius, Lucius Pomponius, in his Roman will made on his deathbed left Marcus Cottius Atticus and also Canuleius as guardians to Lucius Pomponius his son, above named; and since subsequently Canuleius resigned his guardianship, according to the sealed document, leaving Marcus Cottius Atticus as guardian of Lucius: now Lucius Pomponius agrees that neither he nor anyone else on his behalf will sue Marcus Cottius Atticus or Canuleius, . . . since Lucius Pomponius has received back from Marcus Cottius Atticus everything that his father had in his estate.'

It was a part of one's *officium* to one's friends to undertake guardianships, but the principles of mutual duty broke down somewhat in this sphere, exceptionally hard as it was on the *tutor dativus*, appointed compulsorily by the authorities, and we find growing up in our period an ever longer list of *excusationes*, circumstances that would let you off.[85]

Having called *tutela* 'guardianship' we are in difficulty for a word to translate another institution, *curatio* or *cura*; 'caretaker-ship' is not beautiful, but it will have to do. Caretakership of minors, lunatics and spendthrifts must briefly occupy us; the last two of these were ancient Roman institutions with an origin like that of *tutela*, whereas the first grew up within our period to fill in the inadequacies of *tutela*.[86] As early as the middle Republic it was realized that the ending of *tutela* over males at fourteen left youngsters at a very tender age to be in sole control of great fortunes in a wicked world—not to mention that *filii familias* were sometimes cheated into doing foolish things with their *peculium*. A *lex Laetoria* in the second century BC gave an action to anyone of either sex, below the age of twenty-five, whether *sui iuris* or not, against persons whom they alleged to have defrauded them, and an *exceptio legis Laetoriae* if they themselves were sued and wanted to allege fraud. The praetor in his edict went further still:[87]

> 'Whatever transactions are said to have been made with a person under twenty-five, according to the circumstances I will give relief.'

The praetor's relief was *restitutio in integrum*, 'restoration to the *status quo*'; the offending transaction was null and void, any consideration that had passed between the parties must be handed back, and things were as if no such bargain had ever happened. To us this seems excessive; the Romans, having ended their guardianship too early, now take minority and its protection up to too late an age (for at twenty-five a man could hold the first Roman magistracy, the quaestorship). Of course, the young could not escape the consequences of delicts and crimes in this way; and even for commercial bargains there must be some allegation that they had been cheated or imposed upon. As Paulus says:[88]

> 'Not all transactions with minors can be rescinded. They must be referred to equitable principles, otherwise people of this age will labour under great inconvenience, because no one will enter into any transaction with them and they will in a sense be deprived of *commercium*.'

The latter was seen as a very serious point. It began to be met by the minor concerned bringing in a kind of 'best friend' to give sanction to his transactions so that those who hesitated whether to deal with him would have assurance that he was acting with advice. Eventually it became regular for minors to apply to the authorities for a 'caretaker' who could thus authorize all their transactions until they reached twenty-five. Ulpian records a case in which some young men had been given a 'caretaker' but he had ceased to act; the emperor forced him to resume his function.[89]

The right to caretakership of lunatics and (remarkably) spend-thrifts vested originally in their nearest agnate relative, though later a caretaker could be appointed by the authorities.[90] The purpose was the protection of family property; the person concerned was henceforward debarred from controlling his property, alienating it, or making a will. Both cases have a good deal of interest. They comprise the only situation in which a man's relatives could get a complete right to take over his property against his will, and yet, as has been pointed out, the crucial question how to decide whether a man was a lunatic or a spend-thrift (or when he ceased to be so) is never discussed in the law texts.[91] Control of extravagance, it may be added, is unknown to English law; 'it may be better so in the interests of the com-munity at large, . . . but a wife or a widow and children will not quite accept this view'.[92] At any rate, while we are accustomed to see in Rome an extreme development of the principle that a man is entitled to 'do what he will with his own', in this sphere the Roman law imposed greater limitations than the English.

*

Out of the fifty books of the *Digest*, eleven are occupied by the law of succession, lovingly elaborated by the lawyers; one must admit that in will-making the idiosyncrasies of humanity are at their most abundant and generate a lot of law.

It is expedient to begin with intestate succession, not only because it is by definition automatic and not subject to the oddities of individuals, but also because it was almost certainly the oldest—and originally the only—form of succession in Rome;[93] the family's inheritance had to pass down according to ancient custom and the individual could not influence the succession. Many societies do not go beyond this; they do not have will-making, or only have it for the less important part of the family's substance, the earnings or personal accoutrements of individuals and so on. Roman law of our period had will-making of every-thing, but if there was no will or the will was invalid the old automatic rules applied. To understand them a technical term must be introduced: those persons in a man's *potestas* or *manus* who became *sui iuris* by his death were his *sui heredes*. The oldess rule of civil law said that if any *sui heredes* existed they automatically became heirs (hence, indeed, the name), in equal shares irrespective of sex; if none such existed the agnate relatives, of the nearest degree only, could take the estate; if none of those existed it went to the dead man's *gens* or clan. Here is agnatic succession, in the line of *potestas*, at its most rigid; emancipated children, for example, and relatives on your wife's side, even your wife herself (unless *in manu*), were excluded. The praetor, exercising *ius honorarium*, had already modified it a great deal by the beginning of our period; he allowed certain other people to apply for 'possession of the estate on intestacy', which they could retain at first only if there were no civil law heirs in the relevant degree of succession, but later even if there were, so as to come into a share alongside them: in the first degree all *liberi* could claim (technical again: not only *sui heredes* but those who would have been *sui heredes* if they or their father had not been emancipated); if there were no *liberi* then blood-relations down to the sixth degree could claim; and if there was still nobody, at long last a widow could claim her husband's estate or he hers. This praetorian intestate succession is where *collatio bonorum* came in; if you claimed to share with civil law heirs you had to bring into account your property acquired since emancipation (since you had had opportunities of acquisition denied to the *sui heredes*) or your dowry. Finally by legislation, though not until the second century AD, a mother came to be allowed to succeed to her children on intestacy and children to their mother.

By our period, Romans could—and probably normally did— set aside these automatic rules by making a will. With the history of how testation grew up we are not concerned; by Cicero's day Roman *patresfamilias* had wide freedom to dispose as they liked of all the family owned, limited only by the pressure of what was socially expected (which is a powerful limitation). What they could not do was what in many legal systems is normal and actually unavoidable; they could not make a will as to part of their estate and leave the rest to devolve by the rules of intestacy. This is because of the Roman concept of an heir, *heres*. Your heir or heirs were not just people to whom you left particular bits of property; the heir was 'universal successor', stepping into almost the entire legal role of the deceased, including responsibility for the family cult and for his debts as well as his assets (and debts in full, not merely as far as the assets would go). The primary function of a will was to appoint one or more heirs; it need do no more, but if that was not done, and not done first, the will was null and void. If there was more than one heir they were not inheritors of particular things but joint 'universal successors' to everything, according to the fractions named by the testator. They might very well continue in common ownership, if they were brothers and sisters, for example; but at any time any one of them could get an action in the courts for division according to the fractions (which would mean a valuation). If the testator had given a 'prior legacy', *legatum per praeceptionem*, of some particular thing to any one of them, he would get it without it counting against his share in the division. 'Prior legacy' was important,[94] because the joint universal succession insisted on by the law ran counter to the natural desire of testators to leave the house to John and the best tea-set to Mary, and so on.

There were numerous limitations on who could make a will and who could be heir under a will (or otherwise). We shall not consider them exhaustively.[95] First, as to making a will: some people were barred as a penalty for conviction in the courts; some others we have already noted—lunatics, spendthrifts, Junian Latins; infants could not make wills; and women not only had to have guardian's authorization but, until Hadrian,[96] also had to go through a complicated rigmarole of changing guardians by *coemptio*—the 'Gnomon of the Idiologos' is formal as to this:[97]

'It is not allowed for a Roman woman to make a will without a so-called *coemptio*; and a legacy left by a Roman woman to a female Roman infant was forfeited.'

One of Cicero's letters also reveals the late Republican lawyers engaged in a wrangle over it.[98] Secondly, as to heirship; some people were debarred simply from being heirs, others from taking legacies also. Most important is that peregrines could neither be heirs of, nor take in any way from, a Roman citizen. Perhaps equally important (for reasons which will appear) is that 'uncertain persons', *incertae personae*, could not be made heirs or take under a will—which meant, above all, unborn generations, persons not already at least physically conceived when the will was made. In Cicero's day women could not be instituted heirs by people in the highest property class; this ceased to be true under the Principate. Corporations (cities and guilds) could not be made heirs, but they could take legacies (though not *per praeceptionem*),[99] from Nerva's time onwards. Finally, there were complicated rules, stemming from Augustus' attempt to encourage larger families amongst the upper class, imposing disabilities on the unmarried and the childless. They could take little or nothing, not even childless husbands and wives as between one another. 'Now you are a father and can be heir in a will, as a result of my activities', says the adulterer to the husband in Juvenal; 'You get legacies whole, and even luscious lapsed bequests.'[100] The unmarried and the childless could certainly make wills; one of the evils of Roman society most familiar to readers of the classics is *captatio*, the way in which 'legacy-hunters' ingratiated themselves with the unmarried, the childless, and the senile. The fifth Satire of Horace's second book is about nothing else.

The testator could make as many people heirs as he liked, in any fractions he liked. He could also provide for the possibility that named heirs might predecease him or be unwilling to accept the inheritance, by 'substitution': 'let Titius be my heir, or if he has not accepted within *x* days let him be disinherited and let Seius be my heir'. Thus a will might contain grades of heirs, the lower only coming in if the higher did not take; it was customary to mention friends (or the emperor) in a will in this sort of way, in second or third grade, as a *politesse*—no doubt what Trimalchio meant when he said he was 'co-heir with the emperor' in his master's will.[101] What testators could not do was tie the hands of an heir who did accept; they could not say 'let Titius be my heir and when he dies (or 'when my son grows up') let my son be my heir'. Only one such thing was allowed, namely to substitute for infant children by saying 'Let my son be my heir, but if he does not reach the end of his period of wardship then let Titius be my heir.' The reason for these rules, coupled with the rule that you could not make unborn generations heirs, was the great reluctance of Roman law to permit entailing—the tying up of property by a man in ways that could not be untied by his successors. Each generation must have its unimpaired right to make its own decisions and dispositions. It is feudalism that fosters the entail, and Rome was fundamentally un-feudal; nevertheless, testators hanker after power over the future, and it will presently be seen that the law was here standing against a strong current.

The Roman *paterfamilias* in our period was also entirely free in law to disinherit his children. It is true that formalities had to be observed, which amounted to this, that he could not just pass them over in silence; any *liberi* in the technical sense, existing when the will was opened, who were not specifically accounted for in it either by institution or by express disherison (either because they had been passed over or because they had come into the agnatic line since the will was drafted, by birth or *manus* or adoption) had the effect of upsetting the will and were brought in to shares in the estate.[102] Wills therefore commonly contained a clause 'and let all others be disinherited'. Provided this was seen to, disherison was perfectly valid. On the other hand, social feeling in Rome was against a man cutting out his children, unless they were plainly bad and unfilial. So there arose during our period (the exact history of the matter is, as usual, hotly disputed) an important action that could be brought against the heirs named in a will by a man's (or woman's) children who claimed they had been unjustly disinherited, the *querela inofficiosi testamenti* or 'complaint of undutiful will'.[103] It was one of the suits that came before the *centumviri*; Pliny gives an account of a celebrated *querela* in which he represented the plaintiffs.[104] The chance to upset wills in this way had dangers, indicated by Ulpian:[105]

'It must be realized that suits of undutiful will are frequent;

for everybody, parents and children, can argue what constitutes "undutifulness".'

What the plaintiff actually got if the action succeeded was his intestate portion; but he could not bring the action at all if he had been left a quarter of that amount.[106]

Many other things could be done in a will besides the making of heirs, such as granting freedom to slaves and appointing guardians to infants and women, and especially leaving legacies. Legacy was the leaving of specific things to people—what testators of every age spend most of their time doing—and was an entirely different matter from making heirs, though the fate of the whole will, including the legacies, depended on the due entry of heirs. Since every legacy was a diminution of the inheritance, if their total was too great the heirs might not wish to enter. The interest for social history is to see the wide variety of things besides just pieces of property that were left, and could be left under all sorts of conditions, by legacy.[106a] We hear a good deal about legacy of life-interests and of the right to occupy houses, left to widows[107] or widowers:[108]

'he is to have the habitation and the remaining rooms of the house and courtyard for the term of his life without house-tax',

or to freedmen:[109]

'I request you to allow Negidius and Titius and Dio my freedmen, who are aged and infirm, to live out their old age in the places where they now dwell.'

We get annuities and pensions (a whole title on them, *Digest* 33. 1), which might have to be given a cash value on a life-expectancy basis;[110] on the humblest scale they are *alimenta*, 'keep' (with another whole title, 34. 1), or the purchase of a ticket of entitlement to the free corn distribution at Rome.[111] Then there is legacy of the *operae* of a freedman, legacy of her dowry to a wife, legacy in the form of a release from debts owed to the testator. As for pieces of property, there is fascinating social background information (and Latin vocabulary) in the minute analyses by the lawyers of what was included when a man gave a legacy of 'my house' or 'my books' or 'my furniture' or 'my farm fully stocked' or 'my dye-factory with all appurtenances'.[112]

Through a mass of legacies or a mass of debts, or both, heirs might find themselves with a *damnosa hereditas*, an inheritance 'more expense than it was worth'. They might simply decide not to accept heirship; thus, as to debts, Pliny writes to a lady called Calvina:[113]

'If your father had owed money to several people, or indeed to anyone but me, you might well have had a problem whether to enter an inheritance that even a man would find burden-some.'

As to legacies, the praetor would not allow heirs to exercise a dodge by letting the will go void by their non-entrance and then taking their shares of the estate as an intestacy; he promised an action to legatees to secure their legacies in this event.[114] But already in the Republican period there was a run of legislation, culminating in a *lex Falcidia* of 40 BC, which may have improved but certainly complicated the law by laying down that a quarter of the assets must be left to the heirs, so that if legacies exceeded three-quarters each of them must be cut down *pro rata* (that is one reason why such things as annuities might have to be calculated out actuarially). Even then heirs might not be keen. Quite apart from the rule that legatees could demand security,[115] Ulpian points out that:[116]

'people's motives are various: some are frightened by the business side, some of the trouble they will be put to, some of the mound of debts (even if the estate is a rich one), some of the quarrels and jealousies that may arise . . .'

Some heirs, however, were not allowed to refuse to be heirs. *Sui heredes*, whether there was a will or an intestacy, could not. If there was a mound of debts what they could do was to apply for a 'privilege of abstaining' from the actual physical assets; the creditors would sell up the assets as a bankrupt estate, but could not touch the *sui* for the remainder. The Romans also practised what seems to us a particularly rotten trick: a man who knew he was dying in debt, in order to save his own name from disgrace, would free a slave and institute him heir, and this freedman could neither refuse the inheritance nor get a 'privilege of abstaining', but was liable in full, both to the debts and to the stigma of insolvency. All other heirs could refuse, and as a corollary of this, if they wanted the inheritance they must take specific formal steps to enter, usually by a declaration called for by the testator, a *cretio*. This process of *cernere hereditatem* is attested not only by Cicero[117] but by an Egyptian document of AD 170 (in very shaky Latin):[118]

> 'Valeria Serapias, spinster, of Antinoopolis, testifies through her procurator, to wit her brother Lucius Valerius Lucretianus Matidius, known also as Plutinius, of Antinoopolis, that she has entered upon and formally accepted the inheritance of her mother Flavia Valeria, and is her heir according to the tablets of her will.'

At this point it is necessary to go back and examine one more thing that Roman testators were accustomed to do. Making heirs and giving legacies were formal acts, void if wrongly carried out, with strict legal consequences if carried out correctly, and subject to irksome restrictions. But suppose you just made an informal request to your heir in your will or to the person who would succeed you on intestacy, to carry out some act, entrusting it to his good faith to do so? Suppose you simply said, for example, 'Please see that my friend Aristo of Chios gets the house', or 'It is my earnest hope that you will pass everything to my son when he marries'? Nothing could prevent you making such *fidei commissa* or 'trusts', but the law would not originally do anything to help you get them honoured. Nevertheless, for anyone prepared to accept the risk that his trust might be misplaced and his request ignored, *fideicommissa* were a means of getting round the restrictions on inheritance and legacy. You could entrust your heir with the passing of property to a peregrine,[119] or to a woman (to defeat the *lex Voconia*);[120] or you could create the perpetuities so hated by the jurisprudents, or get slaves manumitted in excess of the numbers allowed by the *lex Fufia Caninia*.[121] You could request your intestate heirs that if your will failed they should carry out the whole of its provisions as a *fideicommissum*. And by *fideicommissum hereditatis*, 'trust of the inheritance', which meant instituting someone heir with a request to pass the entire estate on (to be an 'executor', in fact), you could in effect leave everything to a peregrine or to unborn generations.

Two things happened to the law about *fideicommissa* during our period. The first is described in Justinian's *Institutes*:[122]

'In early days all trusts were risky, because no one could be forced to carry out the trust if he did not want to. . . . Augustus, induced more than once by personal favour, or because people were said to have made their requests with a plea "by the safety of Augustus", or because of notorious cases of breach of trust, for the first time ordered the consuls to interpose their authority. And since this seemed equitable and was popular it gradually turned into a standard jurisdiction.'

So from Augustus onwards trusts became enforceable and a man could, for example, leave his estate to a peregrine in a way protected by the courts—not, be it noticed, the ordinary courts, but first a special consular jurisdiction and, from Claudius onwards, either the consuls or a special 'fideicommissary praetor' or the provincial governor.[123] The *fideicommissum hereditatis* in particular was given support by further legislation. The *senatus-consultum Trebellianum* of AD 56 made sure that creditors of the estate would sue the actual beneficiary and not trouble the nominal heir who had handed everything over as requested.[124] The *senatusconsultum Apronianum* of Hadrian's time made *fidei-commissum hereditatis* to municipalities enforceable;[125] it was already being done before that, as a remarkable letter of Pliny shows:[126]

'A certain Julius Largus from Pontus, my lord, whom I have never met or even heard of (I suppose he is relying on your judgement of my soundness) . . . has asked me in his will to be his heir and enter, and then to transfer the whole, less a

prior legacy to myself of fifty thousand sesterces, to the cities
of Heraclea and Tyana . . .'

On the other hand, for its support of *fideicommissa* the law exacted
a price, no less than the gradual imposition upon them of some of
the most important restrictions that applied to legacies. We are
told in the 'Gnomon of the Idiologos' that fideicommissary
inheritance from or to peregrines was stopped by Vespasian,[127]
and a *senatusconsultum* going by the name of Vespasian's urban
prefect, the *Pegasianum*, made *fideicommissa* subject to the rules of
the *lex Falcidia*. Finally, Hadrian laid down that you could not
leave by *fideicommissum* to an 'uncertain person', thereby once
again stopping the loophole for entails. The law still struggled
with what it regarded as the fraud of the 'tacit *fideicommissum*',
which was not put in writing at all:[128]

> 'Those persons are making their trust available in fraud of the
> law who give tacit promises that they will hand over what they
> have received—or other things—to persons who cannot
> legitimately take under a will.'

Digest 49. 14 'on fiscal law' is much taken up with this; it was a
fraud on the treasury, which was entitled to pounce on estates to
which there was no legitimate heir.

The treasury also came into succession questions in another
way. Augustus, looking for an extra source of revenue out of
which to pay a professional army, invented a new tax falling
exclusively on *cives Romani*, the *vicesima hereditatium* or five per
cent estate duty. It applied to all but small estates and fell upon
all heirs except close relatives; how bitterly it was hated can be
seen from the praise lavished by Pliny on Nerva and Trajan for
allowing more exemptions for blood relations.[129] The legislation
establishing the tax also laid down rules for the opening of wills (a
sort of probate),[130] presumably because there had to be a clear
point at which the companies to whom the tax was farmed for
collection could get in and make their valuations. A pair of letters
of Pliny are relevant: as heir to five-twelfths of an estate, he sold
his share to an old friend for less than its full value, she agreeing

to pay the estate duty; and she had to pay the duty on the full value as assessed by the collectors, not on the purchase price.[131] Normally it was the heirs who paid; they could deduct from legacies accordingly, though out of benevolence or at the testator's request they might not.[132]

The proper Roman will was not merely a document but a ceremony, an 'imaginary sale by bronze and balance', with a 'purchaser of the estate', a 'holder of the balance' to weigh out the price, and five witnesses who must be citizens and adult.[133] The testator held up the written tablets of his dispositions and orally proclaimed their validity. The witnesses did not have to know the contents, but there was no harm in their knowing; when asked to peruse the will, says Horace:[134]

> 'say no, and put the tablets aside; but get a quick glance at page one line two—whether you are sole heir or co-heir with a multitude.'

So there was nothing to prevent beneficiaries being witnesses, though Gaius said it was better not to use your heirs as witnesses.[135] It is hard to tell whether people actually went through the ceremony; the surviving wills mostly allege it and refer to it, but that was probably enough. The *ius honorarium* went a little further; the praetor allowed 'entry to the estate' on the basis of any testament properly sealed with the seals of seven witnesses, whether it had the *per aes et libram* form or not—though even in Gaius' time such an entry could not be upheld against a counter-claim by any lawful intestate heirs.[136] Testators were sometimes anxious to keep their dispositions especially secret, and wrote 'codicils', informal written dispositions; but the law was strict about these. If they were expressly confirmed in the will such documents counted as part of it; if they were not they could not purport to act as a will and could only pass fidei-commissary requests.[137]

The wills of soldiers came to be free from all formal requirements. According to Ulpian, Julius Caesar had occasionally allowed anomalous wills by soldiers to stand; astonishingly, Augustus and the Julio-Claudian emperors did not follow suit, but the Flavians were sometimes indulgent, and the privilege became a rule by a constitution of Trajan which was quoted in Chapter I.[138] The reason given by Trajan for this privilege to soldiers, their 'simplicity', can hardly be the whole story. Soldiers were no simpler than civilians—though they were perhaps the only simple people the law much bothered about; and besides, the privilege extended through centurions right up to the tribunes, who were *equites*. Genuine emergencies might, of course, occur, and so even governors and legates had the same dispensation if actually on enemy territory.[139] And unavailability of technical legal advice might be relevant. But the fact is that soldiers' wills were free from much more than merely formal requirements. Above all, they could make peregrines their heirs or legatees;[140] since during all the long years of their service they could not contract a *iustum matrimonium* their children must in most cases have been born of peregrine concubines, and hence peregrine. Soldiers could also institute the unmarried and the childless (*e.g.* their fellow-soldiers); they could make one heir for a period and substitute another for when the period was up; they could make one will for their property acquired by service and another for their other property; the Falcidian rules did not apply to them, nor did the 'suit of undutiful will'; and the *filiusfamilias* who was a soldier could devise his *castrense peculium*. The basic purpose of these indulgences must have been to stimulate recruitment;[140a] Hadrian also allowed intestate 'entry into the estate' to children of soldiers born during service.[141] There was one crucial limitation: the military will only retained its validity for one year after discharge—so long and no more did you have to put your affairs in order and make a proper ordinary will with all its limitations. Naturally, a soldier who did not wish to exercise his privileges could make an ordinary will at any time, as did the author of the most celebrated surviving will, which will be quoted presently.

We possess information about the wills of many individual Romans, and some of the actual documents survive in whole or part. There are the wills of the powerful, such as those of Julius Caesar and Augustus, quoted by Suetonius,[142] or of the eminent in literature, such as Virgil's will from the Donatus 'Life of

Virgil' (heirs: his half-brother to a half, Augustus to a quarter, Maecenas to a twelfth, Várius and Tucca to the residue, with a prior legacy of his manuscripts on condition that they published nothing not already made public by himself).[143] There are the wills of the wealthy: Cluvius the banker of Puteoli (Cicero's share, as co-heir with numerous others, was house property bringing in a hundred thousand sesterces a year),[144] Domitius Tullus ('such marvellous properties, such staggering riches!', exclaimed Pliny, who was no pauper),[145] Dasumius, the friend of Pliny and Tacitus, part of whose complex bequests survives on stone,[146] or the unknown provincial magnate from Gaul whose will is partly preserved in a manuscript.[147] (In this category an honourable mention must go to Trimalchio, who read out his entire testamentary dispositions to his dinner guests from begining to end 'accompanied by the sobs of the household'.)[148] Most impressive and significant, however, are two wills of very ordinary men indeed, a private soldier and a veteran, preserved by the sands of Egypt—significant precisely because they are no botch jobs or humble scraps, but dispose of their little patrimonies with all the formality of the testament *per aes et libram* exactly as the emperor did.[149] Here first is Augustus' will, recorded by Suetonius:

'He instituted as heirs: in Grade 1 Tiberius to two-thirds and Livia to one-third (requiring them to take his name); in Grade 2 Drusus the son of Tiberius to one-third and the residue to Germanicus and his three male children; in Grade 3 various relatives and friends. Legacies: to the Roman people forty million sesterces, to the tribes half a million, to the praetorian guard one thousand each, to the urban cohorts five hundred each, and to every legionary three hundred (all this to be paid at once in cash, for he had it already banked for the purpose); various other legacies, some going up to two million (for which there was a year's grace for payment, Augustus apologizing that his personal fortune was not large). . . . He ordered that the two Julias, his daughter and granddaughter, should on decease not be buried in his tomb. In three separate documents he left instructions for his funeral, a list of his achievements to be inscribed on bronze and placed before his mausoleum, and a set of statistics about the empire . . .'

Elsewhere in Suetonius[150] we learn the famous opening sentence:

'Since harsh fate has snatched my sons Gaius and Lucius from me, let Tiberius Caesar be my heir to two-thirds of my inheritance,'

and the humble position of the future emperor Claudius:

'he was only an heir in Grade 3 amongst what were virtually outsiders, and only to one-sixth,'

and the name of the 'purchaser of estate', confirming that it was a will *per aes et libram*.

At the opposite pole must be quoted in full that marvellous survival, the five waxed wooden tablets containing the entire will of Antonius Silvanus, dated AD 142, in slightly ungrammatical Latin:[151]

'Antonius Silvanus, trooper of the 1st Mauretanian squadron of Thracians, prefect's batman, troop of Valerius, made his will. Of all my property, military and civilian, let M. Antonius Satrianus be my sole heir. Let all others be disinherited. And let him formally accept my inheritance within the first hundred days; if he has not thus accepted let him be disinherited, and then in the second grade let (. . .) Antonius R(. . .)lis, my brother, be my heir and formally accept my inheritance within the next sixty days. To him I give as legacy, if he does not become my heir, seven hundred and fifty silver denarii. As agent for my military property, to get in my assets and hand them over to Antonia Thermutha the mother of my heir aforementioned, I appoint Hierax the son of Behex, corporal of the same squadron, troop of Aebutius; and she is to hold the property until my son and heir becomes free of guardianship and receives it from her. To Hierax I give as legacy fifty silver denarii. To Antonia Thermutha, mother of my heir aforementioned, I give as legacy five hundred silver denarii.

To my commanding officer I give as legacy fifty silver denarii. As to my slave Cronio after my death, if he shall have dealt correctly with everything and handed all to my heir afore-mentioned or to my agent, I wish him to be free, and I wish the five per cent tax on him [i.e. on his manumission] to be paid out of my estate.

Let all fraud be absent from this testament.

Purchaser of the estate for the purpose of testation: Nemonius, corporal of the troop of Marius; balance-holder: M. Iulius Tiberinus, corporal of the troop of Valerius; foreman of witnesses [this is a bit uncertain]: Turbinius, standard-bearer of the troop of Proculus.

Will made at Alexandria-beside-Egypt, in the Augustan camp, winter quarters of legion II Traiana Fortis and the Mauretanian squadron, 27 March, consulships of Rufinus and Quadratus.'

There follows in Greek, presumably in the testator's own hand:

'I, Antonius Silvanus, the aforementioned, have perused this my will above written, and it has been read and I approve of it as it stands above.'

Ancient families surviving for many generations in genetic and property continuity are not characteristic of Rome; neither society as a whole nor any special noble class practised primo-geniture. The rules of intestate succession reveal a 'partible' inheritance system by which all a man's agnatic descendants could expect their share, and though the rules of testation made a system of primogeniture conceivable in theory they do not seem to have been used to that end. And if upper-class society had valued property continuity highly it is unlikely that the law could have held out so firmly against perpetuities. The desire not to partition their estates into too many fragments may have been a factor in the notorious infertility of the Roman upper class; but in an era of high mortality if you do not produce many children you may easily be left with none, and then adoption alone will enable you to preserve the family name.

*

We must not leave the subject of family and succession without
a few words about Roman tombs and the law that applied to
them. It is an aspect of the relation between life and law which
was of concern to great numbers of people and a meeting-place
of many concepts—the nature of the Roman family, the dichotomy of sacred and secular law and of law and custom, the
establishment of memorial foundations, and so on.[152] Also it
raises one of the oddest puzzles in all Roman law. In this field
especially archaeology and epigraphy come into their own, since
actual tombs and their inscriptions survive in large numbers. The
emperors had their family mausolea; the nobility had family
vaults along the roads leading into the cities; and the middle
class, hardly less rich, owned similar vaults forming streets of
cemeteries (such as those of the 'Isola Sacra' at Ostia[153] and those
recently excavated under St Peter's itself in Rome);[154] or they
too might set up huge free-standing monuments like the 'baker's
monument' at the Porta Maggiore.[155] For their slaves and
freedmen the nobility sometimes provided *columbaria*, vaults
with niches for scores or hundreds of crematory urns; the most
famous is that of Livia Augusta.[156] The rest of the humble plebs
and slaves, who in Cicero's day were still cast into open graves on
the Esquiline,[157] later took to becoming members of funerary
societies owning *columbaria* in which members were entitled to a
place, or else they bought a niche in a *columbarium* constructed by
a speculative builder. Many hundreds of inscriptions from all
these kinds of tomb, and from others now lost, record their
establishment and the rules their founders wished to be applied
to them.

The puzzle about Roman tombs derives much of its acuteness
precisely from the fact that the majority of them were structures
intended to hold many burials or sets of ashes, of people who did
not all die at the same time. The most famous rule of Roman
funerary law is given by Gaius:[158] the place containing human
remains put where they have a right to be is *locus religiosus*,
subject to divine law and therefore not susceptible of human
ownership or possession or alienation of any kind (by sale or
gift or legacy or anything else). It is *res nullius*. And yet the tomb

inscriptions record people constantly selling and giving away tombs and parts of tombs and shares in tombs and urns in tombs;[159] and no less frequently they record people imposing prohibitions on their successors against such alienation.[160] One text in the *Digest* says:[161]

> 'Not the whole *locus* intended for burial is *religiosus*, only the place where remains actually lie.'

One might argue, therefore, that the unoccupied parts of a tomb are still *locus purus*, susceptible of ownership and buying and selling. This is attacked as absurd: 'what? a tomb two-thirds of which is not sacred and can at any moment be sold as a pigeon loft or a dwelling?' And yet the contrary is equally absurd: 'what, a *columbarium* built for profit which becomes *locus religiosus* as a whole the moment the first niche is filled and can no longer be owned by anyone?' Many attempts have been made to answer this dilemma. Unless we are to suppose that there was a complete opposition between what the law said and what people did, which went on without compromise or adjustment for century after century, the only alternative is to conclude that in some way the law and the public were talking about different things. One answer is that what was being bought and sold was not the tomb itself but the right to dispose of a place in it, the *ius sepulchri*. The praetor in his edict recognized such rights,[162] and they were probably regulated as a part of sacred law, not civil law, by the *pontifices*,[163] who certainly had functions connected with tombs (for example, you had to have their permission to repair tombs, otherwise you were committing *violatio sepulchri*).[164] But although some inscriptions speak in these terms:[165]

> '. . . Aelius Dignus, Paccius Charito and their partners have been in possession of this garden cemetery with its surrounding wall, with all its rights according to the authority and decision of the *pontifices*,'

most talk baldly about buying and selling the tomb, not the rights in it. The latest answer[166] says, rather differently, 'Tombs were indeed unsusceptible of human ownership, but only in one special sense, that they could never be diverted to non-sepulchral uses; once a tomb, always a tomb. Apart from this, they were as subject to ordinary ownership and alienation as anything else.' About this too the difficulty is that the legal and inscriptional texts show no sign that they are using words like 'buy' and 'sell' of tombs in any but the same sense[167] (though in one recently discovered inscription from the 'Isola Sacra' a man describes a piece of a hereditary tomb which he has walled off for his own descendants as *aediculam puram*, *i.e.* not *locus purus* in the civil law sense, free of all taboo, but *purus* so far as he is concerned, unencumbered with other burials).[168]

Public authority did not concern itself much with sepulchral law. There was a rule, going back to the Twelve Tables, that no one's remains must rest within the *pomerium* of the city of Rome, and the cities generally had the same rule,[169] which explains the lines of tombs outside the walls. The praetor gave actions to ensure that people's proper funeral expenses would be met,[170] and that corpses should not be dumped on other men's land;[171] he also gave the *popularis actio* for 'misuse of a tomb' (which included living in it).[172] But as to the determination of who was entitled to dispose of tombs and space in them there was certainly conflict between the public and the law.

The Roman family of early days carried with it from generation to generation a cult of tutelary spirits, which included upkeep of a family tomb. One of the main reasons for having an heir was to secure perpetuation of these *sacra*, and as long as the heir was automatically a member of the agnatic family upkeep of the *sacra* coincided with perpetuation of the family name. With the growth of free testament, and the resulting possibility of 'extraneous' heirs, there arose the problem that, the heir having the *sacra*, in which he might take little interest (for they involved some trouble and cost), there would be no one to uphold the memory of the family name. Consequently there came to be, in our period, two recognized régimes of right to the tomb:[173]

'Tombs which a man has set up for himself and his *familia* are called *familiaria sepulchra*; tombs which he has set up for himself and his heirs are called *hereditaria sepulchra*.'

The 'family tomb' (overwhelmingly the commonest from Augustus on, to judge from the inscriptions) was intended to descend specifically and exclusively to those who bore the family name. It commonly bore the words 'this tomb will not follow the heir'[174] or '. . . the extraneous heir'; and it is of this category of tomb that alienation was usually prohibited by the founder. Those who bore the family name included—and might soon include nobody but—your freedmen and their descendants:[175]

'L. Hostilius Fortunatus made this tomb for himself and his daughter Hostilia Ianuaria and for their freedmen and freedwomen and their posterity.'

This reception of the freedmen into the family tomb is indeed in a sense evidence of the solidarity of the patron-freedman relationship; those who had been unfaithful were sometimes excluded.[176] As usual, however, there is another side to the question. The freedmen had imposed on them the onus of maintaining the tomb when other members of the family had gone. As the valuable right of burial in the family vault might not be sufficient inducement, one means of further assurance of perpetuity was to impose a penalty for non-compliance, to be paid to some permanent body—the local municipality or the *pontifices* or the treasury—which would thus have an interest in keeping an eye on the monument:[177]

'. . . and if anyone after me raises any controversy about this tomb or tries to remove it from my name, let him pay to the treasury of the Roman people five thousand sesterces.'

In addition you could create a reversion:[178]

'T. Aelius Primitivus, freedman of the emperor, senior chef, and Aelia Tyche, freedwoman of the emperor, his wife, erected this for themselves and their children, their freedmen and freedwomen and their posterity. Let no one interfere with residence for custody of the tomb [meaning a bit uncertain].

But if no one of this our memory survives it shall belong to the guild of imperial chefs, headquarters the palace. We do not permit it to be given or sold; if anyone contravenes the above rule he shall owe to the said guild fifty thousand sesterces.'

A yet further device, which coincided with the desire of the rich to create whole cemetery areas, with gardens and buildings in which sacrifices could be prepared and sacral meals consumed, was to add to all this properties bearing revenue, such as shops and houses, from the income of which the costs of upkeep and of regular sacrifices might be reimbursed:[179]

'The street called Spurianus . . . is attached to this tomb'; 'this shop with building attached is support for the tomb'; '. . . so that from the income of the flats they shall celebrate his memory with sacrifices four times a year.'

From such arrangements as these it is scarcely a step further to those perpetual foundations for poor-relief, local games, cash distributions and the like, in memory of the deceased, which have been the object of important legal and social studies.[180] Two splendid examples of funerary foundations have recently been added to the sum of our knowledge: the cemetery of Pompeia Musa at Alexandria[181] and that of Iunia Libertas at Ostia. There is room to quote only the latter, in a rather abbreviated translation:[182]

'Iunia Libertas has given and granted to her freedmen and freedwomen and those manumitted by them, and their posterity, her right in, and the usufruct of, the gardens, houses and shops known as Iuniani, enclosed in their own boundary wall. None of the beneficiaries is to sell, alienate or grant away the usufruct of his share until the said usufruct descends to one survivor only. In which event I wish the entire property to pass into the ownership of the people of the Colonial City of Ostia. From the income of it I wish sums to be spent by the City of Ostia for the adornment of the tomb and for sacrifices, as follows . . .'

The law had doubts about much of this. Quite apart from conceptual difficulties about permanent foundations in general, it was reluctant to see these sepulchral foundations as unitary institutions. On the one hand it insisted that tombs, as *res religiosae*, were inalienable anyway, while on the other hand it insisted that, whatever people might say, all these appurtenances could not just be 'attached to the tomb' but were subject to ordinary property rights and rules, and could be bought and sold[183] and sold up for debt (which was important, because people evidently tried to save valuable properties from lapsing to creditors or the treasury by 'attaching' them to *res religiosae*; Trajan had to put a stop to this).[184] The law was also suspicious of the legal status of tomb-inscriptions; after all, *sepulchra familiaria* claimed to derogate from the ordinary rules of succession. Were they simply copies of provisions in wills? Certainly they sometimes were; the funeral inscription of Dasumius was in fact his entire will, and a recent inscription from the Vatican cemetery begins:[185]

'From the triple codicils of Popilius Heracla. C. Popilius Heracla to his heirs, greeting. I request and require and commit to the faith of you, my heirs, that you build me a tomb . . .'

But it is unlikely that all the hundreds of tomb inscriptions were duplicates of testamentary provisions, though people perhaps conceived of them as a kind of codicil on stone establishing *fideicommissa*. To perpetuities created by *fideicommissum* the law, as we have seen, was hostile, and the authorities were in conflict with the public; a rescript of Severus Alexander is characteristic:[186]

'Tomb inscriptions do not transfer either rights over tombs or ownership of non-religious land to freedmen.'

The public proceeded in this battle undeterred, doing what the law said was null and void and hoping (which would no doubt usually be the case) that their arrangements would never have to be put to the test of the courts—undeterred, but sometimes a little nervous, as we can see from the inscriptions:[187]

'From this tomb let all fraud and all lawyers be absent.'
'From all these things let fraud and the civil law be absent.'

CHAPTER V

PROPERTY

Perhaps more than with anything else the function of the law is concerned with distinguishing *meum* from *tuum*, that is, with the rights of property, its ownership and conveyance, with those rights other than ownership which people may have over things, such as life interest or tenancy, and with the protection of property against assaults on it like theft or damage. The fundamental concept is obviously ownership or 'title', *dominium*, and of this the Roman law in our period took what one might call a 'strong' view. Jurisprudentially speaking, ownership is a complicated notion to analyse (the question being basically 'right to the thing, yes, but as against whom?'), and different legal systems do so in different ways, even if the results they reach are not always so very different. Such problems arise, for example, as: does there here exist relative ownership (as in a feudal society, where one man owns land, but owns it 'of' his lord, who, so to speak, owns it even more)? Or how far is lawful possession of a thing the same as—or as good as—ownership of it? Ownership is an abstraction, a term of art of the law, the relationship of which to the practical fact of holding something has to be determined for any given legal system; and possession also may be—and in Roman law was—no less a legal term of art, so that you were not necessarily possessor of a thing merely because you had it in your pocket. Or again, how far is ownership good as against the government, the state, the community? We cannot begin to examine things here from this jurisprudential point of view,[1] though something will be said about the last of the above questions in Chapter VIII; by saying that the Romans took a 'strong' view about ownership, what we mean is, first, that they distinguished it sharply from possession—*dominium* was 'title', abstracted from the facts of holding. It was also, except as against the state, absolute; the Roman jurists hardly developed at all a notion of a hierarchy of ownerships, though they had it beneath their noses all the time in the regime of municipal and public land, as we shall see.[2] On the other hand they gave substantial protection to lawful possession short of ownership, sometimes even as against the owner—which is indeed a necessary corollary of regarding owner-ship as absolute; and this meant that there were many situations in which a man might have over things only 'bare' ownership or title, *nudum dominium*, that is to say ultimate title but nothing more, while someone else had all the practical rights enabling him to hold and make use of the things.

Many things were not susceptible of private ownership at all. Gaius gives a list of them (which is rather inadequate and needs to be supplemented from the *Digest*);[3] they are a very mixed bag. *Res religiosae*, tombs, we have met already; *res sacrae* were things publicly dedicated to the gods—temples and altars; and *res sanctae* were the walls and gates of cities. Then there were things belonging to all men (and hence individually to no one): the air, the sea, rivers and most harbours, and the seashore and river-banks as far as use (fishing, towing) was concerned. And there were things belonging to the (or to a) community, like public roads and buildings. Even of those things that were susceptible of individual ownership it must be realized that full private absolute *dominium ex iure Quiritium* was a strict civil law conception. Peregrines could not own anything in this full sense. What is more, the only real estate that could be thus fully owned, even by Roman citizens, was real estate in Italy, except that by a legal fiction certain communities of Roman citizens in the provinces (of which a list, though not systematic or exhaustive, is given in the *Digest*—roughly it was the bigger *coloniae*)[4] were allowed to count their land as 'Italian soil' and so have full *dominium* over it and pay no land-tax on it.[5] However, it must not be concluded that peregrine possession was unprotected or peregrine land rightless (any more than that peregrines were all unmarried because they could not have *iustae nuptiae*).[6]

Amongst those things susceptible of private ownership a natural practical distinction lies between real estate and movables. It did inevitably play a part in Roman legal arrangements, but it was unhappily overshadowed by a quite different distinction, deriving from the primitive habits of early Rome, which had in our period no real economic or social basis but survived as a useless but ubiquitous complication. According to this division, things were either *res mancipi* or not. Gaius tells us what things were *res mancipi*:[7] land and houses (provided on 'Italian soil', of course), slaves, certain animals (oxen, horses, mules and donkeys are named), and one kind of easement, the 'rustic praedial servitude' (which will be explained later). The name means 'subject to *mancipium*', and the crucial feature of the distinction was that whereas ownership of all other things could be passed from one person to another by simple delivery, *traditio*, ownership of *res mancipi* could only be passed by one or other of two elaborate formal acts, either *mancipatio* (the 'imaginary sale' with the coin and balance which we have met already)[8] or 'cession in court', *cessio in iure* (a sort of 'imaginary vindication').[9] Thus, if you merely delivered a slave you did not transfer ownership of him. If we add to this the natural point that no man could transfer more right to a thing than he himself had (*i.e.* if a man who had not got *dominium* of something conveyed it to you, however correctly as to form, even by *mancipatio*, you did not become *dominus* of it either), it will be seen that some further principle was needed to cover two situations that might regularly arise in good faith: first the situation of the man to whom a *res mancipi* was delivered without *mancipatio* by someone who was properly its owner (the recipient had it 'in his goods', *in bonis*, but how could he ever obtain full ownership of it?), and secondly the situation of the man to whom anything whatever had been delivered or mancipated by someone who was not and perhaps could not be its owner *iure Quiritium*, for example a peregrine slave-trader (the recipient was *bona fide possessor* of the thing delivered, but how could he ever obtain full ownership of it?). The principle was found in the concept of 'ripening' ownership—becoming owner by having unchallenged actual control of the thing, based upon a proper transaction in good faith that intended to pass the ownership, for a specified time. This was *usucapio*, 'acquiring (*dominium*) by use'. The specified time was quite short: two years for real estate, one year for movables. At the end of it you were full *dominus ex iure Quiritium* of anything capable of being so owned. Proof of title was therefore reasonably simple in Roman law. There was no need to go back to title deeds of the distant past, for all you needed to prove was undisturbed control for the relevant short period, and the nature and genuineness of the transaction by which you had acquired. One exception is important: ownership of anything that had been stolen could not be acquired by *usucapio* even by someone who had obtained an object of this description in good faith.

There were other ways of acquiring title to things besides conveyance (quite apart from inheritance, which we have already seen, and assignation by the authorities, to which we shall come). For example, there being no game laws, game and fish were the property of those who caught them; though in the case of creatures such as bees, pigeons or deer, so long as they had their hives or cotes or natural haunts on a man's land they were his, but if they moved permanently away they were then open to first taking.[10] Of what was found underground, in the sense of mining rights, we shall speak later; for treasure trove a rule was laid down by Hadrian (the earlier state of the law is much disputed).[11] Hadrian's rule was that what a man found on his own ground was his own, but in what he found elsewhere he must go halves with the landowner. This leaves difficult questions about what constituted treasure trove and how far searching for it was allowed (in ancient graves, for example; would a Roman Schliemann have been allowed to dig Grave Circle A at Mycenae?). The subject is too controversial to go into here. Another mode of acquisition was *alluvio*, increment of land resulting from silting or the shifting of rivers, important in an agricultural society whose rivers were 'not the placid, orderly streams to which we are accustomed'.[12] And yet another, about which the jurists loved to wrangle, was 'accession and specification': who was owner of the resulting object if A wrote in gold lettering (with his own gold) on B's paper, or painted a masterpiece on B's wooden panel, or made wine out of B's grapes or a ring out of B's silver? The wrangles were very abstract, and the important practical question was the one least discussed, namely how you could obtain compensation for your materials if they were incorporated in something which the law held now to belong to the other fellow. It was achieved by a combination of the *exceptio doli* which you could oppose against his claim to have the thing handed over if he did not reimburse you,[13] and the *actio ad exhibendum* by which you could sue for return of your material or the value of it.[14] Premises, finally, were the object of two rules of some consequence. *Superficies solo cedit*, 'that which stands on the land goes with it', was the Roman rule; a house built on my land, by whomsoever, belonged to me. A corollary of this is that ownership was, so to speak, vertical—from the ground up to the sky *ad infinitum*; so you could divide ownership up vertically, *e.g.* divide a house into two by a party wall,[15] but not horizontally —you could not own one floor of a house. You can in English law, though it has not hitherto been common ('the thing exists in various places, notably on the south side of New Square, Lincoln's Inn'),[16] and you could in Greek and Egyptian law, and at least in Egypt it continued to be done, even by Roman citizens.[17] But in Rome itself the strict rule applied; we find it being bluntly reasserted by Caracalla to some petitioner in AD 213:[18]

'If you can prove that the lower floor of the building, which rests on the ground, belongs to you, there is no doubt that the floor above, which your neighbour has added, accrues to you as owner.'

And the public (muddled perhaps, as usual) applied it to parts of tombs:[19]

'Ti. Claudius Buccio in his lifetime mancipated to C. Avillius Leschus 4 *columbaria*, 8 urns, from ground to ceiling.'

The existence and persistence of the rule is extraordinary in view of the fact that most people in Rome lived in blocks of flats (as at

Ostia); but it is so. Of upper stories nothing was to be had but tenancy.[20]

For the protection of title Roman law gave a famous action; a man who claimed that he was *dominus* of something had for its recovery the *vindicatio*, the most ancient form of which is described by Gaius:[21]

'the claimant, holding a rod and seizing the thing, said "I claim that this thing is mine by the *ius Quiritium* according to its title. As I have declared, so, behold, I have placed the rod upon it." And the opposing party did the same . . .'

The *vindicatio* was a powerful action:[22]

'for when I have proved that the thing is owned by me the possessor must restore it, unless he has pleaded an *exceptio*.'

And if the possessor refused to defend the thing (which—or a bit of it—had to be produced in court) the praetor simply handed it over to its vindicator; there was an interdict called *quem fundum* to secure that land thus undefended was restored.[23] Vindication had, however, a weakness, brought out by the fact that, as Gaius says, the opposing party had to 'do the same', *i.e.* had also to claim that he was owner; this meant that it was only available against someone who had possession in the formal legal sense. People who actually physically controlled things were not, in Roman law, necessarily possessors—particularly those who controlled them under subsidiary rights such as loan or tenancy or life-interest;[24] it has been said that possession was controlling a thing 'in the manner of an owner'.[25] Consequently, against your tenant or the holder of your thing under a life-interest you could not have a vindication,[26] but must proceed by some other means. Also it might be hard to discover who *was* the present possessor in the formal legal sense (if, for example, a thief had passed something quickly on to a fence, who had sold it to someone, who had resold it . . .). To remedy this defect one could indeed make use of the *actio ad exhibendum*, which would oblige whoever actually had the thing to produce it or pay up, and would no doubt in

most cases effectually lead you to the possessor, but there is a
very important warning given by Gaius:[27]

> 'Anyone who has decided to have an action to recover some-
> thing ought to consider whether he can obtain possession by
> some interdict; for it is much more convenient to be in
> possession oneself and make the other man take on the diffi-
> culties of being plaintiff than to be plaintiff when the other man
> is in possession.'

Possession was 'nine points of the law'; if you could get it you
had no need to worry about proving title, for it was the other
fellow who must prove his.

Ownership was protected by the *ius civile*; legal possession as
such was under the protection of the praetor and his *ius honorarium*.
He used it most notably in the two cases of 'ripening ownership',
by giving the *actio Publiciana*, a remedy invented probably in
Cicero's time, to the man who had acquired a *res mancipi* without
mancipatio and held it *in bonis* and to the *bona fide possessor* of
something obtained from a non-owner, if they were deprived of
their thing during the time while their *usucapio* was running
(since vindication was not open to them because they could not
yet say 'I claim that this thing is mine by the *ius Quiritium*').
The *formula* of the *actio Publiciana* was a legal fiction; you vindicated 'as if' your period of *usucapio* was complete. And there
was more; the main danger for the man who held a thing *in
bonis* might be from the *dominus* himself, who although he had,
say, sold it, still had title and could therefore vindicate it. So the
praetor gave the *exceptio rei venditae et traditae* which could be set
up against such a vindication. (It is in this case that Gaius, though
he alone of the jurists, and in no other case but this, does use
language of relative ownership; he says that A 'owns *ex iure
Quiritium*' and B, the purchaser, while *usucapio* is proceeding,
'holds *in bonis*' and 'the ownership is divided'.[28] Nowadays the
rather unfortunate term 'bonitary owner' is used. In any case, it
was an ephemeral position, because full ownership would 'ripen'
by *usucapio*.) It is clear that already by Cicero's day *mancipatio* had
become a bore, and the praetor, by granting the Publician action,

K

'transformed Roman ownership. Henceforward the recipient of a *res mancipi* by *traditio* was for nearly all practical purposes in the position of an owner.'[29]

This is not the end of praetorian protection of possession. There were the famous interdicts, known by the opening words of their announcements in the praetor's edict (and indeed, the only way ultimately to define legal possession in Roman law is to say that it was such possession as would have the protection of the Publician and the interdicts). There was, for example, *quorum bonorum*, given to people to whom the praetor allowed 'entry to an estate' on intestacy so that they could actually get in the assets from whoever had them.[30] There was *unde vi*, to get back possession of what had been seized by force; Cicero's speech *pro Caecina* was in a suit under this heading.[31] And there were the two interdicts to settle the vital question who was to be possessor and who plaintiff in a vindication: *utrubi* for movables and *uti possidetis* for real estate (which will serve as a specimen):[32]

'as you [plural] now possess, I forbid force to be used to stop you now possessing.'

This, then, is what you actually did if you wanted to recover something you claimed to be yours: you went to the praetor and put to him a *prima facie* case for possession; if satisfied, the praetor granted you possession and the interdict to prevent its disturbance —and then it was up to the other man. It must be noticed, however, that these interdicts were not just 'injunctions' (though some others in effect were); they were themselves a kind, a very elaborate and complex kind, of lawsuit.[33] The complexities are of no modern interest, but one point is important—they involved the ancient 'wagers of law', the money that you forfeited if you lost the case,[34] and hence the disincentive or penalty for litigation that was spoken of in Chapter III. Consequently one wonders whether the poor man could risk an interdict on these terms against a rich one (which may be relevant to the expropriation of yeomen farmers which troubled the Gracchi), even supposing he could actually get possession (which is even more relevant).

*

Overwhelmingly the most important kind of property in the Roman world was land. It was upon the rents of land that a man must live if he was to cut a respectable figure in the community, and those who made money in trade or manufacture hastened to invest it in real estate, like Trimalchio and Trimalchio's friend, the 'son of a king':[35]

> 'I don't owe anyone a penny. I've never had to compound; no one's ever said "pay up" to me in the forum. I've bought a bit of land and some plate, and I feed twenty bellies and one dog.'

One interesting demonstration of this was made by looking at the rules about what guardians must do to administer a ward's property; they had to purchase land as far as they could, and, for this purpose only, they were allowed to accumulate money in a deposit account instead of putting it out at interest.[36]

The enormous work begun by Augustus, the taking and maintaining of a full census in all parts of the empire, produced a system of land registration, of which a little is told us in the *Digest* title 'on the census':[37]

> 'name of property, in what state and locality situated, with names of two adjoining properties; arable: acreage sown in past ten years; vines in vineyards: number; olives: acreage and number of trees; ley: acreage cut in past ten years; pasture: acreage; commercial woodland. Valuation: by person making the return.'

The same kind of return can be seen in the 'Table of Veleia', the list of landholders on the basis of whose property Trajan's scheme for the maintenance of poor children was based:[38]

> 'P. Atilius Saturninus, by his agent Castricius Secundus, returns the property called Fonteianus in the territory of Veleia, subdistrict Iunonius, neighbours Atilius Adulescens, Maelius Severus, and public land.'

From early times, whenever Rome gave new land (whether in Italy or abroad) to Roman citizens she did so by the strict appor-

tionment of lots on a grid system, the so-called 'centuriation', done
by surveyors, traces of which are still being seen from the air and
on the ground all over the lands of what was once the Roman
empire.[39] The resulting cataster was not merely listed by names
and drawn out on paper but incised as a map on bronze, one copy
kept locally and one in Rome; large sections have turned up of the
catastral map (on stone) of the territory of *colonia Arausio*, Orange
in Gaul,[39a] in which rivers, roads and other features can be seen
winding across the inexorable grid which largely ignores them.
In each section of the grid the acreages of private land, city's
rent-paying land (*ager vectigalis*) and Roman public land are
indicated. The tenants of the *ager vectigalis* are named, and their
rents given, and one can see their holdings sometimes spreading
into several sections of the grid; unfortunately, of the private
land no individual plots or owners are mentioned—presumably
either because it was 'Italian soil' and paid no land-tax, or else
because this particular document was only concerned to regulate
the rents of *ager vectigalis*—so we cannot tell whether account was
taken in the cataster (which is of Vespasian's time) of changes in
the ownership pattern of private land since the original distribution of lots. Except in Egypt, which had, as usual, a minutely
pedantic system of land registration,[40] conveyances were not
(or not everywhere) registered as they took place,[41] so rectifica-
tion of the register would have to wait till the next full census.
Consequently, if land-tax was in question, interim arrangements
about its payment would have to be made in contracts of sales:[42]

> 'If a vendor of land makes no mention of land-tax, knowing it
> to be subject to such tax, he will be liable on the contract.'

Land-tax seems to have been thought of as a charge on the fruits,[43]
and therefore normally fell to be paid by whoever had the right
to them, *i.e.* a tenant if there was one—but not always,[44] and not
if the lease specified that the landlord was to pay, as seems to have
been regular in Egypt.[45] In litigation about boundaries of land
(which evidently could not always be settled by the good offices
of an *arbiter ex compromisso* such as we have met at Herculaneum)
the judge, we are told, must look to ancient records, if any,

otherwise he must follow the evidence of the most recent census unless subsequent alienations or other changes are proved;[46] it is interesting that this shows that even the census-list, being based on individual declarations, was only evidentiary, not automatically proof. In all these catastral matters there appears on the scene the rather grand professional figure of the surveyor, the *agrimensor*:[47]

> 'Against a land-surveyor [*i.e.* who is alleged to have surveyed wrongly] the praetor gives an action on the facts. For we ought not to be cheated by surveyors; it is very important not to be misled in statements of area if, for example, there is boundary litigation or if a buyer or a vendor wants to know what area is up for sale. It is an action on the facts because in former days it was held that there was no contract of hire of services with a surveyor but that his services were rendered as a gratuitous benefit and any remuneration was an honorarium. . . . And the action is only for fraud; it is thought to be quite enough pressure on surveyors if they are liable for fraud only, since they have no contractual liability. If a surveyor has just been incompetent the man who employed him has only himself to blame; even if he was negligent he will be safe, and even if he has taken a fee he will not be liable for negligence because of the words of the edict [for the praetor of course knows that surveyors do sometimes in fact take fees].'

*

A certain inroad upon ownership was made by those very necessary sets of rights known by the Romans as servitudes, *servitutes*. Many of these were connected with real estate, 'praedial servitudes', and were of great antiquity; rights of way and water are the characteristic cases—the right to go across someone's property or drive a cart or cattle over it:[48]

> 'Private road of C. and Q. Largus, sons of Lucius, and C. Olius Salvus. Owes right of way to the estate known as Enianus and . . .';

the right to draw water from it, or dig sand or lime on it, or to

make a neighbour's building bear the weight of your wall. Some
of them were negative rather than positive—to prevent a neighbouring property from obscuring your light or its rain-water
spouts from dripping on your building. But none could be *in
faciendo*, that is, you could have a servitude to make someone put
up with acts done by you,[49] or to restrain him from acts affecting
you, but not to make him do something himself. Another main
rule was that servitudes, once established, ran with the land;
whoever was, or became, owner of the 'servient' property must
for ever allow the holder of the 'dominant' property the relevant
right. The right must, however, be 'useful' to the dominant
property—perhaps we should rather say 'necessary', *i.e.* for its
proper running; for servitudes could not be used for a commercial
advantage. You could create them against your property by will
or by formal conveyance ('rustic' praedial servitudes were *res
mancipi*), or you could alienate your property retaining a servitude
over it (*e.g.* sell half your estate but keep a right of way over the
piece sold). Provincial land only admitted of contractual arrangements, 'pacts and stipulations',[50] but in all other cases the man
who had a servitude had a 'real' right to it, a right *in rem*, like an
owner, not just a contractual right, and could vindicate his
servitude against the holder of the servient property. To protect
some of the ancient servitudes there were also interdicts given by
the praetor: *de itinere, de aqua*, even *de cloacis*:[51]

> 'I forbid force to be used to prevent A from clearing and
> repairing the drain that leads from his building into yours,
> object of suit.'

Some praedial servitudes, again probably because they were the
ancient agricultural ones, could be brought into being by use
from 'time out of mind';[52] all could be lost by non-use, or non-
resistance to breaches of them, for two years.[53] The *Digest* titles
on servitudes also contain some discussion of the problems of the
common wall (a source of urban friction). It was perhaps thought
of as servient and dominant on both sides; neither party has a
right of demolition for repair, says Gaius,[54] because both parties
are *domini*. Thus, someone wrote to the jurist Proculus:[55]

'A man called Hiberus, who has a block of flats behind my grain-store, has built a bath-house against the common wall. But he is not allowed to attach pipes to a common wall . . . and besides, they are making the wall red-hot. I wish you would have a word with him and stop him committing this illegality.'

Proculus agreed that this was illegal, but we are told in another passage[56] that he was also quite firm that having a bath-house against a common wall was not in itself an offence, even if it led to dampness (*i.e.* that the law did not recognize an offence of 'nuisance'). Neratius seems to have disagreed 'if the wall was perpetually wet and harmed the neighbour'. It is really 'nuisance' again that is being discussed in the diverting passage about the cheese-factory:[57]

'Aristo gave an opinion to Caerellius Vitalis that he did not think smoke could legitimately be allowed to penetrate from a cheese-factory into buildings higher up the road [unless there is the possibility of a servitude of such a kind]. Aristo also says: no more can you throw water or anything else from a building higher up on to those lower down. You may only so behave on your own property as not to send things down on to someone else's, and smoke is just the same as water. So the higher man can have an action against the lower "that he has no right to perform this act". He says that Alfenus somewhere remarks that you can have an action to stop a man hewing stone on his land if the chippings fall on yours. And so Aristo says that the man who ran a cheese-factory under license at Minturnae could be stopped from allowing his smoke to penetrate a building higher up; but he would have an action on his contract against the town of Minturnae.'

There was a second main class of servitudes, which seem so unlike rights of way that one might well wonder what they did have in common; the answer is that they also were *iura in re aliena*, 'real' rights, not just contractual ones, over something of which someone else was *dominus*, protected by a vindication—modifications of ownership, in fact. These were the 'personal' servitudes:

usufruct, the right to enjoy property and take its produce; *usus* without the *fructus*; and *habitatio*, the right to occupy a dwelling. The interest could be for the life of the beneficiary, one's widow, for example, or for any shorter term, such as 'for my widow until she remarries', and it could be set up in numerous ways but especially by will. It ran with the beneficiary, not with the property, and was extinguished with the beneficiary's death, which raised a problem about usufruct to municipalities (which do not die), settled at hundred years:[58]

'because that is the term of a very long-lived individual.'

The most interesting rule about usufruct matches that about praedial servitudes, and illustrates the ancient lack of interest in property development. Not only could you not use the property for commercial purposes (unless it was already so used), but you could not use it for any new purpose at all, nor improve it. A passage characteristic of many is:[59]

'If there was a legacy of usufruct of a house, the younger Nerva says you can put in lamps and pictures and ornaments, but you cannot change the internal partitions . . .'

There could be a usufruct over other things besides real estate—over slaves, for example, who must be used according to their accustomed functions.[60] Moreover, a *senatusconsultum* (of uncertain date) caused the lawyers a good deal of trouble by allowing what seemed logically contradictory—usufruct of fungibles (things consumed by the very fact of using them, notably money); the embarrassment of trying to make working rules for this monstrosity conceived by the legislature is apparent in the *Digest* title about it, but it no doubt met a perfectly sensible social need, as can be seen if one thinks of a man leaving his widow a life interest in his entire estate (which might naturally include consumable as well as non-consumable items).[61]

*

Praedial servitudes were essentially subsidiary to the economic exploitation of property; personal servitudes were essentially alimentary in function. Only with tenancy do we come to the heart

of the economic structure. Now a place such as this is not where
Roman lawyers would have discussed the law of landlord and
tenant; for them it was pure contract, to be dealt with under
'obligations: contract of letting and hiring'. And this is a significant fact; the tenant of land and premises had no 'real' right, no
ius in re aliena, over his land or premises, as the usufructuary did,
but only a contract of tenancy; neither did he have possession in
the legal sense. Consequently, if there was controversy over lights
or nuisance, or even if he was ejected from his tenancy by someone, he had no 'locus standi' to bring any proceedings; they were
the affair of the *dominus*. His only redress was to sue the *dominus*
on his contract. 'Sale breaks tenancy' is one aspect of this; if the
dominus sold the property over your head he was not obliged to
sell it 'subject to existing tenancy' (though he normally would),[62]
and the moment the purchaser became owner he could do what he
liked with it, and you had no redress against him because you had
no contract with him. The point has often been made[63] that the
law of landlord and tenant, like that of hire of services—indeed,
all the parts of that strange confederation of legal rules subsumed
under the 'contract of letting and hiring'—reflects the power of
the rich over the poor in Rome and the lack of interest of the
lawyers, who were rich, in developing protections for the poor.
Being a rather facile point it is not always given the qualification
it deserves.

Let us begin with a little about tenancy of houses and flats.
An advertisement in a street at Pompeii runs thus:[64]

'Apartment block known as Arriana Polliana: landlord Cn.
Alleius Nigidius Maius. To let from 15th July next: shops with
porticoes, high-class flats and one house. Potential tenants
[? in chief] apply to Primus, slave of Cn. Alleius Nigidius
Maius.'

All the more, in the big cities like Ostia and Rome, were people
normally flat-dwellers, as can be seen from the archaeological
remains. The jostling, insanitary life of those narrow streets can
be savoured not only in Juvenal[65] and Petronius but equally in
certain titles of the *Digest*, especially 9. 3, 'concerning things

poured or thrown down'. It must be borne in mind that not only the humble were so accommodated; so were quite well-to-do people, perfectly capable of litigating over their rights, such as the bachelor sons of the nobility.[66] What those rights were in detail would depend on the terms of the contract, and so on the bargaining strength of the parties, but in general for the tenant they were confined to justifications of various sorts for withholding his rent. (Thus, he was entitled to vacant and undisturbed possession for the whole of his term, and to unblocked light.)[67] The literary sources are full of well-known references to fires and collapses; here are just two:[68]

'Two of my shop properties have collapsed and the rest are full of cracks. The tenants have decamped—so have the mice.'

'Town property brings good returns, but it's terribly risky. If there were any way of stopping houses perpetually burning down in Rome I'd sell up my farms and buy town property every time.'

This feature is reflected in the *Digest*, for example in 19. 2. 19. 6 (from which it also appears that rent was sometimes paid for a long period in advance). People like Cicero did not, of course, collect their own rents. It looks as if the normal arrangement was for the owner to let *en bloc* to a contractor or tenant in chief, *conductor*, who then sub-let for profit:[69]

'A man took a lease of a block of apartments at a rent of thirty and sub-let individual flats for a total rent of forty. The owner demolished the block on the ground that it was unsafe. Query, for how much can the tenant in chief sue?'

It was also a principle that the lesser had a lien, even if not specifically contracted for, on the tenant's household effects, his *invecta et illata*, not only against the rent but to cover dilapidations as well.[70] Martial maliciously mocks an enemy 'moving out', as he watches the little procession with a few sticks of broken furniture trail off down the road:[71]

'O blot upon the Kalends of July! Vacerra, I've seen your luggage; I've seen it—the bits that weren't held back in lieu of two years' rent...'

A vital, but controversial, figure on the Roman scene is the *colonus*, the tenant of land. In our period he is not the tied serf of late Rome, though what connexion he has with the latter, and how far early symptoms of serfdom are to be found in his condition, are much argued questions.[72] There are, of course, many possible regimes of land management: the subsistence farmer on his small plot, working it with his family (or the joint family, though that is more associated with pastoralism); the cash-crop farmer with a big acreage farming by means of plantation-slaves; the same big landlord letting to free (or part-free) tenants and living on the rents; the state enterprise. It can be seen that there was a history of change in these regimes in Italy, but it was a very complex history. The decline of subsistence and simple cash-crop farming and the rise of the *latifundia* is an oft-told tale of the middle Republic;[73] the *latifundia* of the late Republic were characteristically slave-plantations, but they were far from being the only farming regimes in Cicero's day.[73a]

Free tenants undoubtedly existed. In the agrarian writers it is only with Columella in Nero's time that they appear as a substantial alternative to the plantation, but a lot depended on geographical location.[74] The younger Pliny, in Nerva's and Trajan's day (from whom we learn most on this subject), let his land to tenants as a matter of course; his only other form of management was an experiment—of which he was clearly nervous—in putting his tenants on to a metayage system instead of a money rent.[75] However, as long as care is taken not to muddle this question up with the quite different question of the survival (or revival) of free small owner-farmers, we can fairly make the generalization that our period saw some increase, beginning perhaps at the end of the Republic, of tenant farming in Italy.[76] Reasons would take us too far from the subject of the present book—except to say (because the legal evidence is relevant) that, since the tenants often used slave labour themselves,[77] the rise of the tenant system need not have any direct connection with a decline in the availability of slaves; it was a change of management.

The law relating to the *colonus* is usually emphasized as showing him to have been a humble fellow—no 'gentleman farmer'—scraping a living under the eye of his landlord's bailiff. No actual contract of tenancy from Italy survives, but the picture is by and large fair, as long as care is taken to see that it is not overdrawn. Here, first, are the main rules:

1 The contract could be in any terms, depending on the bargaining position. We do find oppressive conditions, such as 'no fires liable to damage the neighbour', or even 'no fires',[78] but the shortage of tenants of which Pliny constantly complains must have given them, at least in his time, a scarcity value, the effect of which will be seen when we come to abatements.

2 There was no right *in rem* and no possession, so no security of tenure. The regular tenancy period was short—the old censorial *lustrum* of five years (it was at the end of a *lustrum* that Pliny rearranged his rental system);[79] but if the tenant continued in occupation afterwards and his landlord acquiesced there was an implied continuing tenancy from year to year, not a mere 'occupation at will'.[80]

3 The tenant must cultivate. If he decamped without cause he was liable for the full rent of his term.[81]

4 He only acquired ownership of the produce when it had been gathered, for it belonged to the landlord and required gathering as a sort of *traditio*.[82]

5 He must restore the property exactly as it was, though, unlike the usufructuary, if he made necessary improvements even without express agreement he could claim their cost in an action on his contract.[83]

6 The landlord had an automatic lien on the produce against the rent.[84]

7 The normal system, to judge from the *Digest*, was a money rent, though there is probably nothing the matter with D. 19. 2. 19. 3, which envisages part of it at least being in produce; this was regular in Egypt, at least for wheat and barley land.[85] The

alternative was metayage or the 'partiary' colonate, whereby landlord and tenant each took an agreed share of each actual crop (we hear of half).[86]

Given these rules, it comes as a surprise to find scholars saying that 'the privileged position of the English landlord seems to stand out' (as against the Roman).[87] The main point here is that the Roman tenant, except under metayage, had a legal right to abatement of rent if 'Act of God' destroyed crops or made use of the land impossible,[88] though it is added that it was just because the parties were economically on such unequal terms that the law had to make a rule and not just leave it to the terms of the contract.[89] Pliny's letters make it clear that abatements were the landlord's great bogey;[90] precisely for this reason he determined to try the metayage system, and it looks as if this was a lowering of the status of the *coloni*, for Pliny was going to put in slaves or freedmen over them to keep an eye on their work and on the crops. They do not seem to have been able (or wanted?) to offer any resistance to the change. On the other hand, there is some evidence throughout our period of tenants of a less humble kind. Columella refers to the 'urban *colonus*, who prefers to farm with a slave staff', and quotes the judgment of a much older agriculturalist on such tenants.[91] In some passages of Pliny we hear of tenants of substantial properties: he writes to a tenant (obviously sole tenant) of a 'little farm' worth one hundred thousand sesterces; and he says that his big alimentary estate, worth well over five hundred thousand, will always find 'a *dominus* to manage it'—though it is true that that property had become *ager vectigalis*.[92] The most significant remark comes in a letter to his wife's grandfather about restoring the economic health of a derelict property, because it shows that tenants of larger holdings were not necessarily just agents subletting,[93] nor just absentees:[94]

'Your Villa Camilliana in Campania is in a bad state. But all my friends are urban intellectuals; administering a rustic property needs a rough, country sort of chap who won't find the work heavy and the duties sordid and the remoteness bad for the nerves.'

Finally, *instrumentum fundi* must not be allowed to mislead. It was the equipment of a farm, from olive-presses and wine-vats to slaves, and it is minutely defined, both in the *Digest* title about letting and hiring and in other texts about legacy or usufruct.[95] Landlords often let their farms 'with all equipment'; but it cannot be assumed that they were under a duty to do so or that all tenants were so humble as to require it. The texts never say this; they are concerned only to define *instrumentum*, that is, to settle what it included if it did appear in a contract or a will.

The substantial tenant of land turns up in another way; but this time, though his position was technically a tenancy, in terms of economic exploitation he was really more of a *dominus* than a *colonus* (an ambiguity reflected in the ancient texts, and in the passionate and deeply opposed modern arguments).[96] Much land belonged either to the Roman state or to individual munici-palities—*ager publicus* and *ager vectigalis*, respectively. The normal way of exploiting it was to let it to tenants at a rent. In Julius Caesar's colony of Urso the tenancy was for the ordinary cen-sorial *lustrum*,[97] but the most widespread arrangement, at any rate in the time of the Principate, was to let for a very long period or in perpetuity, which made the tenant to all intents and purposes *dominus* provided the rent was paid. This system, which had parallels in (but was not necessarily derived from) Greece and Egypt,[98] was widespread and important.[99] The cataster of Orange reveals large portions of the territory of that colony under a municipal rent,[100] and many of the landholders in the Table of Veleia declared their estates 'subject to deduction of vectigal' (the rent).[101] Such properties could be very large, for it was a particularly satisfactory way of exploiting marginal land. In spite of controversy, it is reasonably probable that in our period, so long as the rent was paid, the tenant had a 'real' right to the property and could transmit it by inheritance;[102] there was a suit *de fundo vectigali* available to him, like the Publician.[103] Conse-quently, one is not surprised to find that the words 'selling' and 'buying' are used of these properties quite as commonly as 'letting' and 'hiring'. Pliny merely says of his alimentary estate, which he has turned into *ager vectigalis*, that it will be 'worth a bit less because of the rent-charge'.[104]

Much the same kind of anomalous arrangement was *superficies*, the 'building lease', perpetual and heritable on payment of a rent called *solarium*.[105] There was an interdict to protect it, and an action, according to the *Digest*—again, much disputed and no less energetically defended.[106] An interesting inscription records the grant of such a lease to the custodian of the column of Marcus Aurelius.[107] First comes his petition to the emperor, evidently successful, then a letter from the finance department to the works department, dated 6 August, AD 193:

'Aelius Achilles and Cl. Perpetuus Flavianus Eutychus to Epaphroditus, greeting. Assign to Adrastus, the curator of the column of the deified Marcus, all tiles and building materials from huts, cottages and appropriate structures, for him to build a dwelling-house as he wishes, to be his property and transmissible to his heirs.'

There follows a letter to the timber department, to let Adrastus have timber at treasury cost price, and finally a letter to the surveyor's department:

. . . 'we therefore require you to order assignment to Adrastus, freedman of the emperor, of the area indicated by him. He will pay *solarium* in the usual manner.'

The emperors, if they were not at the start, soon became the biggest landowners of all. The mode of exploitation of their lands, which were necessarily run as a government department, is revealed at least for a part of Tunisia (how far it can be generalized is uncertain) by a celebrated series of inscriptions, too long to quote here.[108] Here is a piece of the earliest one:

'For the safety of our Augustus, Imperator Caesar Trajan, princeps, and of all the divine household of him who is entitled best of emperors, Germanicus, Parthicus. Rules laid down by Licinius Maximus and Felicior, freedman of the emperor, procurators, on the precedent of the *lex Manciana*. To those persons dwelling on the estate of the Villa Magna of Varianus, viz. Mappalia Siga, it is permitted to cultivate lands left un-surveyed on the terms of the *lex Manciana*, namely that the cultivator shall have right of enjoyment (*usum proprium*). Of the produce of the said land they shall be required to give fractions to the owners, lessees or bailiffs of the estate on the terms of the *lex Manciana*, . . . a third part of the wheat from the threshing-floor, a third part of the barley ditto, a fourth part of the beans ditto, a third part of the wine from the vat, a third part of the pressed oil, a sextarius of honey per hive . . .'

There follows a mutilated section referring to *superficiei usum* and the right to leave by testament, and then:

'. . . the *coloni* who live on the estate of Villa Magna or Mappalia Siga shall be required to give to the owners, lessees or bailiffs of the same, fully, annually, two days' work per man for ploughing, (. . .) days' work for harvest, and for cultivation of each kind one day's work, viz. two in all.'

Here we have great tracts of country under the oversight of treasury officials, the procurators. There seem to be still some private landowners about, but being surrounded by treasury property they are simply brought under the same rules. The treasury lands are let to tenants in chief or contractors, *conductores*, who sublet to *coloni* (here certainly humble and oppressed, according to their own complaints). On *subseciva*, uncatastrated land of a marginal kind, in order to make cultivation worth while, the *coloni* are given a kind of *superficies*, a heritable and alienable perpetuity subject to rent. The rent here is in kind (indeed it is metayage, on the basis of roughly a third of the produce), but there is also a corvée obligation of six days' work annually on the landlord's or contractor's own portion. It was this latter that got overstepped and was the subject of complaints and petitions, and one can see how easily a tied peasantry might develop.[109] Perhaps the most interesting feature of these documents is the recurrence in them of the *lex Manciana* or *cultura Manciana* as a precedent for this type of exploitation (with the three features of 'partiary' tenancy, perpetuity and corvée); it goes right on into Vandal times, for in the 'Tablettes Albertini' contracts are for the sale of plots 'from the *culturae Mancianae* of X on the estate which is owned by Y' (*i.e.* private as well as treasury land). The usual conjecture is that Mancia must have been one of the great Tunisian landlords in pre-Flavian days, before the state took over most of the African estates, and that he must have invented this regime for his own properties.

Ownership of what lay beneath the surface of private land went with ownership of the land, on the 'vertical' principle. This is important for minerals, especially the precious metals of the coinage, but we know practically nothing else about the matter as far as private land is concerned, which is a great pity, because in Cicero's day some important mining areas were still privately owned.[110] The little we do know is a mixed bag, and unhelpful: a much suspected *Digest* text appears to say that Ulpan thought— and perhaps therefore others disagreed—that a usufructuary could not only work mines on a property if such was the normal exploitation of it, but even open new ones if not to the detriment of cultivation;[111] on the other hand, the elder Pliny refers more than once to a senatorial prohibition of mining in Italy, perhaps confined to precious metals, apparently still in force in his day.[112] Under the Principate mining properties rapidly passed into the hands of the emperors,[113] and of the regime of mines under this dispensation we are better—though still tantalizingly—informed by two inscriptions from the state mining district of Vipasca, Aljustrel in Portugal.[114] They are usually quoted in books on social life for their general regulations governing life in a 'fiscal' community—grants to concessionaires to run baths and barber's shops, freedom of the schoolmaster from rates, and so on; but something has also been wrung from them about the property situation.[115] Here is a brief quotation:

'Silver workings are to be exploited according to the regulations in the present code. The prices shall be governed by the liberal decision of the most sacred emperor Hadrian Augustus, viz. that ownership of that part which belongs to the treasury shall

L

pass to him who first deposits the price of the working and pays four thousand sesterces to the treasury.'

The schema was somewhat as follows: the land belonged to the treasury; by what is described as 'ancient custom' half of what it yielded was a 'treasury part', belonging automatically to the treasury—which reminds one, perhaps significantly, of Hadrian's rule about treasure trove. The staker of a claim could have ownership of the other half of the yield by paying down (a) his license money and (b) a standard sum of four thousand sesterces which, as it were, 'bought out' the treasury's half and made him owner of the whole yield. This is really very like the 'partiary' tenancy of the emperor's agricultural land. The concession had a time-limit, and was withdrawn if the concessionaire failed to work the mine, but while it was valid he had a 'real' and not merely a contractual right to what it yielded. What we are unfortunately not told is what happened to the precious metals so mined; presumably the treasury bought them from the *coloni*.

*

The main offences against property are damage and theft, and the *Digest* titles on these are, next to that on 'letting and hiring', the most interesting of all from the historian's point of view.[116] The law of damage to property was regulated by a statute, the *lex Aquilia*, enacted before the beginning of our period, and extended in its scope and effectiveness by juristic interpretation and by the *ius honorarium*. The offence was *damnum iniuria datum*, 'loss caused contrary to the law', and the original statute dealt very baldly with two cases: killing of a man's slave or cattle, and destroying any other property of his by burning or breaking. It was soon held that 'breaking' could cover any kind of ruining; and though the statute concerned only the direct causing of physical injury by a man with his own hands, the praetors increasingly allowed so many *actiones utiles* (that is, actions granted not by the statute but by the praetor on the analogy of the statute) that it came to cover many indirect ways of causing damage, harm, or loss. For anyone interested in the arguments of the law there is great fascination in studying the extent to which the

Romans conceived and worked out notions about remote causes of damage, damage by negligence, contributory negligence (*i.e.* when both parties are partly to blame), damage by doing nothing at all or by doing something you were entitled to do, and so on. It can be seen from the *Digest* fragments that the lawyers discussed and decided many cases of all these kinds, though they did not produce a general 'theory of negligence', but it is beyond our scope here to give a proper account of the topic from this standpoint.[117] The offence was not a crime; it grounded an action in the civil courts. Roman law did not draw the line between civil and criminal in quite the place where we are accustomed to draw it, and the action for damage was like the action for theft, a civil action, but for a penalty. This comes out in the fact that if the defendant admitted the damage he had to pay just the simple assessed value, but if he contested, and lost, he had to pay double; and also in the fact that liability did not pass to a man's heir (as a debt, for example, would). How the value of the damaged object was arrived at involves much-disputed problems,[118] but it certainly took into account such things as the inheritance a slave would have come into if he had not been killed, or the decline in value of a chariot team if one of the horses was killed. Only a *dominus* was entitled to a statutory Aquilian action, but the praetor gave *utiles actiones* to others, for example to peregrines (and against them), with a fiction that they were Roman citizens,[119] and to usufructuaries, holders of a thing in pledge and *bona fide possessores*. [120] One text gives a father an Aquilian action for damage done to his *filius familias*, and another (usually held to be post-classical) to a free adult for his own personal injuries.[121] But the best way we can suggest the scope of the law of damage is by quoting a few of the fragments (all, therefore, from *Digest* 9. 2):

4 pr. 'If I kill your slave when he is making a burglarious attack on me I shall not be liable, for natural reason allows self-defence against danger.'

7.4. 'If someone kills another in a wrestling match or the pancratium or boxing, if it is in a public contest no Aquilian action lies, because the damage is held to have been done for the sake of glory and valour, not with intent to injure. But this is not true of a slave, because it is freeborn people who go in for contests. It applies, however, to a *filius familias*.'

7.6. 'Celsus raises the case of someone who gave poison instead of medicine, and says he furnished a cause of death [*i.e.* did not actually kill] like one who gives a sword to a lunatic; neither of these, he said, is liable under the Aquilian, only an "action on the facts".'

11 pr. 'Mela says, if some people were playing a ball game and someone knocked the ball harder than usual and propelled it against the hand of a barber, so that a slave under the barber's hand had his throat cut by a jerk of the razor, that the Aquilian lies against whoever was to blame. Proculus says it is the barber; and certainly if he was shaving people in a place where people customarily played games or where many people passed by, blame attaches to him; but one might also reasonably say that a man who commits himself to a barber who has his chair in a dangerous place has only himself to blame.'

27.29. 'If you give a glass cup to have glass filigree attached; if the workman breaks it through incompetence he will be liable for wrongful damage, but if the glass had faulty cracks he can be excused. So craftsmen, when things of this sort are given to them, usually put into the contract that the job is not at their risk.'

33 pr. 'If you have killed my slave I do not think that personal feelings can be brought into the reckoning—as for example if someone has killed your natural son on whom you would put an extremely high value—but only his market value to the public.'

44.1–45 pr. 'When a slave wounds or kills with his master's knowledge the master is undoubtedly liable to an Aquilian action. Knowledge here means sufferance, *i.e.* he who could have stopped it is liable if he failed to do so.'

52.1. 'A shopkeeper had put a lamp on a stone in the road one night. Some passer-by abstracted the lamp, and the shopkeeper pursued him. . . . The man began to beat the shopkeeper with a spiked whip which he carried, and this exacerbated the fight, in which eventually the shopkeeper poked out his adversary's eye. He said "Surely I shall not be held to have done wrongful damage? For it was I who was first struck with the whip." I replied that unless he had put the man's eye out deliberately he did not seem to have committed wrongful damage.'

The protections against damage were not exhausted by the possibilities of the Aquilian action. The praetor offered the action which we have met already, for damage from things poured or thrown down into the streets:[122]

'Against the person dwelling in that place from which something has been thrown or poured on to a place where the public walk or stand, I will give an action for double the damage caused.'

This, says Ulpian,[122a] is unquestionably a most valuable provision, for it is in the public interest that people should be able to walk the streets without fear or danger; it does not seem to have been very effectual in Rome, to go by Juvenal.[123] But a remarkable feature of this edict is that there was a penalty if a free man was killed by the falling object—not 'double the damage', because you could not put a money value on a free man, but a fixed sum —and if injured he could have medical expenses and loss of earnings taken into account. Another very ancient remedy of the law was the *actio de pauperie*, for damage by animals—not wild animals, who had no *dominus*, but ordinary animals misbehaving themselves (dogs biting, horses kicking and so on); again you could recover for medical treatment and loss of earnings.[124]

The crash of falling *insulae* (or the menace of rising *insulae*) might be deleterious to neighbours; two interestingly developed sets of rules gave people an opportunity to anticipate damage to their property or amenities. They were already fully in existence in Cicero's day,[125] and lasted all through our period. The first was 'denunciation of new building', *operis novi nuntiatio*: if anybody appeared to be about to erect or demolish some structure[126] on his or other (even public) land, and you believed you had some right to prevent him, such as servitude or potential damage to your property, you must go to the spot and serve notice upon the workmen or whoever was there. The work must then stop, and the man who had ordered it must give security or promises that the work was not inconsistent with your rights, and that if it was adjudged so to be he would undo it; if he refused, the praetor would make him undo it at once, but if he did give security you could not stop him proceeding but only take him to court on his promises afterwards.[127] (Incidentally, the praetor might require you to take an oath that your denunciation was not merely vexatious.) The second set of rules went under the title of *damnum infectum*, 'damage not yet done'. If you had reason to fear that someone's neglect of his building or other property was likely to do harm to yours you could apply to the authorities and (having sworn that your proceedings were not vexatious) require him to give security or make promises to make good any damage caused; his refusal in this case would lead to your being given possession of the property concerned.[128] It is proper to say 'the authorities' here because, as Ulpian points out:[129]

'Since the case of anticipated damage requires haste, and the praetor thinks it might be a dangerous delay if he reserved jurisdiction for himself, he rightly thought that this could be reasonably delegated to municipal magistrates.'

Some of what Ulpian says about *damnum infectum* comes from the part of his treatise on the edict which dealt with the powers of local magistrates; and the surviving portion of the *lex Rubria*, the statute setting out the powers of local magistrates in the citizen towns of Cisalpine Gaul, begins with two prolix paragraphs about their competence in *damnum infectum*.[130] There is also a papyrus, dated 26 January, AD 121:[131]

'To Demetrius, controller of the Oxyrhynchite district, from Tasionys, also known as Dionysia, daughter of Dionysius, of Oxyrhynchus, and Ammonius son of Paseis, of the Little Oasis—Tasionys with authority of her guardian Demetrius Theon, son of Theon, of Oxyrhynchus: We own adjoining houses in the Metroon quarter, and a neighbouring house is owned by Philo son of Dionysius and [several other names]. This house is in danger of collapse through extreme age; wherefore, foreseeing danger to ourselves and families, especially since the said house overlooks both our courtyards, we request that a copy of this notice be served on each of them by the court runner, so that having warning in writing they may put their house in a safe condition or else know that they will be responsible for all future danger and consequent loss.' (The notice was served on all parties, the same day.)

For works liable to divert flood-waters on to your land there was an ancient suit *aquae pluviae arcendae*; Cicero used its definitions as examples of a mode of argument in the treatise *Topica* written for his jurist friend Trebatius.[132] If a man's property had already been invaded and mishandled, we are back in the sphere of the interdicts, notably that called *quod vi aut clam*:[133]

'What has been done by force or by stealth, object of suit, provided that less than a year has elapsed since suit was possible, I order you to restore.'

This was not only for building or demolishing on your land, but also for cutting trees, polluting wells, and numerous other things, as long as they were directly connected with the soil. Any sort of protest by you, if your adversary persisted nevertheless, justified the claim of violence, and you could have an Aquilian action against him as well. The interdict *unde vi*, to get back into possession of property if expelled from it, we have met already; in the disturbed period after Sulla there was added a further interdict for expulsion by force of arms, *vi hominibus armatis*, which figures prominently in two of Cicero's orations,[134] and was designed to put a man back quickly with all questions about rights left till later. For violence, affray and rapine there was also, from Sulla's time onwards, a criminal prosecution available;[135] the same concurrence of criminal prosecution with civil suit applied, under the Principate, to theft, to which we must now come.

*

Of the civil law of theft, *furtum* (another good *Digest* title to read),[136] it is often said nowadays that it was in classical times 'of little practical importance'.[137] Theft was, like damage, a tort—though a penal one; you sued the thief in the civil courts, for your property plus substantial penalties (the thief caught in the act and the robber with violence were liable for fourfold, most other thieves for double). But, of course, thieves are not usually solvent, not worth the trouble of suing civilly—a modern as well as an ancient problem:[138]

> 'Most citizens would probably say "amen" to the wish of Sir Peter Rawlinson, a former Solicitor-General, to see thieves and robbers be made to pay—in the most literal sense—for their crimes. . . . The trouble is that no one (not even Sir Peter Rawlinson) has yet discovered such a method. It is open to an aggrieved loser to sue the convicted man for the loss of his property or money. In practice this is seldom done. The chances of recovering either the property or money, or the costs of the case, are slight . . . Of all cases of larceny in 1964, only 3% involved sums of £100 or more.'

The interest of the public is partly in recovering its economic loss and partly in the repression of theft by means of a coercive kind, and faced with the perennial difficulty of achieving the former it is likely to concentrate on the latter. Now under the Principate theft did become a crime as well as a civil wrong, though it never had a standing jury-court (not being regarded as an 'upper-class' sort of offence):[139]

> 'The man who has haled a thief before the prefect of the watch or the governor of a province is taken to have made his choice of means to pursue his right; and if the matter is concluded in that court and he gets his thing back or his money single-fold, that is the end.'

Perhaps what the prefect of the watch did under the Principate the *tresviri capitales* had already done a good deal of in Cicero's day; but at any rate under the Principate it is suspected that the civil procedure for theft was little used,[140] though the lawyers went on amusing themselves with it, including a lot of primitive complexities[141] which frequent practical application would soon have abolished. It is said of all these anomalous 'penal torts' that in Roman as in English law they were the product of an age when the remedies of criminal procedure lagged behind those of civil— only English law abandoned them when it acquired something better.

Now we do not know the relative frequency of civil actions and criminal trials for theft during our period. The one remark, attributed to Ulpian, that:[142]

'one must remember that nowadays theft is usually punished in the criminal courts'

is very probably an interpolation by someone of a later age. Furthermore, there were two respects in which the civil law rules gave people a better chance to recover their losses than anything anyone has invented since. First, since upon civil judgment the thief (and his accomplice) became a judgment-debtor, he could ultimately be haled off into private bondage to work off his debt.[143] And secondly, since the action for theft was one of the class known as 'noxal actions', which meant that if the offence had been committed by a slave you sued his *dominus*, who had the choice of paying up or handing over the slave, you could in such a case recover something, if only a saleable slave.[144] These possibilities may well have been enough to give the civil procedure an abiding attractiveness, so that people wanted both. They wanted, and could have, more than one civil action cumulatively against the thief, namely, in addition to the *actio furti* for a penalty, a vindication of the stolen object or *condictio furtiva* for its value. For there was, as Gaius says, a 'hatred of thieves'.[145] You could legitimately kill a burglar, or even a day-time thief if he produced a weapon. And yet in our period the Roman law was not as savage to thieves as English law was down to the nineteenth century. Death or transportation for tiny sums was unknown; deportation (for *honestiores*) and the mines (for *humiliores*) were the outside limit even for aggravated theft such as burglary.[146]

The offence was very broadly (or, as some might say, never adequately) defined, though it was minutely partitioned into special cases. It was not confined to 'taking something away with intent to deprive of whole interest', but any unauthorized dealing with something could be theft, such as receiving stolen goods, appropriating things lost, or even taking something of which you were *dominus* away from the man who held it in legal possession (you could, in fact, steal your own thing). There was a much quoted illustration of theft in the form of misuse of something borrowed:[147]

'a man was convicted of theft because, having borrowed a horse to ride to Aricia, he rode it up the hill beyond.'

It was even theft to use at all something deposited for safe keeping. (And, given this scope of the offence, some thieves would not be humble insolvents.) However, there did have to be proved an intention to do something wrong; you could not commit theft by mere inadvertence, and in fact when people came into possession of something they tended to put up a notice.[148] There were many categories of action, according to the special types of theft,[149] such as 'manifest' theft (thief caught in the act), non-manifest theft, stolen objects found on premises, theft by a slave *familia*, robbery with violence, pillaging from fires, shipwrecks and riots,[150] larceny in inns and ships, and so on. The person who had the right of action against a thief was he who had a (pecuniary) interest in the thing not being stolen, but what that meant is the subject of much learned argument;[151] at any rate it was not necessarily in all cases the owner of the thing. The *condictio furtiva*, on the other hand, was available only to an owner.[152] Fairly early in our period there was great legal dispute whether there could be theft of land; the view prevailed (as in English law) that there could not. So theft was of movables only, though that included not only slaves but also free persons in a man's *potestas*.[153]

*

There is another way in which a man can lose his property—debt. It is well known that indebtedness was an acute problem in the age of Cicero;[154] there were features of Roman Republican society over and above the threat (and sometimes the reality) of civil war which made it unstable from the point of credit. The dominant class was land-owning, living on rents. Its members had, on the other hand, very heavy cash expenses, to maintain a grand standard of living and to play the game of politics which involved huge stakes in bribery, bread and circuses. Hence they borrowed, on the credit, ultimately, of their lands, and the liquid funds went the rounds, constantly changing hands according to who needed cash at any moment. (New funds came in from the mines and from provincial tribute, when not in kind; on them the *publicani* had a hold, so they tended to be big creditors and sources of liquid funds.) Another element in the pattern was *officium* again. If you were to be well regarded it was incumbent on you to help your friends in their temporary embarrassments, either with money, even if that meant borrowing on your own credit, or at least by being a surety, pledging your credit, for their borrowings. It can be seen that this was a vicious circle, a nexus of paying one debt by incurring another, all ultimately dependent on the secure market for land.[155] In times of invasion or political insecurity or agitation for the redistribution of land there might be a calling in of debts all round, and chaos could result. Just a few passages from the correspondence of Cicero will illustrate the whole network:

In 50 BC Cicero's political freedom of speech was menaced by the fact that he owed Caesar money. He writes to Atticus:[156]

'What should I do? Pay up, you say. All right; I'll borrow from Caelius.'

In 49 his brother Quintus was being pressed by Atticus himself:[157]

'Quintus is very anxious to get what he owes you settled by substituting Egnatius as your debtor, and Egnatius is quite willing to take over the debt, and is no pauper. But in times like these, when even Titinius says he can't find the money to travel, and has had to let his debtors go on owing at the same rate of interest [*i.e.* he cannot actually get them to pay up]—

and Ligus is in the same position—Quintus hasn't a penny in cash and can't get any cash out of Egnatius or raise a loan anywhere.'

After Caesar's murder, Cicero from Puteoli begged Atticus:[158]

'Please, my dear fellow, look after my affairs in Rome—but without hoping for anything from me. I've got plenty coming to me on paper to pay my debts, but my own debtors often don't come up to scratch; and if something of the kind occurs, think above all of my reputation. You must put me right not only by borrowing but even by selling, if things force it.'

During Cicero's exile in 58 a lot of his property was destroyed by the authorities and he was very straitened. His wife thought of selling property of her own to meet claims. 'No', writes Cicero:[159]

'let others, who are able enough if the will is there, take on the burden' . . . 'if our friends stand by their duty [officium] there will be no lack of funds.'

The same pattern can be observed in Pliny, a century and a half later. He is attracted by a property, and considers buying it:[160]

'You may ask whether I can scrape together even three hundred thousand. It's true I'm almost wholly in land, but I've got a bit out at interest, and should have no trouble in getting a loan. I can get it from my mother-in-law, whose funds I can call on as freely as my own.'

In Pliny's day there is no air of crisis; the 'Augustan peace' had removed some of the prime causes of uncertainty. Yet small beginnings could still under the Principate cause a panic, as can be seen from the curious tale in Tacitus of the financial crisis of AD 33.[161]

How does the law of debt relate to this pattern? The antique law, based on the Twelve Tables, is notorious for its harshness. If judgment was given against you for a debt you had thirty days to pay. If you failed you were brought before the magistrate, and you must either produce a *vindex* (doubtless your patron) who would be sued for double your debt, or you were 'addicted' to your creditor, who could keep you in private bondage for another sixty days, producing you in public at certain statutory intervals (in case anyone would come forward to relieve you); after that he could sell you into slavery abroad. A *lex Poetelia* of 326 BC abolished *nexum*, by which men in need deliberately contracted debts on the security of their persons,[162] and is supposed to have laid down that only a man's goods, not his person, were liable for debt. But whatever may be the authenticity of this latter provision, there is abundant evidence that 'addiction' for unpaid debts continued all through our period.[163] The rise of the formulary system substituted the *actio iudicati* for the old 'seizure by hand', but the practical effects were the same. We can hardly imagine the Roman nobility doing this kind of thing to one another, and it is natural to suppose that attachment for debt was what happened to the poor who (like the thief) had no assets but could be made to pay off by labour.[164] Quintilian talks of 'the addicted man, whom the law requires to be a slave till he has paid'.[165]

Already before our period began an entirely new procedure had been developed for judgment debts. (P. Rutilius, at the end of the second century BC, played some part,[166] though he probably did not invent the whole institution.) This was 'selling up', *bonorum venditio*;[167] the better view, though this has been much argued, is that it was not an alternative to attachment but could be employed as well in appropriate cases.[168] As soon as a man was adjudged debtor his creditors could apply at once for entry into his entire property (for custody, to prevent his disposing of any of it):[169]

'Those who have entered into possession on the basis of my edict [said the praetor] must be in possession in the following sense: what can be properly guarded on the spot, let them there guard; what cannot, they may remove and carry off. The owner must not be expelled if he wishes to remain.'

At the end of thirty days they could meet and appoint a kind of liquidator—or several, if the property was in different provinces[170] —to auction everything off to whoever offered to pay to all of

them the highest 'figure in the pound' on the debt (it could be
the debtor himself). Cicero's speech *pro Quinctio* is by far the most
detailed text on this institution. He describes how his client's
creditors went to the praetor and got an order for entry the
moment he failed to turn up to a promised confrontation, and
dilates upon the appalling humiliation and infamy that resulted
to a man from being 'sold up'.[171] This powerful and severe
procedure, total selling-up for an unpaid debt, however small,
could be applied also to the debtor who absconded:[172]

> 'The praetor says: "He who hides for the purpose of defrauding,
> if he is not defended according to what a good man would
> think reasonable, I will order his goods to be entered upon and
> sold". . . . And this is a very common case of possession, for
> it is regular for the goods of absconders to be possessed.'

What is more, being sold up did not extinguish any part of your
indebtedness that remained; you were still liable, could still be
'addicted' and sued again later for the balance: 'a man owed his
debts till he had paid them'.[173] Now clearly, unless tricked by
some enemy, as Cicero claims that Quinctius was, no solvent
debtor would get into this position. The law's severity would be
sufficient pressure to make him pay up. And once again it is
hard to see the nobility, constantly in debt to one another, in-
flicting such humiliation on their peers. It has been noticed,[174]
in the kind of Ciceronian passages quoted above, that the anxious
creditors did not seem to contemplate taking their debtors into
court; and though Cicero was in deadly earnest about getting
the last penny of Tullia's dowry back from Dolabella in 44, he
turned over all sorts of possibilities for avoiding a direct suit
against him.[175] The penal harshness of the law had, partly as
consequence and partly as corollary, that it was not much used
as between members of the upper class, though they may well
have wielded it mercilessly against debtors of lower status.
In the civil war period, however, there were nobles who reached
rock-bottom, insolvency; probably for them, a *lex Iulia de
cessione bonorum* (whether of Augustus or of Julius Caesar—

who passed a number of measures to relieve the acute debt problem of his day—remains uncertain)[176] gave some further relief to those who could make a case to the praetor that their insolvency was due to misfortune.[177] The debtor could make voluntary cession of all he had to his creditors; he was still sold up,[178] but he did not incur *infamia* and was not liable to attachment;[179] and though he still owed any balance he could not at any given time be sued for a greater part of it than he had means to pay.[180]

Naturally, debtors did their best to defeat all these rules and their creditors by disposing of property quickly:[181]

'Most of the family property he transferred into his wife's name by a cunning fraud, and so, pauper, denuded, protected only by his ignominy, nevertheless he left Rufinus here, without a word of a lie, thirty thousand sesterces. For that's what Rufinus got from his mother's estate, net of debts.'

Cicero tried a dodge when his property was sold up after he had gone into exile: he informally manumitted his slaves, warning them that they might lose their freedom if the manumission was held to be in fraud of creditors.[182] For the only allowance was that mentioned in an earlier chapter; property sold up did not include a man's concubine or natural children. Various other wangles are heard of, and various remedies were available to the liquidator to put a stop to them.[183]

A characteristic feature of the 'act of bankruptcy' in the technical modern sense is that the insolvent who has paid his dividend, his 'so much in the pound', can in the end be discharged; the balance of his debt is obliterated and he can begin again with a clean slate. Was any such arrangement possible in Roman law? We hear several times in the *Digest* of the pact of composition made by an heir to a *damnosa hereditas* with the creditors of the estate, by which they take a dividend and give him a 'pact not to sue'.[184] The advantage sought by the creditors was to persuade the heir to take the inheritance (which they might wish him to do in order that particular legacies might be good,

and so on); the *quid pro quo* was full discharge on only part payment. The advantage to the heir was that by taking the inheritance and having a pact he protected the memory of the
testator from infamy without suffering insolvency and infamy
himself. There is reason to think that the ordinary insolvent was
sometimes allowed a pact of the same kind; and if one wonders
why creditors should have granted a man such an arrangement
when they had the alternative of selling him up, the answer may
well lie in the notorious difficulty and trouble involved (not only
in Roman times) in recovering anything worth the effort from an
insolvent debtor. It might simply be less bother for a man's
sureties and his creditors to meet, arrange what could be paid,
and be rid of him altogether.[185]

There appears frequently in the literature (but only once by
name in the classical legal writings)[186] a process called *decoctio*,
done by a *decoctor*, who *decoxit creditoribus suis*.[187] The standard
meaning of this 'decoction' was declaration of insolvency. It
might simply be followed by *cessio bonorum* (if allowed); the
honourable thing to do if you could not meet your debts was to
let yourself be sold up[188] (naturally under the provisions of the
lex Iulia when they became available)—to 'take it on the chin',
continue to owe your balance, and (it may be conjectured) not
involve your sureties. Equally, 'decoction' might be what the
heir to an insolvent estate had to do if he accepted it; he could
expect a pact in exchange, and this was admitted not to be
dishonourable:[189]

'Do you remember that when you were only a lad you were a
decoctor? "That was my father's fault", you will say. Very well,
for loyalty to your father's memory is a full defence. But the
thing that shows you were no gentleman is that you went on
sitting in the Fourteen Rows in the theatre, although the *lex
Roscia* had appointed a special place for *decoctores* even if a
man had done it through fortune's fault and not his own.'

But the *decoctor* is often spoken of in terms of contempt and
infamy:[190]

'Some debtors a moneylender will not pursue—the ones he knows to have *decoxisse*; for their honour has reached rock-bottom and to appeal to it would be a waste of effort.'

'When people were flinging bills at him on all sides and he was grabbed by everyone he met and driven crazy, he said 'Pax!' [*sic*], admitted he couldn't pay, gave up his gold rings and all the insignia of rank, and made a pact with his creditors.'

These passages bring out the notion that it was no use pursuing a man who had 'decocted', and also the possibility of pacts of discharge.[191] Not having actually sued the debtor, the creditors were not debarred from applying to his sureties for what they could not get out of him;[192] and herein probably lay the real heinousness and disesteem of 'decoction': it 'let the side down'. Hence the Table of Heraclea includes amongst those persons not allowed to stand for municipal office:[193]

'the man who has declared to his sureties or creditors that he cannot pay in full, or has made a pact with them on the basis that he cannot pay in full, or on whose behalf money has been given or expended.'

The social system involved pledging dignity and reputation as well as financial credit on behalf of others; if they proved unsatisfactory it reflected on the surety as well as the debtor; and it threw into confusion the whole nexus of mutual obligations on which credit depended.

It will seem surprising that the law of our period does not appear to have developed that sensible institution for dealing with the solvent but contumacious debtor, distraint by court order upon such pieces of his property as will cover the debt, and it is in truth the more surprising in that in early Roman law certain special cases had been met in that very way.[194] Something akin to it was established, characteristically in a context of class-distinction, by a *senatusconsultum* of unknown date. We learn from a fragment of Gaius in the *Digest*[195] that:

'where a *clara persona* such as a senator or senator's wife is in
a position in which his or her property would be sold up,'

the authorities would put in a *curator bonorum* to distrain upon
particular items of their goods up to what was needed to satisfy
the creditors. Beyond this the execution of civil judgments under
the formulary system never went, but the *cognitio extraordinaria*
did. A rescript of Antoninus Pius set up at long last a wholly
new general arrangement by which the magistrates in Rome were
to execute the judgments of judges and arbiters themselves instead
of making plaintiff and defendant go through the *actio iudicati*
(and this was extended to the provinces by Septimius and Caracalla).[196] They seized *pignora,* *i.e.* distrained on such items of
property as would meet the judgment debt, and after two months
the *pignora* were sold under the magistrate's direction and the
proceeds handed to the creditor. It was, in fact, the administrative
law that found the intelligent solution.

CHAPTER VI

LABOUR

The labour force of Rome consisted partly of free men (free-born and freed) and partly of slaves. It is not possible to make satisfactory generalizations about their relative numbers, except that obviously, while all slaves were part of the labour force, many free men were purely consumers. The proportion of slaves varied geographically and chronologically and with the type of occupation, and in fact the formal distinction between slave and free is not a true differentiator when it comes to the labour pattern, besides which many (in Rome itself perhaps most) free men in the labour force were freed slaves, not *ingenui*.[1] The chain-gangs of slaves on agricultural estates in Italy, still existing in Pliny's day,[2] represent the nadir, but humble manual labour was often free and managerial labour often slave. What is more even in the same job in the same area free men and slaves are to be found indiscriminately, working under the same conditions. The *Digest* discussion of the famous Aquilian case of the master injuring his apprentice is illuminating about the liabilities involved in dealing with free and slave labour:[3]

'If a master wounds or kills a slave when disciplining him, is he liable under the Aquilian for 'loss caused contrary to the law'? Julianus writes that the man who put his pupil's eye out when disciplining him is liable under the Aquilian; all the more will the same hold if he killed him. Julianus also discusses the following situation: a shoemaker who had a free *filius familias* as apprentice struck him with a last for not doing properly what he had shown him, and knocked the boy's eye in. . . .'

It is also characteristic that the code of regulations for the mining district of Aljustrel, when it lays down penalties for various offences connected with work in the shafts, like damaging pit-props, prescribes them for free workmen and for slaves; and it requires under certain circumstances a return from the contractor of 'the number of slaves and free workers (*mercennarii*) he is putting in for this work'.[4] Of course, the upper class thought working for one's living at all rather sordid, but apart from that only one clear distinction can be drawn—the ancient and ubiquitous reluctance of the free-born to 'do the washing-up', to do, in fact, anything that could be thought of as domestic or household service. In the earlier part of our period, secretarial and accounting work were domestic service (with the curious exception of the ancient and distinguished profession of the *scribae publici*),[5] which is part of the reason why the great offices of the growing imperial bureaucracy were so long staffed right to the top by freedmen. Only from the end of our period does there come one reference in the *Digest* to a private stenographer suing for the balance of his wages.[6]

*

The principal mode of acquisition of slaves, as distinct from having them born and reared in your own household, was purchase from the slave-trader in the market. In one of the great nineteenth-century treatises there was given a masterly picture of the slave-market,[7] with its total humiliation of the human personality taken for granted by all, and there is little to add;[8] perhaps just the sinister—because casual—remark of Labeo in the *Digest*:[9]

'If you have contracted to transport slaves you cannot claim the passage-money for any slave that dies on board;'

perhaps just also the receipt given by the slave-trader from Miletus operating in Ravenna:[10]

'In the consulship of C. Curtius Iustus and P. Julius Nauto, 2 October, I, Aeschines Flavianus, son of Aeschines, of Miletus, have written that I have received from Titus Memmius Montanus, ordinary seaman in the Augustan fleet, six hundred

and twenty-five denarii, the price of a slave woman of Mar-
maric origin. . . . Transacted in the camp of the praetorian fleet
of Ravenna.'

In this large department of ancient business many shady characters
operated. Slave-dealers, *venaliciarii*, says Paulus, get together in
companies so as to 'pass the buck' when customers complain
about the quality of their goods.[11] Consequently the aediles of
Rome, who were responsible for the markets, propounded in their
edict certain special actions and conditions which form a celebrated chapter in the Roman law of sale.[12]

The ordinary principle in sale was *caveat emptor*; it was up to
the buyer to take care that he did not make a defective purchase,
and he could not complain afterwards. Some limit was certainly
imposed on this; for example, fraudulent concealment by a seller
of defects known to him gave an action on the contract. A story
told by Cicero and repeated by Valerius Maximus illustrates
this:[13] Claudius Centumalus had a house on the Caelian Rise,
but was ordered by the augurs to demolish it because it got in the
way of their inspection of the heavens. He sold it to Calpurnius
Lanarius without mentioning this order, and Lanarius, on being
forced to demolish, brought an action against the vendor (with
the *formula* 'whatever it is right for the defendant to pay or do
in good faith . . .', a *bona fide* action). Marcus Cato, the father of
Cato of Utica, was judge, and his verdict was:

'Since the defendant had known the facts at the time of sale,
and had not disclosed, he must be liable to the buyer for his
loss.'

Also, if there was an express guarantee in a contract that the goods
had certain specific qualities, and they did not, the seller was
liable. But the weakness in all this is clearly that it might be
difficult to prove that the seller had known of a defect which you
discovered. Therefore the aediles imposed upon the market for
slaves and cattle a special and extremely severe rule, that (unless
there was specific pact to the contrary—an important proviso)[14]

the seller must openly guarantee against a wide range of defects and was liable for them even if he had not known:[15]

> 'The aediles say: "Those who sell slaves are to inform buyers what illness or defect is in each, who is a fugitive or tends to wander, and who is undischarged from *noxa* (*i.e.* has committed an offence for which whoever owns him must pay up or surrender him), . . . and we shall give to the buyer or whoever it concerns an action that the slave be taken back." It must be realized that the seller must be liable even if he did not know the things the aediles require to be guaranteed; and this is right, because the seller could have found them out, and it is irrelevant to the buyer why he is deceived, whether through ignorance on the part of the seller or fraud.'

As a text of social history on the attitude to slaves, the discussions under this *Digest* title about what constitutes 'illness' and 'defect' are illuminating. One remark, on suicidal habits, was quoted in Chapter II;[16] here are just a few more:[17]

> 'If a slave has had his tongue cut out, there is a question whether he can be regarded as "sound"; the question appears in Ofilius in the case of a horse, and he says he does not think the horse is "sound".'

> 'There is a question about the case of a woman whose offspring are still-born every time, whether she is "unsound"; and Sabinus says that if this is due to a defect of her womb she is "unsound".'

> 'There is also a problem about the enuretic . . .'

But to return to the aedilician rules: discovery of any of these defects gave the purchaser the right to an *actio redhibitoria*, a 'handing-back action', which simply means that he was entitled, within six months, to return the slave or beast and recover his price. (Perhaps, as an alternative, he could have within a year an *actio quanti minoris* for reduction of the price, but many think this post-classical.)[18] Gaius tells us rather surprisingly that the edict of the aediles ran in the 'provinces of the Roman people', where the quaestors had the aedilician jurisdiction, but not in the 'provinces of Caesar', where nobody had it.[19] (It must also be kept in mind that the edict applied only to slaves and cattle.) But the aediles went further. Not only defect but also eviction was a serious problem. Mancipation of *res mancipi* carried with it an ancient liability for double the value if the buyer was deprived of his thing by someone with a better claim, for example if the real *dominus* turned up and vindicated it. But the dealer would often be a peregrine, who could not mancipate anyway; you could acquire ownership by *usucapio*, of course, but, worse still, you did not know how he had come into possession of the slave, who might be *res furtiva* and so not susceptible of *usucapio*. So the aediles made it possible for the buyer to insist on a promise in the contract for reimbursement in case of eviction. Varro tells us what was the custom in his (that is, Cicero's) day:[20]

'There is usually a promise that the slave is healthy and free from theft and *noxa*; or if the slave is not being mancipated a promise of double the value or (if such is the agreement) of the simple value.'

This custom the aediles made obligatory; and the promises thus made were actionable like any contractual promises in any jurisdiction, not only that of the aediles themselves.

There survive several contracts of sale of slaves in which we can see these clauses working. Of particular interest are those which turned up amongst the Herculaneum Tablets, because they make specific reference to the aedilician edict as it was propounded in Neronian days. Here are three passages:[21]

'(if possession is disturbed) then the sum for which the slave was bought, of that sum promise was called for by Hamillus, slave of Vibidia Procula, and duly given by Claudia Musa with authorization of her guardian M. Antonius Phaetus.'

'that the aforesaid slave woman is guaranteed sound, free from theft and *noxa*, not a fugitive or liable to wander, or that whatever sum has been laid down and settled by the authority

of the curule aediles as customary in the buying and selling
of slaves in the present year shall be paid; promise that all these
things shall thus properly be paid and done was called for by
Calatoria Themis and duly given by C. Iulius Phoebus.'

'. . . and that if anyone makes eviction of said slave or any
share in him to the detriment of the lawful possession of L.
Cominius Primus or his heir, the simple value shall be given
for the object; that these things are properly guaranteed as is
customary, promise was called for by L. Cominius Primus
and duly given by P. Cornelius Poppaeus.'

The extent to which the forms were standard will be apparent if
we look at just two more documents, from places far apart in
the Roman world. The first is one of the Transylvanian Tablets,
the wooden triptychs from Verespatak in Hungary, a mining
community in the Roman province of Dacia. Its date is AD
142:[22]

'Dasius, Breucian, has bought and received by mancipation the
slave Apalaustus (or by whatever other name he is known),
nationality Greek, *apocatum pro uncis duabus*, for six hundred
denarii from Bellicus son of Alexander, M. Vibius Longus
being surety. That this slave is guaranteed handed over sound,
free from theft and *noxa*, not a wanderer, fugitive or epileptic;
and if anyone makes eviction of said slave or any share in him
to the detriment of the lawful possession and enjoyment of
said purchaser or whomsoever it may concern, that in such
case, whatever sum the loss by eviction has been, twice that
sum shall be paid in good coin, promise was called for by
Dasius, Breucian, and duly given by Bellicus son of Alexander,
and the same promise duly given as surety by Vibius Longus.
And Bellicus son of Alexander said that he has received and
holds price of said slave, viz. six hundred denarii, from Dasius,
Breucian. Transacted in the township of legion III Gemina,
16 May, consulship of Rufinus and Quadratus.'

The second is a papyrus, dated AD 166, found in Egypt but written
at Seleucia in Pieria.[23] As its editor observed, the soldiers and the

dealers who travelled took their receipts and so on with their impedimenta; and it was their requirements that helped to standardize the forms:

'C. Fabullius Macer, non-commissioned officer of the praetorian fleet of Misenum, vessel *Tigris*, has bought the slave, nationality Mesopotamian from beyond the Rivers, called Abbas or Eutyches (or by whatever other name he is known), about seven years old, price two hundred denarii plus poll-tax on import, from Q. Julius Priscus, ordinary seaman of same fleet, same vessel. That this slave is sound according to the edict, and that if anyone makes eviction of said slave or any share in him, the simple value without denunciation shall be properly paid, promise was called for by Fabullius Macer and duly given by Q. Julius Priscus, and promise fortified by good faith and authority of C. Julius Antiochus, *manipularius* of the vessel *Virtue*. And vendor, Q. Julius Priscus, declared that he has received and holds the aforesaid two hundred denarii in good coin properly paid over from buyer, C. Fabullius Macer, and has conveyed [*tradidisse*] the aforesaid slave Eutyches to him in good condition. Transacted at Seleucia in Pieria, in the winter quarters of the detachment of the praetorian fleet of Misenum, 24 May, consulship of Q. Servilius Pudens and A. Fufidius Pollio.'

Even the 'Tablettes Albertini' from Africa under the Vandals retain these long-lived formulae. Beneath the surface, however, changes are apparent. As the editor of the 'Tablettes' points out, in our classical period these *instrumenta* purport to be simply evidence of the carrying out of a whole series of separate formal transactions—the conveyance, the payment of price, the stipulations of quality and against eviction; whereas by the Vandal age, though the wording remained, the *instrumentum* as a whole had become a written contract.[24] Even within our own period, comparison between the Herculanean and Transylvanian documents is instructive.[25] Already by the time of Nero the edict of the aediles is taken to apply to private sales as well as those in open market, but by a century later development has gone further.

The Dacian buyers and sellers are not—or not all—Roman citizens;[26] provincial peregrines have now picked up, and use, the Roman forms of *mancipatio* and the rest, and what is more, they are basing themselves on the aedilician edict in a 'province of Caesar', for all that Gaius may say.

The *fugitivus* is a slave actually 'on the run'. Slaves naturally attempted to escape from bad masters, just hoping for a change or for some means of securing their freedom or passing as free. Slave-collars survive with such labels as:[27]

> 'I am Asellus, slave of Praeiectus, official on staff of the prefect of the grain-supply. I've got out through the wall. Seize me, for I am a fugitive, and return me to the barber's quarter near Temple of Flora.'

The whole mechanism of society ground into action to restore this all-too-mobile property; *Digest* 11. 4, 'on fugitives', shows how. There was right of entry to lands for search, help of the authorities, and there might be rewards. The search for Giton in the boarding-house has it all:[28]

> 'Into the lodging-house came the crier with a town slave and various other people (not many, though); he waved a torch about, that produced more smoke than light, and announced: "Slave recently escaped in the baths, about sixteen years of age, curly hair, effeminate appearance, handsome, name Giton: anyone returning him or revealing his whereabouts will receive one thousand sesterces".'

And waiting for the fugitive, to assist—or betray—him, was the *fugitivarius*, the 'runaway-man', an ingenious rogue whose activities were unmasked in the pages of the *Corpus Iuris* in a brilliant paper not long ago.[29] The runaway-man would say to the master 'Of course you'll never get him back, but I might; tell you what I'll do, I'll take the risk and buy him from you on the chance of recovering him.' The master would not get much, but it was better than nothing; the runaway-man was now owner of the slave and so not guilty of *plagium* for harbouring him;[30]

and the slave could now be sold for his true price to a master he preferred, or even manumitted if he could afford to pay what the runaway-man would ask. A *senatusconsultum* of unknown date (but within our period) therefore extended the offence of *plagium* to anyone who bought or sold a runaway, so that henceforth both the master and the runaway-man would be liable to a penalty; it was *fugam vendere*, to 'sell a flight'.[31] And there was another rule (conceivably to stop dodges that got round even the *senatusconsultum*), that a slave bought by a runaway-man could not be freed for ten years without the consent of his former master, which made the game not worth the candle for the slave who hoped for freedom.[32]

There is no room in this book to describe the multifarious duties of slaves. As to the humble labourer or domestic, the law is more or less exhausted now that we have considered his acquisition and retention and the rules about damage to him which were dealt with in the previous chapter; but the slave in more responsible functions generated other sets of legal rules, to which we must now turn. He was immensely important in the labour force of Rome as agent and manager. At the highest level was the steward, *servus actor* or *dispensator*, who managed the accounts and carried out the financial transactions of the wealthy families and their estates.[33] Cicero's *dispensator*, Eros, is a good example; Cicero grumbled about his inefficiency, but was clearly dependent on him:[34]

'Eros's accounting is holding up my departure. I ought to have had plenty in current account when he balanced up on 5 April; instead, I'm having to borrow.'

'Hordeonius is pressing—not gentlemanly at all; there's only the third instalment owing, due on 1 August, and most of that he has been paid already, a bit ahead of time. But Eros will look after that on the Ides.'

Free men were willing to pass into slavery to secure this coveted position,[35] and the *dispensator* could expect to receive freedom on properly rendering account to his deceased master's heir.[36] He might be in charge of estates abroad, entirely on his own:[37]

> 'Men often think their assets are greater than they really are. This frequently happens to people who have overseas businesses in remote parts of the world, managed by slaves and freedmen; often the business declines over a long period without their knowing it . . .'

He might, as *actor publicus*, be city treasurer of a municipality.[38] Then, on a rather lower level of standing, there was the *vilicus* or bailiff, managing a particular agricultural property, in charge of all the labour, slave and free. Horace's bailiff, who had once been an indoor servant in Rome and longed for the country, but now, promoted, pined for Rome, is perhaps the best known,[39] but all the technical writers on agriculture expatiated on what kind of a man was needed.[40] Then again, the slave might manage enterprises outside the family range altogether, such as taverns and shops;[41] apparently even 'children' (adolescents, one supposes) ran such places—often, according to Gaius.[42] And, going back to businesses, we hear of a slave (who decamped) managing a mixed affair that included money-lending, pawnbroking, and letting depository space to grain merchants;[43] and Ulpian envisages the possibility (though the way he puts it suggests it is a marginal one) of a slave being a full-scale banker.[44] As a yet further alternative slaves could be allowed to hire out their own services independently, *operas suas locare*, in all sorts of crafts and skills: actor, teacher, nurse, shoemaker, prostitute and so on.[45]

All these situations generated for the slave legal relationships not only with his master but with third parties. You could not engage in such activities without giving receipts and discharges, making contracts, taking tenancies, joining partnerships and so on. How could a mere 'thing', a 'human tool', with no rights, no duties and no access to the courts, fulfil this essential function in society? The law found its answer in *peculium*, and rules that were made to flow from it. We have met *peculium* of the *filius familias*, but its prime economic importance was as the personal fund of slaves. No master was obliged to give his slave a *peculium*,

but no slave who was to have any independent role could manage
without one. Technically it belonged to the master, was revocable
at his will and was part of his assets, but the slave had day-to-day
disposal of it.[46] It could consist of not only such parts of his
earnings as he was allowed to keep but also stock-in-trade, land,
inheritances, even other slaves—a *vicarius* was the slave of a
slave; the slave might have a very wealthy fund at his disposal,
and on this basis he could enter into legal relationships even with
his master—common ownerships and tenancies and the like, with
accounting of credits and debits as against one another (though
settlement would be a purely domestic affair and any obligation
only a *naturalis obligatio*, for the slave could not sue his master in
respect of what in law belonged to his master).[47] Normally a
slave's *peculium* would pass with him if he were sold,[48] and so it
would on manumission *inter vivos* unless expressly withheld.[49]
When a master died he could leave his servants their *peculia* as
legacies. On the other hand, a slave might have to 'buy' his freedom with part or all of his *peculium*, *i.e.* leave it behind as a
sacrifice for his liberty.

The existence of *peculium* enabled the law to develop a series of
rules making the slave an agent pledging his master's credit in
dealings with third parties; it gave, in fact, various actions to such
parties against the master. The simplest was the *actio de peculio*:
on any individual transaction of a slave, whether done with the
knowledge or consent of his master or not, the master could be
sued *dumtaxat e peculio*, up to but not in excess of the value of the
slave's *peculium*. And on any general course of transactions done
with the knowledge of the master (which would be the normal
case of the slave in business) there was a more complicated *actio
tributoria* up to the value of the *peculium*, in which the master was
not allowed to begin by subtracting from that value what he
claimed the slave owed him. (On contracts which he had expressly ordered the slave to enter into on his behalf he was
liable in full in the suit called *actio quod iussu*.)[50] And we must run
on here, beyond the slave context, for the law provided yet more
important agency actions, which applied whether the agent was
slave or free—another blurring of the formal status distinction.

The *actio institoria* for businesses on land, like shops and inns, and the *actio exercitoria* for the man who managed a vessel on behalf of a principal, whether the manager was slave or free, and whether the principal was owner of the vessel or himself only an agent, made the principal liable in full on the contracts connected with the concern, unless he gave express notice that he took no responsibility. Ulpian comments thus on the *exercitoria*:[51]

'The usefulness of this edict is apparent, as everyone realizes. We often, through the exigencies of travel, make contracts with ships' captains with no chance of enquiring about their status or *bona fides*, so it is only fair that the principal who puts a master in charge of a vessel should be liable like the principal who has put an agent in charge of a shop or business. Indeed, the necessity of contracting with a ship's captain is greater than that with an agent, for it is possible in the nature of things to enquire as to the status of an agent before you contract with him; not so in the case of the ship's captain, for time and circumstances often leave no room for deliberation.'

He also gives, under the title on the *institoria*, the rule about notice:[52]

'The man about whom a public notice has been put up that no contracts are to be made with him does not count as an agent.'

With many slaves acting in positions of financial trust it is not surprising that the praetor in his edict offered a special action *de servo corrupto*:[53]

'He who is alleged to have harboured the male or female slave of another, or with unlawful intent persuaded such slave to some course making him a worse slave than before; against him I will give an action for double the value.'

Persuading or advising a slave to leave his master was one offence under this heading; so was persuading him to commit assault or theft, or tamper with another slave, or embezzle his *peculium*, or wander off in pursuance of a love-affair, or dabble in magic, or spend too much time at the games, or take part in political agitation. So also was persuading an *actor* to strike out or mix up entries in his master's accounts or those of his own business.[54]

Permitting a slave to hire out his own craft labour was probably not as common as hiring him out yourself and taking the proceeds. This latter would be the natural arrangement in the case of gangs, teams or parties hired as a group, such as builders, miners, orchestras, gladiators and agricultural workers. *Operae servorum* could be left to someone as a legacy (indeed, this is the only heading under which the *Digest* discusses them); the legatee or usufructuary could exploit them himself or hire them out to others. What you were hiring out was actually, of course, the slave himself, the *res*, but for many purposes, such as letting for a period, usufruct and so on, it was desirable to be able to convert the use of a slave for such-and-such a period into a monetary value; and this was achieved by talking not about the *res* but about the *operae*, an *opera* being a 'man-day', a work-unit with a money value, so that one could deal in terms of 'five *operae*' or 'a hundred *operae*' or their cash equivalent. And this provided a basis for contracts of work with free men (freeborn and freed), in whose case it was not possible to talk about letting and hiring a *res*.

★

The freedman doing his obligatory work for a *patronus* was, in labour terms, just an extension of the slave in the less sordid levels of his activity; most of what little we hear about the rules of labour comes from *Digest* discussion about *operae liberti*. He is found working for his patron as bailiff, *exercitor*, and all the rest of such jobs; very characteristic are the letters of Cicero to Ser. Sulpicius Rufus, Caesar's governor of Greece in 46 BC, recommending to him the freedmen of his friends who had business in the province.[55] There is a curious passage in the *Digest* about mistake as to the obligation of *operae*:[56]

'A freedman, thinking he owed *operae* to his patron, has paid them. Julianus in Bk. X of his *Digesta* says the man cannot recover (under 'things paid by mistake', which is the subject of discussion), even though he thought he had bound himself expressly; for there is a natural obligation on a freedman to do *operae* for his patron. But suppose he has not done *operae* for the patron but, being asked for services, has commuted them for money and paid the money? Even then he cannot recover.'

We have already seen that he could not be required to do degrading or sordid things,[57] and that, unlike a master, a patron could not in principle hire out his freedman's *operae* for reward to third parties. But to this latter rule there were numerous qualifications, especially to cover services that could not be exercised at all unless they were available to people outside the family circle, such as those of the doctor or the ballet-dancer (a point which elicited that rarest of phenomena in the *Digest*—a joke):[58]

. . .'for it is not required of a patron, in order to make use of the *operae* of his freedmen, that he should spend all his days watching theatrical performances or being ill.'

*

What, then, of the fully free man, under no prejudicial obligations, hiring out his services under contract?[59] It is not self-evident that he should have existed at all, or not, at least, in any but a formal legal sense. It must be left to the course of discussion to bring out how far, and in what spheres, he really did exist, and in no other question is it more important than in this one to relate our scraps of legal evidence to our scraps of economic and social evidence. From all the principal Near Eastern societies, and from very early times, there survive contracts of labour, but (as has recently been forcefully emphasized),[60] those societies were characterized by the 'spectrum of statuses': few men and women were absolutely free, few were absolutely slaves, and labour contracts were an entry into some degree or other of personal subjection to the employer. Arrangements of this kind went on in the Near East in Hellenistic and Roman times. In the Egyptian 'apprenticeship' contracts parents bound their children (and masters their slaves) to service for periods of years. This was one aspect of *paramoné*; but *paramoné*, as recent work has shown, was a contract of service that covered, without clear distinction, wide ranges of arrangement from virtual self-hire to hire of services for specific jobs and periods with terms of protection for the worker as well as the employer.[61] We must not now be over-influenced by the famous papyrus of the time of Cleopatra:[62]

'. . . for 99 years, that is 1,204½ months; . . . to do all that is commanded by you and your household; . . . wherever you bid me, and I will stand upright in your presence; . . . remain in your house and that of your work night and day,'

nor by the Dura contract of 'squireship' as *quid pro quo* for a loan never likely to be repaid.[63] What, instead, needs emphasis is that what all parties wanted was the labour, and the terms varied over a 'spectrum' related simply to diverse economic bargaining positions.[64] Formal legal change of status was not, socially and economically speaking, the relevant consideration. Thus we have plenty of contracts of what seem to be entirely free persons hiring their services for specific engagements and ordinary periods, and there is some Roman law on the rules that were applied, though not much; we get little out of the *Digest*, because it talks of labour in terms of *operae*, and in discussing them does not distinguish between slaves and obligated freedmen and voluntarily hired workers.

It is true that the world was a rather different place from what the upper class, the writers and readers of our surviving literature, knew much about.[65] That their denigratory attitude towards labour, business and trade was not shared by the middle, let alone the labouring, class can be seen by anyone who looks at the Igel monument and the many other Gallo-Roman sculptures recording people's professions and jobs, or at the wall-decorations of the House of the Vettii at Pompeii,[66] or who examines the composition of the town council at a commercial city like Ostia.[67] These people, however, were the *entrepreneurs*, they owned the shops and ships and hired the labour, slave or free; and the fact that they were not ashamed of themselves does not tell us much about the status of the labourers.

N

It has become a standard opinion that the conditions of free labour were influenced—that is to say, debased—by the concurrence at every level of slave labour. With respect to wage rates this opinion has been properly challenged,[68] but the bargaining power of labour was certainly very limited. Apart from the 'strikes' of the Egyptian peasantry we hear virtually nothing of free labour unrest,[69] and virtually nothing of combination. Ancient society did not develop to a point where technical skills of high specialization were essential enough to its maintenance for its possessors to start calling the tune; 'it is not only the opening analysis of *The Wealth of Nations* which is fifteen hundred or two thousand years ahead in the future, but the pin factory itself'.[70] Hence the argument has usually been accepted that the pattern of contracts of free labour was based on notions deriving from the letting out of a slave, a *res*.[71]

But we must in any case narrow the field. To begin with, the 'professions' or 'liberal arts' do not count; there were certainly some jobs whose practice was not thought of as a case of hire of labour. In the second place, another distinction must be made;[72] it is not made explicitly in any legal texts of our period, does not correspond to anything that would nowadays be regarded as a dividing line, and has rather blurred edges, but it does correspond to the ancient reluctance of the free-born to work 'for' someone else. Roman lawyers of later ages recognized it as the distinction between *locatio operarum*, hiring your *operae* out as a servant, to work 'for' someone, and *locatio operis faciendi*, in which the customer hired out a job to be done to a craftsman. The latter, the contract of the fuller, tailor, glassblower, shipmaster and so on, had 'more responsibility in it',[73] and involved law about competence, negligence, custody and the like which we shall examine under the head of 'business' in the next chapter. There were, of course, borderline cases; is the contract of an Egyptian woman to serve as a wet-nurse[74] a hire or an undertaking (or even a mandate)? But this should not lead to the conclusion[75] that there was no social and economic difference; it is clearly made by Cicero, even within his celebrated denigration of most of the things done by all except his own class:[76]

'Illiberal and sordid are the means of livelihood of all hired workers (*mercennarii*), whose labour, not their arts, is bought; their wage is itself the contractual symbol of their servitude.'

If, then, we subtract all the people who worked 'for' themselves in their own ships, shops, laundries and back-parlours, the sphere of the hired free worker at a wage, the *locator operarum*, is very restricted. He is to be found as a casual field-labourer, mostly at agricultural peak seasons, in a well-known passage of Varro.[77] The labour force is partly slave and partly free, says Varro, and the free are partly independent subsistence farmers and partly:

'. . . *mercennarii*, when the heaviest farm jobs like vintage and haymaking are done by hired labourers. . . . It is better to cultivate poor land with hired men than with slaves, and even in more healthy parts to give them the bigger jobs like storing the fruits of vintage or harvest.'

We are reminded of the workers on a building contract for Cicero at Tusculum, who went off to do harvesting in April.[78] In Columella, on the contrary, there is little mention of such casual work; the *colonus* was perhaps supplying the need.[79] Mining is another occupation in which free labourers appear; we have seen that at Aljustrel in Hadrian's time contractors employed free and slave workmen in the mines, and the most famous labour contract of all, to be quoted presently, comes from the Dacian mines. Building labour was sometimes free,[80] and so were the personnel of hotels and the crews of ships.[81] Pliny writes to Trajan about a man who had hired his services to a bakery firm at Nicomedia and whom—significantly—they had tried to detain (he actually *was* a slave, posing as free, but they did not know that).[82] And it would be a shame to omit Corax, Eumolpus's hired porter in the *Satyricon*:[83]

'Corax, the hired man (*mercennarius*), who was always moaning about his job, kept putting the luggage down and cursing us for hurrying and saying he would chuck the bags away or make off with the lot. "What do you think I am?" he said, "a pack-horse, or a marble-ship? I hired out the labour of a man,

not a cart-horse; and I'm just as free a man as you are, even if
my father did leave me a pauper." And not content with
cursing, every now and then he lifted up his leg and let an
appalling. . . .'

It looks as though Eumolpus and his companions could not afford
a slave odd-job man; and Corax, though he would not (and
legally could not) sell himself into slavery, was doing a servile
job probably for less than a slave would have cost. Some kinds of
locatio operis faciendi were at a scarcely less miserable level—the
jobs mentioned by Juvenal, for instance, in a fine descending
sequence: contracting for a temple, rivers, harbours, funerals,
auctions, . . . public lavatories;[84] and yet they do not have quite
the ring of slavery about them that sounds whenever the word
mercennarius is mentioned. One legal text says:[85]

'A free man, who has control over his own status, can make it
worse or better; and thus he hires out his services for day work
and night work.'

The free servant in the agricultural *familia* is *loco servorum*, he
counts amongst the slaves;[86] he is subject to the commands of the
master or the bailiff, may be able to plead superior orders if he
had done damage under the *lex Aquilia*,[87] and (astonishingly) will
not be liable for theft against his hirer, presumably because it will
be dealt with by domestic chastisement just as if he were a
slave:[88]

'If a freedman or client has committed theft against his patron,
or a hired man (*mercennarius*) against his hirer, no action of
theft lies.'

It is a fair point that the terms 'hired for wage', *mercede con-
ductus*, and 'to hire onself out', *se locare*, do not in themselves
necessarily point to the hiring out of slaves as the origin of free
labour contracts.[89] After all, in English law 'what we hire is the
servant. At the now obsolete hiring fairs the hind or maid let
himself, or herself, rather than his or her services. We find no
difficulty in thinking of a man as hiring himself out'.[90] And it is

probably the case that in early Rome the polarity of statuses was less marked than in the late Republic, the heyday of chattel slavery, and slave and client and *filius familias* were all on a spectrum, neither wholly subject nor wholly free. But be that as it may, the law in the classical period talked of the work of all of them in terms of *operae*, 'man-days'. We get a few rules; *operae* had to be complete days, for example,[91] and there was a right to wages for the whole contracted period if it was not 'up to the worker' that his services were not used:[92]

'He who has hired out his services ought to receive wages for the whole period if it was not up to him that he could not provide his services.'

(This did not mean illness or incapacity of the worker but such things as the death of the employer.) There is also one remark about the right to reasonable time off:[93]

'Not only the freedman but anyone else giving services must be given meals or enough time to obtain meals, and in all cases they must be left adequate time for physical needs.'

More could be stipulated in the individual contract, of course, if the worker was in a position to demand it, such as days off for festivals.[94]

This is the time to look at the one substantially preserved labour contract in Latin: a single wooden waxed tablet from the Transylvanian mines, dated AD 164:[95]

'In the consulship of Macrinus and Celsus, 20 May. I, Flavius Secundinus, have written at the request of Memmius son of Asclepius, who claims to be illiterate, to the effect that he has declared himself to have hired, and has hired, his labour in gold mining work to Aurelius Adiutor from today until the Ides of November next, for seventy denarii and his keep. He shall be entitled to receive his wages in instalments. He shall be obliged to provide his labour in full health and strength to the contractor aforesaid, and if he wishes to resile or retire without consent of the contractor he shall owe five sesterces per diem in cash out of his total wage. If flooding intervenes he shall reckon this *pro rata*. If the contractor at the end of the period is in arrears with payment of wages he shall be liable for the same penalty, except for grace of three days. Transacted at Immenosus Maior.' (Signatures of Memmius son of Asclepius and two other persons.)

In a similar but very badly damaged tablet from the same place, instead of 'he has declared himself' we read 'he confesses . . .', a word which carries some implication that these miners, once they had signed on, felt they were abandoning their freedom for the six-months' term of the contract—and would perhaps have done so for longer if they had been able to get a longer contract; nevertheless, note that the *kind* of work was fixed by the contract. For comparison (and entertainment) here is a contract from Philadelphia in Egypt which could be analysed either as hire of services or as *locatio operis faciendi*, but in which one can sense a different relationship between the parties;[96] the date is AD 206:

'To Isidora, castanet-dancer from Artemisia of Philadelphia. I wish to have you and two other dancers to dance for us for six days from the 24th of Pauni [old style], receiving thirty-six drachmas for each day as pay and for the whole period six artabae of barley and twenty double loaves of bread; and whatever garments or gold ornaments are brought, we shall guard safely. We shall also provide two mules for you, both in coming and going.'

*

A major subject of modern legislation has been compensation for injury to workers in the course of their employment. Did Rome know of such a principle, as far as free men were concerned? Damage or injury to slaves by third parties would give ground for an Aquilian action by their master; and wilful, purposeful injury or assault upon a free man by anyone constituted the offence of *iniuria*, civil and criminal, which it was up to the man himself to pursue (we shall study it later). But the question here is about injury caused through negligence or failure to take care or even without fault on the part of the employer, and as far as free persons were concerned Roman legal doctrines stood in the way of action in such cases. The *lex Aquilia* gave an action only to the owner (or more or less owner) of the thing damaged, and 'no man is owner of his own body', said the Romans. They also said 'no one can put a monetary value on a free man'—a noble principle, but one which helped to produce the consequence that if a free workman fell into a boiling vat his dependents had no claim on anyone. And for *iniuria,* intent to injure was required. Now there are four passages that suggest the possibility of actions available to free men. Three of them we have actually met already:[97]

1 In the story of the master and the free apprentice, an Aquilian action is given to the *paterfamilias* for injury to his *filius familias* on the basis of loss of earnings.

2 Gaius says that for *pauperies,* injury by animals, free persons can have actions for medical expenses and loss of earnings, and it looks as if again this was for a *paterfamilias* for injury to his *filius.*

3 In the rules about 'things poured or dropped' there is a fixed penalty for the death of a free man; but this is not very relevant to conditions of work. The first two of these passages takes us no further than that negligent injury to someone *in potestate* during his work might have grounded an action; a *paterfamilias* did not exactly own his son, but one can see the chain of ideas. We therefore come with surprise to the fourth passage, from a fragment of Ulpian:[98]

'A free man on his own behalf has an action on the analogy of the Aquilian—not a direct statutory one, because it is held that no one is owner of his own limbs.'

And of this text it must simply be said that the common opinion of modern authorities regards it as a post-classical interpolation.[99] We cannot accept it as law for our period. As commentary on all this, however, it is worth remembering that in early modern times things were no better, and they were worst under the common law: 'only in the common law countries, which were first industrialized, were servants made to take the risk not only of accidental damage but of damage done to them by the negligence of their fellow-servants'.[100] When, in recent times, change finally came, it began by way of workmens' insurance, another institution which the Romans failed to invent; doubtless the propertied classes never thought of it and the workers were not organized, but in any case the Romans would probably not have been able to assemble the information or work out the statistics.

*

It is a pity that all our surviving documents on apprenticeship come from Egypt.[101] The story of the master injuring his apprentice, in the *Digest*, confirms the reasonable supposition that it existed everywhere,[102] shows that slave and free youths alike underwent it, and underlines that in most of the labour field there was no distinction when it came to jobs, and which you were was just an accident of fate. There were differences, however, in the form of apprentice contracts, between the more 'highfalutin' trades like flute-playing and stenography and the more banausic like weaving and hairdressing. In the former kind the trainee was pupil rather than apprentice, and was no use at all until he had passed the course,[103] and so the teacher must be paid for his instruction and the candidate maintained by the parent. Here is an example, dated AD 155:[104]

'Panechotes, also called Panares, quondam *cosmetes* of the city of Oxyrhynchus, by the hand of his friend Gemellus, to Apollonius the stenographer, greeting. I have placed with you my slave Chaerammon to learn the shorthand-system of which your son Dionysius is an expert for a period of two years from the current month of Phamenoth, eighteenth year of the lord Antoninus Caesar, for the fee agreed between us of one hundred and twenty silver drachmas, which does not include the cost of holidays. Of this sum you have already received the first instalment, viz. forty drachmas; the second you are to receive when the slave has completed the whole textbook, viz. forty drachmas; the third I [mistake of writer for 'you'] will receive at the end of the period if [or perhaps 'when'] the slave can take down from any ordinary speech and read back faultlessly. If you get him through the course in less than the period I shall not delay till the agreed date for payment. It shall not be open to me to withdraw the slave within the period; and he shall remain with you beyond the period for any days or months he has been absent.'

In the second kind of apprenticeship the trainee could be of some use about the workshop from the beginning, and in such contracts we find the teacher paying the pupil's keep, or even a wage. There can (as above) be stipulations as to holidays, making up lost time, and so on, but the word 'apprenticeship' must not mislead the reader into thinking that the purpose of these arrangements was wholly or even primarily educational. As has been pointed out,[105] they are a subspecies of *paramoné* (the penalty for withdrawal is significant), and are a means whereby the craftsman gets his labour force and the parent or master gets an income out of the work of his child or slave, or in some cases pays for a loan of money by this means. Of this second kind of apprenticeship one document will be quoted which turned up comparatively recently. Its date is AD 48:[106]

'Menodorus, son of Apollonius, of the district Althaea, to Lucius Pompeius Miger [he means 'Niger'], greeting. I confess that you have handed over to me your son Fuscus, not yet adult, to be taught the trade of seated linen-weaver in every aspect as I myself am expert in it, in the two [years] from the month Germaniceius, eighth year of the Emperor Claudius Caesar Augustus Germanicus, on these terms: I am to pay you for him the wage of four silver drachmas per month, you his father undertaking his keep and clothing. And I will keep him at his lessons every day as an apprentice in the trade. He shall have three days' holiday in each month, and I will deduct nothing from his wage; but for more, I will hold back the appropriate part of the wage, and will keep him at the same job after the agreed period for the equivalent number of days. And you are not to withdraw him from me during the period, nor shall it be permitted to me to dismiss him within the same period. And at the end of the time I will display him to you along with three fellow-workers . . .'. (In a rough hand at the end, after the date, are the words 'I Menodorus, son of Apollonius, will teach and do as set out above.')

*

Forced labour, except for penal hard labour, is not much in evidence in our period. The subjects of Rome could certainly be called upon for all sorts of services, such as providing mounts for the government postal service and billeting troops, and of these more will be said in Chapter VIII. A very ancient principle was the occasional call-out for the upkeep of roads and city walls. Cicero's client Fonteius was alleged to have made money out of blackmail in connection with this compulsory levy when governor of Gaul.[107] It was formally enshrined in the charter of Julius Caesar's colony at Urso in Spain:[108]

> Whatever road-work the decurions of this *colonia* have decided on, so long as a majority were present on the council when the decision was made, let it be lawful for it to be carried out; provided that they do not order more than five *operae* per year per adult male, and three *operae* per yoke of draught-animals, . . . and provided that no one be required to perform services, except voluntarily, who is less than fourteen years of age or more than sixty. Persons with domicile or land in the *colonia* or within its territory who are not citizens of the *colonia* shall be liable for this road-work as if citizens of the *colonia*.'

Such work is also occasionally referred to in inscriptions and in the *Digest*.[109] But the great bulk of the road and wall building of the Empire, military in function, was actually done by the military.[110] Egypt was a special case; the maintenance of the vital irrigation system by de-silting the canals had always fallen to the peasantry as corvée, and continued to do so. A series of documents survive, known as the 'Penthemeros-Certificates', from the Fayum, each certifying that so-and-so has completed his annual five days' corvée;[111] this is naturally compared with the five *operae* of Urso, but it is risky to deduce a general rule on this tiny point, spanning the whole Roman world. If one wonders about private, as opposed to public, labour requirements (whether, that is, landlords ever imposed corvée on tenants), evidence is scantier still. Nothing is said in the *Digest* about the possibility of rent being partly in labour on the landlord's 'home farm'; on the other hand there seems no strong reason for thinking that, if the parties so contracted, *operae* (which, as we know, were convertible into a money value) could not have been accepted in part lieu of rent, and one passage of Columella is taken by some scholars to provide evidence for such an arrangement:[112]

> '(The landlord) should behave politely to his tenants and show that he is open to representations, and he should exact work (*opus*) with greater avarice than he exacts rent; for this gives less offence and yet pays better in the long run.'

This text may not be very cogent, but the point is just worth taking because we have seen that on the imperial domain lands in Tunisia corvée was a regular obligation on the *coloni* and was enshrined in the terms of the *lex Manciana*, which may have been invented by a private land-owner. On the whole, however, Rome in our period does not seem to have obtained any sub-stantial part of its labour requirements by conscription.

*

One of the most controversial topics of Roman law in recent years has concerned the remuneration of what we should now call 'professional services'.[113] There were certain cases or categories of dignified services which the Romans were reluctant to think of in the same breath as that of the *mercennarius* or even to regard as *locatio operis faciendi*, hire of services for a reward; but difficulty begins as soon as one tries to get clear, on confusing and con-tradictory evidence, what the professions or liberal arts were of which they took this view. Substantial changes took place during our period in the status of some of these elements in the labour force. In Republican times, for example, doctors and teachers of higher education were mostly slaves and freedmen, but though there continued to be such persons in those professions free-born doctors and teachers became more and more prominent and the *éclat* of their disciplines rose, until by Flavian times they were exempt from taxation and there were salaried chairs of literature at Rome and elsewhere with such incumbents as Quintilian. (In Trajan's day Suetonius could even write a book of potted biographies of celebrated schoolmasters.) In any case, the Roman notion of liberal arts was different from ours; there is no sign that painters or sculptors or musicians came into any special category of dignity. Discussion amongst Romanists centres on the question under what contract payment was made to persons of professional standing. Was it ordinary hire of services after all? Or was it mandate, the arrangement for services as between status-equals, supposed to be gratuitous (though you could sue for expenses) and rewardable only by an honorarium? Or was it neither, but some *tertium quid*?

We can say that we know definitely that philosophers and *iuris prudentes* had a special place above all others; their advice was supposed to be free and they were allowed no means at all of suing for any reward.[114] We know also definitely that surveyors were held not to be governed by 'hire of services' nor their remuneration treated as a *merces* or wage (though it was known that they sometimes acted for a reward).[115] We know that advocates were under a special regime, which was described in an earlier chapter and which meant that they were not in any event to bargain in advance for remuneration.[116] But beyond these reasonably clear cases we are dependent on a difficult text of the *Digest*, in which Ulpian (if it is he and not a post-classical interpolator) tells us that the remuneration of a list of people was sued for *extra ordinem* before the provincial governor.[117] This, it has been maintained, strongly suggests a *tertium quid*, otherwise why not an ordinary *actio locati* or *actio mandati*?[118] But the list is in any case baffling, because it goes so far down the social scale. Teachers of higher education (*rhetor* and *grammaticus*); *geometrae* (another name for surveyors); doctors and midwives, with the exception of certain kinds of quack; ordinary schoolmasters 'by custom', and librarians, notaries and accountants; members of a governor's official entourage (though elsewhere in the *Digest* this is surprisingly treated as a *locatio*);[119] advocates; and wet-nurses (though the Egyptian nursing contracts are a kind of *paramoné*).[120] It can be said at least of the medical profession that there never ceased to exist slave and freedmen doctors, whose *operae* were subject to the ordinary contract for hire of services.[121] And what of the procurator, not in the list, who could sue *extra ordinem* for his salary?[122] The whole problem remains curiously unsolved; no coherent set of rules to cover all the cases can be discovered, and the reason is probably connected with the changes over a long period in the relative social dignity of various branches of labour,[123] and also with the progressive abandonment in practice of the 'gratuitousness' of services which had in origin been given free on a basis of *officium* between status-equals—a point which will be considered further in the next chapter. The field of labour exhibits at every point that the tight and precise categories of the Roman law both of status and of contract are (and were) inadequate to characterize the rich and fluid diversity of social and economic situations in the Roman world.

CHAPTER VII

COMMERCE

Trade and business are the theme of this chapter, and contract, agency and security are the legal modalities under which they will be discussed. As to the theme, it is only fair to warn the reader that trade and business, though the chapter about them will be long, were insignificant in importance in ancient times compared with the land.[1] As to the modalities, correspondingly, the Roman law exhibits gaps, compared with modern systems, which would be very surprising if this warning were not borne in mind. Roman economic life remained overwhelmingly based on agriculture as its primary product; no industrial revolution, no 'take-off', ever occurred, and no significantly big business ever appeared. And the law both reflected this situation and, reciprocally, helped to condition and maintain it.[2] Here, first of all, are a few generalizations, the basis of which will be strengthened as the chapter proceeds:

1 Modern commerce is regulated largely by big block statutes (such as our *Sale of Goods Act, 1893*). For Roman commerce there was singularly little statute; apart from the aedilician edict on the sale of certain goods the law of commerce was built up, like all the other branches of the law, out of the old *ius civile* by a combination of *ius honorarium* and juristic interpretation.

2 Company law remained at a primitive level of development. Partnership grew out of, and retained characteristics of, ancient family common ownership; limited liability never got beyond an embryo stage; and legal personality was not granted to business corporations.[3]

3 The concept of agency, by which 'if an agent enters into a contract on behalf of his principal with a third party, he creates

rights and duties directly between principal and third party, and himself incurs neither',[4] was (it is not very clear why) an awkward hurdle for Roman jurisprudence, and so never systematically developed. On the other hand, even in Roman conditions it was so essential that it found its way into the law in numerous places under various guises, and its lack should not, therefore, be over-stressed.

4 There was no law of patent or copyright, no protection for property in ideas.[5]

5 Accounting remained primitive. Accounts were of course kept carefully enough, especially by the tax-farming companies and by bankers; but they were never more than lists of receipts and expenditure (the Romans did not invent double-entry), and so were of little use for economic planning—even agricultural.[6]

6 Banks performed important functions in the community; they held money on deposit, made payments on behalf of customers on the basis of written instructions, and made transfers of funds as between their own customers or persons known to them. But they never got as far as the negotiable paper instrument or the overseas book-transaction between unknown persons.[7]

7. Above all, ancient society as a whole never hit on the notion of putting capital to work to increase productivity. Modern capital, it has been said,[8] is based on production and spent on more production; ancient capital came either from rents or from money-lending at interest, and was spent on unproductive ends. The difference can very clearly be seen in the field of mortgage. One of the major features of modern business development has been the use of the mortgage to acquire capital for industry, whereas in Rome mortgages were not used for such a purpose, but only as one (and not the most common) of the ways of giving security for a debt.[9]

*

Probably the oldest, and therefore the longest-lived, kind of Roman contract was the 'stipulation', an oral request and promise.[10] One party 'stipulates', that is, says 'Do you promise that such-and-such shall be given (or done)?', and the other party duly promises. Any form of words would do (though there was one solemn ancient form, using the word *spondeo*, which was confined to Roman citizens), so long as the promise was a relevant and consistent answer to the request. It was a 'verbal contract'; the mutual conversation *was* the contract, and writing was in no way necessary—though a written record might be the best way of keeping evidence of it. Apart from impossibilities of various sorts, and immoralities, there was virtually no bargain you could not legitimately make by means of stipulations. They had, however, some disadvantages. First, the contract being oral, both parties must be present; and for the same reason neither the deaf nor the dumb could make it. Secondly, there was no agency here; a third party could not make the request or the promise on your behalf so as to bind you—except that your slave or *filius familias* (since he automatically acquired not for himself but for you) could validly make the request on your behalf, but not the promise. Thirdly, the stipulation was unilateral (producing in one party a right and no duty, and in the other a duty and no right), and the action upon it was *stricti iuris*, not *bona fide*, so that the judge could not take mitigations into account unless they were pleaded as a formal *exceptio*; his *formula* ran: 'if it appears that X owes ... then condemn'. It is true that from early in our period all the important *exceptiones*, e.g. for fraud or coercion, could be formally pleaded for the judge to take account of; but he was still not entitled, as he was in the 'consensual' contracts (to which we shall come), which led to *bona fide* actions, to condemn the defendant to what seemed reasonable when all claims and counter-claims were balanced up (the *formula* being: 'whatever it appears on a basis of good faith that X ought to pay or do ... to that condemn him'). Nevertheless, stipulation was in universal and constant use. You could, for example, create a sale by means of it (A stipulated for the thing and B promised its transfer; B stipulated for the price and A promised its payment), and you could add it to innumerable other transactions: lend something and stipulate for interest, or buy something and stipulate for undisturbed enjoyment, and so on. It was the basis of debt and security.

*

Another kind of contract was the 'real' contract, which came into being not *verbis* but *re*, by the handing over of a *res*; deposit for safe-keeping, *depositum*, was one main case, and loan the other. These arrangements were very old, like stipulation, and they retained a feature characteristic of the early Roman society in which they were born: they had to be gratuitous, for no fee or reward. If you charged me for keeping something safe or for lending me a slave or a spade, that was a perfectly good contract, but it was 'letting and hiring', not deposit or loan. This is the old *noblesse oblige*:[11]

'loan is an affair of good-will and *officium*.'

The labour force, the tools, the precious objects for display, passed round the community as required, and the reward was simply the reciprocal obligation on the other man to do likewise when called on.

With deposit, Rome remained in this climate of thought. Not that deposit was of trivial or declining importance; given the slow rates of travel in the ancient world, the shortage of police, the need to go off to vote or trade or litigate, men had a frequent need to call on the goodwill of a neighbour to look after their property. One of the nastiest and most dishonourable things a man could do was to deny a deposit, to brazen it out that he had never received the thing. Juvenal's thirteenth satire is cynical consolation to someone who had suffered in this way:[12]

'What, at your age, with sixty years behind you, you get mad because a friend will not hand you back a solemn (*sacrum*) deposit?'

As for cash, that you deposited at the bank, and it is significant of the ancient economic attitude that during the whole of our period that meant actual deposit for safe-keeping, sealed up in bags or chests.[13] Only late in Roman law is there talk of 'irregular *depositum*', whereby the bank took and used the money and was ready on demand to return not the actual coins but the equivalent sum. And one recalls the rule about guardians, that they might only leave the money of their wards non-interest-bearing if it

o

was being held in deposit for the purpose of purchasing land; it could not be doing both.[14]

One of the two kinds of loan was in many ways akin to deposit. (For there are economically two kinds of loan, for which the Romans, unlike ourselves, conveniently had different names: if I lend you a slave or a spade I remain its owner, and want the self-same slave or spade back—and that was *commodatum*; but if I lend you ten pounds or a bottle of wine it is for you to consume, which can only be done by my making you owner of it, and what I want back is the equivalent—that was *mutuum*.) *Commodatum*, loan for use, without payment, belonged to the 'mutual help' sphere of social ideas. You could sue for the return of your deposited or loaned object by the *actio depositi* or the *actio commodati*, and the only important difference between them was in the degree of liability for the object while it was in the hands of the 'bailee', the man to whom it had been entrusted. The commodatary, who benefited from the arrangement, was liable not only if he failed to restore the object unharmed through his fault or negligence, but even if it was stolen or damaged through no fault of his (barring certain extreme cases like violent robbery or earthquakes). The depositee, on the contrary, who was doing you a favour and not benefiting—for he must not use the object, which would be theft—was liable only for fault or negligence.[15] Conviction in an action on deposit resulted in legal *infamia*, whereas in an action on *commodatum* it apparently did not; the reason for the distinction is not known,[16] but it may have been a *quid pro quo* for the stiffer formal liability that faced the commodatary anyway. 'No fault' situations might involve liability, but could not reasonably involve 'infamy'.

Commodatum was not commercially important; neither was the other sort of loan, *mutuum*, as such. Though you could, of course, lend people measures of corn and such things, the principal case of *mutuum* was loan of money. Loan of money—on security—is the very foundation of modern commerce, and it was not unimportant in Rome, but because *mutuum*, being a 'real' contract, was gratuitous (the handing over of the money produced no contract for anything except the return of its equivalent; you could not charge for the loan), if you wanted to contract for interest it had to be done by stipulation. As people do not, in the way of business, lend money for nothing, the important contract for money and debt was therefore the ordinary verbal stipulation. (Hence there was no such thing as an *actio mutui*; the creditor sued with a standard *formula* as on a stipulation, such as the *formula certae creditae pecuniae* which was quoted in Chapter III.)[17] Consequently we need not bother with the question whether the gratuitousness of *mutuum* was due to another ancient attitude of Roman society, the hatred of usurers, because usury and *mutuum* had nothing to do with one another, and *mutuum* was gratuitous simply because it was 'real'.

As for the hatred of usurers, it is certainly possible to produce a long chain of celebrated passages showing that people regarded with distaste the professional moneylender, the man whose whole livelihood was derived from loans at interest, such as Plautus' *Curculio*, where the moneylender is equated with the brothel-keeper as a plague on society, or Horace's Epode on Alfius.[18] But the much more interesting fact is that everybody did lend money at interest quite without embarrassment, even the highest nobility (who had most to lend). 'Here we are with a civil war on', says Cicero in 49,[19] 'with Pompey under siege by a Roman army; and yet there is the City the same as usual, the courts in session, the games in preparation, and, as usual, the great and good are clocking up their interest'. Pliny, the ultra-respectable, tells a friend that though his property is mostly in land, he has some funds out at interest.[20] And it might even be a legal duty, as for guardians, who were required to put the funds of their wards out at interest. Rates of interest were not normally much greater in Roman times than we are accustomed to, though they were a bit greater, and fluctuated over rather wider limits; there is a curious tendency amongst scholars to exaggerate them.[20a] In 62 BC Cicero wrote:[21]

'Actually there's plenty of money to be had at six per cent, and one thing about my achievements to date is that I'm regarded as a good risk.'

On the other hand, from Atticus' uncle Caecilius, a hard man:[22]

> 'not even his relations can squeeze a shilling at less than twelve per cent.'

On 15 July, 54 BC such a lot of cash was going into bribes for the consular elections that:[23]

> 'money's gone up from four per cent to eight per cent. I can hear you saying "I can't say I mind that". What a noble fellow! What a public-spirited citizen!'

According to Tacitus, who gives a confused account of the matter,[24] the Twelve Tables had laid down a statutory maximum rate of interest, *unciarium faenus*, which is now usually believed to have meant one hundred per cent per annum,[25] not inconceivable or without parallel in an early agricultural community; and there were penalties for 'usurers' (presumably people who exceeded the maximum). At some later date interest had been forbidden altogether, which naturally became a dead letter. In Tacitus' own day the situation was supposed to be governed by a law of Julius Caesar, but he does not tell us its provisions, merely saying that it too was not observed. We hear in the *Digest* about the non-actionability of interest above a legal maximum,[26] and this was *centesimae usurae*, which had nothing to do with the old *unciarium faenus* but was one per cent per month, *i.e.* twelve per cent per annum. Within this limit it was the business of governors of provinces in Cicero's day to settle the maximum for their province; what he did (probably the normal thing) was to make it the same, twelve per cent.[27] According to the Gnomon of the Idiologos that was the rate in Egypt under the Principate.[28] According to Ulpian interest over one hundred per cent and compound interest were void;[29] perhaps what he meant was the two things taken together, *i.e.* compound interest that raised the total owing to more than twice the original debt, for compound interest was not in itself prohibited—Cicero allowed addition of interest to principal annually in his province.[30] The *Digest* also tells us that a judge who had to assess interest in a *bona fide* action had to take into account the 'custom of the

region'.[31] In addition there were rules about interest on debts
not settled by due date, the details of which we cannot embark
on.[32] There was no National Debt; the state did not, except in
rare moments of emergency, borrow from private individuals.
On debts of individuals to the treasury the normal rate in Paulus'
time was six per cent.[33]

The activities of the hated professional moneylender are
illustrated by a group of the Transylvanian Tablets, which record
certain transactions by a small-time practitioner of this necessary
but despised trade in the Dacian mining villages, one Julius
Alexander.[34] In AD 167 we find him in a moneylending partnership with another man;[35] their entire capital was a bit under
three thousand sesterces and the partnership was for four months
only—just to make a little quick profit out of local poverty,
no doubt. In two documents of a few years earlier we get his
actual contracts of loan, at the standard maximum of twelve per
cent interest; in one case he is lending and in the other he is
himself borrowing. Here is the lending contract:[36]

'For sixty denarii to be given on the day requested (for repay-
ment) in good coin: promise called for in good faith by Julius
Alexander, duly given in good faith by Alexander, son of
Cariccius, who declares that he has received the sixty denarii
in cash as a loan and owes them. And for the interest upon
them from this day per thirty days one per cent to be given
to Julius Alexander or to whomsoever it may concern, promise
called for in good faith by Julius Alexander, duly given in good
faith by Alexander, son of Cariccius. Surety for payment of
aforesaid principal and interest, properly and in good coin:
Titius Primitivus. Transacted at Alburnus Maior, 20 October,
consulship of Rusticus for the second time and Aquilinus.'

*

To us, to whom entering into a contract means signing on a
dotted line, so that the layman would say that, on the one hand, if
there is no writing there is no contract and, on the other, a piece
of writing if produced cannot be gainsaid, the Roman idea of
writing as being inessential, mere evidence, is at first perplexing.
The reader might be pardoned for turning with relief to the next

kind of contract we must come to, the contract 'by writing',
litteris (in which, as Gaius explains,[37] the writing did constitute
the contract), and for wondering why it was not brought in first,
and perhaps supposing that it must have been the commonest
form of Roman legal bargain. He would, however, be quite
wrong.[38] It was a very specialized arrangement, and though
it existed in Cicero's time the absence of later evidence for it
except Gaius' rather inadequate description[39] suggests that it
actually faded out of use. It was not made 'by writing' in general,
but by entries in account books; A entered a sum of money as
owed him by B, and that constituted the contract (but, though
Gaius does not say this, there must have been required some
evidence of reciprocal agreement or consent by B). Its purpose
was auxiliary: to turn contracts from one form into another (*e.g.*
a *bona fide* consensual contract of sale into a *stricti iuris* written
contract) or from one person to another (*e.g.* to transfer a debt).
Cicero's defence of Roscius the actor ought to be our best guide
to the contract *litteris*, because it turns a good deal on entries in
account-books; but we cannot tell whether he is talking of
entries as contract or entries as evidence (he is making a case and
perhaps deliberately muddying the waters, and we have not got
the plaintiff's side).[40] It is possible that this form of contract
proved unsatisfactory because the Romans did not have double-
entry bookkeeping; it does not seem to have been particularly
used by the banking houses, who kept the most systematic
accounts.

Gaius notes that in the Greek-speaking world (which had long
been used to treating contract as a writing) deeds of hand,
acknowledging debt and promising payment, were accepted as
contractual in force.[41]

★

We come to the final group, known as the 'consensual' contracts,
which include three sorts of bargain of particular importance for
commerce: sale, hire, and partnership. Every contract is consensual in the sense that it involves agreement between people,
but these particular ones were consensual in the special sense that
nothing but *consensus* was needed to constitute the contract—no

writing, no particular words, no presence of parties, no handing over of anything; none of these were of the essence, and the contract was 'on' from the moment of agreement. It is a great question of Republican legal history just when these fully consensual contracts achieved acceptance,[42] but we can talk about them freely because they were there at least by Cicero's time. They contained nothing that could not be done by stipulations, but for many purposes they had great advantages. They were bilateral, creating both rights and duties in both or all the parties by a single act of agreement (as is implied by the double name of two of them; 'buying-selling', *emptio venditio*, and 'letting-hiring', *locatio conductio*). More important, they gave rise to *bona fide*, instead of *stricti iuris*, actions, so that any balancing of sums or interests and any other agreements relevant to that in dispute could be taken into account by the judge, and the *formula* needed no *exceptiones*.

Some documents of sale have already been quoted in connection with slavery; here are just two more, again from widely separated parts of the Roman world. The first is from Dacia, its date AD 159:[43]

'Andueia, daughter (? son) of Bato has bought and received by mancipation half a house, the right half going in, which is at Alburnus Maior, in the hamlet of the Pirustae, between the neighbours Plator Acceptianus and Ingenuus son of Callistus, for three hundred denarii from Veturius Valens. This half-house, object of contract, with its fences, surrounding walls, bounds, entrances, doors and windows, locked with keys and in best condition, Andueia daughter of Bato is to possess lawfully. And if anyone makes eviction of said house or any share in it, so as to prevent Andueia daughter of Bato or anyone whom it may concern from holding, possessing or usucapting it lawfully, then for proper payment of such sum as represents the value of what has been prevented, promise has been called in good faith by Andueia daughter of Bato and duly given in good faith by Veturius Valens. And as price of the said half house Veturius Valens declares that he has received and holds from Andueia daughter of Bato three hundred denarii. And it has been agreed between them that Veturius Valens shall pay taxation on the aforesaid house until the next census. Transacted at Alburnus Maior, 6 May, consulship of Quintillus and Priscus.'

The second is from somewhere in Egypt, and its date is AD 77:[44]

'C. Valerius Longus, trooper of the Aprian Squadron, has bought one horse, Cappadocian, black, for two thousand seven hundred Augustan drachmas from C. Julius Rufus, centurion of legion XXII. That said horse eats and drinks as veterinary animals customarily do, apart from [. . .] described openly visible on its body, and if anyone makes eviction of him, that double [? single] the value shall be properly paid in good coin as is customary, promise was called for by C. Valerius, duly given by C. Julius Rufus. And C. Julius Rufus, centurion, declares that he has received and holds from C. Valerius Longus, purchaser, said two thousand seven hundred Augustan drachmas, and [has transferred said horse to him]. Transacted at [. . .], 7 June [or 9 July], consulship of the Emperor Vespasian, eighth time, and Domitian, son of the Emperor, fifth time.'

We observe that it was normal to add to the contract of sale *stricti iuris* stipulations for undisturbed enjoyment and quality of the goods, even outside the cases required by the aedilician edict, and to record receipt of the price. It may be that the *bona fide* element in sale left purchasers a bit unhappy, so that they preferred the security of *strictum ius* for their essential guarantees (though the standard clauses may just reflect the hidebound practice of local notaries). A number of anecdotes in Cicero illustrate the problems in the field of house-buying. We have already had the story about the house burdened with an undisclosed demolition order; there is another about one sold without express mention of a servitude (it was sold to a man who had owned it once before and so was alleged to know anyway).[45] In these cases the *bona fide* nature of the action gave all needed scope to the judge, but the case of the unfortunate C. Canius was different.[46] He bought a 'little property' at Syracuse in the belief, induced by fraud, that it was a marvellous place for fish; but he allowed the price to go down as a book debt against him, a contract *litteris—stricti iuris*. So when he discovered there was no regular fishing for miles he had no remedy, for, says Cicero:

'my friend and colleague C. Aquilius had not yet invented the formulas *de dolo malo*.'

A famous rule of sale in Roman law was that, unless there was express agreement to the contrary, the risk of accidental destruction of, or damage to, the object passed to the buyer as soon as the contract was made. It is true that the seller was under a duty to transfer it to the buyer, and was liable (on what seems the best view) for *custodia* of it until he did so, but this still leaves damage or destruction by violence or natural forces—if the house was destroyed by an earthquake the buyer nevertheless had to pay the price. Risk has to lie somewhere, of course, but normally it passes when ownership passes,[47] whereas in Roman law transfer of ownership awaited the necessary *traditio* or mancipation. And about transfer of ownership there is one additional and truly vexing problem which at first sight looks very fundamental but surely cannot have mattered as much in practice as it seems: Justinian in his *Institutes* gives a rule (not copied from Gaius) that even when the object of sale has been transferred (by *traditio*, he says; but then he had abolished *mancipatio*), ownership of it only passes when the price has been paid or security given for the price.[48] Justinian quotes the Twelve Tables for this rule, but he ends his statement by adding lamely that 'if the seller accepts the good faith of the buyer, then ownership does pass straight away'. A *Digest* text from Pomponius gives the same rule—with the same feeble pendant that reduces the rule to a nullity (but of course the pendant might be an interpolation);[49] and in the *Digest* even Gaius seems to imply the same.[50] But in his *Institutes*, Gaius says firmly that *res nec mancipi* handed over by one who owns them become the property of the buyer at once.[51] Virtually every possible view has been expressed by scholars about this set of passages.[52] It is really a question about sale on credit, and it may be best to hold that the rule existed but did not long have practical importance, because (*a*) every seller in his senses would require some security if the price was not paid at once, otherwise he just would not convey, and (*b*) the praetor protected possession *ad usucapionem*, so ownership for that short period did not matter.

Another thorny set of problems (not only for Roman law) concerns mistake in consensual contracts like sale. Many kinds of mistake can be analysed; a typical one is if you think you are buying this bed and the other man thinks he is selling you that bed. The subject is deep and complex and we cannot embark on it.[53]

Most things could be objects of a valid sale, including inheritances, servitudes, and the right to collect debts. You could have sale of something from a stock of things, or sale of a future thing, like the next harvest,[54] or a real gamble (though we do not hear much about lotteries, only of the small 'raffle' sort occasionally at imperial festivals in Rome). You could have sale subject to all sorts of conditions; two need mention. *In diem addictio* was in effect 'sale subject to a better offer':[55]

'If he gets a better offer the vendor must notify the first bidder, so that if someone has added more he himself may add yet more.'

And the *pactum displicentiae* was in effect 'sale on approval':[56]

'Labeo has a question: suppose I have handed you horses to try for sale on condition that you return them in three days if not satisfied, and you run a vaulting-race on them and win it and then refuse to buy, is there an action of sale against you?'

A common field of application of this was the sale of wine with a right to taste it.[57] As to one kind of transaction which the texts never discuss under (and which, it is assumed, was not amongst the possibilities of) *emptio venditio*, scholars sometimes make a song and dance. This is what is nowadays called *emptio generis*, sale not of a specific thing or part of a specific stock but just 'a horse'—as opposed to 'one of those horses'—or 'twenty dozen

Arretine cups of standard size'. Now this is just the kind of sale that modern large-scale commerce mostly deals with, and its absence from the texts on *emptio venditio* is sometimes said to correlate with the lack of mass-production and mass-consumption in the Roman world. But it must be remembered that the bargain could always be achieved by stipulations, and there is some evidence that it was:[58]

> 'If someone calls for promise of "one hundred modii of good African wheat" or "one hundred amphorae of good Campanian wine", this, it seems, is a stipulation for a "thing uncertain", because you can find something better than good, so that "good" does not signify any absolute standard. But if you call for promise of "best quality" you are taken to mean something the goodness of which is the highest grade of goodness, and consequently that adjective signifies something "certain".'

It is interesting to be told that 'English experience in connection with bulk sales, which are usually governed, not by the Sale of Goods Act, but by standard contracts, seems to show that . . . parties prefer to set out all the terms afresh. The *stipulatio* was peculiarly fitted for this purpose.'[59]

For a contract to be an *emptio venditio* there had to be a money price—otherwise it was barter; it had to be a real, not a nominal, price—otherwise it was gift; and it had to be definite price. We cannot go into the detailed application of these rules.[60]

A regular feature of Roman life was the auction sale. One aspect of it was the selling up by public auction on behalf of the treasury of the property of condemned persons (including Emperors);[61] but the private auction was common and important, especially for land or the contents of inheritances—guardians, for example, were under a duty to get the best price for property of their wards. During our period the custom was for these sales to be done through an intermediary, *argentarius coactor*, the banker-auctioneer.[62] A recent study has elucidated the triangular legal relationship between buyer, seller and middleman.[63] Caecilius Iucundus, the banker and moneylender of Pompeii, some of whose files survived its catastrophe, was engaged in these transactions; they could be for quite substantial sums, given the middle-class ambience of that small city. Here is a specimen, of AD 54:[64]

> 'One thousand nine hundred and eighty-five sesterces, which sum was object of stipulatory contract by L. Caecilius Iucundus on account of auction of box-plantation of C. Iulius Onesimus, payable by next 15 July: this sum, less auction fee, C. Iulius Onesimus has declared himself to have received from M. Fabius Agathinus on account of L. Caecilius Iucundus. Transacted at Pompeii, 10 May, consulship of M'. Acilius Aviola and M. Asinius Marcellus.'

The standard purchase tax was calculated on the price as paid (or promised) by the purchaser to the middleman.[65]

The reader will naturally enquire how far the Romans used deposit in our common modern sense—the advance on the price, which the buyer will forfeit if he does not go through with the bargain. It can serve many purposes in different systems, from simply giving a man a 'first refusal' on something to being the actual clinching moment of a contract. Rome used for it the Greek word arrha[66] (or its Semitic form, also used in Greek, arrhabo); in the Greek law of sale arrha was clinching, and this role persisted sturdily, at least in Egypt.[67] Greek law stuck to sale as a handing of something over for cash; mere agreement to buy and sell imposed no duties and grounded no actions. Consequently arrha was a form of security that the agreement would be turned into actuality. The Romans, once they had developed consensual sale, in which the consensus was the contract and grounded the actions, did not need arrha in a clinching role. It was used, indeed, and Plautus is full of it (perhaps because his plays were written before consensual sale had been fully recognized),[68] but in our period it was treated as merely evidentiary:[69]

> 'Sale is contracted when the price has been agreed on, even if it has not been paid and even if no arrha has been given. For

what is given under the name of *arrha* is evidence of a contract of sale.'

(Gaius sounds here as if he is warning against an erroneous opinion into which people—in the East, for example—might be prone to fall.) Roman Egypt had a 'law of *arrhabo*' which was penal; the vendor was liable for double the deposit if he failed to fulfil (the buyer simply forfeited the deposit).[70] Naturally, if you did give a deposit it counted as an instalment of the price;[71] and in general, payment by instalments was perfectly proper if the parties so contracted,[72] as was also agreement that if the whole price was not in by a given date the sale was rescinded.[73]

The contract of *locatio conductio* covered such a variety of transactions that we have met some of its rules in two different chapters already—tenancy in Chapter V and hire of labour in Chapter VI. We are left with what one might call the 'business' aspects of it—the bargains for carrying out some specific task for a reward, such as transport of goods or people, cleaning, repairing or storing goods, building houses, and manufacturing things out of customers' materials. This branch of *locatio conductio* is not sharp-edged; it fades off into sale,[74] and may be difficult to distinguish in certain cases from hire of labour and hire of premises.[75] Like sale, it was a consensual, *bona fide* contract and there had to be a money reward; but to a much greater degree than with sale there entered into this contract difficult problems about custody and risk, as to the Roman law's solutions for which modern scholars are still much at odds;[76] there is no doubt that those solutions underwent modification with time, but great doubt as to which direction the modifications moved in. It must be kept firmly in mind that people could make what arrangements they liked about these points if they chose specifically so to contract; what we have to ask is, what was the law in our period about custody and risk if no specific provisions had been agreed? Everyone who held something under this contract would be liable to make good his deliberate fault or carelessness (on the fault of his employees there is doubt owing to suspicions of interpolation in a text of Ulpian).[77] Gaius tells us that *fullo* and *sarcinator*, the Roman cleaner and repairer of clothes, respectively, were liable for *custodia*,[78] which is much more severe, because it includes situations in which a man would not normally be said to be at fault—notably, theft. Now many scholars believe that Gaius' *fullo* and *sarcinator* were intended by him as typical cases, and that therefore all 'bailees' under the contract of *locatio conductio* were liable for *custodia*; but not everyone agrees. Unfortunately, whatever Justinian's professors found about this in the texts they used for the *Digest*, they altered it all to fit in with a quite different scheme of relative liabilities, and this makes it impossible to be sure what the classical texts said. The dividing line, at any rate, is theft. On one side of it (certain liability) we hear a lot about lack of care[79]—the careless laundry that lets your clothes be nibbled by mice, the careless navigator, and so on—and it was firmly stated that incompetent workmanship counted on this side of the line.[80] On the other side (certain non-liability), are the events called *casus* and *vis maior*, that is, accidents of nature or of human violence such as robbers stealing goats, passing armies, fires, blight and landslides. About ordinary wear and tear we are not informed; one text makes it sound as if this was normally specified in contracts, where appropriate.[81]

From this point on it will be better to look at one or two commercial situations more specifically, beginning with building. First, we are told (it is not self-evident) that building contracts were *locatio*, not sale.[82] You might begin with a mandate to the builder to quote you a price;[83] then you would agree the contract, including of course the price and sometimes a completion date.[84] The contract might be for a lump sum, *per aversionem*, in which case all risk was on the builder until the moment of final approval by the client; or, in the modern way, the payment might be by stages based on quantity survey of the amounts completed, *per pedes mensurasve*, and the builder then took the risk only of the uncompleted parts (and the client must not deliberately delay the necessary surveys).[85] The builder was not in any event liable for *casus* unless the contract stated so.[86] There is talk also of payment by the day, but it would not be likely for house-building;

perhaps it was for small things like garden walls or sheds. There might or might not be approval by the day, but this was not *locatio operarum*: approval was necessary if the workman was to qualify for his price.[87] 'Approval by client', we are told, meant 'satisfaction as a good man would judge';[88] and there is one passage, on the consequences of changes due to client's impromptu orders on the site, which will remind the modern architect vividly of his own problems.[89]

If we look next at the transport system of the Roman world we shall be involved in one or two sets of legal rules besides those of *locatio conductio*. Maritime arrangements were pre-eminently a field in which the Romans were preceded, and always outclassed and outnumbered, by the Levantines and Greeks, and it used to be held by everybody and is still widely held that the Romans just borrowed the set of maritime rules which they found existing in the Mediterranean world, especially two typical branches, the law of bottomry loans, *nauticum faenus*, and the law of jettison or 'average', *iactus*. That there was a group of rules going by the name of the 'Rhodian Sea Law', known in our period to the Romans[90] and surviving into the Middle Ages,[91] cannot be denied, but there are reasons for being sceptical whether the Romans borrowed these rules (notwithstanding the existence in the *Digest* of a title (14. 2) 'On the Rhodian Law of Jettison') and did not rather reach similar results on a basis of their own legal principles of *mutuum* and *locatio*.[92]

Nauticum faenus, or *traiecticia pecunia*, was the loan of money to a man to enable him to buy a cargo to ship and sell abroad, risk being on the lender so that he could only sue for his principal and interest on the safe return of the ship, and the cargo (and often the ship too) being security for the loan.[93] It was a form of maritime insurance. Great profits could be made, but the risks were great, and so the interest that could be charged was not subject to any statutory maximum, provided that the creditor took the whole risk (*i.e.* that the contract really was *nauticum faenus* and not just an ordinary loan).[94] There is in the *Digest* an argument based on a set of facts which include what looks like a standard bottomry contract:[95]

'Callimachus received a bottomry loan from Stichus, slave of Seius, in the province of Syria, city of Beirut, destination Brindisi; sum in credit: two hundred sesterces for each day of the voyage; pledged as security: the goods bought at Beirut for carriage to Brindisi and any goods to be bought at Brindisi for return carriage to Beirut. And it was agreed between them that on arrival at Brindisi Callimachus should before 13 September following buy other goods, load them, and sail back to Syria, or that if by due date he had not bought other goods and left that city he should repay the whole sum as if the voyage were now terminated, and provide all necessary expenses for those persons carrying the money to enable them to take it to Rome. Promise for proper performance of all these things was called for by Stichus, slave of L. Titius, duly given by Callimachus.'

Iactus, 'jettison', is the rule whereby, if goods have hastily to be cast overboard to save a ship (or handed over to pirates to ransom it), the man whose property was sacrificed is entitled to a contribution from those whose property was thereby saved. In the Byzantine 'Rhodian Sea Law' this principle of 'all in the same boat' was carried very far on a kind of partnership notion, but the Roman law of our period seems to have kept it within narrow bounds (insisting, for example, that the rules only applied if the ship *was* saved), and to have thought of it as arising out of the contract: the loser had an action against the captain who had ordered his things to be thrown over, and the captain was entitled to recover from those whose goods he had saved, the whole being judged on a *bona fide* basis:[96]

'A number of merchants had on board the same ship a variety of cargoes; in addition there were numerous passengers, slave and free. A great storm rose and they had to jettison. The following questions arose: must all parties contribute to make up the loss, even those whose cargoes added no weight to the ship, such as gems or pearls? And what is the basis of apportionment? And must there be contribution on behalf of free passengers [*i.e.* without cargo]? And by what action is all this to be achieved?

The answers were: all who had a [pecuniary] interest in the jettison taking place must contribute, because things thereby saved owe contribution; therefore the owner of the vessel is himself liable for a share. The sum of loss is to be apportioned *pro rata* to the values of the respective cargoes. No financial estimate can be made of free persons. The owners of the goods sacrificed will have an action on their contract of hire with the captain, *i.e.* the ship-master.'

This passage illuminates the ordinary sea transport arrangements (as well as perils)[96a] in the Roman world. One finds very little reference to exclusively passenger vessels—perhaps only the 'packet-boat' on the busy Brindisi–Dyrrhachium crossing;[97] and merchants normally voyaged with their cargoes. There is much else of interest in the *Digest* on freight transport. One text is about lack of care by a lighterman transferring cargo; the importance of these *navicularii* on the rivers in general and especially at river mouths, like Ostia, is well known.[98] Another concerns the 'irregular *locatio*' of grain ships (compare the 'irregular *depositum*' in banks) whereby several shippers poured their grain into a common hold and were entitled to delivery by quantity.[99] And a third, a rare and valuable passage, quotes the cargo quantities in a ship carrying oil and grain from Cyrene to Aquileia.[100]

Road transport makes its appearance a little more frequently than the usual disdainful references to it might lead one to expect. It was slow, inefficient, subject to brigands and to frequent tolls; apart from the *cursus publicus*, the government post and supply service, it was probably not used much for long-distance travel, which relied on rivers and the sea. But it existed; you had to get goods to the rivers and the sea. The ox-waggon was ubiquitous, and so was the mule-waggon: 'all vehicles on the roads are drawn by pairs of them', says Varro, who also mentions trains of pack-donkeys bringing produce to the sea.[101] Thus in the *Digest* we get pack-mules hired with agreement as to maximum load,[102] the mule-waggon paying toll at a toll-bridge,[103] and road transport of columns, tree-trunks and wine-vats,[104] not to mention

P

the case of the careless cabby (whose fare, tipped out and injured, was someone's slave).[105]

Travellers were offered certain special protections. The praetor's edict propounded two actions against 'shipmen, innkeepers and stablekeepers'.[106] One was a special action of theft;[107] the other said:[108]

'Whatever property of any person shipmen, innkeepers and stablekeepers have received for safe custody, unless they return it I will give an action against them.'

These were all people at whose mercy the traveller was. He could not stop to choose—and usually there would be no choice.[109] He had to carry his money on him, and the goods he carried might be valuable and might be someone else's. Innkeepers were notoriously liable to be in league with local thieves,[110] and shipmen were a no less shady lot;[111] and all of them were likely to be *institores* or *exercitores*, agents for an absent owner. The special liability under theft is straightforward: the ordinary *actio furti* lay only against the thief (or accomplice), but this praetorian action lay against the innkeeper, etc., for theft committed by any of their servants or the permanent inhabitants of their premises (not by other travellers, if Ulpian's statement is free from interpolation).[112] But the special liability for safe custody is a subject of extreme controversy, directed mainly to (a) whether it applied only to goods specifically accepted for custody, and (b) why it was needed at all, if 'bailees' under *locatio conductio* were liable for *custodia* in any case, as many think they were.[113] The texts are contradictory, as can be seen by comparing *Digest* 4. 9. 5 pr. with 47. 5. 1. 4 on question (a) and with 4. 9. 3. 1 on question (b). What follows must therefore be understood to be very dogmatic and very far from an 'agreed opinion'. First, this liability was fundamentally concerned with the baggage of travellers, not with carriage of freight in general;[114] it is a mistake to think that it was originally or ever part of shipping law as such. Secondly, whether or not 'bailees' were in any case liable for *custodia*, innkeepers, etc., were singled out because of the special position of travellers. The traveller's contract was for lodging or conveying himself; it was not obvious that he was entitled on that to an *actio locati* for the baggage. What is more, *locatio conductio* being a *bona fide* contract, allowing considerations of set-off, an *actio locati* for the baggage might become entangled with argument about the bill. Or the traveller might be carrying someone else's valuables for which only their owner could have an *actio furti*. Thirdly, there was probably no special pact of custody.[115] If it seems unfair on the innkeeper, if his guest was travelling with priceless undeclared ropes of pearls, it should be recalled that the English 'common innkeeper' was under just such an unrestricted liability until the 1860's. Perhaps the *Hotel Proprietors Act, 1956*, may afford a guess as to what actually happened; the notice, which every hotel must display, makes the hotel liable 'to make good any loss or damage to a guest's property even though it was not due to any fault of the proprietor or staff', but the liability is limited to £100 per guest, except for items specifically deposited. Now Labeo discusses a case in which:[116]

'the manager of a repository put up a notice that he did not receive gold, silver or pearls at his risk.'

It may be conjectured that innkeepers, etc., protected themselves in the same way, *i.e.* by saying 'of the following things I do not accept *custodia*'. It is a guess, but we do hear of shipmasters excluding liability for damage in this way.[117]

The question arises in a particularly acute form in the case of this institution of the law: how real in practice was the protection it afforded to travellers, who *ex hypothesi* needed to get on about their business? There were no grand hotels;[118] the rich travelled via their own chains of private villas or those of their friends,[119] so these provisions would benefit (if at all) middle-class people, the business community. We have no record of any actual case of prosecution under this heading; and yet it is not plausible that this kind of rule, a special invention, not just an assertion of some old principle, was for nothing and to no effect. The traveller had one thing on his side: the innkeeper would always be there to proceed against; and one must not underestimate the willingness of the 'man in the street', in a reasonably orderly society, to pursue his rights.

Repositories were provided by private enterprise for the storage of foodstuffs and other goods in a very general way; see the placard, from somewhere in Rome:[120]

> 'In these private repositories, owner Q. Tineius Sacerdos Clemens, . . . are for hire grain space, lock-up space, close storage, safes, column-safes and space for safes, from today and from 1 July.'

They were naturally commonest in the big commercial centres like Ostia,[121] and Rome itself. A couple of further passages in the *Digest* give hints as to the law about them.[122] It seems that, as usual, the owner let out the running of the premises to a contractor, who did the detailed letting of space. This middleman, the *horrearius*, was liable to his customers for *custodia*, naturally enough (though we have seen that he might post notice of exceptions); he could not push his liability back on to the owner unless *their* contract specified this.[123] A fragment from a work on the duties of the prefect of the watch adds that if the tenants of space in a repository did not appear or pay the charges for a long time permission could be obtained to open their safes and take an inventory.[124] The government itself provided similar premises, and there survives a famous 'notice of terms' of an imperial repository:[125]

> 'In these repositories of the emperor [. . .] Caesar Augustus are for hire grain space, lock-up space, safes and space for safes with service of custodians from today and 1 [January]. Rules of the repository: Anyone wishing to retain for a further year the safe or whatever else he rents must have rent paid up and give notice before 13 December. . . . No liability is undertaken for gold and silver. All property stored in these repositories will be subject to a lien to the contractor against due payment of rent. . . . If anyone renting space in these repositories leaves his property there without making it over under seal to the custodian, the contractor will not be liable.'

As there was a contractor in here there is no reason to think that the rules laid down were different from what would have applied in a privately owned repository.[126]

A discussion of the Roman law of partnership should contain what can be said about Roman company law. It is not very much. Except in one category, that of the *publicani*, we do not hear of big commercial enterprises; perhaps the best evidence for the sort of joint businesses that did exist is provided by the potsherds from the 'Monte Testaccio', that extraordinary hill near the Protestant cemetery in Rome composed entirely of the remnants of the jars in which foodstuffs, mostly from Spain and Africa, were brought to Rome and offloaded at the Tiber wharves.[127] Both the potters' stamps and the painted abbreviations of names of the producing firms survive in some numbers, and when they are not just a single name they are combinations like 'the two Aurelii Heraclae, father and son', 'the Fadii', 'Cutius Celsianus and Fabius Galaticus', 'the Caecilii and freedmen', 'the two Junii, Melissus and Melissa',[128] 'the partners Hyacinthus, Isidore and Pollio', 'L. Marius Phoebus and the Vibii, Viator and Restitutus'. It does not follow, of course, that 'Snooks and Son' may not be a huge firm, but the Monte Testaccio pattern suggests small 'workshop' businesses into which men brought their sons and their skilled workmen (freedmen, in fact) to share the profit and the loss—a sort of 'partiary' arrangement in lieu of a wage, perhaps. As a matter of legal history it is generally agreed that *societas* derived ultimately from the ancient automatic common ownership of family property by undivided heirs. Voluntary *consortium* of brothers goes on being found all through our period;[129] and very similar to it is the most characteristic form of partnership, the *societas omnium bonorum*, partnership of entire property, which was not commercial at all but based on the family notion. Even when business partnerships became common, their legal rules retained some of the familial atmosphere.

Societas was a consensual, *bona fide* contract. It could be between any number of people, for many purposes (not necessarily financial), though not every joint activity was in law a *societas*.[130]

Apart from *omnium bonorum*, we hear in Gaius of slave-trading as a typical partnership activity;[131] moneylending we have met in the Transylvanian Tablets and shall meet again; the facts in Cicero's speech *pro Roscio comoedo* were about a *societas* between a man who had a gifted slave and Roscius the actor—the latter to teach his art to the slave and the partners to share the proceeds of their protégé's stage career. In the *Digest* we have men running a school in partnership, and an architect teaming up with a land agent.[132] And Cicero's *pro Quinctio*, it is important to recall, was about an agricultural partnership. The agreement must not be for a criminal purpose: robbers could not have an action *pro socio* for division of spoils.[133] Otherwise any terms whatever could, as usual, be agreed between the partners, especially about shares of profit and loss, except that it was not lawful so to arrange that one partner shared losses but took no profit at all (and anyone who wonders why such a rule was needed should remember the patron-freedman partnerships of the Monte Testaccio and the position of the *necessarius heres*). In default of express agreement shares in profit and loss were assumed to be in the same proportion.[134] Every member must contribute something, but it need not be money or goods, but could perfectly well be skill, knowledge or standing. Agreement was between a fixed number of specific people, each to each; there was no possibility of 'sleeping' partners with financial shares just coming in and out, nor did a partner's heir automatically succeed him in the firm.[135] Indeed, the death, *capitis deminutio* or selling up of any partner brought the whole business technically to an end, and so did the retirement of any one partner. This did not matter much, for tacit agreement of the rest to continue was enough; what did matter (and brings out the climate of the whole concept) was that any litigation on the partnership brought it to an end—the *actio pro socio*, in other words, was an action to liquidate the firm, and you could not wrangle in the courts about subsidiary questions without destroying the business.

Nor was that all. Two important legal features of modern companies are agency and limited liability. In Roman law a partner was not an agent for all;[136] his acquisitions and contracts accrued to and bound only himself. He was naturally liable *pro socio* to bring acquisitions into the agreed joint management and exploitation, and his colleagues were liable *pro socio* to reimburse him, according to their shares, for his contracts, but that is quite a different matter from these things automatically accruing to or binding the firm as such. Secondly, in Roman law no rule was ever made confining the liability of a partner for the debts of the firm to the extent of his financial contribution. Partners were liable for the firm's whole debts in proportion to their shares in the partnership, or, to put it another way, here as always a man's debts were owed in full, but he could have an action to recover from his colleagues *pro socio* according to the proportions agreed in the partnership contract. Naturally, you could not legitimately retire from the firm in such a way as to escape your liabilities, but the structure made it all too possible for partners to let their colleagues down:[137]

> 'It's his ruddy freedmen; they've walked off with the whole show. You know what I mean; the firm's pot never gets to the boil, and the second things begin to run down hill your pals get out from under.'

It does not look as if the partners in the Transylvanian money-lending business regarded each other with much *bona fides*; we find them almost at the expiry of the partnership taking stipulations:[138]

> 'A partnership of moneylending was entered into between Cassius Frontinus and Julius Alexander, from 23 December last, consulship of Pudens and Pollio [AD 166], to continue to 12 April next. Terms: that any profit and loss from said partnership be borne in equal proportions. Into which partnership Julius Alexander contributed, in cash or out at interest, five hundred denarii, and Secundus, *servus actor* of Cassius Palumbus, contributed two hundred and sixty-seven denarii on behalf of Frontinus. . . . In which partnership if anyone is found to have committed fraud by malice he shall pay one denarius per as, twenty denarii per denarius. At end of term, with deduction

of debts, each is to recover the sum above stated, or, if there is a profit, to divide it. For these things so to be done promise called for by Cassius Frontinus, duly given by Julius Alexander. Concerning which two pairs of tablets have been signed. Also owed to Cossa: fifty denarii, which are due to him from the above partners. Transacted at Deusaris, 28 March, consulship of Verus, third time, and Quadratus' (AD 167).

A bit more is to be said about financial business, though it is in a way parenthetical, because finance was not necessarily carried on in partnership. It was essentially money-changing, money-holding and money-lending, and its operators appear under various names, probably with rather different functions which cannot be very clearly distinguished because they over-lapped in practice. The wealthy families all did moneylending with their own spare cash, and this sometimes took the form of a small private bank, *kalendarium*, in charge, perhaps, of a slave—or even several, on their widely scattered properties—for the convenience (or exploitation) of tenants.[139] Then there is the *daneista* or *faenerator*, the professional moneylender. Higher up we come to *nummularii* and *mensularii*,[140] who were bankers, doing both deposit and lending business, but (as the names suggest) in a small way; and at the top are the *argentarii*, the big-scale bankers, who might well be *publicani* doing private business. A picture can be got from Cicero of their international functions. They made payments to public officials in the provinces on presentation of government bills of exchange,[141] and, for known customers, similar payments on private drafts; the story of how young Quintus was paid his allowance at Athens University through Atticus' bankers there can be traced in the letters.[142] Another picture, of later date, is furnished by the files of Caecilius Iucundus, who not only carried on at Pompeii the auction business which we have seen, but also ran a laundry under license from the municipality[143] and paid public dues on behalf of other similar contractors.[144]

The *argentarii* were sufficiently important to generate some special rules of law. Women were excluded from the profession.[145] A partner here was agent for the firm, in the sense that you could sue any of his colleagues on a contract made by him.[146] The praetor gave a special action to enforce a kind of agreement which was no doubt commonly undertaken, called *receptum argentarii*, namely that the banker would pay a customer's debt over to his creditor (not, apparently, by the book transaction *litteris*);[147] the agreement effectively transferred the debt, so that the creditor could now sue the bank if it was not settled.[148] Another set of special rules appears in the *Digest* title 2. 13 'On Disclosure'. The books of *argentarii* were regarded as unimpeachable legal evidence, and, on grounds of public policy (we are told), were the subject of an edict[149] in which the praetor required bankers to disclose their entries as evidence on behalf of anyone to whose case they were relevant, provided he swore that his application was not vexatious; if disclosure was wrongfully withheld there was an action.[150] (*Nummularii*, says Pomponius, are not covered by the edict, but they ought to disclose like *argentarii*, for their business is essentially the same.)[151] Yet another rule is given by Gaius, discussing *bona fide* actions:[152] business between a bank and its customers was on a basis of the *bona fide* contract of mandate, not stipulations, but in claims against customers bankers must do their own calculation of debits and credits and sue only for the balance. If they overclaimed they lost all—a fierce rule, which shows why their books had to be so accurate. The *Digest* invents a typical banker's letter to customer:[153]

> 'From your bank account with me, at present date you have a balance on various transactions, in hand at the bank, of three hundred and eighty-six and appropriate interest. This sum which you now have in credit with me, uncontested, I shall refund. Any document under your hand for any sum on any transaction, still remaining with me, will be treated as null and cancelled.'

The only substantial exceptions to the general legal rules about partnership were designed for the *publicani*.[154] These companies, to whom was farmed out in the Republican age the collection of all indirect taxation and the direct *tributum* of some of the wealthiest provinces (and companies they had to be, for individuals did not dispose of the great sums required), were indispensable in the absence of an extensive civil service. Their general history is well known; in their heyday, the time of Cicero, they wielded political power; the early emperors took much of the taxation out of their hands and deprived them of political influence, but they still farmed all the indirect taxes for a long time, and had to be subjected to new regulations by Nero. In the second century AD they gradually dropped out of the taxation structure—though not entirely, in our period, for Septimius Severus is still found struggling with their abuses. Cicero's speeches, especially the *Verrines*, are the main evidence for their elaborate international organization. We must summarize the modifications in partnership law which facilitated their business and the rules made to curb their excesses. In the Republican period the taxes were farmed by the censors on the basis of their *lustrum*, that is, for five years at a time, and this continued under the Principate;[155] so the *societates publicanorum* were, as such, quite short-lived, since they had to be reconstituted anew each time, and the censors had power to exclude anyone from participation. It is probable that the same groups tended to reassemble, but presumably they could not carry any accounts over.[155a] Within the period, however, they had two advantages: death of a partner did not dissolve the company (unless he happened to be the managing director), neither did litigation.[156] It is customary to add a third point, that people could come in and out as shareholders, *participes*. The evidence is in truth very thin. It depends first on a well-known remark of Polybius (in the second century BC), that every citizen in Italy had a stake in the state contracts,[157] which must at the very least be a fantastic exaggeration, and secondly on a quotation by Cicero of one of Verres' edicts:[158]

'. . . let him not admit as partner nor give a share . . .,'

with a late, but ancient, gloss saying that it meant 'having a fixed share and no action for division like a partner'.[159] This latter is evidence that if there were shareholders they did *not* come in and out, buying and selling from day to day, but were in for the whole term of the *societas*. The idea of the little man having his flutter on equities can be dismissed, but it is quite likely that the very wealthy *nobiles* participated on a 'sleeping' basis, helping the companies to meet the huge security that was demanded for these public contracts. A fourth point might be added: the *senatus-consultum Macedonianum* did not apply, so there was no bar to *filii familias* being partners.[160] There is question also as to a fifth point: were the companies of *publicani* at some stage recognized as corporations? We shall not tackle the difficult jurisprudential problems about the nature of 'legal personality' and how far the Romans had such a concept;[161] but the municipalities and certain *collegia*[162] were corporations in the sense that they could have a common chest, own property, manumit slaves, receive legacies and so on. Whether the *publicani* gained the same privilege really rests on *Digest* 3. 4. 1 pr., where they are equated by what purports to be Gaius with 'certain *collegia*' as being permitted to 'corpus habere'.[163] It is a much suspected text, and not a strong enough peg to hang an assertion on. They certainly had a common chest and common slaves; in their heyday, the age of Cicero, the juris-prudential question had hardly been formulated.

The only title in the *Digest* about the *publicani*, 39. 4, concerns certain abuses:[164]

'The audacity and temerity of the factions of the *publicani* are known to all.'

The praetor promised a special action for theft or damage com-mitted by the servants of the *publicani*, whether slave or free, and in the case of slaves the employers did not have the choice of noxal surrender—they must pay up.[165] Nero's new rules for curbing the 'avarice of the *publicani*', the most important of which was to bring suits against them into the courts *extra ordinem*, met with the scorn of Tacitus, who declares that they were soon evaded.[166] It is possible, however, that the reduction in the profitability of the occupation that resulted from the rules helped to condition their gradual abandonment of it. There was still trouble, though, at least in Egypt; one of the *responsa* of Septimius Severus runs as follows:[167]

> 'To Isidorus, son of Deius: The audacious behaviour of Comon will be examined by his excellency Fulvius Plautianus, the praetorian prefect, my [?] kinsman. As for Apion the *publicanus*, if he is not implicated in the charges against Comon you will have the prefect of the province as judge.'

The publicans were sinners to the last.

We have one more kind of consensual contract to examine: mandate; but it can best be appreciated in the light of another typical Roman institution which was not mandate nor even technically a contract at all, but had effects of the same kind, namely *negotiorum gestio*, acting in a man's affairs unasked and for nothing. The notion may seem odd, for nowadays we should be unlikely to meddle in our neighbour's affairs unasked, at least in anything of such magnitude that it might lead to litigation afterwards. But in Rome the same considerations as made safe-keeping important applied to this also; the slowness of communications might put your friends and neighbours, when absent, in peril of assaults upon their property and families of which they were unaware until too late, so it was a part of *officium* for you to take steps, without authorization:[168]

> 'lest through lack of defence they suffer possession or selling up of their property.'

You must announce yourself as their agent, defend actions on their behalf, and so on; propping up a dangerous building and undertaking the medical expenses of a slave are cases used as typical in the *Digest*—things, in fact, which might involve you in expenses as well as litigation. People prepared to do this were entitled to reimbursement if their friends later refused to 'stump up', and their friends were entitled to reimbursement if they mishandled affairs—or made a profit. So the praetor offered the *actio negotiorum gestorum*, both ways, to and against those who had undertaken without authorization the affairs of an absent or dying man.[169] A recent writer has argued for the view that in our period *negotiorum gestio* was not always gratuitous and unauthorized,[170] on the ground that the action between a man and his general agent or *procurator* was *negotiorum gestorum* (not, or not necessarily, mandate or *locatio conductio*). The procurators of Cicero's day seem to have been mostly *procuratores absentium*, appointed to look after a man's affairs at home while he was abroad or vice versa; this general appointment may, however, have been a mandate, but not regarded as constituting specific authorization in emergencies (that is to say, *procurator* a mandatary, but sometimes having to perform emergency acts of *negotiorum gestio*). Alfenus in Cicero's *pro Quinctio*, of whom more will be said, was such a *procurator absentis*, and he took emergency steps which it was not certain his principal would ratify (but Alfenus was not a paid employee). The texts which couple procurators with *negotiorum gestorum* rather than mandate are all susceptible of interpretation as emergency situations; and Gaius is firm that *negotia gerere* with authorization is mandate.[171] (Also banks, which look much the same as procurators, were under mandate, not *negotiorum gestio*.) The lesson seems to be that the borderlines in practice were fluid; mandates could be more or less specific, and procurators were of different kinds.

Mandate, then, was the contract by which one man undertook affairs of another on instructions. It was consensual, *bona fide*, and (being an exercise of *officium*)[172] in theory gratuitous. It constituted the mandatary your agent, though as usual his transactions bound himself and not you, and so there had to be mechanisms whereby each party could secure proper performance, transfer over of acquisitions, reimbursement and so on; hence the *actio mandati*, both ways. The lawyers erected an elaborate structure of categories of mandate, but it is of no modern interest. Liability in mandate was probably only for *dolus*, deliberate breach of faith,[173] and conviction in the *actio mandati* resulted in legal *infamia*.

The figures who appear most as mandataries in the *Digest* title, 17. 1, are the surety and the procurator.[174] The procurator, as general agent, if employed at a salary, was presumably a status inferior, and your contract with him should have been *locatio conductio*; if he did it free he was either your freedman acting on the basis of *operae* owed to you, or else a status equal accepting your instructions, and taking perhaps an honorarium *ex gratia*; and the commission might be designed to benefit him as well as you. But the borderlines were fluid; it is as important not to envisage all procurators as humble instruments of the nobility as it is not to cast them all in the mould of the equestrian *procuratores Augusti* of the Principate. Amongst the many letters in Cicero's correspondence commending the procurators of his friends to the good offices of provincial governors there are to be found not only obviously humble agents, probably freedmen and probably salaried, such as Caerellia's procurators in Asia,[175] but also obviously high-status ones, like L. Oppius the banker at Philomelium, 'my close friend', says Cicero:[176]

> '. . . whom I specially commend to you, the more so first because I am so devoted to him and second because he looks after the affairs (*negotia procurat*) of L. Egnatius Rufus, my best friend of all amongst the *equites*.'

And the facts in Cicero's defence of Quinctius reveal another far from humble procurator. Quinctius and Naevius quarrelled over a partnership; Naevius got an order for possession against Quinctius in the latter's absence in Gaul, and Quinctius' procurator, Sextus Alfenus, at once tore down the possession notices and announced himself ready to defend actions against his principal. Alfenus was a friend of both parties, a relation of Naevius, a rich *eques*,[177] and had often before acted for Naevius in *his* absences.

   Not every mandate was a general agency; it probably originated in the social custom of asking one's friends to do particular commissions. There are plenty of vague mandates in Cicero which he obviously did not intend to be contractual at all, such as to Atticus to see to his affairs in his absence, or to Tiro to make payments and collect moneys due.[178] There are, on the other hand, precise ones. Thus, a certain Vettienus was commissioned to act as purchaser of a country lodge for Cicero:[179]

'He's just written: bought for thirty thousand, to whom do I want conveyance made, payment date 13 November.'

And Fadius Gallus got into hot water for buying the wrong sort of statues for his exacting friend.[180] We also find Cicero himself under a mandate to buy something for M. Marius from the auction of an estate to which (as it had piquantly turned out) Cicero was part heir:[181]

> 'I'll take good care of your mandate. You're a clever chap; you've given the commission to the one man who has an interest in it fetching as high a price as possible. Very knowing of you to fix an upper limit, . . . for now I know your ceiling I shall make very sure you don't get it for less.'

Pliny's letters contain mandates of much the same sort, including one (interesting because of its slightly 'distant' tone) to an architect about rebuilding a small temple on one of his estates.[182]

We are led in the end to pose a rather subversive question about the social reality of the principle of gratuitous services in our period. One need not deny the likelihood that in early Roman rustic-aristocratic society many things that later became subject to contract were done on the *noblesse oblige* principle, nor the likelihood that this coloured the contractual rules when they arose. And though it seems odd to us, for whom contract and 'consideration' go hand in hand, that such neighbourly acts as safe-keeping or making a purchase for a friend could become contractual and subject to litigation without sacrificing the aura of neighbourliness and ceasing to be gratuitous, not all that is odd is unhistorical. Nevertheless there are reasons for suspecting that in our period, which begins with the already complex and sophisticated Ciceronian age, gratuitousness and *noblesse oblige* in contract were an old tradition less and less honoured in the observance, as services became more and more specialized and what had once been amateur became professional. Public service, for instance, from Augustus on, was not in the least gratuitous: equestrian prefects and procurators, and even the grand senatorial

generals and governors, received thumping salaries.[183] And when
we look at the supposedly gratuitous contracts we find the need
to make many qualifications and exceptions (excluding only the
innocent *commodatum*). *Mutuum*, for example, was strictly loan
without consideration; but in practice money was not lent for
nothing, and little understanding of the financial pattern of Roman
society would be achieved by anyone who confined himself to
the gratuitous contract of *mutuum*. Or consider *depositum*:
repositories did not work under it at all but under *locatio conductio*,
for a rent; and as for banks, you could get interest on money in
the bank, even if this was not common—we may say that it must
have been by special pact because 'irregular *depositum*' is post-
classical, but the social fact is that it at least sometimes happened.[184]
Or we can go back to mandate. Caecilius Iucundus was not in the
auction business for nothing: he paid up 'less fee', *mercede minus*.
Merces is supposed to be the sign-manual of the humble *locatio
conductio*, but it is scarcely to be imagined that Iucundus was
thought of as a mandatary in banking matters but a paid employee
under his other hat as auctioneer; he was in fact carrying out
mandates for a reward. Barristers we have discussed; they often
worked for a fee, but no one dared to call them employees. And
how—once more—about procurators? It depended on status, and
changes in status—on individual *dignitas*. Some procurators were
wage-earners, some were not; there are texts about salary of
persons who appear to be acting under mandates which require
much agility to argue away, and we have faced Ulpian's curious
list of 'professional' people suing for fees *extra ordinem*. The difficulties with which scholars have struggled in trying to sort out
negotiorum gestio and mandate and their relation to different kinds
of procurator perhaps reflect a social fact: that the distinction
between the gratuitous services of status-equals and the paid
services of status inferiors had partly ceased to be real even in
Cicero's day and grew steadily more unreal. The jurisprudents
continued to assert flatly that such-and-such a bargain must be
gratuitous to constitute such-and-such a contract, because it was
their conceptual framework and otherwise they would have been
obliged to re-draw the boundaries of the whole system; but make-

shifts were found, and the *cognitio extraordinaria*, about which they did not have to make the rules, came to the rescue.

*

With mandate and procuratorship we are already within the field of agency, a topic which deserves a general *coup d'œil* because in modern commerce the principle of agency, that a man can be a legal conduit-pipe between two other men, is extremely important. If we examine Roman law from two aspects, (*a*) acquisition and alienation (can A's transaction with C as agent for B result in B acquiring ownership of something directly from C or vice versa?), and (*b*) binding and benefiting in contract (can A's transaction produce a contract directly between B and C?), we shall see that it started from a fundamental notion that had both a negative and a positive side: a man could not be a conduit-pipe, unless he were a slave or a *filius familias*, in which case he could not be anything but a conduit-pipe. 'It is not possible for us to acquire through an extraneous person', and 'A stipulation is void if we stipulate for conveyance to anyone except to one whose power we are in': these are the maxims quoted by Gaius,[185] and with this basic concept the Romans found it hard to part, though they were resourceful in expedients to facilitate agency in practice in spite of it. Thus, in contract we have already seen the rules by which (*a*) a *dominus* or *paterfamilias* was made liable on the 'binding' transactions of his slave or *filius*, either fully or to the extent of *peculium*, and (*b*) a principal was made liable on the 'binding' transactions of free persons *sui iuris*, as well as slaves and sons, if he put them in charge of businesses or ships. Such free persons *sui iuris* were agents, but one way only; the principal was bound by, but could not benefit by, their transactions; they acquired contractual rights only for themselves, and he must invoke his contract with them to make them hand over. We hear of some further advances: if a firm of partners put in a manager, people who had contracted with him could sue any partner in the firm,[186] and there is some (unfortunately rather dubious) textual evidence to suggest that by the end of our period partners were treated as agents for each other,[187] which nearly reaches the point of making the 'firm' a legal entity. For

Q

the municipalities, which had corporate status, the rule was that receipts and discharges could be given by their *actor publicus*, but had to be signed or sealed by the magistrates.[188] So much for 'binding'; as for 'benefiting', one's slave or *filius familias* could certainly make contracts 'benefiting' oneself—he could, for example, stipulate.[189] But there agency stopped: no *extranea persona*, no one not in your *potestas*, could stipulate so as to benefit you directly.

In property (acquiring and alienating ownership) we come back to the procurator or general agent (noting that he was not necessarily covered by the *actio institoria*). Could a procurator directly acquire for or alienate from his principal? We are hindered from knowing the truth about this by the malignant fate which has damaged the text of Gaius' *Institutes* at the two crucial points.[190] At II, 64, speaking about alienation by non-owners, he says something (which is lost) about a procurator, and the general opinion is that at any rate by his time, and at least in some circumstances, a procurator was competent to pass ownership in his principal's property; but we know nothing about the essential point, how far knowledge or authorization by the principal would have been needed. As for acquisition, Gaius says at II, 95, 'we cannot acquire through an extraneous person; but there is just some question as to the possibility of acquiring possession through a —'. The word is lost, but is probably 'procurator', for what Gaius still found so doubtful had become settled by legislation by the time of Ulpian at the extreme end of our period.[191] And if you could get possession through a procurator you could reach ownership by *usucapio*; you would have to know and authorize.

Akin to agency, and equally important in modern commerce, is delegation and assignment of debt. A owes money to B and is ready to pay, but B, who owes money to C, would like to settle by getting A to pay straight to C—and so on. Much business depends on having fluent and flexible means of achieving this kind of arrangement; Roman law seems again to have been rather stiff-jointed about it. Obligations were personal, not easily to be transferred; also, it has been suggested, there was reluctance, when the law of debt was harsh, to make a debtor accept a new creditor

(who might be stickier than the old) without his consent.[192]
The 'novating' stipulation could produce a delegation or an
assignment in practice: 'That which you owe to me do you
promise that it shall be paid to X?', or 'That which X owes to me
do you promise that it shall be paid to me?'; though technically
this resulted in a new debt altogether. Then there was an ingenious
'penal' stipulation to get round the rule that you could not
stipulate to benefit a third party: 'Do you promise that such-and-
such a sum shall be paid to me if you do not give such-and-such to
X?' There was *constitutum debiti alieni*, the promise to pay someone's debt for him, of which one form was the banker's *receptum*
which we have seen. But the main device was a special kind of
mandate, in which A, to whom B was debtor, gave C a commission to undertake his suit for the debt, with an agreement that
C need not hand over what he got; C was *procurator in rem suam*.
This did not require the agreement of B. It was 'cession of action',
and it was useful in a number of other ways also.

*

A reading of the Roman law sources gives one the impression that
the giving and taking of security was a universal feature of Roman
life; it constituted a network of interrelationships in which
everyone was perpetually enmeshed. The special characteristic
of Roman as compared with modern society in this regard is
usually said to have been that the security they gave and took was
comparatively rarely 'real' security (money or land or other
objects of value) and comparatively frequently 'personal' security,
that is, the personal standing and credit of their friends and
patrons brought in as a guarantee of their own transactions. The
cement of their daily financial relationships was people, not
things; we need not labour again the relevance of the concepts of
officium and *dignitas* to this pattern,[193] but one must only utter the
warning that there is no sound basis for estimating the relative
frequency of these two kinds of security; sometimes both were
used (and required).

Security was a regular feature of numberless transactions in
both private and public law. In the private law, loans of money
were secured, usufructuaries had to give guarantees for proper use

of what they took over, marriage arrangements commonly involved security for the due return of dowry, sale on credit involved security for the price, and so on and on. In public law, all contractors with the state had to give guarantees for their contracts in a double form, both 'personal' and 'real'—*praedes* and *praedia*.[194] A curious surviving contract for building a wall at Puteoli shows that contractors with the municipalities were under the same obligation:[195]

> 'Contract for building wall in front of the Temple of Serapis, far side of road: the successful bidder for the contract is to give sureties and put properties under seal according to the judgment of the magistrates. . . . Payment date: half the price will be paid as soon as adequate properties have been put under seal; the remaining half will be paid on completion and approval of the work.'

The earliest of the municipal charters of Italian towns after the Social War, the *lex municipii Tarentini*, requires *praedes* and *praedia* from candidates for municipal office, as guarantee for their proper handling of public funds,[196] and this must have been general, for the charter of Malaca, of Flavian date, has the same provision, besides one for contractors (the rules of which are said to be the same as those applied by 'those who are in charge of the treasury at Rome').[197]

Looking at the mechanisms of security, we shall consider first 'real' security or the pledge or mortgage, and begin by repeating what was said earlier, that Roman mortgage was simply and solely a kind of security for debt, and was not used as a means of obtaining capital and plant for, or a long-term investment of funds in, industrial enterprise. Perhaps the oldest Roman form of real security was *fiducia*.[198] This was the actual making over of full ownership of a *res mancipi* to your creditor, by mancipation or cession in court, with a pact of *fides et fiducia*, faith and trust, for its reconveyance if the debt was paid, and usually another pact (*lex commissoria*) that if the debt was not paid by the agreed date the creditor might sell up the mortgaged thing to meet it. *Fiducia*, though antique, was clearly found useful, for it lasted all

through our period and has left a curiously large body of documen-
tary evidence. There is, for example, the 'formula Baetica', the
standard contract that hung in some notary's office in Spain
(which we can only summarize);[199]

> 'A has received the estate X in good condition by mancipation,
> and the slave Y by mancipation, from B, on transaction of
> *fiducia*. Pact between A and B: above pledges shall stand as
> *fiducia* until all sums credited, lent, promised, etc., by A to B
> have been duly paid; if not paid by due date, above pledges
> are to be sold for cash by A or his heir. . . .'

The structure is essentially the same in an actual mancipation of
two slaves as security for a loan of one thousand four hundred and
fifty sesterces from Pompeii in AD 61;[200] it contains also an oath
that the slaves are not already pledged for debt or owned jointly
with anyone else, and after the clause permitting sale it enacts that
if the sale fetches a sum inadequate to cover the debt the remainder
will still be owing, but if it fetches more than enough the surplus
will be refunded to the debtor. To these testimonies we can now
add several from Herculaneum, which have moved their editor
to suggest that in first-century Campania *fiducia* must have been
actually the standard form of 'real' security. Here are two
passages:[201]

> 'M. Nonius Fuscus swore by Jupiter and the spirits of the gods
> and the spirit of Nero Claudius Caesar Augustus that the said
> slave woman Nais is his and owned by him and he has possession
> of her and does not own her jointly with anyone else and that
> she is not pledged publicly or privately. Whereupon M.
> Cominius Primus accepted said slave woman Nais by mancipa-
> tion for one sesterce on transaction of *fiducia* for a debt of
> six hundred sesterces. *Libripens* (balance-holder) T. Blaesius
> Saturninus.'
> '. . . re-mancipation of three slaves by M. Nonius Crassus to M.
> Nonius Fuscus . . .'

(Very strikingly exemplified in all this is the slave as a commodity,
being passed from hand to hand like a pound note.) *Fiducia*, with

its transfer of full ownership, gave massive protection to the creditor and was hard on the debtor, who wholly lost, while the debt was owed, a chattel of perhaps much greater value than the debt (for if he was badly in need of money he might be squeezed into giving something valuable as *fiducia*). It is not surprising that conviction in an *actio fiduciae* for recovery of such a pledge was infaming.

The other kinds of 'real' security had much in common; they were *pignus* and *hypotheca*.[202] The whole of Book 20 of the *Digest* concerns them, and treats them essentially as a unity. *Pignus* was pawn—the handing over of something (not confined to *res mancipi* or even to corporeal things) to the creditor, who thereby had possession, not ownership, to be returned when the debt was discharged—usually, no doubt, with a 'commissary' pact to allow the creditor to sell if the debt was unpaid (or the debtor could sell it if the creditor agreed). *Hypotheca* was a lien.[203] The debtor in this case did not hand anything over; he continued to occupy his house or use his slave and so on, but they were forfeit if the debt was not paid. As with modern mortgages, property could be saddled with more than one charge of this sort, the creditors having rights according to the chronological order of establishment of the successive liens. (In later law there arose an elaborate and vexatious system of 'privileged' creditors, particularly the treasury.) Based on this principle of *hypotheca*, and probably its original and always its main use, was the landlord's general lien on his tenant's goods for the rent, which was automatic;[204] but the same kind of general lien could equally well be established by express contract.[205] The creditor who held a *pignus*, having legal possession, was entitled to the praetor's interdicts that protected it—that is, he had a 'real' right to it, and, as will be remembered, it was theft for the debtor to take it away even though he was technically still *dominus* of it. (In the Eastern parts of the Roman dominions, including Egypt, the standard pledge was a bit different, a form we call 'antichresis', which means that the creditor had the right to use the pledge—live in the house, take the fruits of the land and so on—but must set the proceeds off against the debt.[206] Putting oneself into *paramoné* for a loan was really a kind of 'antichresis'.)[207] In the case of *hypotheca*, as far as Roman rules were concerned, the landlord-creditor, not yet having possession,[208] had to be given a means of asserting his right to get the pledge from the debtor if he defaulted. Already in Republican times he too was given an interdict by the praetor, the *interdictum Salvianum*, and later (but at least before the codification of the edict under Hadrian) he got an action by the *formula Serviana*, a 'real' right, to recover his pledge from any-one.[209]

About the details of 'personal' security, important though it was, not very much needs to be said. In general it is worth noting that sureties are ubiquitous in our surviving documents, many of which record the transactions of people far below the grand walks of life; which shows that the concept of *officium* was not confined to the 'upper crust'. The mechanism of suretyship was the accessory promise. 'Do you promise *x*?', said the creditor to the debtor. 'I promise'. 'Do you promise the same *x*?', he said to the surety. 'I promise'. The effect was to make debtor and surety (or sureties) equally liable for the debt; the relationship of debtor and surety between one another was one of mandate. The oldest kinds of surety, the *sponsor* and *fidepromissor* (who were the only kinds in Cicero's day) could only be brought in to support the stipulation, the 'verbal' contract; but from the time of Labeo (say, the beginning of the Principate) there came in a third, more flexible kind, the *fideiussor*, who could make a promise in support of a bargain of any kind—a 'real' or 'consensual' contract, sale and so on. There was a lot of uninteresting legislation about sureties and co-sureties of which Gaius gives quite a long account, but one very important question concerning all three kinds of surety seems unsettlable on existing evidence. Payment of the debt by any party, debtor or surety, naturally released the rest, and so did discharge (*acceptilatio*) by the creditor. More crucially, a standard opinion of scholars is that suit against the principal debtor, if it got to the vital moment of *litis contestatio*, released the sureties,[210] so that the creditor must ask himself carefully whether to take the risk of suing the debtor and finding him insolvent, for he could not then turn to the sureties. (He could, of course, sue the debtor for part, and turn to the sureties for the remainder.)[211] But what of suit against the surety first? It was perfectly possible; it was a blow to the debtor's *dignitas* since it implied his insolvency, and might be actionable as defamation, but then the debtor might have sacrificed his *dignitas* and proclaimed his insolvency. The question is, did it automatically release the debtor? There is no good evidence that suit against a *fideiussor* barred a subsequent suit against the principal debtor; the obligation of the *fideiussor* was technically an independent one, being based on a quite separate stipulation of his own.[212] But it is usually held that suit against a *sponsor* or *fidepromissor* did release the principal debtor because their obligation was not an independent one: they promised 'the same x', on the same stipulation just repeated. However, the soundness of this argument has been doubted, and the texts do not settle the matter.[213] *Dignitas* probably supplies the answer in practice; a surety, even if his principal had 'let the side down' by insolvency, would pay up without suit to protect his own standing.

In order to round off the picture of Roman security we must briefly describe one other field of its application: it was required very frequently by the legal authorities themselves from parties to litigation or when litigation was likely—from the usufructuary for proper use, from the guardian for proper management, from the heir for due payment of legacies, in *damnum infectum* and *operis novi nuntiatio* and so on. Gaius gives an account of the 'praetor's stipulations', and the *Digest* contains some titles about them.[214] The guarantee demanded by the courts was in some cases just an unsecured promise on a stipulation, but in others a promise with security—which had to be 'personal' security:[215]

'Praetorian guarantees require persons to enter in support of them; neither by pledges nor by the payment into court of money or gold or silver is correct security given.'

We have seen how litigants took contractual bail from one another for initial appearance before the praetor; it was required obligatorily by the praetor for reappearance whenever actions had to be adjourned, and in proceedings for 'aggravated *iniuria*' the amount of bail demanded by the praetor for reappearance in effect determined the damages in the suit.[216] Agents also had to give bail for the attendance of their principals.[217] Agents again, and guardians and caretakers, might have to promise *iudicatum solvi*, *i.e.* not only that they would make a proper defence but that if they were condemned their principal would pay up. This was the point at which Quinctius's procurator, Alfenus, jibbed:[218] he refused to *satisdare iudicatum solvi*, which has raised the same suspicion in the minds of modern readers as no doubt filled the breasts of Quinctius's adversaries, that the case of Cicero's client was perhaps not as cast-iron as the great barrister feigned to believe. If the agent was plaintiff in a suit he had to give security 'for ratification', namely that his principal would accept the action and the judgment as properly concluded on his behalf and not bring any further suit in the same matter on his own account (for, as will be recalled, the agent's suit was technically his own). We meet this security *amplius non peti* several times in Cicero;[219] perhaps the best example comes in a letter to Atticus (though the background is not clear):[220]

> 'I have spoken to Acutilius. He says he has had no written communication from his procurator and is surprised that there has been this quarrel because the procurator refused to give security "that no further suit will be entered".'

CHAPTER VIII

THE CITIZEN AND THE STATE

This final chapter begins at a tangent, with an account of the civil wrong called by the Romans *iniuria*. The real reason is that, though important, it does not fit conveniently anywhere else; however, it does touch our main theme tangentially, and will in due time lead us to it. For the action of one man against another for *iniuria*, which began as a means of redress for personal physical assault and battery, widened in scope until it became available for every sort of offence against dignity or standing, including defamation, verbal assault. Now defamation, as everyone knows, though it may simply be an affair between private individuals, moves at one end of its spectrum into seditious or criminal defamation, the bringing into contempt of the state or its officers, and so disturbing the peace and order of the community at large; and when it reaches that point it is very relevant indeed to the relation of citizen and state, because it raises the issue of freedom of speech.

There is no place here to go into the early history of the Roman law of *iniuria*, for its important extensions had already taken place by the beginning of our period.[1] The Twelve Tables had laid down penalties in money for physical assault on free men and slaves, and they contained the general clause, 'If he shall have done an *iniuria* let there be a penalty of twenty-five' (*i.e. asses*), a sum which went down in value until it became derisory—hence the famous anecdote copied from Labeo by Aulus Gellius:[2]

'There was a certain L. Veratius, a terrible nuisance and fearfully irresponsible. He used to take delight in slapping the faces of free men with the palm of his hand, and he went around

followed by a servant with a purse of *asses*, and when he had
slapped a man he would order twenty-five *asses* to be paid out
on the spot. Therefore, says Labeo, the praetors afterwards
decided that this law should be abolished and abandoned,
and laid down in their edict that they would give "recoverers"
for estimating injury.'

It was indeed the praetors, exercising *ius honorarium*, who built a
whole law of redress for personal affront out of these unpromising
materials. They added clauses to their edict widening the scope of
iniuria, including one 'that nothing be done for the purpose of
defaming'; and ultimately any wilful damage to a man's dignity or
standing, even indirectly through persons in his *potestas*, was
capable of grounding an *actio iniuriarum*. Gaius in the *Institutes*,
and the *Digest* in a well-known title, testify to the great, and open-
ended, scope of the action:[3] assault (or pretended assault) on the
moral reputation of a man's wife or daughter or son; doing
things to imply that a man could not meet his debts; flogging his
slave; preventing him from fishing or sitting in a public place;
raising an outcry against him; defaming him. (One thing, however, it did not cover: the killing, whether deliberate or negligent,
of a free man. For that there was no civil action in damages for
the man's wife and family; their only recourse was to the criminal
law.) The *actio iniuriarum* had a number of important features.
According to Gellius it went before *recuperatores*, though that was
clearly not always the case.[4] It was also technically 'estimatory';
the plaintiff named a figure for his damages, which the judge could
reduce but not exceed.[5] Thirdly, conviction resulted in 'infamy';
fourthly, the suit, being regarded as very personal to the injured
party, was not available to his heirs and did not lie against the
heirs of the assaulter; and fifthly, you must not delay or swallow
your injury, but pursue it at once, otherwise you lost your right
to sue.

The Twelve Tables treated as criminal not only the casting of
spells on people by incantations but also *occentare* (which was to
raise a hostile demonstration in the streets against someone),[6]
thus blocking the only way open to the plebs in early days of

bringing to notice and branding with public shame a wickedness or unfairness of one of the great men. This also was taken over into the civil law of *iniuria* by the praetor's edict; it receives careful definition in the *Digest*.[7] A court *de iniuriis* was amongst the standing jury courts established by Sulla; technically it was not a criminal court, according to Paulus:[8]

> 'for an action for *iniuria* under the *lex Cornelia* a representative can be put in (*i.e.* as defendant), for although the court is there for the public utility it remains a private suit.'

Its scope is plainly stated in the *Digest*:[9] assault and battery, and forcible entry upon private premises. A recent attempt[10] to prove that it covered defamation as well is unconvincing; it was in line simply with much other legislation 'concerning armed violence' in those troubled decades. But at some uncertain date a *senatusconsultum* did add to it libel and slander, whether by name or not, and included under this head persons who sold and propagated defamatory writings.[11] What was the date of this *senatusconsultum*? It is generally held that it was passed under the influence of the emperor Augustus, late in his principate, and is referred to by Suetonius:[12]

> 'Even libels about him distributed in the senate-house failed to disturb him—though he took great trouble to refute them—and he did not even investigate their authorship. All he did was to propose that in future there should be prosecution of anyone who put out flysheets or lampoons to the defamation of people under pseudonyms.'

Though admittedly there are doubts and difficulties this is probably right;[13] if so, then from Augustus onwards (but not in Cicero's day) defamation, like other *iniuriae*, could be proceeded against either for civil damages or before the jury courts. As for seditious libel, the perennial problem about which is that it may be just political satire regarded with hostile eyes, a famous and difficult passage of Tacitus[14] implies that Augustus on one occasion at least treated it as falling within the scope of the criminal law of treason, *maiestas*, which had hitherto, says Tacitus, been confined

to deeds, not words (it had in fact been concerned with the
punishment of disobedience or incompetence on the part of
officers of state). This too is probably right;[15] words had been
immune—immune, that is, from prosecution under the statutes of
maiestas. Henceforward (but not in Cicero's day) there was always
a danger that outspoken criticism of the regime or its personnel
might count as treason.

The mark left by all this on literature should be considered.
Lucilius in the good old days had 'got away with murder';
apparently like many satirists he did not much care for his own
medicine, for we hear of him as plaintiff in a suit against an actor
for defaming him on the stage. He lost it.[16] In the late Republic
the angry young men like Catullus flung their insults about with
deliberate defiance. But the famous satirists of the classical age
did not attack contemporaries. 'No Roman writer, playwright
or satirist either enjoyed or thought himself entitled to exercise
the right of free speech. If he attacked or defamed people, he did
so at his peril.'[17] Horace made a joke out of the situation, bringing
in good old Trebatius (once the butt of Cicero's avuncular legal
quips, now the 'embodiment of the law') to keep him on the
straight and narrow path:[18]

> 'Just take heed of warnings, lest ignorance of the inviolable
> laws should cause you trouble; if a man makes wicked verses
> against another the law and the courts await him.'

'Think before you enter the fray', says Juvenal's imaginary inter-
locutor:[19]

> 'It's too late to repent of the battle once you've got your helmet
> on.' 'Very well, I'll chance what I'm allowed to say—about
> the fellows already in their tombs along the *Via Flaminia* and
> the *Via Latina*.'

Nor did Tacitus, for all his contentment with the regime under
which he wrote, when you could 'say what you thought',
openly defame any contemporary.

It is customary to say—in rather modern language—that
'truth was a complete defence' to a charge of *iniuria*. In so far

as this assertion is based, as it appears to be, on one text in the
Digest, it goes too far and makes nonsense of the whole Roman
principle of damage to dignity and standing. What Paulus says
in that text is:[20]

> 'It is not equitable for a man who defames a harmful person
> (*nocentem*) to be convicted for so doing, for the crimes of the
> harmful ought to be published and it is in the public interest
> for them to be.'

This may be accepted as far as it goes, that truth was a good
defence to the charge of publicly accusing someone of being a
criminal;[21] but there are many things that you can publish about
a man with intent to injure his dignity that fall short of alleging
him to be a 'harmful person'—you can say he is illegitimate, or in
financial straits, or squints, or is henpecked, or that his daughter
has run away with a sailor. Nothing suggests that the truth of
remarks of this kind would have been a good defence.

The reader may be puzzled about what has so far been said
about defamation. 'Surely', he will ask, 'we have in published
political and forensic oratory of the Republic the most savage and
unbridled defamation; and was not outrageous personal abuse a
stock-in-trade of political controversy?' This is undeniable, and it
may be added that while there is on the one hand no shred of
evidence that political or forensic speeches were protected by any
formal legal 'privilege', on the other hand no actual case is ever
heard of in which anyone sued anyone else for defamation on the
basis of what was said about him in the courts or the senate or
coram populo. It seems to have been thought more proper for
established barristers to defend than to prosecute,[22] and Quintilian
has a discussion about the desirability of reasonable politeness, in
which he refers to Cicero's practice; but he never says or implies
that there was any danger of prosecution for slander[23]—and
speeches for the defence might, of course, contain just as much
incidental defamation as those for the prosecution. Nor does
Cicero's usage bear out the contention sometimes advanced[24]
that the phrase 'whom I name for honourable reasons' was slipped
in, when counsel had occasion to refer to people incidentally,

in order to dispel the danger of a slander action. We must assume that there was in this matter a distinction of *genre* and a distinction of class, and that politics and the law courts were accepted by the upper class in Republican times as a game with its own special rules, such that they thought it beneath their dignity to appeal to umpires outside the game about what was said of them by their peers in the course of it. What the humbler man could say with impunity no doubt depended on the strength of his friends and enemies.

*

The next task is to look briefly at 'citizen and state' from the formal point of view of legal rights and duties. We begin with rights. The *civis Romanus* had a special position in the Roman state. He had, first of all, the suffrage; what happened to this right is part of the general political history of Rome, and here it need only be said that in Cicero's day it was largely controlled by the patronage and bribery of political bosses, that in the early Principate it was maintained (even, to start with, the vote in the election of officers of state) but was a shadow rather than a reality,[25] and that the last known occasion on which the *populus Romanus* was called upon to vote legislation was under the emperor Nerva. The second right of the *civis Romanus* (a very real and practical one for the upper class) was that he alone could stand for public office. Freedmen, however, were debarred; on the other hand much of the executive grade of the growing bureaucracy from Augustus onwards was staffed by freedmen, and the highest of these posts were capable of carrying massive political influence. But after the Julio-Claudian age, in which Pallas, Narcissus and others were notoriously powerful, the headships of the executive grade came also to be kept for freeborn persons— *equites*, in fact. The right of appeal was a third prerogative of *cives Romani*; the story of the decline of its practical usefulness has already been told.[26] Fourthly come the exceedingly important private law rights of *commercium* and *conubium*. These, especially in opening the way to inheritance of estates of other *cives Romani*, must be regarded (along with the right to hold office) as the major incentives that moved peregrines in their constant desire to acquire Roman citizenship. Peregrines were subjects; they had only such privileges as the Roman state chose to afford them. In general, however, Rome protected the legal rights, public and private, which peregrines had in their own communities with as little interference—beyond public safety and the maintenance of upper-class control—as possible.

The first duty was military service. All free inhabitants of Rome's dominions were liable to this, and in the first century AD, at least, the compulsory levy was still used—it is hard to tell with what frequency, because the levy also recruited volunteers.[27] However, throughout our period much of the army was enlisted and professional, divided into legions (of *cives Romani*) and *auxilia* (of peregrines).[28]

Taxation was a second universal liability, but its incidence as between citizens and peregrines varied. Far and away the most important item was land-tax, *tributum* or *stipendium*. It fell only upon 'non-Italic' land, and therefore mainly upon peregrines, though it must be remembered that as more and more provincials became *cives* there were more and more *cives* owning 'non-Italic' land (and also, on the other hand, that most of the big *coloniae* of Roman citizens in the provinces had the *ius Italicum*). Indirect taxation (on market sales, sale of slaves and manumission of slaves, and customs dues) fell on all the relevant transactions, by whomsoever made, with one exception: estate duty, the *vicesima hereditatium* or five per cent tax on inheritances, which was charged upon *cives Romani* only. Begun by Augustus, it had a long history of perpetual complaint and adjustment;[29] according to Cassius Dio the real motive of Caracalla's extension of Roman citizenship by the *constitutio Antoniniana* was to bolster the treasury with an increased revenue from this tax.[30] Into the history of the Roman treasury departments it would be irrelevant here to enquire;[31] what needs to be said is simply that during our period the 'Fiscus' inevitably became a major government department with a good deal of administrative law attached to it, concerned especially with debts to the treasury and estates escheated to the treasury.[32] But in considering the financial liabilities of the people in Rome's dominions there is another factor to take into account: the free inhabitants of the empire, being for the most part members of local communities, were liable also for local taxation, unless exempted by status, as were senators of Rome[33] and those professional persons let off by legislation of Vespasian and Hadrian.[34] The personal acquisition of Roman citizenship did not of itself release former peregrines from local taxes (though such release might be granted as an extra privilege).

Besides the ordinary 'liturgies' or *munera*, which were an ever more oppressive burden on the landowning class in the muncipalities (and corvée, which we have touched on already) there fell upon people two other hated prestations, closely connected with each other: billeting, and the provision of transport for the government postal and supply service. The arrival of the army or of the emperor and his entourage (which meant troops as well) was a dreaded imposition, involving the instant provision of supplies of every sort. Already in Cicero's day billeting led to abuses:[35]

'Every year, before I got here, this season was taken up with this sort of graft: rich cities were paying huge sums to avoid the army being quartered on them for the winter.'

And from Egypt there survive a whole series of documents about 'royal progresses';[36] the most astonishing and illuminating one of all belongs to the time of Diocletian, long after our period—a newly edited papyrus that deserves mention nevertheless for its sheer enormousness:[37] corn, meat, wine, vegetables, bread, bedding, shipping for the troops and the emperor all requisitioned in haste and alarm. The *Digest* reflects these conditions: under usufruct it refers to 'contributions from the produce for the passing of an army',[38] and under *locatio conductio* there is one discussion of what happens if the tenant 'decamps upon the arrival of troops' (who proceed to remove windows, etc., from their billet), and another in which the depredations of the military are held to count as a kind of *vis maior*.[39] Maintenance of the *vehiculatio*, the official posts and transports,[40] involved billeting again, and upkeep of roads, provision of pack and draught animals and post-horses, each community being responsible for specific

R

stretches of road out to its boundaries. With several recent accessions[41] we now have a large body of evidence for the abuses (especially of unauthorized persons using the system),[42] for the quarrels over responsibility,[43] and for the efforts of the emperors (uttering cries of despair at the incorrigibility of human villainy)[44] to correct the abuses. Nerva abolished the *vehiculatio* charges upon Italy, Hadrian took some part of the provincial charges upon the shoulders of the treasury, and so on. But they remained a burden and source of complaint all through our period and beyond.

Finally, upon *cives Romani* were incumbent the civic responsibilities of guardianship and acting as judges and jurors in the courts of Roman law. Persons on the official list of *selecti iudices* had to have an excuse to avoid acting if called upon, and the long lists of *excusationes* from guardianship have already been referred to.[45] A papyrus from Caranis records a petition to the chief district officer of the Thebaid in AD 172–3, by a Roman citizen who was also a citizen of Hadrian's much-privileged foundation, Antinoopolis, for exemption from guardianship on the ground that Antinoites were not liable to be guardians of anyone except other Antinoites; he appends copies of previous decisions to this effect, including a transcript of some court proceedings in 148:[46]

'To Iulius Lucullus his excellency the epistrategus, from Gaius Apollinarius Niger, also called Hermaeus, of Antinoopolis, Osorantine district. Marcus Antistius Gemellus, veteran, when he died, expressed the wish in his will that his daughter Valeria Tertia, also called Thaesarion, a minor, should be heir to his property in the Arsinoite nome, and left as guardians of this orphan myself, Apollinarius Niger, and Valerius Comon, and as [?] associate her grandmother Valeria Sempronilla. But, my lord, in view of the rule laid down by Herennius Philotas, sometime epistrategus, and equally by Antonius Macro, that Antinoites are not to be guardians over anything not in the nomarchy of Antinoopolis, I myself am unable to accept this guardianship laid upon me. I ask, therefore— appending for you, my lord, a copy of these parallel cases— to be relieved of this according to the rules, and that you will order to be done what you think proper that I may be assisted. Yours faithfully. Here is the copy:

'Year 11 of the emperor Caesar Titus Aelianus Hadrianus Antoninus Augustus Pius, 6th of the month Mesore. Eudaimon son of Hermaeus having been summoned according to the petition for suit, and Dionysius having appeared in court, and the petition submitted by him having been read, Philotas said, "Of what origin was the man who left Eudaimon as guardian?" Apollinarius junior said, "He was a *civis Romanus* domiciled at Ibio Panycteris." Philotas said, "It was proper for him to decline, even if the man who made him guardian was a citizen of Antinoopolis. For he cannot be liable to be guardian for anyone else, and the testator's property is not within the nomarchy." Apollonius said, "We shall bring evidence to show that these persons have meddled in the guardianship and have behaved in all ways as guardians . . .".'

*

From the formal duties of the citizen it is a short step to the next question: to what extent did the state interfere in the private lives and property of individuals? In general the Roman government throughout our period (as opposed to later) had a very liberal attitude; on the whole, a free Roman's house was his castle, his labour not directed, his children not appropriated for purposes either secular or religious, and his movement and change of domicile unrestricted. On the other hand, there is no reason to think that the state was not held competent to interfere with individual freedom in any of these matters if it chose, and in certain respects it did. The Twelve Tables of the Republic's early days, if the information that survives about their contents is correct, contained an unashamed mixture of private law, public law, and administrative rules about public conduct, hygiene and safety. They laid down, for example, that people were liable for the maintenance of proper metalled roads at the bounds of their property; that no burials or cremations were allowed in the city (for hygiene and fire-protection), and that limits of various kinds were to be placed on the elaboration of funerals (a 'sumptuary' rule very characteristic of the Roman Republic, which all through its history kept vainly trying to curb conspicuous expenditure);[47] they prohibited hostile demonstrations and nocturnal assemblies, and enacted that 'societies'—groups of people—could have only such private constitutions as were not in conflict with the law.[48] These provisions of the Twelve Tables represent very well the spheres in which the more developed state continued to exercise powers of compulsion.

Town-planning bye-laws were regular in many large cities of Greco-Roman times;[49] Julius Caesar's regulations, partly preserved in clauses of the 'Table of Heraclea',[50] were probably designed as a code for all the Italian towns as well as Rome, and they include the following: (a) Repair and maintenance of public streets is to be done by the proprietors of the buildings that flank them, except that where public buildings are on one side the state will pay part. If proprietors fail to maintain, the job will be put out to contract and the proprietors will be liable to the contractor for the bill; (b) Keeping the streets free from rubbish is the responsibility of special officials under various legislative provisions; (c) There are celebrated traffic regulations, keeping heavy waggons out of the city during daylight hours except for those carrying material for public buildings or removing refuse; (d) No erection of structures is allowed in public spaces or porticoes (for the booths of shopkeepers tended to encroach) except in the case of certain public contractors and of temporary structures for the games. Augustus made some regulations about height of buildings,[51] and in his principate important Water Acts were promulgated for Rome.[52] After the great fire of AD 64 Nero legislated carefully for the parts of Rome that had to be rebuilt: —wider streets, lower *insulae*, every proprietor required by law to keep fire appliances on the premises;[53] and Domitian made some more rules, apparently reinforcing the prohibition against traders spilling into the streets:[54]

'The bold shopkeeper had swallowed the whole of Rome, and within her threshold no threshold could be seen. You, my lord Germanicus, have ordered the narrow alleys to grow, and what was a street has become a road. No longer is every pillar festooned with roped wine-jars, nor the praetor forced to walk in the middle in the mud; no longer are unsuspected razors sharpened in the midst of the crowds nor the entire street taken up with a sordid tavern. The barber, the publican, the cook and the butcher keep behind their thresholds, and behold! we have Rome again, where yesterday there was nothing but one great filthy shop.'

In Rome the aediles and other minor officials were charged with carrying out some of these rules; Papinian wrote a short commentary on the law relating to them.[55] In addition, as we know from a series of titles in the *Digest* ('That nothing be done in sacred places', 'Concerning public spaces and roads', 'On the repair of public highways and roads', etc.),[56] the praetor's edict was the mechanism of enforcement of many city by-laws, and Labeo was already engaged in interpreting these clauses of the edict. One bit of the aediles' edict besides their well-known market regulations also turns up rather *mal à propos* in the *Digest*:[57]

'The aediles then say: "Let no one be found to have had a dog, pig, hog, boar, wolf, bear, panther or lion in any place where the public customarily walk so as to be capable of damage or loss to anyone. If this provision is contravened and a free man has died in consequence let him be condemned to pay two hundred *solidi*; if a free man is alleged to have been injured let him be condemned in what sum the judge decides to be equitable; for other damage, double the actual damage."'

The aediles were responsible not only for the market but for the public shows, which must have brought many a consignment of dangerous wild animals into the city.

One particular rule of urban planning occurs with reiterated insistence at Rome and in the *municipia* whose statutes were modelled on those of Rome, but does not seem to have had a parallel in the Hellenistic cities: namely, that houses must not be demolished (either wholly or in part) without permission of the authorities, which would only be given if something was put in their place. We meet the rule for the first time in the earliest municipal charter, that of Tarentum, and it is echoed at Julius Caesar's foundation of Urso.[58] An enactment of Claudius' principate, the *senatusconsultum Hosidianum*,[59] laid down for Rome and Italy that buying a building in order to make a profit by demolishing it and selling the materials should be a punishable offence for both buyer and seller, and the transaction a nullity— and it did so in curiously excitable language that sounds like the authentic voice of the emperor Claudius himself:

> 'Since the care of our best of emperors has taken thought even for the buildings of our city and of Italy, that they may be ever-lasting, coming to their aid not only with most august precept but with his own example; and since the felicity of the coming age, the more it is contributed to by public buildings, the more it demands the preservation of private ones; and since all men ought to abstain from this most bloodstained form of trafficking and not cause a spectacle most unsuitable to peace by the ruins of houses in town and country . . .'

The prohibition makes numerous appearances in the *Digest*,[60] one text of which says that you cannot leave a building by legacy or *fideicommissum* with instructions for it to be demolished, and another that a further *senatusconsultum* in AD 122 made it illegal to leave by legacy the attachments of buildings—columns and so on—and extended the whole principle over the entire empire and over other buildings besides houses.[61] The psychology of this is not easy to fathom; it does not seem to have been so much preservationism of antiquities as a deep distaste for the appearance of derelict structures on waste ground—a dislike of ruins.

It is natural to enquire at this point how far private property was liable to expropriation by the state for public purposes. Directly opposite answers have been given to the question, which tends to be treated as a highly theoretical issue about the content of *dominium ex iure Quiritium*.[62] Here we are simply concerned to state what actually happened during our period. It is proper to distinguish between penal expropriation (*i.e.*

confiscation of property for crime), expropriation for public necessity, such as pulling down a man's house to prevent a fire from spreading or ordering its demolition because it interferes with the auspices, and expropriation for public utility (for example, to build an aqueduct or provide land for time-expired soldiers). The first two are not in dispute; we must here be dogmatic, and say that expropriation for public utility was also legitimate but in our period sparingly used and, when so used, accompanied by some (not necessarily full) compensation. To say that 'the Roman owner had a general residuary, not an unrestricted, right' to his property[63] is too legalistic, and no Roman jurist ever laid down anything of the sort; but it is no less excessively legalistic, from our standpoint, to argue away all the known cases of expropriation on grounds of 'only establishing a servitude', 'not concerning land susceptible of *dominium*', 'referring to *ius sacrum*, not *ius civile*', and so on. If owners were powerful men they might stop a project—not *qua* owners but *qua* powerful men;[64] or a tactful person like Augustus might prefer to restrict his new forum rather than demolish too many of the humble dwellings of the plebs.[65] The state normally came to arrangements with owners:[66]

> 'Caesar's friends (yes, I mean me and Oppius, however sick that makes you!) have decided to make no bones about sixty million for the public work you were so laudatory about—opening up the Forum and clearing it right to the Atrium of Liberty. We haven't been able to settle with the private owners for less.'

But the powers could be taken. The Augustan Water Acts, for example, took materials from private land and established rights of way where necessary:[67]

> 'Decision of senate for repair of aqueducts; . . . that from the land of private owners earth, clay, stone, bricks, wood and all other necessary materials may be taken, value estimated as a good man would estimate, from the nearest places from which they can be removed without damage to private property, and that for the purpose of removing such materials and achiev-

ing such repairs, rights of way and carriage must be granted
when required through the land of private owners, without
damage to it.'

And the charter of Urso laid down in terms that if an aqueduct
was decided on by a majority of the city council it could not be
stopped from proceeding over private land.[68] (Aqueducts were
naturally the standard case, being the one kind of big public
structure that must, so to speak, go this way rather than that.)
As to land for veterans, it was a notorious political issue in the
late Republic. It was not denied that the state could call in *ager
publicus*, however questionable the expediency of doing so; as for
ager privatus, apart from the wickedness as well as folly of Sulla's
expropriations and the triumviral proscriptions, the assumption
was that if the state took private land it would buy what it could
get in the market.[69] Augustus, though he took land for his troops,
at least paid for it.[70] We hear occasionally in the *Digest* and the
gromatici of expropriation of provincial land for veteran settlement.[71]

★

No less subject to controversy is the question of the right of
free association in Rome. Many kinds of voluntary groups of
people flourished at every period of Roman history;[72] we hear
most, through masses of inscriptions, of the 'burial societies' of
the poor and of the guilds of artisans and merchants, each centred
upon the cult of some patron deity. These latter play a famous role
in history, because just at the very end of our period the first steps
were taken to turn them into tied and ultimately hereditary trade
corporations which would eventually take their place alongside
the tied land-workers in the regimented economy of the late
empire;[73] our present question, however, is a different one: how
far could people join together voluntarily without restriction for
the promotion of their political objectives, the exercise of their
religious beliefs, or the protection of their economic interests?
The Roman state, all through its history until the late empire,
tended to take a *laissez-faire* view of private activities; but this
tendency was strongly countered, where association was con-

cerned, by another, namely that to the first of the above-men-
tioned aims the government was always deeply hostile, and the
others tended to get mixed up with it. The *populus Romanus*
was never allowed free political assembly; not only its voting
assemblies but even public meetings for political speeches had to
be presided over by a magistrate, who controlled the proceedings.[74] The tribunes, indeed, counted for this purpose—so far
was political opposition possible; but it is characteristic that when
historians in the late Republic tried to give an account of the early
struggles of the Roman plebs under their tribunes for political
power they pictured them in terms of 'agitators' and 'mob'.
For by Cicero's day politics *was* a jungle; on one side the upper
class had political pressure-groups for the purpose of 'managing'
elections,[75] and handed out money through *divisores* to groups
of humble citizens for their vote, and on the other side there
arose the real 'mob', bands of thugs, free and slave, operating to
intimidate, to break up elections and so on. Hence a tale of legislation and counter-legislation: a *senatusconsultum* of 64 BC suppressing *collegia* and a law put through the assembly by Clodius in 58
restoring them;[76] a *senatusconsultum* in 56 suppressing *sodalitates
decuriatique*[77] (which sounds like the pressure-groups of the aristo-
cracy) and a *lex Licinia de sodaliciis* of 55,[78] apparently again
directed against mass bribery; and finally a *lex Iulia* which seems
to have settled the law fairly effectively for the future. Whether
this statute should be attributed to Julius Caesar or to Augustus
remains unsettled; Suetonius seems to attribute it to each of them
in turn,[79] but the fact that the ancient ban on independent
political meetings turns up in the charter of Urso[80] perhaps tips
the balance in favour of giving this important Julian Law to
Caesar. It enacted that, except for certain time-honoured formal
societies, every other association whatsoever must henceforward
be licensed.[81] One of the numerous guild inscriptions throws a
little more light on the licensing process:[82]

'To the Gods of the dead: In honour of the Society of Bands-
men who perform at the public rituals, whom the senate has
allowed to meet, be summoned, and be gathered together under

the Julian Law by authorization of the emperor for the purpose of the festivals.'

It is probable that the statute was originally for Rome and Italy, and the senate the licensing authority; when its scope expanded the emperor was no doubt the practical arbiter, but when it expanded it must also have become unmanageable, for the empire pullulated with little associations. Consequently, at some time in the first century AD there was one further final shift of policy; the innumerable small groups of the humble folk who paid small sums for an occasional beano and a proper burial were permitted to exist unlicensed, by a *senatusconsultum* of which we learn from the surviving constitution of such a club at Lanuvium in the 130's:[83]

'Clause from the *senatusconsultum* of the Roman people: Persons allowed to meet and gather and have an association: those who wish to pay a monthly sum for [? funerals] may form an association for this purpose, but they must not meet more than once a month under the terms of the association, for making their contributions out of which they will receive burial on their decease.'

The rules thus became as stated in a late passage of the *Digest*:[84]

'Governors of provinces are forbidden by imperial mandate from permitting *collegia* and *sodalicia* or allowing soldiers to have camp societies. But the humble are allowed to contribute a monthly sum provided they meet only once a month, lest under such a pretext as this they initiate an illicit society. This applies not only in Rome but in Italy and the provinces, as was laid down in a rescript of the late emperor Severus. But they are not prevented from meeting for religious purposes as long as they are not in contravention of the *senatusconsultum* that forbids illegal associations.'

If we were to go by a text in the *Digest* that purports to come from Gaius,[85] the licensed associations were few: the *publicani*, guilds of miners, certain guilds at Rome, notably that of the bakers, and the guilds of shippers in the provinces. This leaves in a kind of middle ground very large numbers of associations, of merchants, craftsmen, showmen and so on, of which the inscriptions give testimony. Were they under license or not? The answer is that they probably were, and Justinian's compilers have deleted from a longer list of Gaius all except the ones that were significant in the late empire, or all except the ones that had corporate status.[86]

What were the purposes of the licensed associations? The most prominent, and perhaps genuinely much the most important, was a combination of cult to a patron deity and social get-together, with plenty of hierarchy and precedence such as people love. In this role they had a special status and place of honour in the life of the municipalities.[87] Did they, then, never pursue economic or political aims? They are found occasionally petitioning the government about their interests,[88] and the 'election posters' of Pompeii testify that there at least they played a vigorous part in local politics, proclaiming their support for candidates for office; though precisely at Pompeii there were illicit *collegia* which were dissolved after disturbances in AD 59.[89] But common action in pursuit of economic or political aims (especially if it led to rioting) might be regarded by the government as subversive; strike meetings by the bakers' union at Ephesus, for example, were sternly repressed,[90] and at Ephesus again the reader will recall not only Paul's clash with the silversmiths' union who saw their livelihood in danger but also the warning of the town clerk that public demonstrations about this would look to Rome like a political riot.[91] One surviving set of rules of association, that of the society of salt merchants at Tebtunis in Egypt, dated AD 47, divided between its members the areas in which they should have a monopoly of the trade, and fixed an agreed minimum price for the product.[92] We cannot say how regular such agreements were; the Tebtunis merchants were lessees of a state monopoly under licence, and so hardly count. All we know is that in the case of the grain-supply they were forbidden on grounds of public policy:[93]

'By the *lex Iulia de annona* a penalty is laid down against anyone

interfering with the grain supply or entering into any partnership to increase the price of grain.'

Apart from this, government action in the economic field was
mainly confined to the curing of particular abuses brought to its
notice by petition.[94] And much the same can be said of strikes;
if workers withdrew their labour that was a matter between them
and their employer.[95] Organized action, however, as has already
been said, might be treated as riot or conspiracy, and there is in
fact little evidence for it.[96]

*

The most obvious sphere in which the state impinges upon the
individual is the criminal law. The system of the Roman criminal
courts was described in Chapter III, and it was there shown how
during the Principate the standing jury courts were gradually
supplanted by the 'extraordinary' jurisdiction of the emperor's
delegates. The jury courts came to an end with a whimper rather
than a bang; the jurist Paulus at the beginning of the third
century said:[97]

'The ordinary jurisdiction of the capital courts has ceased to
be in use; [but the standard legal penalties survive although the
crimes themselves are now investigated *extra ordinem*].'

They were probably never formally abolished by legislation.[98]
Books 47 and 48 of the *Digest* contain a mass of evidence about the
offences that were tried under the criminal law, still mostly
grouped under the headings of the old statutes that set up the
standing jury courts; one might wonder why the great Severan
jurists like Ulpian, writing when the jury courts were in practice
obsolete, chose to group the criminal law in this way, but the
answer is no doubt partly that it was traditional and partly that
they were only defining offences—so that even Justinian could
continue to employ the antique system of classification.[99] The
picture is in any case confusing; some offences seem to have been
transferred from one court to another, the addition of new
offences to the sphere of this or that court seems to have been
done quite unsystematically, and some very similar looking

crimes were apparently triable under more than one heading. One thing they had in common, besides the rules of procedure laid down for them by the *leges Iuliae iudiciariae*: conviction in all of them resulted in legal 'infamy':[100]

'Infamy is not produced by conviction for all crimes, but for those of the *iudicia publica*. Infamy therefore does not follow condemnation for a crime not under the *iudicia publica*, unless it is one for which condemnation in a civil action would have resulted in infamy, such as theft, violent seizure of goods, or *iniuria*.'

Of treason, *maiestas*, nothing need be said except to remind the reader that seditious libel came to be attached to it. It was the political crime *par excellence*, and its history belongs to the sinister story of palace politics, intrigue and assassination told by Tacitus, Suetonius and Dio. *Repetundae*, extortion of money by provincial governors, remained a common offence in the first century AD[101] (and perhaps later—it is the evidence that dies out). Pliny records numerous trials; in his day the offenders were tried by the senate, their peers, but upon conviction the case went to a board of *recuperatores* to determine the sum at issue. Judicial bribery also came under this head.[101a] The court for murder took parricide, poisoning and magic arts, but seems to have lost its old original 'walking with a weapon with intent to kill or steal' to the court for *vis publica*.[102] On the other hand it picked up arson, wrecking, castration, and engineering of testimony, if a magistrate, to procure a death penalty.[103] *Vis publica* dealt with illegal possession of arms, false imprisonment, affray, rape, prevention of burial, tampering with the courts (presumably by intimidation) and breach of the citizen's right of *provocatio*;[104] and it seems that violation of tombs might also come under it.[105] The court *de adulteriis* dealt also with *stuprum* and with unnatural sexual practices, including incest. The court *de annona* was confined to punishing combinations to raise the price of grain. And as to the old offence of *ambitus*, election bribery, it was still being legislated against in the first century AD, but later, as Modestinus says:[106]

'This law is obsolete in Rome today, because the creation of magistrates belongs to the care of the emperor, not the favour of the people.'

Theft and *plagium* we have already said enough about, and also the non-civil court for *iniuria* (not, it appears, technically a *iudicium publicum*), which concerned assault and battery and forcible entry. But some further particularity must be given to the interesting complex of offences that crystallized round the old *lex Cornelia testamentaria*. Its original scope was false dealing with wills—suppressing them, forging them, even opening and resealing them.[107] An edict of Claudius and a *senatusconsultum Libonianum*[108] made it a particular offence to write yourself into a man's will, and the *Libonianum* seems to have been important enough to warrant a special treatise by Paulus.[109] By another *senatusconsultum* of unknown date the *lex Cornelia* was extended to cover forgery of any kind of document.[110] Then it picked up falsifying of edicts and constitutions[111] (though if done by an official this was *peculatus*,[112] and the praetor had always had a clause protecting his own edict from being tampered with).[113] Also there came in here all the law about counterfeiting—adulteration, clipping, forging, uttering false money and refusing to accept good money[114] (though again, if done by officials this might be *peculatus*).[115] The use of false weights and measures was subsumed under the *lex Cornelia* by Trajan,[116] which is natural enough; but a curious collection of other falsifications gets put by the *Digest* at least under the same heading: bribery in the legal process appears here also; so does neglect of imperial constitutions by a judge; assuming a false name; foisting upon someone a supposititious child; falsely behaving as a member of the military and using faked *insignia* or passes.[117] *Peculatus*, as we have seen, was very similar to *falsa*; in fact it was much the same offences when done by persons holding public or sacred office—retention of public money, conversion of public and sacred funds and the like were covered by it.

There was a constant need during the Principate to define new criminal offences, for the criminal law of the Republic had remained elementary. Some, as was shown above, were subsumed under the old statutes, others were treated as *extraordinaria* from the start, going before the emperor's delegated tribunals: black-mail (*concussio*), cattle-rustling (*abigeatus*), harbouring of brigands (*receptatio*), burglary (*effractio*), and what seems to have been a special provision against snake-charmers.[118] The most striking-sounding of these new 'extraordinary' offences, though little is really known about it, was *stellionatus*, behaving like a lizard; it was the criminal version of *dolus*, put alongside the civil *actio de dolo* just as theft and *iniuria* got their non-civil counterparts, and it carried the same peculiarity as the *actio de dolo*, that it was a residuary procedure, only to be resorted to if no other charge would fit.[119] It must be remembered, in any case, that the magisterial *cognitio* did not depend on the allegation of a named and defined offence; any set of alleged criminous acts was good enough ground for *cognitio*. The definitions no doubt arose out of the frequency of certain sets of facts.

For completeness we must add that gambling and betting were the object of a long tale of legislation from early Republican times onwards,[120] though they were not, in our period, criminal offences. A *senatusconsultum* said you could put money on athletic contests 'which are done for virtue', but not on other games.[121] It was the praetor's edict which applied the sanctions; the praetor, it appears, refused actions to recover gambling debts, and refused them also to the proprietors of gambling premises for assault or for theft committed on the premises, and he gave an action to people forced into gambling against their will:[122]

> 'for there are those who force people to gamble, either initially or, when they themselves are losing, to keep their opponent at the table.'

This seems in the end to have been visited with criminal penal-ties.[123]

Everyone is struck by the apparent contrast between the simplicity and lack of savagery of the penalties for crime in the Republican age of Rome and the diversity and increasing brutality of those under the Principate. Appearances, as to brutality, may be a bit misleading, and diversity testifies to a more sophisticated and flexible criminal system. Under the system of the *quaestiones perpetuae* the penalty was fixed by the statute which established the court; if the jury convicted, the *poena legis* followed invariably, though where it was pecuniary there might have to be a *litis aestimatio* or assessment of amount. Penalties were either pecuniary or they were capital—there was nothing else. The capital penalty (execution with the axe—later with the sword) was seldom inflicted, to judge from what we hear, because the defendant normally went into exile, which was not a penalty of the law but an accepted way of avoiding the penalty. He lost his citizenship and freedom, so far as Rome was concerned,[124] and he lost whatever property he could not take away with him; and behind him the door was shut by the decree that, he being now 'in exile', he was 'interdicted from fire and water'—none must harbour him, and if he returned anyone could put him to death with impunity. Judging from what we hear may, however, be misleading; we do not know how much chance the lower classes had to slip away into exile, and a good many people may in fact have suffered the death penalty to the letter.

Jurisdiction *extra ordinem* was a wholly different affair. It depended on no statutes, and the penalties were at the discretion of the magistrate; even if the defendant was up on a 'statutory' crime, if it was being judged *extra ordinem* and not by a standing jury court (as was increasingly the case under the Principate), the emperor or prefect of the city or provincial governor could please himself and inflict penalties greater or less or of a different kind.[125] The results were not in the end as arbitrary as they sound, for what happened was the growth, by the end of our period, of a fairly standard set of 'extraordinary' penalties, because judges tended to follow the precedent of imperial rescripts.[126] There was, to begin with, exile—as a true penalty, not just an escape route— in two main forms: *relegatio*, a negative form, meaning expulsion from Rome or from a province, and *deportatio*, a positive and much more severe form, involving loss of citizenship and banishment to some specific remote place (Tomi, Pandateria and so on);

this latter was not within the competence of provincial governors.[127] These forms might or might not involve loss of property (normal with deportation but not with relegation), and they might be permanent or temporary. Another creation of the Principate was condemnation to labour[128]—public works or the mines or the gladiatorial troops. The first of these, the least severe, did not affect free status, and might be temporary; but *damnatio in metalla* was for always (the 'next thing to death'),[129] and as a gladiator you were bound to be killed sooner or later—moreover, in these two cases a man lost liberty as well as citizenship, becoming a 'penal slave'.[130] Exile in its various forms was on the whole for the upper class, hard labour for the lower. Beyond this came the death penalty (which in the 'extraordinary' jurisdiction really meant death) by decapitation, and beyond even that came the *summa supplicia*, aggravated death by crucifixion, burning, or being thrown to the beasts in the circus.

Now the *summa supplicia* were emphatically not an invention of the Principate, for all that they are associated primarily in everybody's mind with the Christian martyrdoms, including the first of them all.[131] The first two, at least, are very old, going right back to the 'barbarism' of early Rome, when crucifixion was a penalty for incest and treason. Of course, everybody knows that all through the Republic revolted slaves were crucified. Verres put to death in this way a Roman citizen in Sicily; Cicero complained of the breach of *provocatio* and the shamefulness, but not of the illegality of the method of punishment as such, and probably he would not have turned a hair if the man had been a peregrine.[132] Burning too was an ancient punishment for treachery and arson. (It should be added that the antique special punishments of the 'sack' for parricides and the walling up alive of criminous Vestal Virgins went on.) The earliest certain evidence for casting to the beasts is a reference by Strabo to the fate of a robber chieftain from Sicily in his own time.[133] Naturally, like the others, it was not normally inflicted on high-ranking persons.[134] This became, in fact, the sphere *par excellence* of the distinction between *honestiores* and *humiliores*. Where the latter were condemned to the *summa supplicia* the former were just

S

executed; where the latter went to the mines the former were merely
relegated, and so on. But whether a sharp distinction ought to be
made between a 'liberal' Republic and a progressively more
brutal Principate seems doubtful. It is vital to remember that we
do not know much about what was done to humble criminals in
Republican times. In the late Republic the only criminal courts
were the *iudicia publica*, mostly for 'upper-class' offences, so that
it is not surprising that the penalties were mild in practice; but the
lower plebs, and peregrines, and slaves, were at the mercy of
magisterial *coercitio*, which is unlikely to have been liberal-minded.
With the criminal law of the Principate we are at least looking
across the spectrum of the whole population. At any rate, returning to the great distinction between *honestiores* and *humiliores*
as it was formally set out from the second century AD onwards:
Hadrian ruled that decurions (the bottom of the *honestiores*,
so that what applied to them applied *a fortiori* to those above)
could not receive capital punishment at all except for parricide,
but this did not last.[135] Decurions could not be condemned to the
mines or to crucifixion or burning. Flogging, too, a very common general punishment for minor offences,[136] which it had
originally been a Roman citizen's privilege to escape, was now
escaped only by the *honestiores*;[137] we are back, in fact, to what
was said at the end of Chapter III, that the *humiliores* came to take
the place once occupied by peregrines.

Imprisonment was not, in principle, a legal penalty in Rome,
and was probably not much used in practice, though the principle
could at times be disregarded:[138]

'Governors often condemn people to be held in prison or kept
in chains, but they are not supposed to do so, for such penalties
are forbidden; prisons ought to be for detaining men [*i.e.*
for trial], not for punishing them;'

and people may have had to languish in gaol awaiting the
infrequent assizes, in the provinces particularly.

Nor, apart from the *summa supplicia*, was torture a legal penalty.
To the Romans it was not a category of punishment but a method

of interrogation of witnesses.[139] In the case of slaves, their evidence was not admissible *except* under torture.[140] Numerous rules were evolved about this, such as that of Augustus that 'you cannot begin with torture',[141] *i.e.* that there must be a *prima facie* case of some kind before slaves could be interrogated, some prior evidence for them to refute or corroborate. Augustus, indeed, seems to have wanted to confine slave torture to evidence in 'capital and atrocious' crimes, and Antoninus Pius laid down that in pecuniary suits torture was only to be used if the truth could not be reached otherwise.[142] We have already noted that if a master was killed all the slaves of his *familia* had to be put to the torture.[143] What of free persons? Torture was one of the things against which a *civis Romanus* could exercise appeal, and it seems that apart from flagrant sporadic illegalities free persons were not tortured for evidentiary purposes in the late Republic. In the age of the Principate, however, we hear often enough of free persons, even *cives*, being tortured in trials for treason. Marcus Aurelius ruled that the highest class of all and their families were to be exempt from torture,[144] and by the end of our period this privilege had been extended to all *honestiores*; but conversely treason always remained an exception,[145] and other grave crimes tended to be added to it.

As is well known, suicide was not regarded by the Romans with any horror or disapprobation, and many people of the upper class, feeling that for one reason or another life was not worth living any longer, escaped from it; we do not know how common suicide was amongst the lower classes. Now the historians of the early Principate refer a good deal to suicide as a means of avoiding the terrors of a trial for treason:[146]

'This kind of death was often put into people's minds by fear of the executioner, and also because, if convicted, a man's property was confiscated and his burial forbidden, whereas those who settled their own fates had their bodies buried and their wills respected—a bonus for getting it over quickly.'

The rule that death before conviction forestalled the conviction, so that the consequences of ignominy and confiscation did not fall upon your family, is borne out for Cicero's day by an anecdote of Valerius Maximus:[147] Licinius Macer, on trial for extortion, waited on a balcony till the votes began to be counted, and when he saw Cicero, who was president of the court, taking off his magisterial toga he sent a message to him saying 'I have died not condemned but still under trial, so my property cannot be sold up', and at once committed suicide; on receipt of this message Cicero pronounced no verdict. By the end of our period the rule was different: suicide before conviction did not save a man's will, according to Ulpian:[148]

> 'except in the case of those who do it out of weariness of life or impatience with ill health, or for self-advertisement, like some philosophers.'

If you wanted to save your property you must be still more prompt, and commit suicide before any charge had been preferred, that is, before you were even on trial.[149] It is uncertain when this change came about. It has recently been argued,[150] on the basis of a new piece of evidence about what happened to the property of Macro, Caligula's praetorian prefect, after he had been driven to commit suicide, that it had already come about in the reign of Tiberius (which would suggest that the change was connected with the spate of treason trials); this may well be right, but the evidence adduced does not actually prove that the new rule rather than the old governed the case of Macro.

The principles of procedure for the standing criminal courts, as codified by Augustus in the *lex Iulia iudiciorum publicorum*, were 'accusatorial'; there had to be a named accuser and a proper statement of charge. The authorities had no power, of themselves, to charge and try people. Any citizen—with a few exceptions— could bring a criminal charge, and there were rewards for the accuser if the trial resulted in a conviction—which was liable to conjure into being the professional *delator*; but on the other hand the accuser was responsible for his charge and liable to penalties for calumnious accusation. To judge from the fact that Paulus is found in the *Digest*[151] quoting the proper statutory form of 'charge-sheet' in connection with the crime of adultery, we may assume that the 'accusatorial' procedure continued to be proper for the statutory offences even when they came to be judged by tribunals other than the standing courts. (The *Digest* also contains a list of people debarred from preferring charges:[152] women and wards, soldiers, magistrates in office, 'infamous' persons, and freedmen as against their patrons; but to this rule in turn there were exceptions (thus, anyone at all could bring a charge of treason),[153] which headed the law in a new direction, towards a principle that anyone should be entitled to bring an accusation on behalf of his own interest or family—a sort of private prosecution for crime.)[154] The magistrate judging *extra ordinem*, on the other hand, at any rate for non-statutory offences, could proceed 'inquisitorially'; there need be no formal named accuser and charge, and he could simply investigate on 'information received', hale into court on his own responsibility, and judge whomsoever he chose (subject to the rules of appeal). Pliny proceeded, in dealing with Christians, on the basis of an *index* or informer as well as on formal accusations, and Trajan's objection to the use of anonymous informations, 'they are a bad example and not in tune with the age we live in', implies that there was nothing *ultra vires* about Pliny's use of them. No doubt it was the lower orders who got thus treated.[155] It is instructive to compare the procedure of the proconsul of Africa before whom Apuleius pleaded his defence on a charge of magic arts; here there was a formal named accusation and charge-sheet, and the governor actually required it to be resubmitted on the ground that the real accuser was sheltering behind someone else's name.[156] At the top of the tree of crime was the unquiet world of intrigue and bloodshed about the imperial court; in the political trials for treason and its appended charges the rule of law did not always run, and we must not expect them to be always explicable in terms of, or to illuminate neatly, the rules of criminal justice. Such details as proper charge-sheets and named accusers were hardly to be expected at such times, for example, as the aftermath of the Pisonian conspiracy:[157]

'No charge, no accuser was available. Nero, unable to clothe himself in the appearance of a judge, had to turn to naked force.'

Professional *delatores* flourished on the rewards to be gathered. The emperors knew well enough the dangers of unleashing the informer, but, not without justification, they feared treason more. As Tiberius insisted:[158]

'better to subvert the law than to abolish its custodians.'

And Domitian, who is reported to have said 'If you do not chastise *delatores* you are giving them positive encouragement', is also reported to have said that the great difficulty for emperors was that nobody believed them when they complained of plots against them until they were actually assassinated. He was proved correct.

*

We have touched upon the fate of the Christians, which brings us once more face to face with the issue of freedom—this time, freedom of religion. 'The law and the Christians' has been studied exhaustively in recent as in former years by scholar after scholar.[159] It may seem grotesquely impertinent to make summary remarks about the subject here (especially since they will reveal robust independence—or *inflexibilis obstinatio*, according to the point of view); the only excuse is that the scope of this study demands that the problem shall not be omitted altogether, and it must be accompanied by a plea to the reader not to read what follows and nothing else. The view about the legal position to which scholars have been gradually leading us is that Christians in the provinces, when disturbances of one kind or another brought them to the attention of the authorities, were proceeded against by the magistrate (unless he preferred to ignore them) in the exercise of his unfettered *cognitio*, so that we do not have to subsume Christianity under some great legal heading like treason or unlawful assembly in order to understand why Christians were tried. To this account, which is a great advance, one difficulty seems still to adhere: the Christians *were* a special category. Magisterial *cognitio* over *mali homines* (as almost everyone in the first two centuries regarded them) cannot explain why, when Christians were punished, they were punished 'for the name', simply for being Christians; if you said you were one you were executed or, if a citizen, sent to Rome, but you had only to deny you were one to secure release. 'If a Christian, *a fortiori* a *malus homo*'; very well, that could make sense; but 'if not (now at this moment) a Christian, *a fortiori* not a *malus homo*'—that does not make sense. The equation 'Christian = man to be punished' can only have been established by government directive. It is allowed that Nero's punishment of Christians after the fire of Rome in AD 64[160] may have constituted some kind of precedent for the assumption that 'badness' was inherent in the 'name'.[161] This is not enough. There must have been a legal order, a rescript to the urban prefect or something of the sort, laying down that henceforward persons brought before him *as Christians* were to be capitally punished;[161a] otherwise we still have no explanation why the fact that Christians were punished in 64 as incendiaries was a precedent, not merely for their being punished later as Christians but for their not being punished if they demonstrated that at the moment of trial they were not Christians.

The legal position was, of course, the outcome of mingled currents of opinion—the attitude of the governing class, of the man in the street, of the Christians themselves. Scholars have traced the course of many streams that flowed into the river of hatred against Christians and intransigence by Christians; on the one side, fear of subversion, dislike of contumacy, contempt for exclusiveness; on the other, intolerance of pagan syncretism, messianic hope, the tradition of martyrdom. It is important that the old view has recently been restated (in new dress) that the Roman governing class minded about the traditional Roman religion, so that Christianity presented a special specifically religious challenge to Roman society.[162] The occasional outbursts of persecution against other contemporary religions are on the whole explicable on grounds of politics or concern with morals and public order (though vaguer and more 'ideological' dislikes are not to be ignored even in their case); astrologers were also banished *en masse* from Rome or Italy now and then,[163] and so were 'philosophers'—mostly the Cynic moral preachers, if their allegations and comminations became too subversive. But Christians and Jews were different, because they refused to participate in the civic religion of the Roman state, the 'faithful ritual', *pius ritus*,[164] upon which the most sceptical and agnostic never quite lost the feeling that the empire might depend—upon which, for example, even the emperor Caracalla ostensibly based his bestowal of citizenship on all free men:[165]

> '. . . wherefore I think that I can best make just acknowledg-ment of their majesty if I bring together all those persons who come to be numbered amongst my subjects into the [?] worship of the gods.'

Now the Jews of Judaea were a *natio*, a clear ethnic group, and their special habits of religious thought well known throughout the Mediterranean world from of old; their cult was given special license and sanction by the Romans as a national idiosyncrasy. The Jews of the Dispersion were accorded the same license as a 'permitted religion' *a fortiori*, as it were; though the Romans did not like Jewish proselytizing it was mostly in the east and led to no disturbances (if Jews were thought to be responsible for dis-turbances they got into trouble like everybody else). Judaea was destroyed after several national rebellions, but even so the Jews of the Dispersion were never persecuted for their religion. It has been plausibly suggested that they were a specially protected, exempted and sanctioned religious minority because it was admitted by all that they were loyally adhering to their ancestral tradition— their own 'faithful ritual', however repugnant it might seem to outsiders. The Christians, on the other hand, were the rejecters of the state religion not on the basis of an ancestral and recognizable tradition, but in rejection of that too; they were therefore (and we cannot escape from this) followers of a *religio illicita*, alone punishable as such.

★

The problems of freedom of thought and speech and action in society are many-sided, and have been the subject, for Rome as for other historical societies, of many studies.[166] They radiate in many directions, far beyond the sphere of the law, but in so far as they do belong to that sphere they are relevant to the subject with which this book can most fittingly conclude. 'The excellence of the Roman law is justly extolled', writes a recent scholar (as a prelude to setting out its defects);[167] indeed, it is a cliché to talk about the greatness of the Roman law and to see in it the one major historical achievement of the Roman genius. On the other hand, we are in an iconoclastic age, and before long it will be fashionable (one can see this coming) to allow the Roman law no merits at all. The foregoing pages provide at least some material for reflection on this topic, but they are limited by chronological period and in other ways; the purpose of what follows, therefore, is to direct the reader's attention to some other features of the pattern which need to be taken into account.

First of all, what has been said above is inadequate to provide evidence for estimating the Roman legal achievement in one important aspect, because there has been no description or discussion of the quality of argument and methods of interpretation of the Roman jurists, though some notion of this may emerge from the passages that have been quoted from their writings.

In the second place, the reasons for talking about the greatness of Roman law cannot be adequately judged by looking only at the period in which we have studied it; that estimate is bound up with its entire subsequent history. It became, from roughly AD 1200 to roughly AD 1600, in a greater or less degree the living law of all European states except England,[168] and has left its mark on the ways of legal thinking in Europe and the states to which Europe expanded, even though they have now abandoned its formal framework in favour of national codes. Though emphasis has recently been given to the view that the reason for the 'reception' of Roman law in Europe was not so much any intrinsc marvellousness as the desire of the aspiring successors of the Roman empire to acquire the law of the Roman empire,[169] we can see that just because its principles have been revered, taught, and interpreted to give living law by so many generations of lawyers in so many countries, their universality has helped to

convince people of their quality. If, on the other hand, we direct
our attention (as we have been doing) not to the huge Corpus of
Justinian in its grand historical perspective, nor the great dogmatic
structure built upon it by generations of jurists, culminating in
the awe-inspiring 'Science of the Pandects' of eighteenth- and
nineteenth-century German legal scholarship, but to the actual
impact of Roman law upon society in the limited period from
Cicero to Ulpian, a more qualified judgment imposes itself.
First there is the well-known point that the elaboration and
subtlety and intellectual power were nearly all poured into the
mould of the pure private law. It is an exaggeration to say that the
criminal law of Rome 'never passed through a stage of strict
law',[170] but it did remain bound up with the exercise of executive
imperium, and administrative law grew up with little help or
interest from the jurists, until the end of our period. Moreover,
there were chinks in the intellectual armour; the reader will have
noticed a kind of 'a priorism' in the Roman jurists, a tendency to
play best the deductive games with the rules and the 'case-to-
case' games with particular sets of facts, and to shy away from
more empirical problems like inventing rules of evidence, or
keeping proper records of legislation, or going out and seeing
how people in the empire were actually behaving. And this
brings us on to the clear class-factor; much of the law was directed
to the maintenance of those rules of private property which
mainly interested the possessing classes. It would be wrong to
draw this line too narrowly; we have seen many examples of
comparatively humble people in all walks of life successfully
ordering their affairs through the rules of Roman law. But we
have also seen, for example, how little there is in the *Digest*
about the terms of labour or the protection of tenants' rights, and
how severe were the obligations of freedmen—not to mention
slaves. Connected with this again, but going beyond it, are all
the questions about the real availability of the remedies of the
law: absence of a professional tradition of impartial justice, and
of adequate public force to keep the writ of the law running in
remote places where the boss or the thug might hold sway with
impunity; the vexations and the delays. . . . And there were

broader defects still (defects, really, of Roman government and society as a whole, though emerging in the law): the very narrow limits of free speech and political action and the tendency to treat other freedoms as subversive. All these things must be set in the historical scales.

A third consideration is that, quite contrary to what one might tend to suppose, in our period Roman law was decidedly non-ecumenical.[171] This is in many ways a merit; Rome believed in her mission to govern peoples and to maintain the 'Roman Peace', and one can find many tributes to the blessings of that peace,[172] but she did not believe in any mission to spread the institutions, as opposed to the protection, of Roman law beyond the range of those who wished (and were judged worthy) to accept her citizenship. Citizen and peregrine, till the end of our period, had fundamentally different rights and duties, and what is more, as Rome gave citizenship—lavishly enough—with one hand, so she diminished its rights, for all save *honestiores*, with the other. Peregrines, as between one another, were mostly left to their own legal systems—an admirable principle, though it is not to be supposed that Rome would have tolerated in the peregrine cities the turbulent and kaleidoscopic democratic life of classical Athens; Rome took care everywhere to secure upper-class control. The topic of interaction between the local laws and the law of Rome, *Reichsrecht* and *Volksrecht*, is much too difficult to treat here.[173] Scholars have pointed to cases in which peregrines as between each other seem to have adopted Roman legal forms (such as the mancipations we have seen in the Transylvanian tablets);[174] and they have pointed to cases in which Romans in the provinces, and the Roman provincial courts, seem to have accepted peregrine rules, which would be natural enough in the latter part of our period when many Roman citizens in the provinces were first-generation enfranchised peregrines whose whole tradition of legal relations was Hellenic.[174a] But two provisos are necessary. The bulk of the evidence for this process comes from Egypt, which was a special case in very many ways; and in any case the great event most vital to produce a fusion of laws, the *constitutio Antoniniana* making almost all free people Roman citizens, did not occur till the end of our period, so that quite apart from the extremely controversial nature of its effects they lie outside our consideration. No doubt it would be desirable to distinguish, even in our period, in the provinces, between Roman law proper between citizens, provincial Roman law when peregrines came into the Roman courts, 'provincial practice' (*i.e.* the adoption of local institutions by the Roman courts), peregrine law proper as between peregrines in their own courts, and 'peregrine practice' (*i.e.* the adoption of Roman rules by peregrines).[175] But what weight to give to these bridges is very doubtful; in the age with which we have dealt the Roman magistrate on the spot had to make such extempore synthesis as he thought fit, and did so with no help from the jurists, who had no eyes for the problem.

The complex theoretical and dogmatic structure of the Roman law, to which the treatises on Roman law mostly introduce us, with its fine distinctions of contract and quasi-contract, of *locatio conductio rei* and *operis faciendi* and *operarum*, and so on, was largely a product of ages later than that which we have studied; but it is that structure at which people are inclined to look with admiration (mingled perhaps with some distaste) when they talk of the greatness of Roman law. In our period it was, for all its deficiencies and blind-spots, a more down-to-earth affair, proceeding on a basis of a few rigidly held principles, from case to case and example to example. But the fair-minded observer may be inclined to feel that, given their patterns of society and habits of thought (which neither the law nor anything else can just wish away), and given the fundamental perennial problem of the need to reconcile consistency and certainty of law with equity and flexibility of law, the Romans made a not altogether contemptible effort to provide, for a vast area of diverse peoples, a legal framework in which orderly lives could be led.[176]

'Recently in a case before the emperor, when someone had cancelled the names of his heirs from his will, and his property was claimed as *bona caduca* by the treasury, there was a long discussion about the legacies, especially those to the heirs whose names had been struck out. Most thought that the legacies must go too, which I would have agreed with if the testator had cancelled the entire will. . . .

'Decision of the emperor Antoninus Augustus, consulship of Pudens and Pollio: "Since Valerius Nepos, changing his mind, cancelled his will and struck out the names of his heirs, his inheritance, according to the constitution of my deified father, is held not to pass to those who were written down." And he said to counsel for the treasury, "You have your court." Vibius Zeno said, "I beg you, my lord emperor, to hear me patiently: concerning the legacies what will you decide?" Antonius Priscianus, counsel for Zeno, said, "He only cancelled the names of the heirs." Calpurnius Longinus, counsel for the treasury, said, "No testament can be valid which does not contain an heir." Priscianus said, "He manumitted some slaves, and left legacies." Antoninus Caesar dismissed all, deliberated, recalled the court, and said, "The present case seems to admit of the more humane interpretation, that we should hold that Nepos only intended those parts to be void which he actually struck out." '

NOTES

ABBREVIATIONS

The following abbreviations will be used for references to books and periodicals after the first (which will always be quoted in full):

AJP: *American Journal of Philology*.

Apokrimata: W. L. Westermann and A. Arthur Schiller, *Apokrimata. Decisions of Septimius Severus on Legal Matters* (1954).

Berger, *Dictionary*: A. Berger, *Encyclopedic Dictionary of Roman Law* (Transactions of the American Philosophical Society, N.S. XLIII, part 2) (1953).

BGU: *Berliner Griechische Urkunden* (Aegyptische Urkunden aus den koeniglichen Museen zu Berlin, Griechische Urkunden).

Bömer, *Untersuchungen*: F. Bömer, *Untersuchungen über die Religion der Sklaven in Griechenland und Rom*, I (Akademie der Wissenschaften und der Literatur in Mainz, Abhandlungen der geistes- und sozialwissenschaftlichen Klasse, Jahrgang 1957, nr. 7) (1958).

Buckland, *Textbook*: W. W. Buckland, *A Textbook of Roman Law* (3rd ed. revised by P. Stein, 1963).

Buckland and McNair: W. W. Buckland and A. D. McNair, *Roman Law and Common Law* (2nd ed. revised by F. H. Lawson, 1952, repr. with revisions by J. C. Hall, 1965).

BIDR: *Bullettino dell' Istituto di diritto romano*.

Cl. Qu.: *Classical Quarterly*.

CR: *Classical Review*.

Econ. Survey: Tenney Frank, ed., *An Economic Survey of Rome*, 6 vols. (1933–40).

Fontes I, II, III: S. Riccobono, G. Baviera, C. Ferrini, G. Furlani and V. Arangio-Ruiz, eds., *Fontes iuris Romani anteiustiniani*, 3 vols. (vol. I in 2nd ed.) (1940–43).

ILS: H. Dessau, *Inscriptiones Latinae Selectae*, 3 vols. (1892–1916).

Jolowicz, *Hist. Introduct.*: H. F. Jolowicz, *Historical Introduction to the Study of Roman Law* (2nd ed., 1952).

JRS: *Journal of Roman Studies.*

Jones, *Studies*: A. H. M. Jones, *Studies in Roman Government and Law* (1960; partly a collection of periodical articles published at earlier dates).

Kunkel, *Introduction*: W. Kunkel, *An Introduction to Roman Legal and Constitutional History*, transl. J. M. Kelly (1966).

Nicholas, *Introduction*: Barry Nicholas, *An Introduction to Roman Law* (1962).

PBSR: *Papers of the British School at Rome.*

P. Fam. Tebt.: B. A. van Groningen, *A Family-Archive from Tebtunis* (*P. Fam. Tebt.*), Papyrologica Lugduno-Batava, vol. VI (1950).

Proc. Camb. Phil. Soc.: *Proceedings of the Cambridge Philological Society.*

Realencyclopädie: Pauly's *Realencyclopädie der klassischen Altertums-wissenschaft*, ed. Wissowa, Kroll, Mittelhaus *et al.*

RHDFE: *Revue historique de droit français et étranger.*

Rostovtzeff, *SEHRE*: M. Rostovtzeff, *The Social and Economic History of the Roman Empire* (2nd ed. rev. by P. M. Fraser, 1957).

Schulz, *CRL*: F. Schulz, *Classical Roman Law* (1951).

Schulz, *Principles*: F. Schulz, *Principles of Roman Law* (1936).

SEG: *Supplementum Epigraphicum Graecum.*

Sherwin-White, *RSNT*: A. N. Sherwin-White, *Roman Society and Roman Law in the New Testament* (1963).

Sherwin-White, *Pliny*: *The Letters of Pliny. A Historical and Social Commentary*, by A. N. Sherwin-White (1966).

Tab. Herc.: The Herculaneum Tablets, ed. V. Arangio-Ruiz and G. Pugliese Carratelli in *La Parola del Passato* (for details see Chapter I, note 33).

Tijdschrift: *Tijdschrift voor Rechtsgeschiedenis.*

Wenger, *Quellen*: L. Wenger, *Die Quellen des römischen Rechts* (1953).

Wieacker, *Textstufen*: F. Wieacker, *Textstufen klassischer Juristen* (1960).

ZSS: *Zeitschrift der Savigny-Stiftung für Rechtsgeschichte*, romanistische Abteilung.

CHAPTER I

1 The principal general works in English (and the editions in which they will be quoted) are: W. W. Buckland, *A Textbook of Roman Law* (3rd ed., rev. by P. Stein, 1963, retaining the pagination of the 2nd ed. of 1932) [*Textbook*], and *The Main Institutions of Roman Private Law* (1931); H. F. Jolowicz, *Historical Introduction to the Study of Roman Law* (2nd ed., 1952) [*Hist. Introduct.*]; F. Schulz, *Principles of Roman Law* (English ed., 1936) [*Principles*], and *Classical Roman Law* (1951) [*CRL*]; B. Nicholas, *An Introduction to Roman Law* (1962) [*Introduction*]. The most recent grand-scale textbook is in German: M. Kaser, *Das römische Privatrecht*, I (1955); II (1959); *das römische Zivilprozessrecht* (1966). An invaluable reference guide is A. Berger, *Encyclopedic Dictionary of Roman Law* (1953) [*Dictionary*], and a most important source of comparisons is W. W. Buckland and A. D. McNair, *Roman Law and Common Law* (2nd ed., rev. by F. H. Lawson, 1952; repr. 1965 with revisions by J. C. Hall, without change of pagination), which will be cited simply as 'Buckland and McNair'

2 For example: M. Rostovtzeff, *The Social and Economic History of the Roman Empire* (2nd ed., rev. by P. M. Fraser, 1957) [*SEHRE*]; Tenney Frank, ed., *An Economic Survey of Ancient Rome*, 6 vols. (1933–40) [*Econ. Survey*]; A. H. M. Jones, *The Cities of the Eastern Roman Provinces* (1937), and *The Greek City from Alexander to Justinian* (1940), and *The Later Roman Empire, 284–602. A Social, Economic and Administrative Survey* (1964)

3 On the sociology of law in general, see the work of M. Weber in M. Rheinstein, ed., *Max Weber on Law in Economy and Society* (1954); E. Ehrlich, *Fundamental Principles of the Sociology of Law*, transl. W. L. Moll (1936); Sir Carleton Kemp Allen, *Law in the Making* (7th ed., 1964); G. Sawer, *Law in Society* (1965). Buckland's way of thinking about Roman law took not much account of its social context, but Schulz in *CRL* and Nicholas in *Introduction* say important things about it. J. M. Kelly, *Roman Litigation* (1966), deals extensively with the question of the real availability of legal remedies in Rome

4 Sawer, *Law in Society*, 183–9

5 H.-I. Marrou, *Histoire de l'éducation dans l'antiquité*⁴ (1958), 380ff

6 The best chronological treatment is Jolowicz, *Hist. Introd.*

7 See the introductory note to the Oxyrhynchus Papyrus, *P.Oxy.* 2565

8 A case is made against it by F. Millar in *Journal of Egyptian Archaeology*, 1962, 124ff.; he would move it to AD 214, so from our point of view the difference is unimportant, except for the loss of a famous 'landmark' date

9 See the growing work of A. Watson, the first stage of which is *The Law of Obligations in the later Roman Republic* (1965)

10 Collected in S. Riccobono *et al.*, ed., *Acta divi Augusti*, I (all published) (1945)

10a The author does not delude himself that he is here writing sociology. Those who study that subject will miss here the theoretical discussions, concepts and structures which they desiderate. Perhaps at least the facts in this book may be useful as data for a more rigorous approach

11 Certain categories of inscriptions exist in sufficient numbers to be tractable. Thus, (a) some demographic or biometric analysis is done (see, for example, A. R. Burn in *Past and Present*, IV, 1953, 2ff; M. K. Hopkins in *Population Studies*, vol. XVIII, 1965, 309ff); but one should note the very pessimistic conclusions of Hopkins in *Population Studies*, vol. XX, 1966, 245ff. And (b) the possibilities of analysis of class structure are exemplified by L. R. Taylor in *American Journal of Philology* [*AJP*], 1961, 113ff; the papers of P. R. C. Weaver quoted in Chapter II below, at note 119; B. Rawson in *Classical Philology*, 1966, 71ff; and the papers of R. P. Duncan-Jones in *Papers of the British School at Rome* [*PBSR*], 1962, 47ff; 1963, 159ff; 1965, 189ff

12 For example, drawing conclusions about early Rome from the 'Indo-European joint family'; see *Classical Quarterly* [*Cl. Qu.*], 1967, art. 'Patria Potestas', forthcoming

13 Schulz, *Principles*, Chapter 3

14 E. P. Parks, *The Roman Rhetorical Schools as a Preparation for the Courts under the early Empire* (1945), ch. 3; S. F. Bonner, *Roman Declamation in the late Republic and early Empire* (1949), Chapters V and VI

15 Sawer, *Law in Society*, 60 and 152

16 Such questions as these are gone into by Kelly, *Roman Litigation*

17 There is one reference in the *Digest* to the Celtic and Punic languages: D. 32. 11 pr.

17a Rescripts in the Justinian Code are sometimes addressed to quite humble folk: soldiers, freedmen, a builder (4. 65. 2), a flat-tenant (4. 65. 3), and so on

18 For a selection, see J. B. Pritchard, ed., *Ancient Near Eastern Texts* (1950), 217ff

18a See, however, G. R. Driver and Sir John C. Miles, *The Babylonian Laws*, I (1952), 23–4 and 56–7: 'nor is there any reason why at a future date . . . as much should not be known of it as Roman Law'

19 On which the standard textbook is R. Taubenschlag, *The Law of Greco-Roman Egypt in the Light of the Papyri*[2] (1955). For relating it to its economic background the best aid is the second volume of *Econ. Survey*, A. C. Johnson's *Roman Egypt to the Reign of Diocletian*; and for its historical background see E. Seidl, *Ptolemäische Rechtsgeschichte*[2] (1962)

20 L. Wenger, *Die Quellen des römischen Rechts* (1953) [*Quellen*], takes just under a thousand large pages to do so

21 For speculations upon whom see A. M. Honoré, *Gaius, A Biography* (1962). The essential text, translation and commentary are F. de Zulueta, ed., *The Institutes of Gaius*, I (1946) (text and facing translation); II (1953) (commentary); but important also is the latest edition, in progress, by

M. David and H. L. W. Nelson, *Gai Institutionum Commentarii IV* (1954–) (*Studia Gaiana*, vols. II and III). The work as we have it has a complex history; it may be a post-classical 'epitome' of Gaius' actual text or even posthumous notes, and it is not free from interpolations and glosses. See F. Wieacker, *Textstufen klassischer Juristen* (1960) [*Textstufen*], 186ff

22 See H. F. Jolowicz in *Journal of the Warburg and Courtauld Institutes*, 1952, 88ff

23 It also contains the 'New Laws' promulgated by Justinian later in his reign, which will not concern us at all. The standard edition is *Corpus Iuris Civilis*, I, *Institutiones*, ed. P. Krueger and *Digesta*, ed. Th. Mommsen and P. Krueger; II, *Codex Iustinianus*, ed. P. Krueger; III, *Novellae*, ed. R. Schöll and W. Kroll

24 Going 'upwards', the titles are grouped into fifty books. Going 'downwards', the fragments (unless very short) are paragraphed on a traditional principle like the floors of an English building: the 'ground floor' is called *principium* and then come paras. 1, 2 and so on. Thus a typical *Digest* reference will be D. 26. 6. 4. 3 (= *Digest*, Book 26, Title 6, 'who may apply for guardians', fragment 4—from Book 13 of the *Disputations* of Tryphoninus—para. 3); or D. 43. 27. 1 pr. (= *Digest*, Book 43, title 27, 'concerning felling of trees', fragment 1—from Book 71 of Ulpian's commentary on the edict—initial para.) There linger different, and at first confusing, older habits of citation, and on such matters H. J. Roby, *Introduction to the Study of Justinian's Digest* (1884) is still a useful guide

25 See M. Kaser in *Zeitschrift der Savigny-Stiftung für Rechtsgeschichte*, romanistische Abteilung [*ZSS*] 1952, 60ff.; W. Kunkel, *An Introduction to Roman Legal and Constitutional History*, transl. J. M. Kelly (1966) [*Introduction*], 136ff; and for advanced discussion Wieacker, *Textstufen*, passim

26 The *Controversiae* of the elder Seneca and the pseudo-Quintilian *Declamationes* are evidence in plenty. Petronius thought them drivel: *Satyricon*, 1

27 D. 29. 2. 86 pr.; 36. 1. 48; and 34. 9. 16. 1 (it is hard to believe that the last of these was not some relative of the historian Cassius Dio Cocceianus)

28 D. 4. 4. 11. 2; 16. 1. 19. 1; 17. 2. 52. 7; 28. 5. 35 pr.; 31. 83; 36. 1. 18. 5

29 D. 4. 2. 9. 3

30 D. 4. 4. 38 pr.; 14. 5. 8; 32. 27. 1; 36. 1. 76. 1; 49. 14. 50

31 *Fontes iuris Romani anteiustiniani* I, *Leges*, ed. S. Riccobono² (1941); II, *Auctores*, ed. G. Baviera *et al.* (1940: includes Gaius's *Institutes* and the 'Vatican Fragments', 'Titles from Ulpian', 'Opinions of Paulus', etc.); III, *Negotia*, ed. V. Arangio-Ruiz (1943) [References will be to *Fontes* I or II or III]

32 This last is not in *Fontes*. The first edition is by W. L. Westermann and A. Arthur Schiller, *Apokrimata. Decisions of Septimius Severus on Legal Matters* (1954); but for the text revised by H. C. Youtie and revised comments by Schiller see *Chronique d'Egypte*, 1955, 327ff [Reference will be to *Apokrimata*]

33 Not in *Fontes*, but published by V. Arangio-Ruiz and G. Pugliese
Carratelli in the periodical *La Parola del Passato*, as follows: nos. I–XII
in vol. i, 1946, 373ff; nos. XIII–XXX in vol. iii, 1948, 165ff; nos. XXXI–
LVIII in vol. viii, 1953, 454ff; nos. LIX–LXXV in vol. ix, 1954, 54ff;
and nos. LXXVI–LXXXVII in vol. x, 1955, 448ff [Reference will be to
Tab. Herc.]

33a Not in *Fontes*, but published by B. A. van Groningen, *A Family-Archive
from Tebtunis* (*P. Fam. Tebt.*), Papyrologica Lugduno-Batava, vol. VI
(1950). [Reference will be to *P. Fam. Tebt.*]

34 Not in *Fontes*. See Ann Perkins, ed., *The Excavations at Dura-Europos*,
Final Report V, Part I, The Parchments and Papyri, ed. C. B. Welles,
R. O. Fink and J. F. Gilliam (1959). Law documents from the Dead Sea
caves are discussed by E. Volterra in *Iura*, 1963, 29ff

35 Interestingly discussed by Wenger, *Quellen*, 878ff

36 Berger, *Dictionary*, 802ff gives a bibliography of works written about the
contributions to legal knowledge derivable from the writings of various
Latin authors

37 *Pro Quinctio, pro Roscio comoedo, pro Caecina* and the débris of *pro Tullio*

38 An analysis of them is given by Zulueta, *The Institutes of Gaius* II, 13ff

39 Cicero, *Topica*, 28

40 Gai. *Inst.* I, 2

41 They are collected in G. Rotondi, *Leges Publicae Populi Romani* (1912,
reprinted 1962)

42 The post-Augustan *leges* are in Rotondi, op. cit., 463–71

43 By M. W. Frederiksen in *Journal of Roman Studies* [*JRS*], 1965, 189f

44 Of the mass of literature (the whole controverted topic of '*imperium* and
auctoritas' is relevant) we need only quote the survey of M. Hammond in
The Antonine Monarchy, 336ff and the notes thereto. The view that the
Principate was from the beginning constitutionally different from all
merely magisterial powers was argued by R. Orestano, *Il potere normativo
degli imperatori e le costituzioni imperiali* (1937) and also in *Bullettino dell'
Istituto di diritto romano* [*BIDR*], 1936–7, 219ff

45 D. 1. 4. 1 pr.

46 Gai. *Inst.* I, 5. The phrase may be a later interpolation, to make Gaius
match Ulpian, who gives a similar but more cogently expressed reason.
Hammond's book shows how a generalized notion of 'sovereignty' grew
up over the years

47 Different scholars have a variety of systems, see Hammond, *Antonine
Monarchy*, 339

48 The third Edict of Cyrene, *Fontes* I, no. 68 (p. 408)

49 *Fontes* I, no. 72. *Cf.*, more recently discovered, the *epistula* of (probably)
Augustus to Vardacate, *L'année épigraphique*, 1947, no. 44 and A. Degrassi
in *Athenaeum*, 1948, 254ff

50 See Schiller in *Apokrimata*, 45; and, on the *libellus*, the note in *The Letters of*

Pliny. A Historical and Social Commentary, by A. N. Sherwin-White (1966) [Sherwin-White, *Pliny*], 716–7

51 D. 36. 1. 30

52 D. 29. 1. 1 pr.

52a See Sherwin-White, *Pliny*, 589–91

53 D. 5. 3. 20. 6

54 D. 2. 15. 8 pr.

55 *Fontes* I, no. 60

56 D. 1. 1. 7

57 See Jolowicz, *Hist. Introduct.*, 95ff

58 The phrase 'civil law' was (and is) used in several different senses, but they are easily enough distinguished by context: (*a*) the whole law of Rome, as when we speak of 'Professors of Civil Law'; (*b*) *ius civile* as opposed to *ius publicum* (the law of constitution and administration); (*c*) *ius civile* as opposed to *ius honorarium*; and (*d*) *ius civile* as opposed to *ius gentium*, which will be explained later

59 For Verres and the urban and provincial edicts see the whole passage *II in Verrem* I, 104 to the end of the speech

60 Cicero, *ad fam.* III, 8, 4

61 Cicero, *ad Att.* VI, 1, 15; and the sequel is important

62 The attempt of A. Guarino (in *Studi in memoria di E. Albertario* I, 1953, 625ff and *Atti del congresso internazionale di diritto romano, Verona, 1948*, II (1951), 169ff) to displace this standard view has not met with acceptance. In its codified form the praetor's edict has been reconstructed out of the many *Digest* fragments taken from commentaries upon it. The standard work is O. Lenel, *Das Edictum Perpetuum*3 (1927, reprinted 1956); but the text can be read in *Fontes* I, 335ff

63 *Codex Theodosianus*, 1. 4. 3 (see 1. 4. 1 and 2 for earlier official authorizations). On the significance of the 'Law of Citations' see Wieacker, *Textstufen*, 156ff

64 D. 1. 2. 2. 48–9

65 On this endlessly argued *ius respondendi* the principal bibliography down to 1952 is given in Berger's *Dictionary* on p. 532. For some more recent items see G. Provera in *Studia et Documenta Historiae et Iuris*, 1962, 342ff

66 Gai. *Inst.* I, 7

66a For Gai. *Inst.* I, 7 as interpolated see Wieacker, *Textstufen*, 38 and 157

67 The two books are: F. Schulz, *Roman Legal Science* (1946; there is a revised edition in German, *Geschichte der römischen Rechtswissenschaft*, 1961) and W. Kunkel, *Herkunft und soziale Stellung der römischen Juristen* (1952). The process is summed up by Nicholas, *Introduction*, 29–30

68 *Auctor ad Herennium*, II, 19

69 'Equity' was not, as in England down to the Judicature Acts, administered in a separate set of courts, and the Romans did not use the word *aequitas* as a label for the *ius honorarium*. But on the nature and growth of 'equit-

able' rules in Roman law see W. W. Buckland, *Equity in Roman Law* (1911), and Allen, *Law in the Making*, 392ff

70 *E.g.* Jolowicz, *Hist. Introd.*, 359ff, Schulz, *Principles*, 20ff, Allen, op. cit., 80ff

71 D. 1. 3. 32. 1

72 See J. A. C. Thomas in *Tijdschrift voor Rechtsgeschiedenis* [*Tijdschrift*], 1963, 39ff

73 D. 21. 2. 6

74 D. 26. 7. 7. 10

75 Pliny, *Ep.* X, 108–9 (*cf.* 112–13)

76 See F. H. Hinsley, *Sovereignty* (1966), 179ff

77 On what was meant by a Roman citizen see Chapter II

78 See E. Volterra, *Diritto romano e diritti orientali* (1937), and also below, Chapter VIII, p. 283

78a Unfortunately, only for Egypt do we know much about this fusion: Taubenschlag, *Law of Greco-Roman Egypt*, 27ff

79 On which see Chapter III. What is said here, and not its contrary, is implied by Pliny, *Ep.* X, 72–3. See also F. Millar in *JRS*, 1966, 156ff, especially 160

80 For an example see Gai. *Inst.* I, 47 (if the clause 'senatus ita censuit . . .' is not an interpolation)

81 Hammond, *Antonine Monarchy*, 340. For a case of specific change see D. 48. 18. 1. 19

82 Pliny, *Ep.* X, 58, 10

83 See E. Volterra in *Studi di storia e diritto in onore di Enrico Besta*, I (1939), 449ff and G. I. Luzzatto in *Scritti di diritto romano in onore di Contardo Ferrini*, ed. G. G. Archi (Milan, 1946), 265ff

84 Pliny, Ep. X, 97, 1

85 This is settled by the first Edict of Cyrene, *Fontes* I, no. 68, and the Leiden inscription, *Supplementum Epigraphicum Graecum* [*SEG*], vol. XVIII, no. 555

86 *Fontes* I, no. 73. (Almost the whole of this preamble is R. Herzog's conjectural restoration of missing lines, but the point here being made is not affected.)

87 *Cf.* Cicero, *de legibus*, III, 46. On the publication and preservation of the law see Fritz, Freiherr von Schwind, *Zur Frage der Publikation im römischen Recht* (1940), and Frederiksen in *JRS*, 1965, 184ff

88 Pliny, *Ep.* X, 58

89 *Ibid.*, 65–6

90 *Ibid.*, 72–3

91 *Ibid.*, 79, 5

92 Tacitus, *Histories* IV, 40, 2; Suetonius, *divus Vespasianus*, 8, 5

93 Pliny, *Ep.* VI, 33, 3–4

94 Juvenal, *Satires* VIII, 79

95 The Horace passages are, respectively: *Epistles* I, xvi, 40; *Satires* I, ix,

passim; *Satires* II, vi, 23ff
96 Pliny, *Ep.* I, 20, 12 and VI, 2, 7
97 For which see R. E. Megarry, *Miscellany-at-Law* (1955), 76–7

CHAPTER II

1 Tarsus had a property rating to qualify for citizenship. On the 'linen-weavers', who did not possess it, see Dio of Prusa, *Orations* XXXIV (the 'Second Tarsic'), 21 and 23. A. H. M. Jones, *Studies in Roman Government and Law* (1960) [*Studies*], 136, gives some other examples
2 See the important study of D. Nörr in *Tijdschrift*, 1963, 525ff
3 *Fontes* I, no. 21, § 126
4 *Fontes* I, no. 24, § 53
5 D. 50. 1. 29. See also *SEG*, vol. XIV, no. 479 (or XVI, no. 408), l. 12
6 Nörr, op. cit., 556, note 50, speaks of the 'well-nigh unsurveyeable literature' on the topic, and gives a lot of it. One side of the controversy is represented by F. De Visscher in *Les Edits d'Auguste découverts à Cyrène* (1940, reprinted 1965), 108ff, the opposite by V. Arangio-Ruiz in *Scritti giuridici in onore di Francesco Carnelutti* IV (1950), 56ff. Nörr himself takes an acceptable view, and A. N. Sherwin-White, *Roman Society and Roman Law in the New Testament* (1963) [*RSNT*], 181ff, should be read (so indeed should the whole passage from p. 175 on, and pp. 144ff as well)
7 Cicero, *pro Balbo*, 28
8 The new evidence, which raised all the discussion, was the grant of citizenship by Octavian as triumvir to the sea-captain Seleucus of Rhosos, *Fontes* I, no. 55, and the 3rd Edict of Cyrene, *Fontes* I, no 68 (p. 408) which was quoted above in Chapter I, p. 21
9 'Rechtszuständigkeiten', Nörr, *Tijdschrift*, 1963, 555. Paul surely thought of himself as having two citizenships
10 See Seleucus of Rhosos, above, note 8
11 A brief description by W. Seston and M. Euzennat is in *Comptes Rendus de l'Académie des Inscriptions et Belles-Lettres*, 1961, 317f
12 See J. Triantaphyllopoulos in *Akte des IV. internationalen Kongresses für griechische und lateinische Epigraphik, Wien, 1962* (1964), 399ff, and in *Iura*, 1963, 109ff
13 Pliny, *Ep.* X, 6, 1. For the official in charge of the *commentarii beneficiorum* see Dessau, *Inscriptiones Latinae Selectae* [*ILS*], no. 1792
14 Though as to Latins, see below
15 'By the rod', see Pliny, *Ep.* VII, 16, 4
16 Gaius, *Inst.* I, 32b–34, gives some
17 *E.g. Fontes* I, nos. 70 and 71
18 *Apocolocyntosis divi Claudii*, 3 (follows Petronius in the Loeb edition)
19 See G. L. Cheesman, *The Auxilia of the Roman Imperial Army* (1914),

32–4; H. M. D. Parker, *The Roman Legions*[2] (1958), 237–46; C. G. Starr, *The Roman Imperial Navy 31 B.C.–A.D. 324*[2] (1960), 89–94

20 *E.g. Fontes* I, no. 27

21 And the auxiliaries lost it about AD 140, except for their senior ranks, perhaps because the legions were complaining: H. Nesselhauf in *Historia*, 1959, 434ff. On the law applying to soldiers in general see the studies of E. Sander in *Rheinisches Museum*, 1958, 152ff and 193ff, and 1960, 289ff

22 Asconius, *in Pisonianam*, Oxford Text, ed. A. C. Clark, p. 3

23 See Dessau, *ILS*, nos. 6779 to 6781

24 Gai. *Inst.* I, 75

25 See Sherwin-White, *RSNT*, 154–5

26 Cassius Dio, LX, 17, 5–8

27 Vespasian gave the 'Latin right' to the whole of Spain, Pliny, *Natural History* III, 30

28 If there was any proof; but see the disgraceful conduct of Cicero, *ad Att.* VII, 2, 8

29 This is dogmatism. H. M. Last in a famous note (*Cambridge Ancient History* X, 888ff) set out the evidence and came to a different conclusion, but the fact remains that the only direct evidence for the date of the statute is that Justinian's *Institutes*, I, 5. 3 call it *lex Iunia Norbana*, which must be a law proposed by the consuls of AD 19. Recent scholars (Arangio-Ruiz, Kaser, Volterra, Nicholas) all put against this statute the remark '? AD 19', except M. de Dominicis in *Tijdschrift*, 1965, 558ff, who rejects 'Norbana', though he does not adduce any new grounds

30 Pliny, *Ep.* VII, 16, 4 and X, 104, respectively

31 *Fontes* III, no. 11

32 *Titles from Ulpian* V, 4, in *Fontes* II (p. 268), and Mommsen's restoration of a lacuna in Gai. *Inst.* I, 79

33 Gai. *Inst*, I, 80

34 Gai. *Inst.* I, 78

35 *Titles from Ulpian* XIX, 4, in *Fontes* II (p. 280)

36 See, for example, E. Cuq, *Manuel des institutions juridiques des romains* (1917), 93; Buckland, *Textbook*, 93; Zulueta, *The Institutes of Gaius* II, 27

37 For example, M. Kaser in *Studi in onore di Vincenzo Arangio-Ruiz* (1952–3) II, 131ff, mostly following M. Wlassak in *ZSS*, 1907, 114ff

38 *Titles from Ulpian* III, in *Fontes* II (pp. 266–7)

39 Nicholas, *Introduction*, 65

40 Implied by Gai. *Inst.* I, 22–3

41 Pliny, *Ep.* X, 5, 2

42 Gai. *Inst.* I, 13–15. See, however, Jones, *Studies*, Essay no. VIII, also Sherwin-White, *Pliny*, 569

42a See D. Nörr, *Imperium und Polis in der hohen Prinzipatszeit* (Münchener Beiträge zur Papyrusforschung und antiken Rechtsgeschichte, vol. 50) (1966), 56

43 Cicero, *pro Archia*, 6–11

44 See F. Schulz in *JRS*, 1942, 78ff, and 1943, 55ff

45 D. 27. 1. 2. 1 and Apuleius, *Apologia*, 89 (quoted below)

46 D. 22. 3. 16

47 *Fontes* III, nos. 1 and 3

48 *Fontes* III, no. 2. For a recent addition to these documents, dated AD 224, see the Oxyrhynchus Papyrus, *P. Oxy.* 2565

49 *Fontes* III, no. 4. This was important for children of serving soldiers (who were of necessity illegitimate); see *Fontes* III, no. 5 and H. I. Bell in *JRS*, 1937, 31ff

50 *Tab. Herc.*, no. V

51 Apuleius, *Apologia*, 89

52 D. 48. 10. 13 pr.; Suetonius, *divus Claudius*, 25

53 *Tab. Herc.*, nos. XIII–XXX. See A.-J. Boyé in *Droits de l'antiquité et sociologie juridique, Mélanges Henri Lévy-Bruhl* (1959), 29ff; but some revisions are needed in the light of Arangio-Ruiz' own last thoughts and corrected readings in *BIDR*, 1959, 223ff

54 *Codex Iustinianus*, 9. 21. 1

55 *Tab. Herc.*, nos. XVI, XX, and XXIV, respectively

56 Buckland and McNair, 186

57 See L. R. Taylor in *AJP*, 1961, 113ff; J. M. C. Toynbee and J. Ward Perkins, *The Shrine of St. Peter and the Vatican Excavations* (1956), 105ff; and on the cultural pattern, F. Bömer, *Untersuchungen über die Religion der Sklaven in Griechenland und Rom* I (Akademie der Wissenschaften und der Literatur in Mainz, Abhandlungen der geistes- und sozialwissenschaftlichen Klasse, Jahrgang 1957, nr. 7) (1958) [*Untersuchungen*], 403ff, 459ff; 563ff

57a Persius, *Satires*, V, 78ff

58 Cicero, *ad Quintum fratrem*, I, 1, 13

59 Comprehensively described by A. M. Duff, *Freedmen in the Early Roman Empire* (1928, repr. with corrections and addenda, 1958), Chapter III

60 For which see below, Chapter III, p. 84

61 D. 47. 10. 7. 2

62 D. 23. 2. 45. 4

63 D. 24. 2. 11

64 Gai. *Inst.* I, 19; D. 40. 2. 13

65 D. 40. 2. 14. 1

66 See P. A. Brunt in *JRS*, 1962, 70

67 D. 38. 1. 38 pr.

68 D. 38. 1. 2. 1 and 38. 1. 4

69 See P. Jaubert in *Revue historique de droit français et étranger* [*RHDFE*], 1965, 5ff

70 Tacitus, *Annals* XIII, 26–7. The *lex Aelia Sentia* had introduced an 'accusation of ungrateful freedman' (see *Acta divi Augusti*, 217); to judge

NOTES

from Tacitus here it led—at most—to relegation

71 Suetonius, *divus Claudius*, 25, 1
72 D. 37. 14. 1
73 Pliny, *Ep.* X, 104
74 Justinian's *Institutes* III, 7, 4
75 Duff, *Freedmen*, 79, note 1
76 D. 38. 5. 9. For details see Buckland, *Textbook*, 597
77 D. 44. 5. 1. 5
78 The *nuances* of which repay reading in the letters, Cicero, *ad fam.* XVI
79 D. 38. 2. 3. 4
80 D. 38. 2. 3 pr.
81 Petronius, *Satyricon*, 81. *Cf.* Tacitus, *Annals* XIII, 27 and D. 12. 4. 3. 5, on the actor Paris
82 D. 40. 16. 4
83 D. 40. 11. The implication was that during the grantee's years of slave service he had really been a *liber homo bona fide serviens* (see below). It was on that basis that Paris sued for the return of money paid for his manumission
84 The law is expounded in massive detail by W. W. Buckland, *The Roman Law of Slavery* (1908). A good and still useful book is R. H. Barrow, *Slavery in the Roman Empire* (1928). For wider contexts see Bömer, *Untersuchungen*; A. H. M. Jones, 'Slavery in the Ancient World', in M. I. Finley, ed., *Slavery in Classical Antiquity* (1960); M. I. Finley in *Comparative Studies in Society and History*, vi, 1964, 233ff; J. Vogt, 'Sklaverei und Humanität' (*Historia*, Einzelschrift no. 8, 1965); E. E. Urbach, *The Laws regarding Slavery as a Source for Social History of the Period of the Second Temple, the Mishnah and Talmud*, in J. G. Weiss, ed., *Papers of the Institute of Jewish Studies, London*, I, 1964, 1ff
85 Finley, *Comparative Studies* (see the note above), 236 and 248–9; and see, for example, Driver and Miles, *The Babylonian Laws* I, 222–3
86 D. 4. 4. 11. 5
87 D. 21. 1. 23. 3
88 On the army see Pliny, *Ep.* X, 29–30
89 Juvenal, *Satires* VI, 222
90 Antoninus Pius, quoted at D. 1. 6. 2
91 D. 5. 1. 53
92 D. 9. 2. 5 pr. and 9. 2. 23. 9
93 K. M. Stampp, *The Peculiar Institution* (English edition, 1964), 15
94 For the law, see D. 29. 5 and the 'Opinions of Paulus', *Pauli Sententiae*, III, 5, in *Fontes* II (pp. 361–2)
95 Tacitus, *Annals* XIV, 42–5
96 Pliny, *Ep.* III, 114, 5
97 D. 18. 1. 5
98 D. 5. 1. 53

99 D. 4. 2. 8. 1

100 Except in Egypt, where it looks as if recovery was not possible: see E. Volterra in *Studi Besta* I (1939), 466–7

101 Pliny, *Ep.* X, 65–6. Volterra, in the article cited above, accepted by Sherwin-White, *Pliny*, 654, argues that the Greek and Roman rules were exactly the opposite way round; but I do not think that the word *ideo* in Trajan's answer to Pliny need necessarily imply 'since there is no rule for Bithynia we must uphold the local custom' rather than 'since there is no rule for Bithynia here is a Roman rule for you to apply'. The rest of the evidence can be interpreted in more ways than one, and *Tab. Herc.* XVI (see above, p. 49) is nothing to do with exposure of children

102 Shown exhaustively by R. Reggi, *Liber homo bona fide serviens* (1958), but stated already with characteristic brevity by Buckland, *Roman Law of Slavery*, 331

103 D. 22. 6. 1. 2 talks about it under 'errors of fact and not of law'

104 Pliny, *Ep.* VI, 25; *cf. ILS*, no. 8506

105 D. 12. 1. 41; *cf.* 45. 3. 34

106 Dio of Prusa, *Orations* XV, 23 and 13, respectively

107 Petronius, *Satyricon*, 57, 4

108 *Collatio legum Mosaicarum et Romanarum* XIV, 2, 1, in *Fontes* II (p. 577)

109 *Pauli Sententiae* V, 6, 14, in *Fontes* II (pp. 395–6). Later a crime: D. 48. 15. 1

110 D. 43. 29 and D. 10. 4. 13

111 D. 18. 1, frags, 4, 5, 6 pr. and 70

112 D. 40. 12, frags. 14 and 20. 4

113 D. 40. 12. 23. 1

114 Buckland discusses the problem, with less than his usual magisterial confidence, in *Roman Law of Slavery*, 427ff

115 See M. I. Finley in *RHDFE*, 1965, 159ff, and the two recent studies of *paramoné*: B. Adams, *Paramoné und verwandte Texte* (1964), especially 44ff and 112–13, and A. E. Samuel in *Journal of Juristic Papyrology*, 1965, 221ff. *Paramoné* covers a complex group of transactions, including, besides things akin to self-enslavement, a common Greek relationship of freedman to patron, and also free labour contracts, not involving diminution of status and not necessarily lasting for long periods

116 Petronius, *Satyricon*, 117, 5–6

117 Gai. *Inst.* I, 159–63

118 For discussion of both the rules and the purposes of the *sc. Claudianum* see P. R. C. Weaver in *CR*, 1964, 137ff and *Cl. Qu.*, 1965, 324–5; see also *CR*, 1967, 7–8.

119 See Weaver in *Cl. Qu.*, 1963, 272ff; 1964, 134ff and 311ff; 1965, 145ff and 323ff; in *JRS*, 1964, 117ff; in *CR*, 1964, 137ff; in *Proceedings of the Cambridge Philological Society* [*Proc. Camb. Phil. Soc.*], 1964, 74ff; and in *Historia*, 1964, 188ff and 1965, 460ff

120 Tacitus, *Annals* XII, 53

121 *Titles from Ulpian* XX, 16, in *Fontes* II (p. 284); and see Buckland, *Roman Law of Slavery*, 325

122 Weaver in *Cl. Qu.*, 1964, 315

123 As to the figure there is some uncertainty; see Jones, *Studies*, 30. For the actual wealth of average senators see Duncan-Jones in *PBSR*, 1965, 178 and 188: a normal 'social' minimum senatorial fortune in Pliny's time was perhaps about 8 million, and in the late second century 20 million was short of real riches

124 Jones, *Studies*, 30ff

125 See M. I. Henderson in *JRS*, 1963, 61ff

126 Cicero, *II in Verrem* II, 120ff

127 Pliny, *Ep.* X, 79, 1

128 The *Table of Heraclea*, *Fontes* I, no. 13, 108ff

129 The *lex coloniae Genetivae Iuliae sive Ursonensis*, *Fontes* I, no. 21, § 105

130 *Tab. Herc.*, nos. LXXXIII and LXXXIV

CHAPTER III

1 Compare D. Daube in *JRS*, 1951, 66ff, with F. Serrao, *La 'iurisdictio' del pretore peregrino* (1954)

2 Jones, *Studies*, 73

3 Gai. *Inst.* IV, 31

4 See, however, Valerius Maximus VII, 7, 6 for a case

5 Cicero, *II in Verrem* I, 119

6 Jones, *Studies*, 72. See Cicero, *pro Quinctio*, 29 and Pliny, *Ep.* I, 23, 3

7 See the *lex Rubria*, *Fontes* I, no. 19, §§ 21–2, and the *fragmentum Atestinum*, *Fontes* I, no. 20, l. 5

8 Jones, *Studies*, 75 and 77

9 Rabirius was prosecuted before the assembly in 63; Cicero would have been the object of a tribunician impeachment if he had not gone into exile in 58; Cicero in 70 threatened to use his aedileship in 69 to impeach anyone suspected of bribery in the trial of Verres; and Clodius as aedile impeached Milo for a fine in 56. The cases are collected in A. H. J. Greenidge, *The Legal Procedure of Cicero's Time* (1901), 353ff

10 Th. Stangl, *Ciceronis orationum scholiastae* (1912, repr. 1964), 201

11 W. Kunkel, *Untersuchungen zur Entwicklung des römischen Kriminalverfahrens* (1962), ch. XII, and *Introduction*, 61–2

12 *Senatusconsultum de Asclepiade*, 78 BC, *Fontes* I, no. 35, Greek text, ll. 17ff; *Epistula Octaviani Caesaris de Seleuco*, 42 BC, *Fontes* I, no. 55, ll. 53ff

13 Jones, *Studies*, 75–6 (*cf.* Cicero, *II in Verrem* II, 36)

14 See A. N. Sherwin-White, *RSNT*, 14ff

15 Recent works on this most difficult topic are Jones, *Studies*, Essay no. V (originally published in 1955); J. M. Kelly, *Princeps Iudex* (1957); J. Bleicken, *Senatsgericht und Kaisergericht* (1962)

16 Suetonius, *divus Iulius*, 44, 2. So did Pompey, according to Isidore of Seville, *Etymologiae* V, 1, 5. On Pompey's intention see E. Pólay in *Acta Antiqua*, xiii, 1965, 85ff, and on Caesar's the same author in *Iura*, 1965, 27ff

17 For what survives see *Acta divi Augusti*, 142ff

17a For the history of this appointment see Kaser, *Das römische Zivilprozessrecht*, 367-8; for a fideicomissary case before a *iuridicus* see D. 40. 5. 41. 5

17b See Pliny, *Ep.* IV, 29, 2 and Sherwin-White, *Pliny*, 309

18 Jones, *Studies*, Essay No IV

19 Tacitus, *Annals* XIV, 41

20 Cassius Dio, LXIX, 18, 3-4. Burrus in Seneca, *de clementia* II, 1, 2 is only carrying out sentences, *pace* Sherwin-White, *Pliny*, 639

21 D. 12. 4. 15

22 D. 1. 15. 3. 1

23 Jones, *Studies*, Essay no. IV. See, however, P. Garnsey in *JRS*, 1966, 174ff

24 D. 1. 16. 9 pr.

25 See the article 'iuridicus' in E. de Ruggiero, *Dizionario Epigrafico*, 1941

25a In *Fontes* I, no. 49, l. 42, legionary commanders are coupled with juris-dictional magistrates; perhaps in the second century they took a share

25b On criminal appeal see Jones, *Studies*, Essay IV, and on civil appeal Essay V, 77-83

25c See Jolowicz, *Hist. Introduct.*, 406 and Kaser, *Das römische Zivilprozessrecht*, 399-401

26 I simplify here by speaking only of the 'formulary system' and not of its historical predecessor, the *legis actio*

27 See, for example, Gellius, *Noctes Atticae* I, 22, 6, quoted below

28 *Fontes* I, no. 65

29 F. Casavola, *Studi sulle azioni popolari romane* (1958)

30 D. 5. 1 and D. 13. 4

31 D. 5. 1. 19. 2

32 Cicero, *II in Verrem* III, 38

33 D. 5. 1. 1

34 D. 13. 4. 1

35 Cicero, *ad fam.* XIII, 14

36 *Tab. Herc.*, no. XIV

37 Cicero, *pro Quinctio*, 22-5 and 48-58

38 Horace, *Satires* I, i, 11 and ix, 36 and 75

39 *Pace* H. Lévy-Bruhl, *La 'denegatio actionis' sous la procédure formulaire* (1924), who denied its existence altogether

40 A loose statement of a rather complicated position; see Buckland, *Textbook*, 634

41 Juvenal, *Satires* XIII, especially ll. 15-16 and 199ff

42 Gai. *Inst.* IV, 39ff and 116ff

42a Cicero, *pro Roscio comoedo*, 24

43 Cicero, *II in Verrem* II, 30. See G. Broggini, *Iudex Arbiterve* (1951), 55ff

44 D. 5. 1. 12. 2; 5. 1. 80; 42. 1. 57; Gai. *Inst.* IV, 105. Quintilian apparently once pleaded a case in the presence (in Rome) of Queen Berenice, and implies that she was a *iudex: Inst. Or.* IV, 1, 19; but see *AJP*, 1951, 169

45 Pliny, *Ep.* VI, 2, 7

46 Quintilian, *Inst. Or.* X, 1, 32; Juvenal, *Satires* VII, 115-17 and XVI, 13ff

47 J. Mazeaud, *La nomination du 'iudex unus' sous la procédure formulaire à Rome* (1933). F. La Rosa in *Labeo*, 1958, 39ff, argues that only persons on the *album* could be chosen as *iudices* in civil suits, but does not discuss the references in lay literature

47a Kaser, *Das römische Zivilprozessrecht*, 43-4 and 141. The distinction is well brought out in Pliny, *Natural History*, Praef., 6ff

48 Broggini, *Iudex Arbiterve*, passim

49 D. 4. 8. 44; the whole title repays perusal

50 *Fontes* III, no. 164

51 *Tab. Herc.*, no. LXXVI

52 *Tab. Herc.*, nos. LXXVII, LXXVIII and LXXIX, respectively

52a See Cicero, *II in Verrem* III, 135

53 *Fontes* I, no. 44. See La Rosa in *Labeo*, 1958, 19ff

54 Cicero, *de oratore* I, 173

55 Cicero, *de oratore* I, 180 and II, 140 and 221

56 See back, Chapter I, p. 33 and note 93

57 Cicero, *ad Quintum fratrem* I, 2, 10

58 See Kelly, *Roman Litigation*, Chapter V

59 Gellius, *Noctes Atticae* XIV, 2

60 Pliny, *Ep.* VI, 2, 7-8; *cf.* Martial, VI, 35

61 D. 2. 13, 'de edendo'. See Buckland and McNair, 406

62 D. 32. 69 pr.; *cf.* Watson, *Law of Obligations*, p. 3 on stipulations and p. 93 on sales

63 D. 22. 6. 9 pr. and 2

64 D. 22, titles 3 and 5, respectively. On 'burden of proof' see, with discussion of several recent papers, G. Pugliese in *Revue internationale des droits de l'antiquité*, 1956, 349ff

65 D. 22. 5. 3

66 D. 22. 3. 10

67 Suetonius, *Nero*, 17

68 *Pauli Sententiae* V, 25, 6

69 D. 5. 1. 79. 1; *cf.* D. 22. 1. 32 pr.

70 Gai. *Inst.* IV, 61-2

71 Buckland and McNair, 412, note 1; but on an earlier stage of specific performance of contract in the common law see H. D. Hazeltine, 'Early History of Specific Performance of Contract in English Law, in *Juristische Festgabe des Auslandes zu Josef Kohlers 60. Geburtstag* (1909), 67ff

72 D. 12. 3

72a On which see La Rosa, *L''actio iudicati' nel diritto romano classico* (1963)

73 Cicero, *pro Flacco*, 48

74 Gai. *Inst.* IV, 103–9

75 Jones, *Studies*, 81–3

76 Cicero, *pro Flacco*, 49

77 A. H. J. Greenidge, *Infamia. Its place in Roman public and private law* (1894); L. Pommeray, *Etudes sur l'infamie* (1937); U. Brasiello, *La repressione penale in diritto Romano* (1937), 152ff; Zulueta, *The Institutes of Gaius*, II, 300–1; M. Kaser in *ZSS*, 1956, 220ff, L. Lombardi, *Dalla 'fides' alla 'bona fides'* (1961), 165ff; A. Watson in *Tijdschrift*, 1963, 76ff; Kelly, *Roman Litigation*, 24ff

78 Even, once, for bad farming, according to Gellius, *Noctes Atticae*, IV, 12

79 See Kaser in *ZSS*, 1938, 74ff

80 Asconius, *in Pisonianam*, p. 8 of Clark's Oxford Text; Livy, XXXIX, 42, 6

81 Gai. *Inst.* IV, 182

82 D. 3. 2. 1

83 Watson (quoted in note 77 above); *cf.* P. P. Zanzucchi in *BIDR*, 1916, 93

84 *Codex Iustinianus*, 2. 11. 2 and 5 and 18

85 See Chapter II, p. 66

86 Brasiello, *La repressione penale*, 546ff

87 Cicero, *II in Verrem* II, 26

88 D. 1. 18. 8

89 D. 3. 5. 46. 1

90 Cicero, *II in Verrem* II, 32 and 37ff

91 Cicero, *pro Flacco*, 47–8, and *II in Verrem* II, 41 and III, 28 and 135ff

91a Cicero, *divinatio in Caecilium*, 56; *II in Verrem* III, 55 and 69

92 Cicero, *II in Verrem* II, 30

93 See the fourth Edict of Cyrene, *Fontes* I, no 68 (p. 409)

94 Taubenschlag, *Law of Greco-Roman Egypt*, 512

95 *Fontes* III, no. 64. See also nos. 100, 170, and 86 (the 'Sententia Senecionis'), and the long report of a trial before a *iudex datus* in AD 124, *P. Fam. Tebt.* no. 24

95a See, however, Pliny, *Panegyricus*, 36, 4

96 Parks, *The Roman Rhetorical Schools*, passim

97 Cicero, *pro Cluentio*, 139

98 Cicero, *Topica*, 51

99 Horace, *Epistles* I, iii, 23–4

100 D. 31. 29 pr.; Cicero, *II in Verrem* I, 73; Suetonius, *divus Augustus*, 33, 2. See P. Garnsey in *JRS*, 1966, 177–9

101 Pliny, *Ep.* VI, 11

102 D. 4. 2. 9. 3

103 Gellius, *Noctes Atticae* I, 22, 6 (the verbal joke slightly adapted)

104 Cicero, *II in Verrem* II, 71ff; *cf.* I, 73–4

105 Gellius, *Noctes Atticae* XII, 13
106 Ibid. XIII, 10, 1; *cf.* Valerius Maximus, VIII, 7, 4 and IX, 3, 2
107 Valerius Maximus, VIII, 12, 1
108 See Cicero's puns on *cavere* in *ad fam.* III, 1, 3, VII, 6, 2 and VII, 13, 2
109 On this process see Schulz, *Roman Legal Science*, 42ff and 102ff
110 Of the problems connected with the *ius respondendi ex auctoritate Caesaris* something has been said in Chapter I; see p. 26
111 See, for example, Schulz, *Roman Legal Science*, 119ff; Honoré, *Gaius*, 18ff; but *cf.* Kunkel, *Introduction*, 106: 'The two schools were not teaching institutions'
112 Gellius, *Noctes Atticae* XIII, 13
113 On which see Jones, *Later Roman Empire* I, 507ff
113a Cicero gets some fun out of the brothers Caepasius, who were only too glad of any brief: *pro Cluentio*, 57
114 Cassius Dio, LIV, 18, 2
115 Tacitus, *Annals* XI, 5 and 7
116 An interesting series of letters, Pliny, *Ep.* V, 4 and 9 and 13
117 Buckland and McNair, 299
118 Juvenal, *Satires* VII, 106ff (paraphrased)
119 Passages quoted by Kelly, *Roman Litigation*, 84, note 1
120 *Fontes* III, no. 57 (*cf.* no. 30)
121 Martial, VI, 19
122 See *ILS*, no. 7750, for a man who 'wrote wills for 25 years without a jurisconsult'
123 *P. Hamb.* 72; see Wenger, *Quellen*, 745, note 110, and 807
124 *Fontes* III, no. 92. See below, Chapter VII, p. 245
125 See *Revue belge de philologie et d'histoire*, 1957, 361, and Ch. Saumagne in Courtois, Leschi, Perrat and Saumagne, eds., *Tablettes Albertini, Actes privés de l'époque vandale* (1952), 81ff
126 R. von Ihering, 'Reich und Arm im altrömischen Civilprozess', in *Scherz und Ernst in der Jurisprudenz*[3] (1885), 175ff
127 Cicero, *de oratore* I, 177
128 Gellius, *Noctes Atticae* V, 13, 2
129 Cicero, *II in Verrem* II, 36. And on *reiectio Romae* see p. 70, above
130 The theme of Lombardi's *Dalla 'fides' alla 'bona fides'*.
131 Cicero, *ad fam.* XIV, 1, 5
132 Cicero, *ad Att.* I, 18, 8
133 Cassius Dio, LIX, 26, 9; see J. A. Crook, *Consilium Principis* (1955), App. 4
134 Crook, ibid., p. 63
135 *Fontes* I, no. 103 (p. 497)
136 *Apokrimata*, no. 5. See also Chapter I, note 17a. Provincial governors were supposed to protect humble litigants and assign them counsel: D. 1. 16. 9. 4–5

137 Jones, *Later Roman Empire* I, 470ff
138 See the judgment quoted by Megarry, *Miscellany-at-Law*, 116–17
139 Tacitus, *Annals* XIV, 28
140 D. 2. 14. 53 and 48. 7. 6
141 Kelly, *Roman Litigation*, 85. For some criticisms see *CR*, 1967, 83ff
142 Juvenal, *Satires* XVI, 36–47; see Kelly, op. cit., Chapter VI
143 D. 4. 6. 23 pr.
144 Pliny, *Ep.* I, 18, 1; Juvenal, *Satires* III, 212–13
145 D. 4. 6. 15. 3
146 Apuleius, *Metamorphoses* (the 'Golden Ass') IX, 35–8
147 For the history see Schulz, *CRL*, 600ff; and on the *actio metus causa* see also Kelly, op. cit., 15ff
148 D. 4. 3. 11. 1
149 D. 22. 5. 3
150 D. 48. 2. 10 and 11 pr.
151 The fundamental treatment of the whole subject is by G. Cardascia in *RHDFE*, 1950, 305ff and 461ff
152 D. 48. 19. 15
153 Jones, *Studies*, 65

CHAPTER IV

1 The well-known system of Le Play ('extended' family: 'stem' family: 'nuclear' family) is briefly described in C. C. Zimmerman and M. E. Frampton, *Family and Society, A Study in the Sociology of Reconstruction* (1935), 97–9. It is a mistake to classify family systems rigidly and exclusively on this or any other basis; see, for example, Olga Lang, *Chinese Family and Society* (1946), 14ff and 135ff. For some comments on this as it affects Rome see *Cl. Qu.*, 1967, art. 'Patria Potestas', forthcoming
2 But for doubts about this see *Cl. Qu.*, quoted in the note above
3 On which see P. E. Corbett, *The Roman Law of Marriage* (1930)
4 Testimony to this latter purpose runs all the way from the ancient censorial oath quoted by Gellius, *Noctes Atticae* IV, 3, 2, to the betrothal document from Africa under the Vandals, *Tablettes Albertini*, no. I, l. 3
5 D. 23. 2. 44 pr.
6 *Fontes* III, no. 19
7 Details in Gai. *Inst.* I, 62–3
8 D. 12. 4. 8; D. 23. 2. 4
9 M. K. Hopkins in *Population Studies*, 1965, 309ff, following up papers by M. Durry to which he gives references on p. 309, note 8
10 Valerius Maximus, IV, 3, 3
11 The considerations of social psychology that result from reflection on this pattern are very well summed up by Hopkins, op. cit., 327. It is fair to note that in the Graeco-Egyptian family of *P. Fam. Tebt.* they seem to have married comparatively late.

U

12 D. 50. 17. 30
13 Gai. *Inst.* I, 63
14 Cicero, *de oratore* I, 183
15 Gellius, *Noctes Atticae* IV, 3, 3. For *manus* see below
16 D. 32. 49. 4
17 Suetonius, *divus Vespasianus*, 3
18 *Scriptores Historiae Augustae, Vita Marci*, 29, 10
19 D. 39. 5. 31 pr.
20 Especially P. M. Meyer, *Der römische Konkubinat* (1895) and J. Plassard, *Le concubinat romain sous le haut empire* (1921)
21 Plassard, op. cit., 160
22 *Pauli Sententiae* II, 20, 1
23 D. 45. 1. 121. 1
24 For example, *Corpus Inscriptionum Latinarum* V, 1918, quoted by Schulz, *CRL*, 139, which makes it likely that in *Corpus* VI, 1906 (to wife, concubine and another wife) the concubine was concurrent with one of the wives—contrary to the view of Plassard, op. cit., 126, note 7
25 D. 48. 5. 14 pr.
26 Plassard, op. cit., 69ff
27 Gellius, *Noctes Atticae* IV, 4
28 Juvenal, *Satires* VI, 25f
29 See the so-called 'Laudatio Turiae', *Fontes* III, no. 69, i, l. 16; and *cf.* Cicero, *pro Flacco*, 84
30 Schulz, *CRL*, 119
31 Gai. *Inst.* II, 63
32 See Buckland, *Textbook*, 325
33 Apuleius, *Apologia*, 71 and 91–2
34 D. 23. 4
35 D. 15. 3. 21
36 D. 23. 3. 10 pr.
37 *Cf.* Apuleius, *Apologia*, 91
38 Valerius Maximus, VIII, 2, 3, describes a nasty little fraud tried out by one man
39 Valerius Maximus, VI, 3, 10–12
40 This is best set out in detail by V. Arangio-Ruiz in *La legislazione*, Chapter III of *Augustus: Studi in occasione del bimillenario Augusteo* (1938)
41 D. 24. 2. 9. See Corbett, op. cit., 228ff
42 *Pauli Sententiae* V, 6, 15
43 D. 24. 1
44 D. 24 1. 40 and 42; Antoninus Pius
45 D. 17. 1. 54 pr.
46 See, in addition to the passages about to be quoted, D. 9. 2. 33 and 19. 5. 5 pr.
47 D. 20. 1. 8 and D. 42. 5. 38 pr.

48 D. 28. 6. 45 pr.

49 Tacitus, *Annals*, XIII, 32, 2; *cf.* Suetonius, *Tiberius*, 35, 1

50 Cicero did not really consult his beloved daughter Tullia, *ad Att.* XI, 3; *cf.* Apuleius, *Apologia*, 77, and, on the limit imposed by Antoninus Pius, note 42 above

51 And see, on betrothal, D. 23. 1. 13

52 Gellius, *Noctes Atticae* II, 7, 20

53 Horace, *Satires* I, iv, 48-50

54 Gai. *Inst.* I, 55

55 D. 1. 6. 9

56 Consuls and governors: D. 1.7. 3; senators: D. 39. 5. 7. 3; local magistrates: D. 15. 1. 3. 13; D. 27. 8. 1. 17; D. 50. 1. 2 pr.

57 Gellius, *Noctes Atticae* II, 2

58 Though for hesitation as to senators see D. 39. 5. 7. 3

59 D. 15. 3. 7. 5

60 D. 14. 6. 1. 3

61 But the evidence is not unequivocal; see *Cl. Qu.*, 1967, art. 'Patria Potestas' forthcoming

62 Pliny, *Ep.* IV, 2

63 *Titles from Ulpian* XX, 10

64 Juvenal, *Satires* XVI, 51-6

65 Gai. *Inst.* I, 93 and II, 135 a

66 Pliny, *Ep.* X, 11, 2

66a The magistrates of Salpensa gaining Roman citizenship *ex officio* got it (*Fontes* I, no. 23, § 22), but this does not seem to have been universal: Pliny, *Panegyricus*, 37, 3. The government was quite capable of taking fiscal advantage of such anomalies, as the 'Gnomon of the Idiologos' shows, passim

67 Gai. *Inst.* I, 97ff; Gellius, *Noctes Atticae* V, 19

68 See, for example, Gai. *Inst.* I, 19

69 D. 1. 7. 17. 3; *cf.* D. 1. 7. 15. 2-3

70 Cicero, *de domo*, 34-5

71 Gai. *Inst.* II, 138

72 Schulz, *CRL*, 145

73 Tacitus, *Annals* XV, 19

74 Gai. *Inst.* I, 132

75 *Cf.* D. 37. 12. 5

76 See *L'année épigraphique*, 1946, no. 123, first fragment—a new piece of the *Lex coloniae Iuliae Genetivae*. The local magistrates can appoint guardians on application

77 Gai. *Inst.* I, 196

78 Apuleius, *Apologia*, 101

79 *Fontes* III, no. 25

80 D. 26. 7

81 On all this see, as well as the *Digest* title, E. J. Jonkers, *Economische en sociale toestanden in het Romeinsche rijk, blijkende uit het Corpus Juris* (1933), 21ff

82 D. 27. 2

83 D. 26. 10. 1 pr. The complaints were of maladministration, not of danger to the ward's life: see Jolowicz in *JRS*, 1947, 82ff

84 *Fontes* III, no. 31

85 D. 27. 1 and *Fragmenta Vaticana* 123–247, in *Fontes* II (pp. 494ff)

86 There is much room for divergent opinions on the detailed development, because the bit of Gaius's *Institutes* that treated of *curatio* is lost

87 D. 4. 4. 1. 1

88 D. 4. 4. 24. 1

89 D. 4. 4. 11. 2

90 *Cf.* Horace, *Epistles* I, i, 102

91 Schulz, *CRL*, 198 and 201

92 Buckland and McNair, 190

93 See *Cl. Qu.*, 1967, art. 'Patria Potestas', forthcoming

94 For the differences between *legatum per praeceptionem* and *praelegatum* see Buckland, *Textbook*, 336 and 352–3, and Kaser, *Das römische Privatrecht* I, 624

95 Lists are given in *Titles from Ulpian* XX and XXII

96 Gai. *Inst.* I, 115 a

97 *Gnomon*, § 33, in *Fontes* I (p. 475)

98 Cicero, *ad fam.* VII, 21

99 As to heirship, *Titles from Ulpian* XXII, 5; as to legacy, *Titles from Ulpian* XXIV, 28; not *per praeceptionem*, Pliny, *Ep.* V, 7, 1 (it is, of course, obvious). Important for the history is G. le Bras in *Studi in onore di Salvatore Riccobono* III (1936), 33ff. See also Sherwin-White, *Pliny*, 330–1

100 Juvenal, *Satires* IX, 86ff

101 Petronius, *Satyricon*, 76, 2

102 For certain modifications in the late Republic and by the *lex Iunia Velleia*, see Buckland, *Textbook*, 323–4

103 See E. Renier, *Etude sur l'histoire de la 'querela inofficiosi' en droit romain* (1942); Schulz, *CRL*, 275ff

104 Pliny, *Ep.* VI, 33

105 D. 5. 2. 1

106 D. 5. 2. 8. 8 and Pliny, *Ep.* V, 1, 9 (where the young man, if not disinherited, would have been sole heir, so $\frac{1}{4}$ of his intestate portion was $\frac{1}{4}$ of the whole estate)

106a On this theme, see L. Boyer in *RHDFE*, 1965, 333ff

107 Oxyrhynchus Papyri, *P. Oxy.* 105, l. 5 and 489, l.5

108 *P. Oxy.* 104, ll. 14ff

109 D. 33. 2. 33. 2

110 D. 35. 2, frags. 68 and 55 and 3. 2. See P. Stein in *Revue internationale des droits de l'antiquité*, 1962, 335ff

111 D. 5. 1. 52. 1; D. 31. 87 pr.
112 *E.g.* books, D. 32. 52; farms and furniture, D. 33. 7
113 Pliny, *Ep.* II, 4, 1
114 D. 29. 4
115 D. 36. 3
116 D. 36. 1. 4. *Cf. P. Fam Tebt.* no. 17, ll. 11ff., '. . . in order not to be put to trouble . . .'
117 Cicero, *ad Att.* XI, 2, 1 and XIII, 46, 3
118 *Fontes* III, no. 60
119 Gai. *Inst.* II, 285
120 Cicero, *de finibus* II, 55
121 *P. Hamb.* 72, quoted in Wenger, *Quellen*, 807
122 Justinian's *Institutes* II, 23, 1
123 Gai. *Inst.* II, 278; D. 1. 2. 2. 32
124 D. 36. 1. 1. 1–3
125 D. 36. 1. 27
126 Pliny, *Ep.* X, 75. See Sherwin-White, *Pliny*, 663–4
127 *Gnomon*, § 18, in *Fontes* I (p. 472)
128 D. 34. 9. 10 pr.
129 Pliny, *Panegyricus*, 37–40
130 See *Acta divi Augusti*, pp. 221–2
131 Pliny, *Ep.* VII, 11 and 14
132 See *Acta divi Augusti*, p. 220, note 2
133 Description in Gai. *Inst.* II, 104. The will of a Roman citizen had to be in Latin: *Gnomon*, § 8; but Greek-speaking testators would have a copy in Greek. For such a copy see *P. Oxy.* 2348
134 Horace, *Satires* II, v, 51ff
135 Gai. *Inst.* II, 108
136 Gai. *Inst.* II, 119
137 Pliny, *Ep.* II, 16. Pliny congratulates himself on his willingness to carry out the provisions in an unconfirmed codicil; it had presumably contained something that purported to be more than a mere *fideicommissum*, which Pliny would have been legally obliged to carry out
138 D. 29. 1. 1 pr. See Chapter I, p. 22
139 D. 37. 13. 1 pr.
140 Gai. *Inst.* II, 110. *Gnomon*, § 34 is probably a local rule for Egypt
140a See Arangio-Ruiz in *BIDR*, 1906, 157ff; *inter alia* it was to give men used to peregrine testamentary habits the assurance that their property could be left in ways which they understood
141 *Fontes* I, no. 78
142 Suetonius, *divus Iulius*, 83, 2; *divus Augustus*, 101
143 *Vita Donati*, §§ 37 and 40, ed. C. Hardie in 'Appendix Vergiliana', Oxford Text (1957). *Cf.* the will of Persius described in his *Vita*, in the Oxford Text of Persius and Juvenal, ed. W. V. Clausen (1959), pp. 32–3

144 Cicero, *ad Att.* XIII, 46, 3

145 Pliny, *Ep.* VIII, 18. On Pliny's place in the scale of senatorial wealth see R. P. Duncan-Jones in *PBSR*, 1965, 177ff

146 *Fontes* III, no. 48

147 *Fontes* III, no. 49

148 Petronius, *Satyricon*, 71–2

149 *Fontes* III, nos. 47 and 50

150 Suetonius, *Tiberius*, 23; *divus Claudius*, 4, 7; and *Nero*, 4, respectively

151 *Fontes* III, no. 47

152 The most recent general work is the important series of essays by F. De Visscher, *Le droit des tombeaux romains* (1963)

153 For a picture, see R. Meiggs, *Roman Ostia* (1960), pl. XXXIII. And for a picture of the 'Street of Tombs' at Pompeii, see A. Aymard and J. Auboyer, *Rome et son empire* (1959), pl. XVII

154 For pictures, see J. M. C. Toynbee and J. Ward Perkins, *The Shrine of St Peter and the Vatican Excavations* (1956), pls. I and IV

155 Aymard and Auboyer, op. cit., pl. XIV

156 *ILS*, no. 117

157 Horace, *Satires* I, viii, 8ff

158 Gai. *Inst.* II, 3 and 6 and 9. This is not just legal theory; imperial constitutions confirm the rule, *e.g. Codex Iustinianus*, 3. 44. 2., and Trajan's ruling in *Gnomon*, § 1, in *Fontes* I (p. 470)

159 See *ILS*, nos. 7893ff, especially 7912–13, and *Fontes* III, no. 80, *e, f,* and *g*

160 *E.g. ILS*, 8226 and 8233

161 D. 11. 7. 2. 5

162 D. 11. 7. 2. 2

163 See Schulz, *CRL*, 342, and *Principles*, 26

164 *ILS*, 8382–3 and *Fontes* III, no. 85, *b–e* (*cf. f* and *g*)

165 *ILS*, 8386

166 De Visscher, *Le droit des tombeaux romains*, 65ff

167 See, for example, the 'Sententia Senecionis', *Fontes* III, no. 86

168 See De Visscher, op. cit., 225ff, and P. Stein in *Studi in onore di Biondo Biondi* II, 115

169 See, for example, the *lex coloniae Genetivae*, *Fontes* I, no. 21, § 73; but *cf.* D. 47. 12. 3. 5

170 D. 11. 7, from frag. 12. 2 onwards

171 D. 11. 7. 2. 1

172 D. 47. 12. 3

173 D. 11. 7. 5

174 Petronius, *Satyricon*, 71, 7

175 An example from hundreds: *ILS*, 7933 *b*

176 *ILS*, 8115, 8283, 8284, and the will of Dasumius, *Fontes* III, no. 48, p. 139

177 *ILS*, 8219; cf. 8226, etc.

178 *ILS*, 1798; *cf.* D. 33. 2. 34 pr. and *ILS*, 8351. (The other copy of this

inscription, *Corpus Inscriptionum Latinarum* VI, 8750, contains a different wife.)

179 *ILS*, 8351, 7536 and 8366, respectively

180 Legal studies: besides Le Bras in *Studi in onore di Salvatore Riccobono* III (1936), 23ff, see P. W. Duff, *Personality in Roman Private Law* (1938), 168ff; E. F. Bruck in *Scritti in onore di Contardo Ferrini pubblicati in occasione della sua beatificazione* (Milan, 1947-9), vol. IV, 1ff (especially 18ff). Problems of trusts and of the growth of the notion of legal personality are involved; for comment on several general studies see R. Feenstra in *Tijdschrift*, 1956, 381ff. On the Roman attitude to peregrine foundations see J. H. Oliver, *The Ruling Power* (1953), 963ff. Social Studies: R. P. Duncan-Jones in *PBSR*, 1962, 47ff; 1963, 159ff; 1965, 189ff

181 Published by P. M. Fraser and B. Nicholas in *JRS*, 1958, 117ff and 1962, 156ff (*cf.* De Visscher, *Le droit des tombeaux romains*, 199ff)

182 *L'année épigraphique*, 1940, no. 94. See De Visscher, op. cit., 240ff

183 D. 18. 1. 73. 1, and the 'Sententia Senecionis' (see note 167)

184 See *Gnomon*, § 1, in *Fontes* I (p. 470)

185 De Visscher, op. cit., 298

186 *Codex Iustinianus*, 3. 44. 6

187 *ILS*, 8365 and *Corpus Inscriptionum Latinarum* VI, 8861, respectively. Mommsen, as usual, put his finger unerringly on all the problems; see his *Gesammelte Schriften* III, 198ff, especially 213–14

CHAPTER V

1 There is a useful discussion in Buckland and McNair, 62ff, with the excursus of F. H. Lawson

2 For our period we do not need to take into account the different view of early Roman law expressed by M. Kaser, particularly in his *Eigentum und Besitz im älteren römischen Recht* (1943) (2nd ed., 1956). On 'layers' of ownership in 'bonitary ownership', the only pure civil law case, and on the *agri vectigales*, see later in this chapter

3 Gai. *Inst.* II, 2–11; D. 1. 8

4 D. 50. 15, frags. 1 and 6–8

5 On the recent discovery of a *ius Italicum* of individuals see Chapter II, p. 40, with note 12

6 On peregrine land see Jones, *Studies*, Essay IX

7 Gai. *Inst.* II, 14a–17

8 Gaius describes it, *Inst.* I, 119–22, in connection with the *mancipatio* of persons

9 Gai. *Inst.* II, 24. What 'vindication' was is explained below, p. 144

10 Hence Virgil's advice to encourage bees to swarm nearby, *Georgics* IV, 21–4. See also D. Daube in *Droits de l'antiquité et sociologie juridique: Mélanges Henri Lévy-Bruhl* (1959), 63ff

NOTES

11 See Sir George Hill in *Proceedings of the British Academy*, 1933, 219ff; Buckland, *Textbook*, 218ff; Schulz, *CRL*, 362
12 Nicholas, *Introduction*, 132
13 D. 6. 1. 23. 4
14 D. 10. 4, frags. 6 and 7. 1. See Buckland, *Textbook*, 210
15 D. 8. 4. 6. 1
16 Buckland and McNair, 101
17 Taubenschlag, *Law of Greco-Roman Egypt*, 239–40
18 *Codex Iustinianus*, 3. 32. 2 pr.;
19 *ILS*, 7908. Note the mancipation; urns were not *res mancipi*! But if they were thinking of them starting with the ground, what then? But even so, what price *res nullius*?
20 *Pace* C. A. Maschi in *Studi in onore di Vincenzo Arangio-Ruiz* (1952–3), IV, 135ff, who argues that *superficies* was a right over a floor protected by the *ius honorarium*. It is usually thought to have been a kind of 'building-lease', and Maschi has not convincingly demonstrated the contrary
21 Gai. *Inst.* IV, 16. For what it all means see the commentary in Zulueta, *The Institutes of Gaius* II, 233–4
22 D. 6. 1. 9
23 Schulz, *CRL*, 372
24 The pledgee did possess; into this anomaly we cannot go
25 Nicholas, *Introduction*, 111
26 See the very characteristic note of Buckland in *Textbook*, 258, note 12
27 D. 6. 1. 24
28 Gai. *Inst.* II, 40–1
29 Nicholas, *Introduction*, 127
30 Gai. *Inst.* IV, 144
31 See H. J. Roby, *Roman Private Law in the Times of Cicero and of the Antonines* (1902), II, 510ff
32 Gai. *Inst.* IV, 160
33 Gai. *Inst.* IV, 161ff
34 See Buckland, *Textbook*, 736ff
35 Petronius, *Satyricon*, 76, 8ff (Trimalchio) and 57, 5–6 (his friend)
36 D. 27. 4. 3. 6, etc. See Jonkers, *Economische en sociale toestanden*, 21ff
37 D. 50. 15. 4
38 The entry quoted is *Corpus Inscriptionum Latinarum* XI, 1147, item no. 8. For other entries from this long document see *Fontes* III, no. 116
39 Of the cataster the most important treatment is still in F. Blume, K. Lachmann and A. Rudorff, eds., *Die Schriften der römischen Feldmesser*, I(1848), II (1852), by Mommsen in vol. II, 152ff and Rudorff in vol. II, 405ff. It was *peculatus* to tamper with the cataster: D. 48. 13. 10. On the Augustan *forma* see *ILS*, 251. For centuriation and its physical traces see J. Bradford, *Ancient Landscapes* (1957) and the references quoted by A. Piganiol, *Les documents cadastraux de la colonie romaine d'Orange* (1962), 38ff

39a See Piganiol, op. cit., and Ch. Saumagne in *Journal des Savants*, 1965, 73ff
40 Taubenschlag, *Law of Greco-Roman Egypt*, 222ff
41 *Pace* Piganiol, op. cit., 404–5 (but he is talking of *ager vectigalis*)
42 D. 19. 1. 21. 1. *Cf.* D. 2. 14. 42; 19. 1. 13. 6; 39. 4. 7 pr.
43 D. 25. 1. 13
44 Cicero, *II in Verrem* III, 55; D. 26. 7. 32. 6
45 Taubenschlag, op. cit., 360, with note 23
46 D. 10. 1. 11. For legislation about illegal moving of boundaries, see *Fontes* I, no. 12 and D. 47. 21. 2–3
47 D. 11. 6. 1 (much suspected of interpolation). *Cf. Rondel v. Worsley*, (1966) 1 All E.R., 467 and (1966) 3 W.L.R., 950, on conduct of cases by barristers
48 *ILS*, 6005
49 One curious and much-argued document records the purchase, on behalf of a municipality, of a right to obstruct certain lights: *Fontes* III, no. 106s
50 Gai. *Inst.* II, 31
51 *De itinere:* D. 43. 19; *de aqua* (with elaborate complications): D. 43. 20; *de cloacis*: D. 43. 23
52 D. 8. 5. 10 pr.
53 On which see Buckland and McNair, 135
54 D. 8. 2. 8
55 D. 8. 2. 13 pr.
56 D. 8. 2. 19 pr.
57 Or perhaps cheese-shop, *taberna casiaria, i.e.* a snack-bar. The whole passage, D. 8. 5. 8. 5ff, is of great interest. The piece put, in the translation, in square brackets is obscure, ungrammatical, and probably interpolated, but the whole is a very characteristic specimen of legal argument from case to case—a paradigm, perhaps, of all legal argument
58 D. 7. 1. 56
59 D. 7. 1. 13. 7. But on usufructuary's right to work mines see G. Pugliese in *Tulane Law Review*, 1966, 542ff, with interesting references to the modern law. See also p. 161, below
60 D. 7. 1. 15. 1
61 D. 7. 5
62 D. 19. 2. 25. 1
63 See Nicholas, *Introduction*, 184, and the celebrated passage of Schulz, *CRL*, 544ff
64 *Fontes* III, no. 143 *a; cf.* Petronius, *Satyricon*, 38, 10 and Martial, XII, 32, 1, which make it probable that we should read '1 July' in the Pompeian inscription
65 Juvenal, *Satires* III, 269 (and the whole context)
66 Cicero, *pro Caelio*, 17; D. 9. 3. 1. 7
67 D. 19. 2. 60 pr. and 19. 2. 25. 2, respectively
68 Cicero, *ad Att.* XIV, 9, 1 and Gellius, *Noctes Atticae* XV, 1, 3, respectively

69 D. 19. 2. 30 pr.; *cf.* 19. 2. 7 and 13. 7. 11. 5. *Conductor* may imply such a chief tenant in the Pompeian advertisement

70 D. 2. 14. 4 pr.; *cf.* 13. 7. 11. 5 and 20. 2. 2

71 Martial, XII, 32, 1–3

72 W. E. Heitland, *Agricola, a Study of Agriculture and Rustic Life in the Greco-Roman World from the point of view of Labour* (1921), remains an indispensable and masterly collection of evidence for agricultural management, though its over-all thesis would not now be acceptable. His section on the law of tenantry is at pp. 361ff. The latest, and revolutionary, theory about the tied colonate is that of A. H. M. Jones, argued in *Past and Present* xiii, 1958, 1ff. See also *The Later Roman Empire* II, 795ff

73 Told again most recently by Arnold Toynbee, *Hannibal's Legacy* (1965), II, 190–312 (with various relevant 'annexes')

73a See K. D. White in *JRS*, 1966, 249

74 H. Gummerus, *Der römische Gutsbetrieb als wirtschaftlicher Organismus* (*Klio*, Beiheft 5), 1906, 64ff and 82ff; Heitland, op. cit., 252ff. One must not forget the five *coloni* on Horace's small farm, Horace, *Ep.* I, xiv, 2ff, nor Domitius, who could man seven ships with the *servi*, *liberti* and *coloni* from his huge estates, Caesar, *Bellum Civile* I, 34, 2. See Brunt in *JRS*, 1962, 71

75 Pliny, *Ep.* IX, 37

76 For a clear contrast with slave-farming see D. 20. 1. 32

77 See Pliny, *Ep.* III, 19, 7; D. 9. 2. 27. 11. *Instrumentum fundi* could include slaves. *Cf.* Sherwin-White, *Pliny*, 256

78 D. 19. 2. 9. 3 and 19. 2. 11. 1, respectively

79 Pliny, *Ep.* IX, 37, 2

80 D. 19. 2. 13. 11

81 D. 19. 2. 55. 2

82 Buckland, *Textbook*, 221

83 D. 19. 2. 55. 1. The text says 'necessary or useful', but the last two words are probably an interpolation

84 D. 20. 2. 7 pr.; but it was usually written into the contract, D. 47. 2. 62. 8. *Cf.* Pliny, *Ep.* III, 19, 6

85 Taubenschlag, op. cit., 358. *Cf.* V. A. Tcherikover, A. Fuks, and M. Stern, eds., *Corpus Papyrorum Iudaicarum* II (1960), no. 420 *a* and III (1964), no. 453

86 D. 19. 2. 25. 6; Pliny, *Ep.* IX, 37, with Sherwin-White, *Pliny*, 520–1

87 Buckland and McNair, 298

88 D. 19. 2. 15. There were complications of set-off

89 Buckland and McNair, 294–5

90 Pliny, *Ep.* VIII, 2 and IX, 37

91 Columella, *Res Rustica* I, 7, 3–4. *Cf.* Martial, IV, 64, 33–4

92 Pliny, *Ep.* VI, 3 and VII, 18, 3 (*pace* Sherwin-White, *Pliny*, 423), respectively

93 *Pace* Schulz, *CRL*, 545, and Sherwin-White, *Pliny*, 358 and 390

94 Pliny, *Ep.* VI, 30. This is the nearest we get to a Squire Western. I do not

quote X, 8, 5, because *novus colonus* there may be singular used to imply plural

95 D. 19. 2. 19. 2; D. 33. 7; *Pauli Sententiae* III, 6, 34ff

96 There is an enormous bibliography on *agri vectigales*; most recently, L. Bove, *Ricerche sugli 'agri vectigales'* (1960), giving the reference (on p. 5, note 8) to the big studies of F. Lanfranchi, *Studi sull'ager vectigalis*, I–III, (1938–40). Schulz, *CRL*, 397–8 states the main area of dispute, rather dismissively—but characteristically

97 *Lex Coloniae Iuliae Genetivae, Fontes* I, no. 21, § 82

98 Bove, op. cit., 68, note 69; Taubenschlag, op. cit., 263ff

99 There is a good deal on tenancy of *ager publicus* in Cicero's *Verrines*; cf. also *ad Att.* II, 16. 4. For Cicero on *agri vectigales* see *ad fam.* XIII, 7, 1 and 11, 1—very remarkable

100 A. Piganiol, *Les documents cadastraux*, 57ff

101 See F. G. de Pachtere, *La table hypothécaire de Veleia* (1920), 93–5

102 Gai. *Inst.* III, 145; D. 6. 3. 1. For the controversy, compare Schulz, *CRL*, 398 with Lenel, *Das Edictum Perpetuum*, 186ff

103 D. 21. 2. 66 pr.; D. 6. 2. 12. 2

104 Pliny, *Ep.* VII, 18, 4

105 The latest discussion is by H. Vogt, *Das Erbbaurecht des klassischen römischen Rechts* (1950). Definition of *solarium*: D. 43. 8. 2. 17

106 D. 43. 18. 1 pr.; cf. 39. 2. 15. 26; and see Lenel, op. cit., 576ff

107 *Fontes* III, no. 110

108 *Fontes* I, nos. 100–103, translated by R. M. Haywood in *Econ. Survey* IV, 89ff. Add *L'année épigraphique*, 1938, no. 72, and *Tablettes Albertini*, 97ff

109 Heitland, op. cit., 209

110 See Tenney Frank in *Econ. Survey* I, 374

111 D. 7. 1. 13. 5. See note 59

112 Pliny, *Natural History* III, 138; XXXIII, 78; XXXVII, 202. See Tenney Frank in *Econ. Survey* I, 180 and 263–4

113 See, for example, Suetonius, *Tiberius*, 49, 2

114 *Fontes* I, nos. 104–5, translated by J. J. van Nostrand in *Econ. Survey* III, 167ff

115 By E. Schönbauer, *Beiträge zur Geschichte des Bergbaurechts* (1929)

116 Damage: D. 9. 2; theft: D. 47. 2. *Digest* 9.2, *ad legem Aquiliam*, is printed with a translation (like Zulueta's Gaius) in F. H. Lawson, *Negligence in the Civil Law* (1950)

117 See Lawson, op. cit., passim; Zulueta, *The Institutes of Gaius* II, 209ff; Buckland and McNair, 362ff

118 See Lawson, op. cit., 8ff. Note particularly that many scholars hold that it was the value of the damage, not of the object, that was in question

119 Gai. *Inst.* IV, 37

120 For argument, see Lawson, op. cit., 65ff, and Schulz, *CRL*, 591

121 D. 9. 2. 5. 3 to 7 pr. and D. 9. 2. 13 pr. See Lawson, op. cit., 21–2

122 D. 9. 3. 1 pr.

122a At least, the fragment is Ulpian's; but these frequent *laudationes edicti* are post-classical. See Wieacker, *Textstufen*, 269, note 253

123 Juvenal, *Satires* III, 269ff

124 D. 9. 1. We shall meet wild animals in Chapter VIII

125 Cicero, *Topica*, 22

126 D. 39. 1. 1. 12

127 D. 39. 1. 20. 9

128 There were complex details; see Roby, *Roman Private Law*, I, 509ff

129 D. 39. 2. 1

130 *Fontes* I, no. 19, §§ 19–20

131 *P. Fouad* 30, edited by J. Bataille, in J. Bataille et al., eds., *Papyrus Fouad I* (Cairo, 1939). The Egyptian rule was evidently slightly different

132 D. 39. 3; Cicero, *Topica*, 38–9

133 D. 43. 24. 1 pr. (with note)

134 *Pro Tullio* and *pro Caecina*. Cf. *ad fam.* XV, 16, 3

135 D. 47. 8. 2. 1

136 D. 47. 2; published with a facing translation and commentary by H. F. Jolowicz, *Digest XLVII. 2, 'De furtis'* (1940)

137 Nicholas, *Introduction*, 211

138 *The Times*, 19 Jan. 1965

139 D. 47. 2. 57. 1

140 Schulz, *CRL*, 573–4

141 Gai. *Inst.* III, 183–94

142 D. 47. 2. 93

143 Schulz, *CRL*, 26–7

144 This point was made by P. W. Duff in *Cambridge Law Journal*, 1954, 86ff. A thievish slave might not be worth much, but he could be sold for chain-gang work

145 Gai. *Inst.* IV, 4

146 D. 47. 18. 1. 2

147 Valerius Maximus, VIII, 2, 4; *cf.* Gai. *Inst.* III, 196 and Gellius, *Noctes Atticae* VI, 15 and XI, 18

148 D. 47. 2. 43. 8

149 For a list, see Schulz, *CRL*, 581

150 For three not being a crowd in Roman law see D. 47. 8. 4. 3

151 Gai. *Inst.* III, 203; D. 47. 2. 10. See Jolowicz, op. cit., xxviiiff

152 D. 13. 1. 1

153 Gai. *Inst.* III, 199

154 See M. W. Frederiksen in *JRS*, 1966, 128ff

155 Kelly, *Roman Litigation*, 74ff refers to this nexus, but uses it to reach conclusions which I do not find acceptable

156 Cicero, *ad Att.* VII, 3, 11

157 *ad Att.* VII, 18, 4

158 *ad Att.* XVI, 2, 2

159 *ad fam.* XIV, 2, 3 and 1, 5, respectively

160 Pliny, *Ep.* III, 19, 8

161 Tacitus, *Annals* VI, 16–17. See Tenney Frank's analysis in *Econ. Survey* V, 32ff

162 Livy, VIII, 28. But *nexum* was probably quite distinct from *addictio* for judgment debts: see La Rosa, *L*'*actio iudicati*', 72ff

163 See Roby, *Roman Private Law* II, 431; La Rosa, op. cit., 93–5; and add Sallust, *Catilina*, 33; Cicero, *pro Flacco*, 48; *Lex Coloniae Iuliae Genetivae, Fontes* I, no. 21, § 61; Quintilian, *Inst. Or.* VII, 3, 26–7

164 Though Buckland, *Textbook*, 643, thinks that 'perhaps it was mainly used for solvent debtors', to make them pay up. Down to the invention of *bonorum venditio* this may well have been so, for *addictio* did not pass the debtor's property to you

165 See note 163

166 Gai. *Inst.* IV, 35

167 Juvenal, *Satires*, VI, 255

168 In the *lex Rubria, Fontes* I, no. 19, § 22, *eosque duci bona eorum possiderei* sounds as if both could be done; and see *Codex Iustinianus*, 7. 71. 1

169 Cicero, *pro Quinctio*, 84

170 D. 42. 7. 2. 2

171 Cicero, *pro Quinctio*, 25–6 and 48–51, respectively

172 D. 42. 4. 7. 1–2; *cf.* Gai. *Inst.* III, 78

173 Buckland and McNair, 302

174 By Kelly, *Roman Litigation*, 75. *Cf.* Cicero, *ad Att.* I, 1, 3 : 'but talk of a liquidator is absurd'—*i.e.* things won't get that far

175 Cicero, *ad Att.* XVI, 15, 2

176 See *Acta divi Augusti*, p. 152, and L. Guénoun, *La cessio bonorum* (1920), 19ff, who, in my view rightly, plumps for Augustus, though not all his reasons are good ones. The opposite view is argued by Frederiksen in *JRS*, 1966, 128ff

177 That it depended on misfortune is not accepted by all scholars. The best evidence is the implications of Seneca, *de ben.* VII, 16, 3 :'in the old days' they recognized a moral distinction between insolvency by misfortune and insolvency through fault, but made no legal distinction. See Guénoun, op. cit., 48ff

178 Gai. *Inst.* III, 78

179 *Codex Iustinianus*, 2. 11. 11 and 7. 71. 1

180 D. 42. 3. 4 pr.

181 Apuleius, *Apologia*, 75

182 Cicero, *ad fam.* XIV, 4, 4; *cf.* D. 40. 9, frags. 10 and 11 and 16. 2–3

183 D. 42. 8. See Buckland, *Textbook*, 596, and *cf.* Cicero, *ad Att.* I, 1, 3

184 D. 2. 14, frags. 7. 17ff. and 10 pr. and 44; D. 42. 8. 23

185 On this and what follows see art. 'Decoction,' in *Latomus*, 1967

186 Gai. *Inst.* IV, 102
187 See, for example, Cicero, *in Catilinam* II, 5 (with the scholium on the passage in Th. Stangl, ed., *Ciceronis Orationum Scholiastae* (1912), 281) and *Philippic* II, 44; Catullus, XLI, 4; Valerius Maximus, VI, 9, 12; Pliny, *Natural History* XXXIII, 133; Seneca, *de beneficiis* III, 17, 4; IV, 26, 3; V, 21, 3
188 Cicero, *pro Sulla*, 58
189 Cicero, *Philippic* II, 44
190 Seneca, *de ben.* V, 21, 3 and Apuleius, *Apologia*, 75, respectively
191 On pacts see D. 2. 14. Not every pact, of course, was of this kind or relevant to this topic
192 See Chapter VII, pp. 247–8, with note 210
193 *Fontes* I, no. 13, l. 114
194 See Roby, *Roman Private Law* II, 115
195 D. 27. 10. 5
196 D. 42. 1, frags. 15 pr. and 31

CHAPTER VI

1 See W. L. Westermann, *The Slave Systems of Greek and Roman Antiquity* (1955), 90–95
2 Pliny, *Ep.* III, 19, 7
3 D. 9. 2. 5. 3
4 *Fontes* I, nos. 104, §§ 5–7 and 105, l. 48 respectively
5 On whom see Jones, *Studies*, 154ff and Pliny, *Ep.* IV, 12
6 D. 19. 2. 19. 9
7 H. Wallon, *Histoire de l'esclavage dans l'antiquité* (1879), II, 51ff. (The first edition was in 1847: 'ce livre a été fait en un temps où la question de l'esclavage était encore (sauf en Angleterre) partout à résoudre')
8 See, however, Rostovtzeff, *SEHRE*, pl. XII, no. 2 (with his commentary); and for the American parallel, Stampp, *The Peculiar Institution*, 196–7, and his Chapter VI, 'Slavemongering'
9 D. 14. 2. 10 pr.
10 *Fontes* III, no. 134, a queer document, in the Latin language but the Greek alphabet. The consular date is uncertain, but before 151: A. Degrassi, *I Fasti Consolari dell'impero romano* (1952), 43
11 D. 21. 1. 44. 1
12 For a summary see F. de Zulueta, *The Roman Law of Sale* (1945), 49–51
13 Cicero, *de officiis* III, 66; Valerius Maximus, VIII, 2, 1
14 D. 2. 14. 31
15 D. 21. 1. 1. 1–2. Gellius gives a pre-codification form of the edict, *Noctes Atticae* IV, 2, 1. The edict on cattle is given at D. 21. 1. 38 pr.
16 See Chapter II, p. 56
17 D. 21, 1, frags. 8 and 14 pr. and 14. 4, respectively

18 See Schulz, *CRL*, 537

19 Gai. *Inst.* I, 6

20 Varro, *Res Rusticae* II, 10, 5. It is worth comparing Babylonian warranties: Driver and Miles, *The Babylonian Laws* I, 479ff

21 *Tab. Herc.*, nos. LIX, LX and LXI, respectively. We meet some old friends in them

22 *Fontes* III, no. 88 (*cf.* nos. 87 and 89, and also nos. 133–4). The phrase 'apocatum pro uncis duabus' is of uncertain meaning, much argued; plausibly connected with *actio auctoritatis* by A. Watson in *Revue internationale des droits de l'antiquité*, 1963, 247ff

23 *Fontes* III, no. 132

24 Saumagne in *Tablettes Albertini*, 90ff

25 See E. Pólay in *Acta Antiqua*, 1962, 385ff

26 Though opinions differ. For the arguments see now Pólay in the article quoted above

27 *ILS*, 8727

28 Petronius, *Satyricon*, 97–8

29 D. Daube in *Juridical Review*, 1952, 12ff

30 A rule amusingly used by Apuleius, *Metamorphoses* VI, 4 (at the end)

31 D. 48. 15. 2. 3; *Pauli Sententiae* I, 6a, 2

32 *Pauli Sententiae* I, 6a, 1

33 See, for example, Apuleius, *Metamorphoses* II, 26

34 Cicero, *ad Att.* XV, 15, 3 and XVI, 2, 1, respectively. He was actually an employee of Atticus, but seconded to deal with Cicero's financial affairs

35 See Chapter II, p. 60

36 D. 40. 7. 40

37 D. 40. 9. 10; *cf. Corpus Papyrorum Judaicarum* II, nos. 419 *a* and *c*

38 Pliny, *Ep.* VII, 18, 2

39 Horace, *Epistles* I, xiv

40 These passages are translated in Toynbee, *Hannibal's Legacy* II, 576ff

41 *E.g.* Petronius, *Satyricon*, 61

42 D. 14. 3. 8

43 D. 14. 5. 8

44 D. 2. 13. 4. 3

45 D. 7. 1. 25. 2

46 That in our period *libera administratio* was inherent in grant of *peculium* was shown in the following papers: G. Longo in *Archivio giuridico*, 1928, 124ff; E. Albertario in *Rendiconti dell'Istituto Lombardo*, 1928, 833ff; G. Longo again, in *BIDR*, 1930, 29ff

47 See Buckland, *Roman Law of Slavery*, 188

48 See, for example, D. 21. 1. 33 pr.

49 D. 15. 1. 53

50 As to chronology, there is no sign of the *tributoria* or *quod iussu* in Cicero's day: Watson, *Law of Obligations*, 185

51 D. 14. 1. 1 pr. See Chapter V, note 122a
52 D. 14. 3. 11. 2
53 D. 11. 3. 1 pr.
54 D. 11. 3. 1. 5
55 Cicero, *ad fam.* XIII, 21, 2 and 23
56 D. 12. 6. 26. 12
57 See Chapter II, p. 52
58 D. 38. 1. 27 (Julianus)
59 Most that has been written on this subject in recent years comes from the
    pen of F. M. de Robertis. See especially *I rapporti di lavoro nel diritto
    romano* (1946), and *Lavoro e lavoratori nel mondo romano* (1963, where, on
    pp. v–vi, he lists other publications of his own). Add J. Macqueron, *Le
    travail des hommes libres dans l'antiquité romaine* (1958), and, for the long
    arguments about the status of the *mercennarius*, R. Martini, '*Mercennarius*',
    Contributo allo studio dei rapporti di lavoro in diritto romano (1958), with its
    review by Macqueron in *RHDFE*, 1959, 600ff, and H. Kaufmann, *Die
    altrömische Miete* (1964), 145ff (a book with a very different approach to the
    origins of *locatio operarum*)
60 By M. I. Finley in *Comparative Studies in Society and History*, 1964, 233ff,
    especially 238, and in *RHDFE*, 1965, 159ff
61 These studies are: Adams, *Paramoné und verwandte Texte*, especially 44ff,
    and Samuel in *Journal of Juristic Papyrology*, 1965, 221ff (quoted above,
    Chapter II, note 115)
62 *Papiri della società italiana*, no. 549, discussed by Adams, op. cit., 44
63 *Excavations at Dura-Europos*, Final Report V, Part I, no. 20 (pp. 109ff)
64 See Adams, op. cit., 76, and (on *Berliner griechische Urkunden* [*BGU*]
    IV, 1126, the 'barmaid's contract' of 9 BC) 50 and 58
65 De Robertis, *Lavoro e lavoratori*, Chapter 2
66 Of the Igel monument there is a little photograph in O. Brogan, *Roman
    Gaul* (1953), fig. 39a; some of its detailed relief panels are included among
    other 'business' pictures in Rostovtzeff, *SEHRE*, Pls. XXIV and
    XXXIX. For paintings from the House of the Vettii see Rostovtzeff, pls.
    XIV–XV
67 See Meiggs, *Roman Ostia*, 189ff and 230–1
68 By A. H. M. Jones in M. I. Finley, ed., *Slavery in Classical Antiquity*, 6 (he
    is talking about Athens here, but the point is a general one)
69 For what there is, see Rostovtzeff, *SEHRE*, 621, note 45. We shall return
    to the point in the last chapter. On the Egyptian strikes see Rostovtzeff,
    677, note 52
70 M. I. Finley in *Economic History Review*, 1965, 39
71 It is the view of de Robertis; see also J. A. C. Thomas in *BIDR*, 1961,
    231ff. The main disagreement is that of Kaufmann in *Die altrömische Miete*.
72 So, properly, by Thomas in the article quoted above, at pp. 236–7
73 Buckland, *Textbook*, 504

74 See *Econ. Survey* II, 286ff, and Adams, *Paramoné*, section IV

75 Which seems to be implied by Schulz, *CRL*, 542

76 Cicero, *de officiis* I, 150 (*pace* de Robertis)

77 Varro, *Res Rusticae*, I, 17, 2–3. See Heitland, *Agricola*, 180–2

78 Cicero, *ad Att.* XIV, 3, 1; *cf.* Suetonius, *divus Vespasianus*, 1, 4

79 Heitland, *Agricola*, 256; but *cf.* the inscription from Mactar, *ILS*, 7457

80 See *L'année épigraphique*, 1916, no. 60

81 D. 4. 9. 7 pr.; 47. 5. 1. 5

82 Pliny, *Ep.* X, 74, 1

83 Petronius, *Satyricon*, 117, 11–12

84 Juvenal, *Satires* III, 31ff

85 *Pauli Sententiae* II, 18, 1. I do not think this means formal legal change of status, but merely social status or even just general conditions of life

86 D. 7. 8. 4 pr.; 43. 16. 1. 18

87 D. 9. 2. 37 pr.

88 D. 47. 2. 90; 48. 19. 11. 1

89 Kaufmann, *Die altrömische Miete*, especially 203

90 Buckland and McNair, 300

91 D. 38. 1. 3. 1

92 D. 19. 2, frags. 38 pr. and 19. 9

93 D. 38. 1. 50. 1

94 See de Robertis, *Lavoro e lavoratori*, 205, and H. C. Youtie on the 'Heidelberg Festival Papyrus' (*P. Heid. Inv.*, 1818), in P. R. Coleman-Norton, ed., *Studies in Roman Economic and Social History in Honor of Allan Chester Johnson* (1951), 178ff

95 *Fontes* III, no. 150*a*

96 *P. Cornell*, 9, translated by A. C. Johnson in *Econ. Survey* II, 300. On the 'artistes' contracts' in general see Adams, *Paramoné*, section V

97 D. 9. 2. 7 pr.; 9. 1. 3; 9. 3. 1 pr., respectively

98 D. 9. 2. 13 pr.

99 Thus Schulz, *CRL*, 591–2 and 599; Lawson, *Negligence in the Civil Law*, 22 and 92 (note); Kaser, *Das römische Privatrecht*, I, 520, note 19; Nicholas, *Introduction*, 222

100 Lawson, op. cit., 45

101 They were discussed by Westermann in *Classical Philology*, 1914, 295ff, but for the most recent list, with important conclusions, see Adams, *Paramoné*, section III

102 D. 9. 2. 5. 3 (see above, p. 179); *cf.* 19. 2. 13. 3. On apprenticeship as an aspect of slave education see C. A. Forbes in *Transactions of the American Philological Association*, 1955, 321ff, especially 334

103 For examinations see the papyrus *BGU* IV, 1125, in Westermann's article quoted above

104 *P. Oxy.* no. 724

105 By Westermann in the article quoted above, also Adams, *Paramoné*, 144

w

106 *P. Fouad* 37, ed. J. Scherer, in J. Bataille *et al.*, eds., *Papyrus Fouad I*, (Cairo, 1939). An even newer example, dated AD 253, is *P. Oxy.* 2586; in this, wages begin after the first six months, and the father gets a loan

107 Cicero, *pro Fonteio* 17–18

108 *Lex coloniae Genetivae Iuliae, Fontes* I, no. 21,§ 98. *Cf.* Pliny, *Ep.* X, 41, 2 and Sherwin-White, *Pliny*, 623

109 See, for example, *ILS*, 5729 and 6887–9; D. 50. 4. 12

110 *Cf.*, however, Tacitus, *Agricola*, 31, 2

111 See P. J. Sijpesteijn, *Penthemeros-Certificates in Greco-Roman Egypt*, Papyrologica Lugduno-Batava, vol. XII (1964)

112 Columella, *Res Rustica* I, 7, 1. See Heitland, *Agricola*, 253-4, who reluctantly refuses to be seduced by this view, though admitting its attractiveness.

113 Here are just a few items: de Robertis, *Rapporti di lavoro*, 183ff; K. H. Below, *Der Arzt im römischen Recht*, 2ter Abschnitt (1953; reviewed by D. Daube in *JRS*, 1955, 179–80); A. Watson, *Contract of Mandate in Roman Law* (1961), 99ff; J. A. C. Thomas in *BIDR*, 1961, 240ff

114 D. 50. 13. 1. 4–5

115 D. 11. 6. 1 pr. and 1

116 See Chapter III, p. 90

117 D. 50. 13. 1. For suspicions of 'Ulpianus, *de omnibus tribunalibus libri decem*' see Schulz, *Roman Legal Science*, 256

118 Watson, *Contract of Mandate*, 101

119 D. 19. 2. 19. 10

120 See *Econ. Survey* II, 286ff, and Adams, *Paramoné*, section IV, especially 155–6 and 165. In Egypt there was no jurisdiction except the *cognitio* of the prefect or his delegate

121 D. 38. 1. 25. 2; *cf.* 9. 2. 7. 8

122 D. 17. 1. 7

123 As suggested by Thomas in the article quoted in note 113 above

CHAPTER VII

1 See A. H. M. Jones in *Recueils de la société Jean Bodin* VII, 1955, 161ff, and M. I. Finley in *Economic History Review*, 1965, 40ff

2 See M. Rheinstein, ed., *Max Weber on Law in Economy and Society* (1954), 130ff

3 Though as to *publicani* see below

4 Nicholas, *Introduction*, 201

5 A. A. Schiller looked hard for it, in *Studi in onore di Salvatore Riccobono* IV, 77ff, but he did not come up with anything very concrete

6 See G. E. M. de Ste. Croix, *Greek and Roman Accounting* (reprinted from A. C. Littleton and B. S. Yamey, eds., *Studies in the History of Accounting*, 1956), 14ff, especially 37–8

7 This is a 'Greek' subject. A view of it can be obtained from de Ste. Croix,

op. cit., 48–9, with the works he quotes on p. 48 at note 18 (to which might be added J. Hasebrock in *Hermes*, 1920, 113ff)

8 S. Brassloff, *Sozialpolitische Motive in der römischen Rechtsentwicklung* (1933), 5

9 Nicholas, *Introduction*, 150

10 Gai. *Inst.* III, 92ff

11 D. 13. 6. 17. 3

12 Juvenal, *Satires* XIII, 15–17 and 200–2; *cf.* Seneca, *de beneficiis* IV, 26, 3

13 See M. Kaser in *Tijdschrift*, 1961, 169ff

14 D. 26. 7. 5 pr. Bankers' interest on money is referred to in D. 2. 14. 47. 1, in a context that seems intended to be typical, and in D. 16. 3, frags. 24, 26. 1 and 28. It could always be arranged, like interest on a loan of money, by independent stipulations, but in view of the guardian situation I do not think it can have been normal. F. Bonifacio, in *BIDR*, 1947, 80ff, argues that 'irregular *depositum*' was not in itself either irregular or post-classical, but admits (89–90) that interest on it, as part of the contract of deposit, was post-classical. The texts are unfortunately all very suspect

15 The problem of liability for *custodia* is one of the most perplexed in Roman law. I am being dogmatic here. See Buckland, *Textbook*, 560–1; Schulz, *CRL*, 515; and, for bibliography, Berger, *Dictionary*, under the word *custodia*. See also pp. 221–2 and note 76, below

16 I am not convinced by A. Watson in *Tijdschrift*, 1963, 76ff

17 See above, Chapter III, p. 77

18 Plautus, *Curculio*, 506–11; Horace, *Epodes* II

19 Cicero, *ad Att.* IX, 12, 3

20 Pliny, *Ep.* III, 19, 8; *cf.* Dio of Prusa, *Orations* XLVI, 5 and 8

20a See Sherwin–White, *Pliny*, 423–4 and 635–6

21 Cicero, *ad fam.* V, 6, 2

22 Cicero, *ad Att.* I, 12, 1

23 Cicero, *ad Att.* IV, 15, 7

24 Tacitus, *Annals* VI, 16

25 The demonstration was made by Ch. Appleton in *Nouvelle revue historique de droit français et étranger*, 1919, 467ff. *Cf.*, however, for Babylon and Assyria, Driver and Miles, *The Babylonian Laws* I, 176. It is certainly not the case in our period, as Kelly maintains in *Roman Litigation*, 77, that 'even this enormous rate was frequently exceeded'. Scaptius's forty-eight per cent was a wild extortion. Pólay (see note 34 below) gets 365 per cent out of one document, but by misinterpretation

26 D. 22. 1, frags. 1 pr. and 29. There was no maximum on 'nautical loans'

27 Cicero, *ad Att.* V, 21, 11. *Cf. ad Att.* VI, 2, 7 for compound interest over 12 per cent on arrears

28 *Gnomon*, § 105. (This clause is not in *Fontes*, which gives only a selection.

For the whole text see E. Seckel and W. Schubart, *Der Gnomon des Idios Logos*, 1919, and for translation see *Econ. Survey* II, 711ff

29 D. 12. 6. 26. 1

30 See note 27 above

31 D. 22. 1. 1 pr.

32 See E. Cuq in Ch. Daremberg and Edm. Saglio, *Dictionnaire des antiquités grecques et romaines* V, under the word *usura*

33 D. 22. 1. 17. 6

34 See E. Pólay in *Acta Antiqua*, 1960, 417ff, but discount his determination to see a sinister one per cent per day; the moneylender's charge was one per cent per month

35 *Fontes* III, no. 157; we shall meet this text again presently

36 *Fontes* III, nos. 122 and 123. The one quoted is no. 122, dated AD 162

37 Gai. *Inst.* III, 128–34

38 There is a good deal of literature, and still much uncertainty. For a good account see A. Steinwenter in Pauly-Wissowa, *Realencyclopädie der klassischen Altertumswissenschaft* [*Realencyclopädie*] XIII, 786ff

39 And perhaps *Tab. Herc.*, no. III

40 See de Ste. Croix, *Greek and Roman Accounting*, 73, note 14, and Watson, *Law of Obligations*, 24ff, with his Appendix to Chapter 3

41 Gai. *Inst.* III, 134

42 See, for example, E. Costa, *Cicerone Giureconsulto* I, (1927, reprinted 1964) 178ff; Jolowicz, *Hist. Introduct.*, 297; Zulueta, *The Institutes of Gaius* II, 146–7; Watson, *Law of Obligations*, 40–1

43 *Fontes* III, no. 90

44 *Fontes* III, no. 136

45 Cicero, *de oratore* I, 178; *de officiis* III, 67

46 *de officiis* III, 58–9

47 Buckland and McNair, 287–8

48 Justinian's *Institutes* II, 1, 41

49 D. 18. 1. 19

50 D. 18. 1. 53

51 Gai. *Inst.* II, 20

52 And the reader will have a good example of a typical exegetical problem in the subject if he will look at the following (all in English except one): Buckland, *Textbook*, 230, note 8 and 240, note 2; Zulueta, *Roman Law o, Sale*, 37–8; Schulz, *CRL*, 350; Zulueta, *The Institutes of Gaius* II, 61–2; Kaser, *Das römische Privatrecht* I, 352–3; Watson, *Law of Obligations*, 61ff

53 See Nicholas, *Introduction*, 176ff

54 Pliny, *Ep.* VIII, 2, 1 (and plenty of other cases; it is a necessary agricultural bargain)

55 D. 18. 2. 8

56 D. 19. 5. 20 pr.

57 Cato, *de agri cultura*, 148; see R. Yaron in D. Daube, ed., *Studies in the*

Roman Law of Sale, dedicated to the memory of Francis de Zulueta (1959), Essay no. 5

58 D. 45. 1. 75. 2.; *cf.* 45. 1. 54

59 Buckland and McNair, 282–3

60 See Nicholas, *Introduction*, 174–5

61 *E.g.* Tacitus, *Histories* I, 90

62 Cicero, *pro Caecina*, 13–17; D. 40. 7. 40. 8

63 M. Talamanca in *Atti dell' Accademia nazionale dei Lincei, Memorie della classe per scienze morali, etc.*, 1955, 35ff

64 *Fontes* III, no. 128 *c*; *cf.* all the texts under nos. 129 and 130

65 *Lex Metalli Vipascensis*, *Fontes* I, no. 105, ll. 1–10

66 Still 'arrhes' in French

67 See F. Pringsheim, *The Greek Law of Sale* (1950), Part 3, Chapter 4 (with comment by M. I. Finley in *Seminar*, 1951, 80); Zulueta, *Roman Law of Sale*, 22–3

68 But see Watson, *Law of Obligations*, 46ff

69 Gai. *Inst.* III, 139

70 Taubenschlag, *Law of Greco-Roman Egypt*, 410

71 D. 18. 3. 8

72 D. 18. 1. 6. 1

73 The *lex commissoria*, D. 18. 3

74 Gai. *Inst.* III, 145–7

75 Labour: D. 19. 2. 51. 1; premises: D. 19. 5. 1. 1

76 See above, note 15. The most important full-scale modern work on the problem is V. Arangio-Ruiz, *Responsabilità contrattuale in diritto romano²* (1933)

77 D. 19. 2. 11 pr.

78 Gai. *Inst.* III, 205–6

79 D. 19. 2. frag. 13 pr. to 6

80 *Imperitia* is *culpa*: D. 19. 2. 9. 5

81 D. 19. 2. 30. 4

82 D. 19. 2. 22. 2; *cf.* Cicero, *ad Att.* IV, 16, 8

83 D. 19. 2. 60. 4

84 D. 19. 2. 58. 1

85 D. 19. 2. 36

86 D. 19. 2. 36 and 59

87 D. 19. 2. 51. 1

88 D. 19. 2. 24 pr.: *viri boni arbitratu*, not far from the 'reasonable man'

89 D. 19. 2. 60. 3. *Cf.* Cicero, *ad Quintum fratrem* III, 1, 1, and H. B. Creswell, *The Honeywood File* (edition of 1964) 157ff

90 Tertullian, *adversus Marcionem* III, 6

91 W. Ashburner, *The Rhodian Sea Law* (1909)

92 For the arguments see (besides Ashburner): A. Berger in Pauly-Wissowa, *Realencyclopädie* IX, 545ff; P. Huvelin, *Etudes d'histoire du droit commercial*

romain (1929), 184ff; V. Arangio-Ruiz in *Studi in onore di Salvatore Ricco-bono* IV (1936), 384ff; W. Osuchowski in *Iura*, 1950, 292ff; F. Wieacker in *Studi in memoria di E. Albertario* I (1953), 515 ff; F. M. de Robertis in *Studi in onore di Vincenzo Arangio-Ruiz* (1952–3) III, 155ff; J. Rougé, *Recherches sur l'organisation du commerce maritime en Mediterranée sous l'empire romain* (1966), 3e Partie

93 D. 22. 2. 6 and 7. See the papyrus *P. Vindobon.* 197926, quoted by Rougé, op. cit., 348, note 4

94 *Pauli Sententiae* II, 14, 3; D. 22. 2. 4 pr.

95 D. 45. 1. 122. 1. It is imaginary; note that the slave is 'slave of Seius' and then 'slave of L. Titius'. But this would not affect the general form of contract. *Cf.* Rougé, op. cit., 350

96 D. 14. 2. 2. 2

96a Rougé, op. cit., 336ff, has an interesting discussion of the law about wrecks; but the texts are very uncertain

97 D. 14. 1. 1. 12

98 See L. Casson in *JRS*, 1965, 31ff

99 D. 19. 2. 31

100 D. 19. 2. 61. 1

101 Varro, *Res Rusticae* II, 8, 5 and 6, 5, respectively

102 D. 19. 2. 30. 2

103 D. 19. 2. 60. 8

104 D. 19. 2. 25. 7. For pictures, see Rostovtzeff, *SEHRE*, pls. XXVIII, 3; XXXIII, 3; XXXIX, 4; XLVI, 3

105 D. 19. 2. 13 pr.

106 *Nautae, caupones, stabularii. Stabulum* often itself means a lodging-house, but in this context it actually means someone who stables horses, etc.

107 D. 47. 5

108 D. 4. 9. 1 pr.

109 D. 4. 9. 1. 1

110 D. 4. 9, frags. 1. 1 and 3. 1

111 *Pace* Schulz, *CRL*, 565. See Horace, *Epodes* XVII, 20 and *Satires* I, v, 4; Juvenal, *Satires* VIII, 172f

112 D. 47. 5. 1. 6

113 For the points of view, see Huvelin, *Etudes*, 135ff; Arangio-Ruiz, *Responsabilità contrattuale*, 103ff; M. Sargenti in *Studi Albertario* I, 553ff; C. H. Brecht, *Zur Haftung der Schiffer im antiken Recht* (1962), especially Chapter 2

114 I am sure Brecht was right about this

115 Here I part company with Brecht

116 D. 19. 2. 60. 6

117 D. 4. 9. 7 pr.

118 Except perhaps the *hospitia* for V.I.P.'s at places like Olympia

119 On the whole, though remember Horace, *Satires* I, v

120 *Fontes* III, no. 145 *b*. The owner was a consul. I do not know exactly

what the different things mentioned were

121 See Meiggs, *Roman Ostia*, pl. XVa, for the 'Horrea Epagathiana', and *cf.* pp. 280–1

122 See J. A. C. Thomas in *Revue internationale des droits de l'antiquité*, 1959, 371ff

123 D. 19. 2, frags. 55 pr. and 60. 9

124 D. 19. 2. 56

125 *Fontes* III, no. 145 *a*; excerpts only, and my choice of readings

126 *Cf.* D. 20. 4. 21. 1

127 The fundamental study is that of H. Dressel, the excavator, in *Annali dell' Instituto di Corrispondenza archeologica*, 1878, 118ff. He edited the sherds with inscriptions in *Corpus Inscriptionum Latinarum* XV, Part 2

128 Note the lady, and *cf.* ILS, 7488, and Toynbee and Ward Perkins, *The Shrine of St. Peter*, 120

129 See, for example, Pliny, *Ep.* VIII, 18, and the references in *Cl. Qu.*, 1967, art. 'Patria Potestas', forthcoming

130 D. 17. 2. 31

131 Gai. *Inst.* III, 148

132 D. 17. 2, frags. 71 pr. and 52. 7, respectively

133 D. 10. 3. 7. 4; and see Chapter I, p. 34

134 Gai. *Inst.* III, 150

135 D. 17. 2. 59 pr. Watson, *Law of Obligations*, 131, holds that in Cicero's day an heir did succeed. In Cicero, *pro Quinctio*, 14–15 there is no mention of a new agreement when the heir came in; but he may not have thought it worth mentioning

136 D. 17. 2. 74; though for some slight evidence to the contrary see p. 241

137 Petronius, *Satyricon*, 38, 13

138 *Fontes* III, no. 157. See Pólay in *Acta Antiqua*, 1960, 417ff

139 D. 12. 1. 41; 32. 34. 1; 32. 64; 33. 2. 37; *cf.* Cicero, *ad fam.* XIII, 72, 1

140 Bankruptcy of *nummularius*: D. 16. 3. 7. 2; of *mensularius*: D. 42. 5. 24. 2

141 Cicero, *ad fam.* III, 5, 4

142 Cicero, *ad Att.* XII, 24, 1; XV, 15, 4

143 *Fontes* III, no. 131, *b* and *c*

144 *Fontes* III, no. 131, *e*

145 D. 2. 13. 12. As to slaves, see Chapter VI, p. 188

146 *Auctor ad Herennium* II, 19, where the rule is given as an example of 'consuetudo', *i.e.* no legislation, but accepted by the courts

147 The passage in the above note is not necessarily a reference to the contract *litteris*

148 See Lenel, *Das Edictum Perpetuum*, 132ff

149 Public policy: D. 2. 13. 10. 1. The edict: Lenel, op. cit., 62ff

150 D. 2. 13, frags. 6. 2 and 8

151 D. 2. 13. 9. 2

152 Gai. *Inst.* IV, 64–8

153 D. 2. 14. 47. 1; but as to its typicality see above, note 14

154 The exhaustive treatise on this is F. Kniep, *Societas Publicanorum* I (all published) (1896)

155 D. 49. 14. 3. 6

155a Though in Cicero, *ad fam*. II, 13, 4 we find them in the province collecting arrears owed to them from a previous *lustrum*

156 D. 17. 2. frags. 59 pr. and 65. 15

157 Polybius VI, 17

158 Cicero, *II in Verrem* I, 143

159 Stangl, *Ciceronis Orationum Scholiastae*, 253, reading (with Kniep) *divisui*

160 D. 14. 6. 3. 1

161 It is the theme of P. W. Duff, *Personality in Roman Private Law* (1938)

162 *Cf. Fontes* III, no. 93, ll. 9–10, where 'immunes et curator et pleps universa collegi eius' is reminiscent of 'the Master, fellows and scholars of St. John's College'

163 See Duff, op. cit., 141ff and 159–161

164 D. 39. 4. 12 pr.

165 D. 39. 4. 1. 6

166 Tacitus, *Annals* XIII, 50–1

167 *Apokrimata*, no. XI

168 D. 3. 5. 1 (another *laudatio edicti*)

169 So limited according to Schulz, *CRL*, 621

170 Watson, *Contract of Mandate*, Chapter 3

171 Gai. *Inst*. III 155

172 D. 17. 1. 1. 4

173 *Pace* Watson, op. cit., Chapter 10

174 Whom I do not think it is right to emend away

175 Cicero, *ad fam*. XIII, 72, 1 (*cf*. I, 3)

176 *ad fam*. XIII, 43, 1

177 Cicero, *pro Quinctio*, 62

178 *ad Att*. XVI, 2, 2; *ad fam*. XVI, 24, 1, respectively

179 *ad Att*. X, 5, 3

180 *ad fam*. VII, 23, 1–3

181 *ad fam*. VII, 2, 1

182 Pliny, *Ep*. IX, 39

183 One remark of Papinian about the right of a governor's suite to their emoluments got into the *Digest* under *locatio conductio*: D. 19. 2. 19. 10

184 D. 2. 14. 47. 1 and 16. 3. 24 (the last clause of which need not be an interpolation), 26. 1 and 28. See above, note 14

185 Gai. *Inst*. II, 95 and III, 103, respectively; *cf*. III, 163

186 D. 14. 3. 14

187 D. 14. 1, frags. 1. 25 and 2 and 3

188 See *Fontes* III, p. 417, and the discharges given to Caecilius Iucundus, which follow

189 And *actor publicus* was a slave of the municipality

190 Gaius's *Institutes* (the Verona text) are in any case the bottom writing of a triple palimpsest (*i.e.* they have had two other texts written over the top of them), and it was marvellous work that enabled them to be first recognized and then read as much as they have been

191 D. 13. 7. 11. 6

192 See Schulz, *CRL*, 626–8; Buckland and McNair, 309–10. Cicero, *ad Att.* XII, 12, 1 may be a case in point

193 See Schulz, *CRL*, 401ff

194 Polybius VI, 17; Cicero, *II in Verrem* I, 142

195 *Fontes* III, no. 153 (excerpt only)

196 *Fontes* I, no. 18, § 2

197 *Fontes* I, no. 24, §§ 60 and 63–5, respectively

198 See A. Watson in *ZSS*, 1962, 329ff

199 *Fontes* III, no. 92

200 *Fontes* III, no. 91

201 *Tab. Herc.*, nos. LXV and LXVI, respectively

202 See Nicholas, *Introduction*, 150ff

203 See, for example, *P. Oxy.* 2134

204 D. 20. 2. 2–3

205 D. 20. 1, frags. 1 pr. and 6 and 15. 1

206 See, for example, *P. Oxy.* 1105

207 See *Excavations at Dura-Europos*, Final Report V, Part I, nos. 20 and 21, and Taubenschlag, *Law of Greco-Roman Egypt*, 286ff; but not every kind of *paramoné* was antichretic

208 Gai. *Inst.* IV, 147; D. 13. 7. 9. 2

209 See Lenel, *Das Edictum Perpetuum*, 490ff; Buckland, *Textbook*, 475; Kaser, *Das römische Privatrecht* I, 395

210 See, for example, Buckland, *Textbook*, 450; Kaser, *Das römische Privatrecht* I, 556. The contrary view is expressed dogmatically by Schulz, *CRL*, 497. The evidence when probed more or less comes down to Cicero, *ad Att.* XVI, 15, 2; that passage can perhaps be interpreted in a way that would destroy its status as the principal support for the rule, but Cicero does seem to be making a point about *litis contestatio*, and it is hard to see what other point he could be making. It is true, however, that the other passages, such as *Pauli Sententiae* II, 17, 16; D. 44. 2. 21. 4; *Codex Iustinianus*, 8. 40. 28 are strictly only about *fideiussor*

211 D. 45. 2. 3. 1 (again technically about *fideiussor*)

212 See W. W. Buckland in *Juridical Review*, 1941, 281ff

213 Buckland, op. cit., 283, cautiously says '*non constat* as to *litis contestatio*', but Schulz, *CRL*, is dogmatic that there was no release

214 Gai. *Inst.* IV, 88ff; D. 46, titles 5 to 8

215 D. 46. 5. 7
216 Gai. *Inst.* III, 224
217 See Gellius' discussion of *sistere vadimonium: Noctes Atticae* II, 14
218 Cicero, *pro Quinctio,* 29
219 Cicero, *Brutus,* 17–18; *pro Roscio comoedo,* 35; *II in Verrem* II, 60; *ad fam.*
    XIII, 28, 2
220 Cicero, *ad Att.* I, 8, 1

CHAPTER VIII

1 See Schulz, *CRL,* 593ff and Zulueta, *The Institutes of Gaius* II, 216ff
2 Gellius, *Noctes Atticae* XX, 1, 13
3 Gai. *Inst.* III, 220ff; D. 47. 10
4 *Auctor ad Herennium* II, 19 and Gai. *Inst.* III, 224 both refer to a *iudex*
5 Gaius, loc. cit.; but on 'aggravated *iniuria*' he tells us that the praetor in
   effect determined the amount.
6 Shown most cogently by E. Fraenkel in *Gnomon* (the periodical), 1925,
   193ff (reprinted in his collected *Kleine Beiträge zur klassischen Philologie*
   II, 407ff). See also Kelly, *Roman Litigation,* 21–3
7 D. 47. 10. 15. 3ff
8 D. 3. 3. 42. 1
9 D. 47. 10. 5 pr.
10 By R. E. Smith in *Cl. Qu.,* 1951, 169ff—an important article, even if wrong
   (as I think) on this and some other points
11 D. 47. 10, frags. 5. 9–11 and 6; *Pauli Sententiae* V, 4, 15
12 Suetonius, *divus Augustus,* 55
13 *Pace* Smith, art. cit.
14 Tacitus, *Annals* I, 72
15 Notwithstanding Cicero, *ad fam.* III, 11, 2
16 *Auctor ad Herennium* II, 19
17 E. J. Kenney in *Proc. Camb. Phil. Soc.,* 1962, 36
18 Horace, *Satires* II, i, 80–1. The reference is to the Twelve Tables, with
   their provisions about 'magic and spells'; it should not be taken seriously
   as a statement of the rules of defamation in Horace's day
19 Juvenal, *Satires* I, 169–71
20 D. 47. 10. 18 pr. If, as some scholars think, the passage has suffered interpolation and cannot be used, there is then no evidence at all for truth
   being a good defence
21 Though see *Codex Theodosianus,* 9. 34. 1
22 Cicero's apologies for prosecuting Verres at the beginning and end of the
   divinatio in Caecilium (1 and 66ff) suggest this
23 Quintilian, *Inst. Or.* XI, 1, 57ff
24 For example, by Schulz, *CRL,* 595. Antony did not call Caesar's assassins

'honourable men' in order to escape an action for defamation. *Cf.* Cicero, *pro Roscio comoedo*, 18

25 For the efforts of Augustus to give it reality, see Jones, *Studies*, Essay III

26 See Chapter III, pp. 72–3

27 For call-up of provincials for local defence in Cicero's day, see, for example, *II in Verrem* IV, 76. And for compulsory levy under the Principate, see Sherwin-White, *Pliny*, 601

28 There were always, to judge from the *diplomata*, a few *cives* in the auxiliary regiments, probably through special personal circumstances.

29 Pliny, *Panegyricus*, 37–40

30 Cassius Dio LXXVII, 9, 5

31 See Jones, *Studies*, Essay VI; F. Millar in *JRS*, 1963, 29ff; Brunt in *JRS*, 1966, 75ff

32 *Gnomon of the Idiologos*, passim; D. 49. 14; *Pauli Sententiae* V, 12; and the *fragmentum de iure fisci*, in *Fontes* II (pp. 627ff)

33 D. 50. 1. 23

34 D. 50. 4. 18. 30

35 Cicero, *ad Att.* V, 21, 7

36 See *Econ. Survey* II, nos. 366ff

37 *P. Beatty Panop.* I, edited by T. C. Skeat in *Papyri from Panopolis in the Chester Beatty Library, Dublin* (1964)

38 D. 7. 1. 27. 3

39 D. 19. 2, frags. 13. 7 and 15. 2, respectively.

40 See H. G. Pflaum, *Essai sur le 'cursus publicus' sous le haut-empire romain* (1940)

41 See *SEG*, vol. XVI, no. 754; M. McCrum and A. G. Woodhead, *Select Documents of the Principates of the Flavian Emperors, AD 68–96* (1961), nos. 457 and 466; *L'année épigraphique*, 1960, no. 334 (with *Revue des études grecques*, 1958, no. 341); 1964, no. 231

42 *Econ. Survey* II, nos. 368–9

43 See *SEG*, vol. XVI, no. 754

44 Thus Claudius: *ILS*, 214; Domitian: McCrum and Woodhead, no. 466

45 See Chapter IV, p. 116, with note 85

46 *Fontes* III, no. 30 (part only)

47 Gellius has a list of 'sumptuary' legislation: *Noctes Atticae* II, 24

48 Though see W. Liebenam, *Zur Geschichte und Organisation des römischen Vereinswesens* (1890, reprinted 1964), 18–19

49 Jones, *The Greek City*, 213. The 'Astynomic Law' of Pergamum is a good example: W. Dittenberger, *Orientis Graeci Inscriptiones Selectae*, no. 483; G. Klaffenbach, 'Die Astynomeninschrift von Pergamon', *Abhandlungen der deutschen Akademie der Wissenschaften zu Berlin*, Klasse für Sprachen, Literatur und Kunst, Jahrgang 1953, no. 6; M. Amelotti in *Studia et Documenta Historiae et Iuris*, 1958, 80ff

50 *Fontes* I, no. 13

51 Strabo 235 C; Suetonius, *divus Augustus*, 89
52 The *lex Quinctia de aquaeductibus*, with accompanying *senatusconsulta*: Frontinus, *de aquaeductu*, 100ff
53 Tacitus, *Annals* XV, 43
54 Martial VII, 61, reminiscent of the case of the Dublin grocer quoted by Megarry, *Miscellany-at-Law*, 363-5
55 See Schulz, *Roman Legal Science*, 247
56 D. 43, titles 6–11
57 D. 21. 1. 40 and 42; see Lenel, *Das Edictum Perpetuum*, 566
58 *Fontes* I, nos. 18, § 4 and 21, § 75, respectively
59 *Fontes* I, no. 45; its date should perhaps be AD 45, see Degrassi, *Fasti Consolari*, 12–13
60 See (besides the references in the next note) D. 18. 1. 52 (with direct reference to the *Hosidianum*); 39. 2. 46 and 48
61 D. 30. 114. 9 and D. 30. 41, respectively. See also *Fontes* I, no. 80, and (already under Trajan) Pliny, *Ep.* X, 70, 1
62 See J. W. Jones in *Law Quarterly Review*, 1929, 512ff; L. Homo, *Rome impériale et l'urbanisme dans l'antiquité* (1951), 363ff; Schulz, *Principles*, 161 (with references at note 3) and 163, note 2; Kaser, *Das römische Privatrecht* I, 343 (with references at note 2)
63 J. W. Jones, art. cit.
64 Livy, XL, 51, 7
65 Suetonius, *divus Augustus*, 56, 2
66 Cicero, *ad Att.* IV, 16, 8
67 Frontinus, *de aquaeductu*, 125 (*cf.* 127)
68 *Fontes* I, no. 21, § 99
69 Cicero, *de lege agraria* II, 82
70 *Res gestae divi Augusti*, 16, 1
71 D. 6. 1. 15. 2; 21. 2. 11 pr.; Siculus Flaccus, *de condicionibus agrorum*, in K. Lachmann, ed., *Gromatici Veteres* (*Schriften der römischen Feldmesser*, vol. I), p. 160, ll. 25ff. On compulsory purchase see also U. von Lübtow, *Das römische Volk. Sein Staat und sein Recht* (1955), 510, note 229
72 See Liebenam, *Römisches Vereinswesen*; J.-P. Waltzing, *Etude historique sur les corporations professionelles chez les romains* (1895/6); F. M. de Robertis, *Il diritto associativo romano* (1938); Sherwin-White, *Pliny*, 608–9
73 Waltzing, op. cit. II, 268ff
74 Livy, XXXIX, 15, 11 (given insufficient weight by de Robertis, op. cit.); Ch. Wirszubski, *Libertas as a political idea at Rome during the late Republic and early Principate* (1950), 18–19
75 See the references to *sodales* and *collegia* in the *lex Acilia Repetundarum*, *Fontes* I, no. 7, §§ 10, 20, 22, and to *sodalitates* in the *Commentariolum Petitionis*, 19 (following the letters *ad Quintum fratrem* in the Oxford Text of Cicero)
76 For both, Asconius, *in Pisonianam*, p. 7 of Clark's Oxford Text

77 Cicero, *ad Quintum fratrem* II, 3, 5
78 Cicero, *pro Plancio*, 36
79 Suetonius, *divus Iulius*, 42, 3; *divus Augustus*, 32, 1; but see J. Linderski in *ZSS*, 1962, 322ff, for an attempt to reconcile by distinguishing. Rougé, *Recherches sur l'organisation du commerce*, 462–3 argues that there was no such statute (concerning commercial groups, at least)
80 *Fontes* I, no. 21, § 106. Josephus, *Antiquitates* XIV, 215 would settle the matter if he could be trusted
81 D. 3. 4. 1 pr.; 47. 22. 3. 1
82 *Fontes* III, no. 38
83 *Fontes* III, no. 35. On the 'burial clubs' there is much of importance in Bömer, *Untersuchungen*, pp. 406ff, 431ff, and especially 461ff
84 D. 47. 22. 1; see Duff, *Personality in Roman Private Law*, 110ff
85 D. 3. 4. 1 pr.
86 Duff, op. cit., 148–9
87 Waltzing, op. cit., II, 183ff
88 *E.g.* ILS, 6987, and see Waltzing, I, 190ff
89 Tacitus, *Annals* XIV, 17
90 See the edict quoted with translation in *Econ. Survey* IV, 847
91 *Acta Apost.* XIX, 23ff
92 *Fontes* III, no. 46
93 D. 48. 12. 2 pr.
94 See, for example, the case of the bankers of Pergamum: *Orientis Graeci Inscriptiones Selectae*, no. 484. Domitian imposed a prohibition on viticulture, but did not persist in it; see *Econ. Survey* V, 141–2; and there was perhaps a prohibition on mining, see above, Chapter V, p. 161
95 The builders at Miletus consulted the oracle: *Econ. Survey*, IV, 837
96 For such as there is, see Rostovtzeff, *SEHRE*, 619, note 43 and 621, note 45. See also above, Chapter VI, p. 194, with note 69
97 D. 48. 1. 8; though see Brasiello, *Repressione penale*, 209; the second half of the sentence (in square brackets) is certainly not true
98 See Brasiello, op. cit., 45ff
99 Compare, as Brasiello says (op. cit., 49–52, especially 50, note 76), the way they are laid out in *Pauli Sententiae*
100 D. 48. 1. 7
101 See Brunt in *Historia*, 1961, 189ff
101a D. 48. 11. 3ff
102 D. 48. 6. 3. 1. See, however, D. 48, 8. 1 pr
103 D. 48. 8, passim
104 D. 48. 6, passim
105 D. 47. 12. 8
106 D. 48. 14. 1 pr.
107 *Pauli Sententiae* IV, 7 and V, 25
108 Attributed to the policy of Nero by Suetonius, *Nero*, 17

109 D. 48. 10. 14 pr., 15 pr. and 22
110 *Collatio legum Mosaicarum et Romanarum* VIII, 7, 1, in *Fontes* II (p. 565)
111 D. 48. 10. 25 and 33
112 D. 48. 13. 10
113 D. 2. 1. 7
114 D. 48. 10, frags. 8 and 9; *Pauli Sententiae* V, 25, 1. See P. Grierson in R. A. G. Carson and C. H. V. Sutherland, eds., *Essays in Roman Coinage presented to Harold Mattingly* (1956), 240ff
115 D. 48. 13. 1
116 D. 47. 11. 6. 1
117 D. 48. 10, frags. 1, 1–3; 13 pr.; 19. 1; 27. 2
118 D. 47, titles 13, 14, 16, 18 and 11.11, respectively
119 D. 47. 20
120 D. 11. 5. 3
121 D. 11. 5. 2. 1
122 D. 11. 5. 2 pr.
123 D. 11. 5. 1. 4
124 *Pace* G. Crifò, *Ricerche sull' 'exilium' nel periodo repubblicano* I, (1961), 312 (his summing up)
125 This is why there must be something wrong with D. 48. 1. 8. See the famous account of Claudius' jurisdiction in Suetonius, *divus Claudius*, 14–15
126 See de Robertis in *ZSS*, 1939, 219ff
127 D. 48. 19. 2. 1
128 First attested, Pliny, *Ep.* X, 31, 2; 58, 3
129 D. 48. 19. 28 pr.
130 Brasiello, op. cit., 416ff.; Pliny, *Ep.* X, 31–2
131 See Th. Mommsen, *Römisches Strafrecht* (1899), 918ff
132 Cicero, *II in Verrem* V, 161–4
133 Strabo, 273 C
134 See Suetonius, *Caligula*, 27
135 D. 48. 19. 15; see Mommsen, op. cit., 943
136 D. 48. 2. 6
137 D. 48. 19. 28. 2
138 D. 48. 19, frags. 8. 9 and 35
139 See A. Ehrhardt in Pauly-Wissowa, *Realencyclopädie*, 2te Reihe, VI, 1775ff
140 See Buckland, *Roman Law of Slavery*, 87ff
141 D. 48. 18. 1 pr.
142 D. 48. 18. 8 pr. and 9 pr., respectively
143 Buckland, op. cit., 94–5. *Senatusconsulta*: D. 29. 5 and *Pauli Sententiae* III, 5
144 *Codex Iustinianus*, 9, 41, 11 pr.
145 D. 48. 18. 10. 1
146 Tacitus, *Annals* VI, 29, 1
147 Valerius Maximus IX, 12, 7

148 D. 28. 3. 6. 7

149 D. 48. 21. 3 pr.

150 By F. De Visscher, in *Bulletin de l'académie royale de Belgique*, Classe des lettres et des sciences morales et politiques, 1957, 176ff

151 D. 48. 2. 3 pr.

152 D. 48. 2. 8

153 D. 48. 4, frags. 7 pr.–2 and 8

154 See M. Lauria in *Atti della reale Accademia di scienze morali e politiche di Napoli*, vol. LVI, 1933, 304ff

155 Pliny, *Ep.* X, 96–7. This view runs counter to those expressed by Sherwin-White, *RSNT*, 17ff, and de Ste. Croix in *Past and Present*, 1963, 15; and is closer to that of Lauria in his paper quoted immediately above. *Cf.* D. I. 18. 13 pr on brigands and D. 48. 3. 6 on second-century rules for police prosecutions

156 Apuleius, *Apologia*, 2

157 Tacitus, *Annals* XV, 69, 1

158 Tacitus, *Annals* IV, 30, 4

159 For a few recent studies of major importance see: Sherwin-White in *RSNT* and in *Pliny*, Appendix V; J. Moreau, *La persécution du christianisme dans l'empire romain* (1956); de Ste. Croix in *Past and Present*, 1963, 6ff; W. H. C. Frend, *Martyrdom and Persecution in the Early Church* (1965)

160 For which see J. Beaujeu, *L'incendie de Rome en 64 et les chrétiens* (Collection Latomus, vol. XLIX) (1960)

161 So de Ste. Croix, *Past and Present*, 1963, 8

161a Sherwin-White, *Pliny*, 781–2 gets thus far but then sheers off into error. 'It lay in the governor's discretion . . .'; whether to accept charges, yes; how to punish, yes; but whether to punish, if Christianity was proved against a man or confessed by him, no. Pliny knew that under those circumstances he *had* to punish

162 See especially J. Vogt, 'Zur Religiosität der Christenverfolger', *Sitzungsberichte der Heidelberger Akademie der Wissenschaften*, philosophisch-historische Klasse, 1962, I, but also de Ste. Croix, *Past and Present*, 1963, 27ff, and Frend, *Martyrdom and Persecution*, Chapter 4

163 See F. H. Cramer, *Astrology in Roman Law and Politics* (1954), Part II, section V

164 Symmachus, *Relatio* III, 8–10 (long after our period, of course)

165 *Fontes* I, no. 88. *Cf.* the speech of the advocate of the Goharenians before Caracalla in *L'année épigraphique*, 1947, no. 182: 'the whole case concerns the sanctity of religion . . .'

166 Important, though concerned almost exclusively with political freedom, are: Wirszubski, *Libertas as a political idea*; M. Hammond in *Harvard Classical Studies*, 1963, 93ff; J. Bleicken in *Historische Zeitschrift*, cxcv, 1962, 1ff. The remarks of Momigliano in *JRS*, 1942, on pp. 123–4, should be pondered

167 Jones, *Later Roman Empire* I, 470

168 Introductory items on this great theme are: F. W. Maitland, *English Law and the Renaissance* (1901), and as a partial corrective, H. D. Hazeltine in *Cambridge Legal Essays written in honour of and presented to Doctor Bond, Professor Buckland and Professor Kenny* (1926), 139ff, especially 165–9; P. Vinogradoff, *Roman Law in Mediaeval Europe* (1904, 2nd ed. by de Zulueta, 1929); P. Koschaker, *Europa und das römische Recht* (1947, reprinted 1958), and the studies in his memory, *L'Europa e il diritto romano, Studi in memoria di Paolo Koschaker* (1954)

169 Koschaker, *Europa und das römische Recht*, 79–82 and 114–15

170 Jolowicz, quoted by de Ste. Croix, *Past and Present*, 1963, 12

171 See A. H. M. Jones, 'The Greeks under the Roman Empire', *Dumbarton Oaks Papers*, XVII, 1963, 1ff

172 The most famous is the *Roman Oration* of Aristides, ed. J. H. Oliver in *The Ruling Power* (1953), 871ff

173 On this vast and complex subject only a few orientations can be given. The pioneer work was L. Mitteis, *Reichsrecht und Volksrecht in den östlichen Provinzen des römischen Kaiserreichs* (1891, reprinted 1935). For more recent studies see R. Taubenschlag's *Opera Minora* I (1959), 421ff; F. Pringsheim in *BIDR*, 1960, 1ff; F. De Visscher in *Cahiers d'histoire mondiale* (= *Journal of World History* = *Cuadernos de Historia Mundial*), II, no. 4, 1955, 788ff; von Lübtow, *Das römische Volk. Sein Staat und sein Recht*, 512ff; Nörr, *Imperium und Polis, passim*

174 And on the stipulations, see Pólay in *Journal of Juristic Papyrology*, 1965, 185ff

174a The point made by Arangio-Ruiz about the 'military will' in *BIDR*, 1906, 157ff; see Chapter IV, note 140a

175 This is the scheme set out by Pólay in *ZSS*, 1962, 54–5

176 The final quotation is D. 28. 4. 3 pr., and the date of the decision recorded in it is AD 166

The Late Republic	90	90–89 Enfranchisement of Italy after the 'Social War'
	80	81 CICERO's first extant oration · 81 The dictatorship of SULLA
	70	70 CICERO's speeches against Verres · *Floruerunt:* SER. SULPICIUS RUFUS · C. AQUILIUS GALLUS
	60	63 CICERO's consulship
		59 JULIUS CAESAR's first consulship
	50	51–49 CICERO's provincial governorship
		49 Enfranchisement of Italy north of the R. Po (the 'Transpadanes')
	40	
	30	VARRO
AUGUSTUS		*Floruerunt:* VIRGIL
27 BC–AD 14	20	HORACE
The Principate		The social legislation of Augustus
	10	and the *leges iudiciorum* · *Floruit:* M. ANTISTIUS LABEO
	BC	*Floruit:* OVID
	AD	
	10	
TIBERIUS 14–37	20	*Floruerunt:* STRABO, VALERIUS MAXIMUS
The Julio- GAIUS	30	
Claudian (CALIGULA)		
Emperors 37–41	40	
CLAUDIUS	50	
47–54		*Floruerunt:* PERSIUS, COLUMELLA, PETRONIUS
NERO 54–68	60	64 The great fire of Rome
THE FOUR EMPERORS		
68–9	70	
VESPASIAN 69–79		
The TITUS 79–81	80	79 The destruction of Pompeii and Herculaneum
Flavian DOMITIAN		
Emperors 81–96	90	
		97–108 PLINY Letters, Books I–IX · *Floruit:* DIO OF PRUSA
NERVA 96–98	100	
TRAJAN 98–117		
	110	?111–113 PLINY Letters, Book X (the correspondence with Trajan)
		c. 117 TACITUS *Annals* · *Floruerunt:* JUVENAL
HADRIAN	120	SUETONIUS
117–138		
	130	SALVIUS JULIANUS quaestor of Hadrian c. 131 Codification of the Edict
	140	*Floruit:* POMPONIUS
ANTONINUS PIUS	150	
138–161		
The MARCUS AURELIUS	160	?160–162 GAIUS *Institutes* · c. 160 APULEIUS *Apologia*
Antonine 161–180		
Emperors	170	c. 169 GELLIUS *Noctes Atticae*
COMMODUS	180	
180–192		
	190	
SEPTIMIUS SEVERUS		The age of the great 'classical' jurists:
193–211	200	PAPINIAN praetorian prefect of Septimius Severus
The CARACALLA 211–217	210	PAULUS · ?212 The *Constitutio Antoniniana*
Severan ELAGABALUS		
Emperors 218–222	220	
SEVERUS		ULPIAN praetorian prefect of Severus Alexander
ALEXANDER		
222–235	230	

INDEX

argentarius coactor, 219–20, 240
army: service, 256; billeting, 257; and see soldiers, auxiliary regiments, military will
arrha, 220–1
assembly, right of, 265
assignment of debts, 171, 242–3
assizes, 70, 96
association, 264–8
astrologers, 279–80
auctions, 219
auctoramentum, 61
Augustus, will of, 130–1
auxiliary regiments, 41, 111, 296, note 21, 331, note 28

bail, see *vadimonium*
bailiff, see *vilicus*
Banasa inscription, 39–40, 48
banishment, see deportatio, exile, *relegatio*
banks, see *argentarii*
bankruptcy, 174–8
barristers, 87–8, 90–2, 204, 240, 254
bastards, see *spurii*
beasts, casting to, 273
beneficium abstinendi, 124
bigamy, 101
billeting, 257
birth registration, 46–8, 74
bona fide iudicia, contracts, 82, 84, 181, 208, 212, 214–16, 221, 227, 229, 233, 237
bona fide possessor, 141, 145, 163
bonitary ownership, 141, 145
bonorum: cessio, see *cessio bonorum; possessio*, 119; *publicatio*, 219, 276; *venditio*, 173–6
building contracts, 195, 222–3

burglary, 34, 72, 169, 271
burning alive, 273
by-laws, 260–1

caelibes, 37, 112–13, 121
capital punishment, 272–4, and see *summa supplicia*
capitis deminutio, 62, 113, 230, 272
captatio, 121
caretakership, see *cura*
casus, vis maior, 222
cataster, 148, 160
causae liberales, see *adsertor libertatis*
Censors: edict of, 23; guardians of morality, 83–4; lustrum, 156, 158, 234
census: Republican, 46; of land, 147–9
Centumviri, 33, 79–80, 123
centuriation, 148
cessio: bonorum, 174, 176, 317, note 177; *in iure*, see *in iure cessio*
childless persons, see *orbi*
Christians, 31, 273, 277, 279–80
Cicero, edict of, 25
citizens, see citizenship, *cives Romani*
citizenship: concept of, 37–8; desire for, 255–6; double, 39; loss of, 272; *potestas*, 111; taxes, 257; by birth, 40; by purchase, 43; by grant, 283; to individuals, 39, 42, 70; to communities, 41; to *auxilia*, 41; to Latins, 42, 44; to Italy and Transpadanes, 8, 69; to all by Constitutio Antoniniana, 8, 97
cives Romani, 31, 39, 283; duties,

852723

Printed in Great Britain by
Amazon.co.uk, Ltd.,
Marston Gate.